The Irish Air Corps
An Illustrated Guide

By Joe Maxwell and Patrick J. Cummins

All rights reserved, no part of this publication may be reproduced, stored in a retrieval system or transmitted in any form or by any means, digital, electronic, mechanical, photocopying, filming, video, scanning, recording or otherwise, without the prior permission in writing of the copyright owners and publishers of this book.

While the authors have managed to trace the owners of most photographs, this has not been possible in all cases.
The authors apologise for any omissions in the photographic credits arising from this.

The opinions expressed in this book are those of the authors and do not necessarily reflect those of the Irish Air Corps or the Department of Defence.

ISBN 978-0-9562624-0-0

Production Designer: Declan Maxwell
Contributing Artists: David Howley, Joe Maxwell, Andy McKay.
This book is typeset in Bembo 9.5 pt.
Printed by W&G Baird, Caulside Drive, Antrim, Northern Ireland.
First published by Max Decals Publications Ltd. May 2009.
© Joe Maxwell and Patrick J. Cummins

www.maxdecals.com

Contents

Contents

Foreword

R. James
Brigadier General
GOC Air Corps

Unless we understand and appreciate where we have come from we cannot hope to know where we are now as an organisation or where we can go into the future. Each generation builds on what has been handed down to it. The Air Corps has a unique history and indeed a unique place in the development and history of Irish and world aviation. To date we have had very few works of reference on the Air Corps and I am delighted to welcome this volume "The Irish Air Corps – An Illustrated Guide". I have no doubt that it will quickly become a major work of reference on the Air Corps and I wish it every success.

The joy of this work though is that it will be valued by both scholar and general reader alike, given the quality of production and the manner of presentation. It fills in many blanks and brings to life in coloured illustrations so much of our past fleet and history in a way that is both interesting and pleasing to the eye. It sheds light on little known areas of our history such as the mapping of our coastline using Seafires or the use of Gliders during the 1930's. Drawing on Air Corps and private archives the Authors have brought together the most complete publication to date.

No work of this scope or quality can be completed overnight and I congratulate Joe and Patrick on their commitment and dedication to the task. The effort and hard work has ensured that the Air Corps story is presented in a meaningful and readable publication. The quality of the drawings is very high and will be of immense interest to many around the globe.

I thank Joe and Patrick and congratulate all those who provided material and moral support with the preparation of this book which is such an important step in chronicling the Air Corps for future generations. I am particularly grateful that all those who died in the service of the Air Corps and the State are remembered and that through this publication their names will be enshrined into the future.

This publication starts to fill a void and marks a wonderful first step academically. I hope, and would strongly encourage, other scholars to help complete the recording of the Air Corps history through publishing studies related to our history to ensure that our past is not lost to future generations.

R. James Brigadier General
GOC Air Corps

Acknowledgements

The Authors could not have brought this book to fruition without the support and assistance of a great many people. We would like to thank Brig. Gen. Ralph James, General Officer Commanding the Air Corps for his support and for providing us with photographs from his own collection. He also made an inspired choice by appointing Lt. Col. Kevin Byrne as liaison officer to the project. Kevin's contribution and enthusiasm has been immense. He has cheerfully answered all our questions, given helpful insights and provided us with photographs from his own collection and from the Air Corps Photographic Section. Peter Hopkins deserves special mention for proof reading all of the sections and assisting us by posing questions for which the answers might have appeared obvious to us as authors, but really required clarifications which we subsequently provided in the text. However any typographical errors that remain are entirely the responsibility of the authors. Thanks also to Tom Mansfield, formerly of the Garda Air Support Unit for clarifications on the text relating to that unit and for providing us with interesting photographs.

We would like to thank Comdt. Victor Laing and his staff at the Military Archives of Ireland, Airman Michael Whelan, Curator of the Air Corps Museum & Heritage Centre at Baldonnel and Comdt. Paul Whelan for relating to us his account of his time with the Silver Swallows Aerobatic Team. Comdt. Con Murphy (ret.) also provided us with a great deal of information and photos relating to the early entry into service of the Gulfstream jet and the first trans-global flight by an Air Corps aircraft.

We are indebted to Annette Peard, daughter of the late Comdt. D.K. Johnston for providing us with access to his logbooks and photographic collection. We would also like to thank Colm O'Rourke for permitting us to use extracts from interviews of Comdt. D.K. Johnston conducted by the late Madeleine O'Rourke.

We also wish to thank Karen Wilsher, John Benjamin, Ken Hyne, Alec Bennon and Betty Bennon of the Shuttleworth Collection for facilitating our visit and providing access to the various cockpits that are featured in the book. Thanks also to Graham Skillen who provided us with samples of original Seafire parts so that we could ascertain the original colour scheme as applied to the Irish Seafires.

At the outset of this project we had useful discussions with a number of people who were extremely helpful including Paul Cunniffe of Irish Air Letter and Simon Nolan, both of whom provided access to their vast collection of Air Corps photos, many of which appear throughout the book. Simon Nolan also provided a great deal of information from his own research on the Westland Lysander. Authors who had previously written about the Air Corps were also very helpful including Donal McCarron, Lt. Col. Michael O'Malley (ret.), Liam Byrne and Tony Kearns. Thanks also to Denis Barry for providing information on the airfield at Fermoy.

We were delighted to be able to utilise the talents of David Howley and Andy McKay in the production of the various colour illustrations that accompany the text. A special thanks to the Production Designer, Declan Maxwell who learned a thing or two about aeroplanes along the way.

Photographers & Photographic Collections
We would like to thank all those who generously provided us with photographs including Liam Aherne, Maurice Aherne, Christopher Bateman of Rotor Leasing, Philip Bedford, John Bigley, Radu Brinzan, P. Branney, Christopher Bruton, John Byrne, Liam Byrne, Kevin Byrne, Dennis Cousins, Brendan Culleton, D. Corcoran, Paul Cuniffe, Gabriel Desmond, Oliver Dowling, Jim Egan, Margaret Farrell, Ray Flynn, George Flood, Jean-Paul Gilbert, Fergal Goodman, Denis Gorman, Frank Grealish of IrishAirPics.com, Peter Hopkins, Ralph James, Donal Leahy, Tom Mansfield, Con Murphy, Bernie Murran, Donal MacCarron, John McFarland, Malcolm Nason, Simon Nolan, George Norman, Michael Oakey at Aeroplane Monthly, Paddy O'Meara, Eamonn Power, Steve Quigley, Stephen Rogers, Geoff Russell at AgustaWestland, Graham Skillen, John Sheehan, Aaron Smith, William Olave Solis, Simon Thomas, Ronny Vogt, Guy Warner, Liam Whelan, Billy Walsh and Eric Thomas at Martin Baker Ltd. We would also like to thank the staff of the Irish Air Corps Photographic Section for their assistance with this project.

Finally we would like to thank our spouses, Margaret Farrell and Maura Cummins for their patience and understanding during the production of this book.

Authors' Note

In tackling a subject such as the aircraft of the Irish Air Corps, the authors have had to make a number of choices with regard to the content in order to cover the subject with some depth but at a level that we hope would interest the general reader, aviation enthusiast and scale modeller. We recognise that to tell the story of the aircraft is really to tell only a small fraction of what makes the Irish Air Corps a distinctive part of Irish heritage. The high calibre people who served and who continue to serve within its ranks are central to what makes the Air Corps such a beneficial organisation to the state and much of their story remains to be told. Other authors have written excellent accounts of the search and rescue aspects of the Air Corps and a full listing of useful further reading can be found in the bibliography.

Throughout the book we chose to give only a brief introduction to the development of each aircraft type as much more information is readily available in other publications and on the internet. The amount of coverage given to each aircraft type varies depending on a number of factors such as what was available (particularly on the early pre-WW2 types) and on the authors' personal preferences. We hope that the introduction to each section will provide a basis from which the reader can place each aircraft in a historical context. Detailed information on the history of each airframe is provided in tabular form in Appendix 1.

In covering the early aircraft used by the Air Corps for which photographic coverage is scarce (colour photos being non-existent) we have provided colour drawings to illustrate how the aircraft may have looked. In some cases, where complex camouflage patterns were used and where we did not have photos showing the entire airframe a certain amount of interpolation has had to be carried out to complete the colour drawings. In some specific cases we based the colour demarcations on known patterns that were in use by the RAF and which were subsequently provided to the Air Corps. We also decided to provide cockpit and other detail of photos of authentically restored aircraft from the Shuttleworth Collection in the United Kingdom. We have no reason to believe that the interiors of Irish Air Corps aircraft would have been significantly different from their RAF counterparts in terms of colour schemes or instrument panel layouts and for that we reason we believe that the photos provide a useful reference to Irish Air Corps aircraft interiors from the first half of the twentieth century.

Irish Air Corps aircraft are painted using paint from a variety of sources. There are three standards for paint colours that are in general use, BS standards in the UK, RAL in many parts of Europe and Federal Standards in the United States. Where appropriate we have stated the relevant BS, RAL or FS paint number where known.

We have attempted in so far as possible to provide accurate information throughout the book. However, in some cases the information on a particular type is incomplete and the authors would welcome hearing from anyone with further information on the history of the aircraft used by the Air Corps. We hope that the publication of this book will prompt members of the public to come forward with photos and anecdotes about the early days of the Air Corps for possible inclusion in future editions of this guide.

Joe Maxwell　　　　Patrick J. Cummins

The Early Years

1.0

The Early Years (1922 – 1936)

Col. James Fitzmaurice who became world famous after the epic flight across the Atlantic in the "Bremen" in 1938.

The Irish Army Air Service was formed in the Spring of 1922, following the signing of the Anglo-Irish Treaty in December 1921 and the establishment of the Irish Free State. The first aircraft to enter service, a Martinsyde Type A1 Mk II, had been acquired in November 1921 to enable members of the Irish delegation to escape from London should the Anglo-Irish peace negotiations fail but it had not been required for this purpose. The initial intake of pilots, mechanics and other personnel for the Army Air Service were mainly recruited from Irish nationals who had served in the RFC and the RAF during the First World War. Based at Baldonnel Aerodrome, the Irish Army Air Service comprised a single flying unit, No. 1 Squadron, which in turn had two Flights: 'A' Flight, which was equipped with training aircraft and 'B' Flight, which was equipped with operational aircraft.

In June 1922, a Civil War erupted throughout the new State between the Provisional Government, which was supported by the National Army, and Republican forces which had rejected the terms of the Anglo-Irish Treaty. As a result of this development, deliveries of aircraft to the Irish Army Air Service, which was a component of the National Army, became a priority and a total of nineteen combat aircraft and four elementary training aircraft were acquired over the next seven months. The first aircraft were delivered in July 1922, some from RAF units stationed in Ireland, but most came from the Aircraft Disposal Co. Ltd., usually abbreviated to Airdisco. Established in 1920 by Handley Page Ltd., this company had acquired stocks of aircraft and aero-engines from the Aircraft Disposal Department, which had been set up by the British Government in 1919 for the disposal war surplus aircraft and aero-engines that had been delivered to the RFC and RAF.

From October 1922 onwards, the National Army was engaged on offensive operations mainly in south-west Ireland, where the Republican forces had concentrated. The former RAF airfield at Fermoy, Co. Cork, was occupied by an Irish Army Air Service detachment, equipped with various combat aircraft types, in order to provide air support for the National Army in south-west Ireland. Over the next eight months, these aircraft were engaged in combat operations over the region, including attacks on Republican troops, patrolling the railway system, reconnaissance flights and dropping propaganda leaflets over territory controlled by Republican forces. There was a shortage of pilots in the Air Service and in December 1922, following an invitation to personnel from other units of the National Army to enlist as student pilots in the Irish Army Air Service, thirteen personnel were selected for flying training. The Civil War ended in May 1923 and the Irish Army Air Service detachment at Fermoy returned to Baldonnel in April 1924.

With the ending of the Civil War there was a considerable reduction in the number of men under arms and some within the Army and Air Service were angered by the way in which reductions in numbers was carried out. The so called Army Mutiny of March 1924 lead to the resignations of approximately 800 officers including the then Commanding Officer of the Air Service, Maj. Gen. W.J. McSweeney and the adjutant, Col. Charles Dalton. A proposed restructuring of the Air Service into two squadrons with effect from 1st April 1928 did not take place. However, following a re-organisation of the National Army in October 1924, the Irish Army Air Service was re-named the Irish Army Air Corps. Comprising a total of 68 personnel of all ranks, the existing flying unit, No. 1 Squadron, was retained in the Air Corps, with 'A' flight and 'B' Flight continuing to be equipped with training and operational aircraft respectively.

The first public display by the Air Corps took place on Friday 15th August 1924 in Dublin's Phoenix Park as part of the Tailteann Games, a sporting festival organised by the Gaelic Athletic Association open to all with Irish ancestry. A flypast at the official opening of the games was followed by an aerobatic display and aerial races around Dublin. In April 1926, the Air Corps' first intake of nine pilot cadets, selected through a recently-established competitive Civil Service examination, commenced training.

Because of its geographical location, Ireland was the focal point of many transatlantic flight attempts during this period and a number of these set out from Baldonnel, where the facilities of the Air Corps were made available. On 12-13 April 1928, Commandant James C. Fitzmaurice, Officer Commanding the Air Corps, together with Captain Hermann Kohl and Baron von Hunefeld completed the first east-west non-stop crossing of the Atlantic in a Junkers W.33 named 'Bremen'. Fitzmaurice was keen to see civil aviation established in Ireland and following his transatlantic success he presided over the Irish Aero Club, which was set up in August 1928. The flying activities of the Irish Aero Club were based at Baldonnel for a number of years, with the first civil aircraft registered in Ireland (Avro Avian EI-AAA) being based there from January 1929. In 1930, Charles Kingsford Smith who had completed the first transpacific flight from America to Australia in June 1928, completed a round the world flight in the Fokker F.VII 'Southern Cross'; in preparation for the transatlantic leg of the journey, the aircraft was based at Baldonnel, although the actual flight itself commenced from Portmarnock Strand near Dublin on 24th June 1930.

Baldonnel was also the home base for the fledgling Aer Lingus, the newly-formed Irish national airline, which operated there from 1936 until 1940 when it transferred its operations to the newly opened airport at Collinstown, north of Dublin. There has been a long association between the Air Corps and Aer Lingus, with many pilots and technicians receiving their training with the Air Corps and subsequently moving to the airline.

Throughout the 1920's and early 1930's the Air Corps was engaged in military exercises with other units of the Defence Forces, conducting photographic surveys of archaeological sites in the State and participating in air displays at military tattoos and other events. The first Search and Rescue mission by the Air Corps occurred in February 1926 in Clifden Bay, Co. Galway, off the west coast of Ireland. Despite adverse weather conditions, pilots flying DH-9s and Bristol F2bs searched for more than four days for a missing trawler and its crew, but no survivors were found.

By 1929, only sixteen aircraft remained in service with the Air Corps and even these were reaching the limit of their useful life. In the same year, a report to the Department of Defence described the Air Corps as "… a worthless organisation, costing £100,000 annually, with junk equipment and insufficient mechanics". However, a re-equipment programme led to total of twenty-two new aircraft being delivered to the Air Corps between 1930 and 1935: eight for army co-operation duties and the remainder for elementary and advanced flying training. The personnel of the Air Corps numbered just 113 in 1931, 17 pilots, 6 observers and 91 mechanics.

Formed in October 1934, and equipped with operational aircraft, No. 1 Army Co-Operation Squadron replaced 'B' Flight of No. 1 Squadron. Also formed in the same month, the Air Corps Schools No. 2 Section: Flying Training consisting of Elementary, Basic and Advanced Training Flights replaced No.1 Squadron's 'A' Flight.

In 1935, at the request of the Department of Industry and Commerce, the Air Corps carried out an aerial photographic survey of the area around Rineanna, Co. Clare. This area had been selected as a possible location for a transatlantic air terminal and construction work on an airfield at Rineanna commenced in January 1937. This would eventually become Shannon International Airport. Air firing exercises by the Air Corps were carried out during this period over an air firing range at Kilworth, Co. Cork. In 1935 a permanent air firing range was established at Gormanston Military Camp, Co. Meath, where air firing exercises have taken place ever since.

In 1936, the Air Corps Apprentice School was established for the recruitment of Boy Personnel for service with the Army Air Corps. The Apprentice School was to provide technical training for these recruits, who would fulfil the Air Corps' future requirements for ground technicians. An initial intake of twenty youths was recruited for the first Apprentice Class in March 1936.

In the early years the air crews wore their parade uniforms while flying, over which they donned heavy protective clothing as seen here. Clockwise F. Reade, T. Hanley, M. Kennedy, K. Curran. (Photo, A.Peard collection)

The aircraft hangars at Fermoy, later demolished in the 1990s. (S. Nolan photo)

1.1

Martinsyde Type A1 Mk. II and F.4 Buzzard (1922 – 1929)

Following the end of the First World War, contracts for various aircraft types in large-scale production for the RAF, including the Martinsyde F.4 Buzzard, were cancelled by the British Government. Powered by a Hispano Suiza engine, the Buzzard was a fast single-seat fighter. Over 300 Buzzards had been constructed by Martinsyde Ltd. when production was terminated in 1919, with approximately 60 having been delivered to the RAF. At that stage, the Sopwith 7F.1 Snipe was selected to equip RAF fighter squadrons in the post-war period, and the Buzzards, being surplus to requirements, were initially offered for sale to other air forces by the Aircraft Disposal Department, a British Government agency. In March 1920, the Agency was taken over by the Aircraft Disposal Company (Airdisco), which delivered a number of Buzzards to several air forces throughout Europe. The Buzzards were also offered for sale to other air forces by Martinsyde Ltd., but with little success. The Buzzard was an excellent aircraft and was the fastest fighter of its day, two actually being used as fast mail transports between Paris and London during 1919.

Throughout 1919 and 1920, the company also continued development of the Buzzard design, which included two civil transport aircraft types, designated Martinsyde Type A Mk.I and Type A Mk.II. Powered by a 275hp Falcon III engine, the Type A Mk.I was a two-seat, long-range transport aircraft, but only four were constructed. The Type A Mk.II was also a long-range transport aircraft, powered by a 300 hp. Hispano Suiza engine, which could carry four passengers in a glazed cabin forward of the pilot's open cockpit, and four of these aircraft (c/ns 215, 216, 217 and 218) were constructed. Apparently one of these aircraft (c/n 217) was a Type A Mk.I (G-EAPN) with a Falcon III engine installed, which was rebuilt as a Type A Mk.II in August 1920 and then placed in storage by the company. Martinsyde Ltd. went into liquidation in 1921, following which this Type A Mk.II, together with the remaining stocks of Buzzards, was acquired by Airdisco.

In June 1921, following a truce in the Anglo-Irish conflict, the British Government agreed to commence peace negotiations with an Irish delegation in London. Michael Collins, who was leading the Irish delegation, had a reward of £10,000 "placed on his head" by the British Government for organising and directing the IRA's guerrilla warfare campaign during the conflict. There was a possibility that the British Government might detain Collins and some other members of the Irish delegation in London if the peace negotiations failed. It was therefore decided to acquire an aircraft that could be used to fly Collins either back to Ireland, or possibly France, if the peace negotiations failed; a Martinsyde Type A Mk.II (c/n 217) was therefore purchased from Airdisco by two members of the IRA, both of whom were former RAF pilots. The Type A Mk.II flew for the first time on November 24, 1921, followed by a second flight of 1 hour and 10 minutes duration on December 9, 1921, and was then kept at readiness at an airfield near London until the Anglo-Irish Treaty was signed on December 21, 1922. Three days later the aircraft was delivered to Croydon Aerodrome and placed in storage to await delivery to Ireland.

Following the formation of the Irish Air Service in May 1922, when Baldonnel Aerodrome was taken over by a detachment from the National Army, the Type A Mk.II was delivered in crates via the port of Dublin on June 16, 1922. The aircraft was re-assembled at Baldonnel Aerodrome and following a test flight of 15 minutes duration on October 11, 1922, became the Air Service's first operational aircraft (a pair of floats was also supplied to allow the aircraft to be converted into a seaplane, but apparently these were never used). Known as the Martinsyde Passenger by the Air Service, the Type A Mk.II was not allocated a serial number, but had the inscription "The Big Fella" (Michael Collins' nickname) painted on the sides of the engine

Far right: well known photo of the Martinsyde at Baldonnel. (A.C. Photographic Section)

A rare shot of the Martinsyde A1 Mark II (photo Donal Mac Carron collection)

cowlings. The Type A Mk.II, which was operated by 'B' Flight, No. 1 Squadron, was intended to be used for transport of the Army High Command when necessary, but had only accumulated a total of 2 hours, 25 minutes flying time by January 5, 1923. The Type A Mk.II flew for the last time on October 11, 1927 and was then used as an instructional airframe by the Air Corps over the following five years. The Falcon III engine was removed from the aircraft on May 12, 1928 and installed in a Bristol F2B Fighter (no.8) on June 7, 1928. From February 1, 1932 the Type A Mk.II was stored in a hangar at Baldonnel Aerodrome, without wings or engine, where "deterioration . . . set in, due to damage by birds". The inscription "The Big Fella" on the engine cowlings had at some stage been replaced by the inscriptions "City of Dublin", on the port side, and on the starboard side, in Gaelic, "Cathair Atha Cliat (i.e., "City of Dublin" in the Irish language). In 1935, the Type A Mk.II was included in a survey of obsolescent aircraft and aero-engines held in storage by the Air Corps, that were valued as scrap and should be sold or destroyed". The Minister for Defence approved the scrapping of the Type A Mk.II in September 1936, after which the aircraft was, in the language of the time, described as having been "converted to produce" in January 1937, despite a recommendation from the Air Corps that it should be preserved in the National Museum.

The Type A Mk. II was only the start of the Irish association with Martinsyde aircraft. In June 1922, a civil war erupted in Ireland between the National Army (supporting the Provisional Government, which had signed the Anglo-Irish Treaty with the British Government) and Republican forces, which had rejected the Treaty's terms. In order to provide air support for the National Army in this conflict, the Air Service acquired a number of aircraft types over the following six months from Airdisco and from RAF units stationed in Ireland. From October onwards, the National Army was engaged on offensive combat operations in the south-west of Ireland, where the majority of the Republican forces were concentrated, and a detachment from the Air Service was deployed to the former RAF airfield at Fermoy, Co. Cork, to provide air support for the Army.

A Martinsyde F.4 Buzzard (ex-RAF, serial no. D4285), acquired from Airdisco, was delivered to Baldonnel Aerodrome on August 15, 1922 and (having been allocated the Roman numeral I as a code) entered service with 'B' Flight, No. 1 Squadron, the operational flying unit of the Air Service. Three more Buzzards (also ex-RAF, serial nos. D4281, D4298 and D4274) were delivered to Baldonnel Aerodrome on October 14, 1922 and (coded II, III and IV respectively) entered service with 'B' Flight, No. 1 Squadron. Constructed by Martinsyde Ltd., the four Buzzards were from the initial batch of 150 (serial nos. D4211-D4360) ordered for the RAF in December 1917, which never entered service and were later acquired by Airdisco. The Buzzards were the Air Service's first single-seat fighter aircraft.

The first Buzzard (I) delivered to the Air Service was deployed to Fermoy airfield on October 1, 1922 and was soon engaged in supporting the National Army on combat operations in the south-west; the aircraft's tasks included patrolling the railway system, reconnaissance flights and dropping leaflets over territory held by Republican forces. On October 14, 1922 the Buzzard was dropping leaflets over suspected Republican strongholds in the mountains east of Killarney, Co. Kerry, but was forced to land in a field on the outskirts of the town following an engine failure. Having repaired the engine, the pilot was able to take-off from the field on the following day, but on doing so was fired on by Republican troops surrounding Killarney; the fuselage and wings were riddled with bullets in this incident. The pilot and engine were not hit, but the Buzzard had to land again outside Mallow, Co. Cork, eighteen miles from Fermoy, following another engine failure. An inspection revealed that a new engine was required to enable the Buzzard to fly again and at that stage the aircraft was dismantled and stored in Mallow Military Barracks. One month later, the Buzzard was transported by road to Fermoy airfield, where a new Hispano Suiza engine was installed in the aircraft, which flew again on December 8, 1922. During this period an inscription in Gothic lettering ("The Humming Bird") was added to the starboard side of the mid-fuselage section of the Buzzard.

Following a restructuring of the Defence Forces in October 1924, the Air Service was re-named the Irish Army Air Corps. No. 1 Squadron, which had a total of eleven aircraft, including the four Buzzards, in service with 'B' Flight, remained the single flying unit. Over the next five years, the Buzzards participated in annual military exercises conducted by the Defence Forces, often with temporary coloured stripes displayed on the fuselage behind the cockpit for identification by other units participating in these exercises. During this period the Air Corps also used the Buzzards for advanced flying training. The serial numbers allocated to each Buzzard were also altered to include the prefix "M" (for Martinsyde) to the Roman numerals. One of the Buzzards (MIV) was written-off in a crash on September 18, 1928, and a second (MI) was also written-off in a crash near Baldonnel Aerodrome on May 16, 1929. The remaining two Buzzards (MIII and MII) were withdrawn from use in September 1925 and April 1929 respectively.

Unique photo of the first Martinsyde F.4 Buzzard in the later overall silver colour scheme. Note the No. 1 on the tailfin. (D. MacCarron collection)

Martinsyde A1 Mk II.

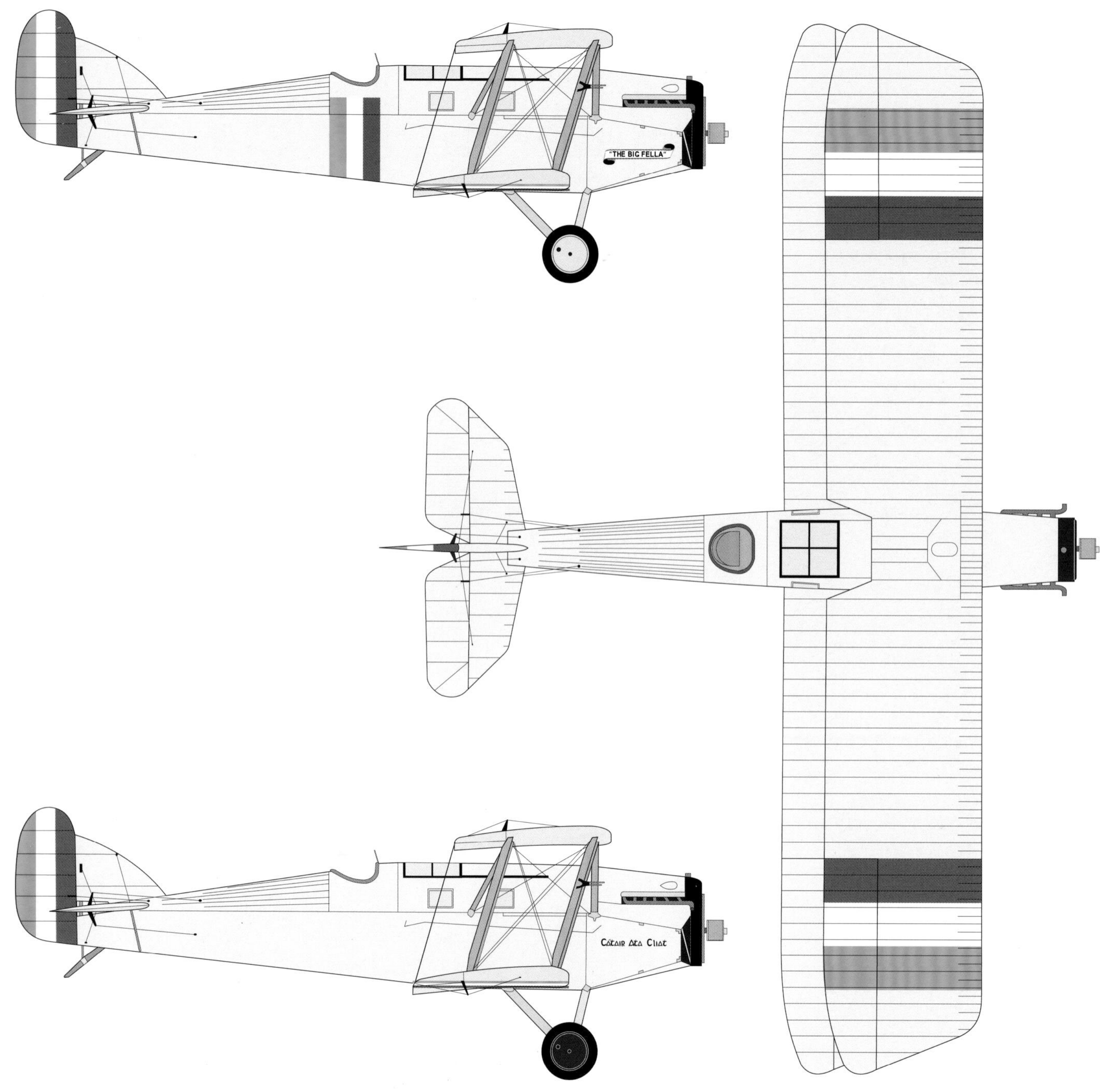

Martinsyde F4. Buzzard

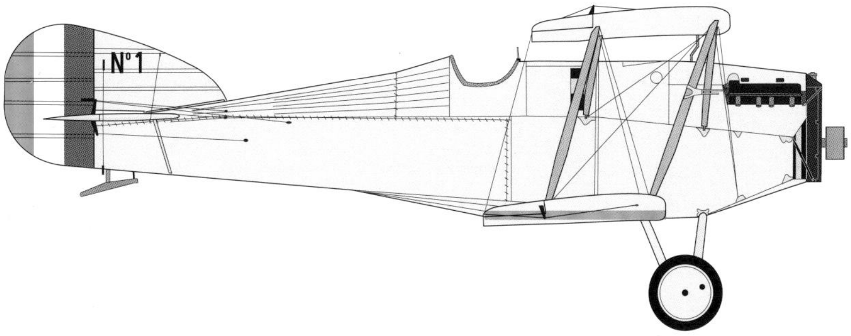

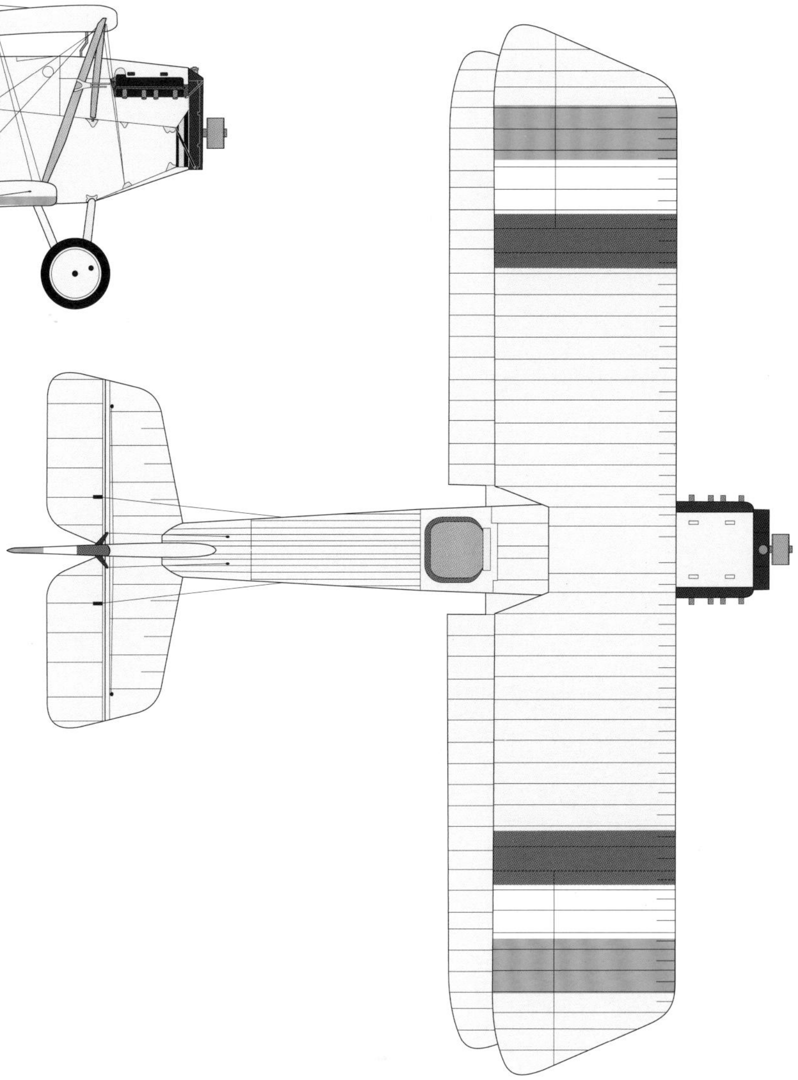

Colours & Markings

The Type A Mk.II had an overall silver dope finish with a large tricolour flag (green, white and orange) displayed on both sides of the fuselage under the cockpit. The tricolour, as green, white and orange vertical stripes, was also displayed on both sides of the rudder.

Initially the Buzzards were finished in the then standard RAF colour scheme of khaki green overall, which was replaced by a silver dope finish after the civil war had ended. The national colours, as green, white and orange vertical stripes, were displayed on the upper surfaces of the top wings, the under surfaces of the lower wings and on both sides of the rudder. Each aircraft's serial number was displayed on both sides of the rear fuselage section, in front of the tailplane. When the aircraft were repainted in the overall silver scheme, the serial number was displayed on the vertical fin ahead of the rudder.

1.2

Bristol F2B Fighter (1922 – 1935)

The Bristol F2B Fighter was an outstanding and versatile machine for its time. Initially entering service with the Royal Flying Corps in April 1917, this aircraft was eventually operated by 14 countries. The initial production versions were powered by Rolls-Royce Falcon III engines, but to overcome a shortage of these powerplants in 1918, Sunbeam Arab, Siddeley Puma and Hispano-Suiza engines also powered several batches of F2B Fighters. Designated F2B Fighter Mk. II, production of these models by the parent company continued in the post-war years, many having a wide range of equipment installed for army co-operation missions - this was a popular type in service with RAF squadrons stationed overseas. When production ended in 1925, a total of 5,300 F2B Fighters of all types had been constructed.

Eight F2B Fighters were delivered to Baldonnel Aerodrome between July and November 1922.

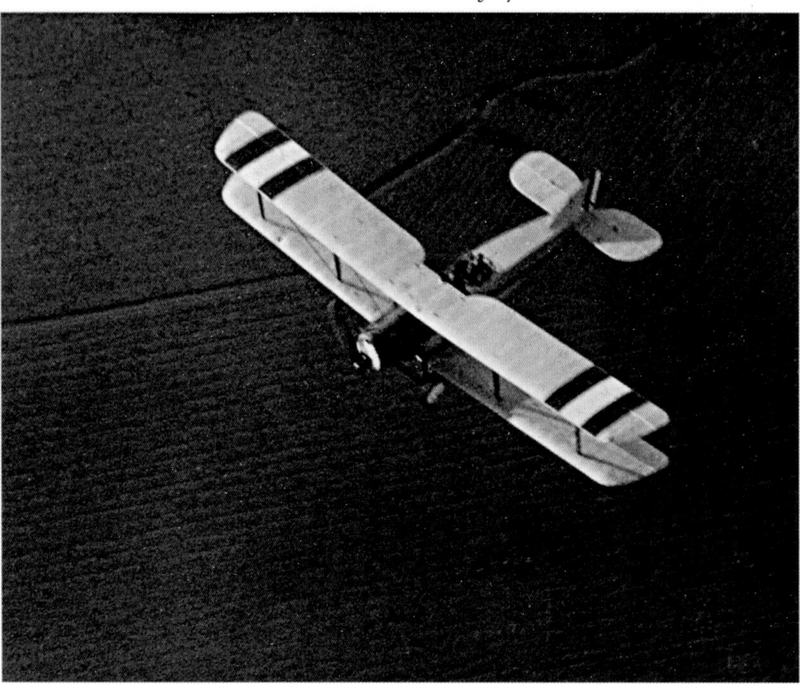

Above: The Bristol Fighter was a popular and reliable type in Air Corps service, flying on a myriad of missions until 1935. (A.C. Photographic Section)

These were acquired from Airdisco and from the Irish Flight, RAF, stationed in Ireland. These aircraft had Roman numerals I to VIII initially allocated as serial numbers and the prefix letters 'BF' were added later. From July 1922 to May 1923 the F2B Fighters were engaged on combat missions supporting the National Army against Republican forces throughout the Civil War. The F2B Fighters were operated by the Air Service on reconnaissance missions, patrolling the country's railway system and dropping propaganda leaflets over territory occupied by Republican forces. Operating from a temporary airstrip near the city of Limerick, the second F2B Fighter (BI) was engaged on reconnaissance flights over south-west Ireland soon after delivery. On August 21, 1922 this aircraft crash-landed following engine failure and damaged the leading edge of one wing and the propeller; however, the pilot and observer were not injured. It was later established that the F2B Fighter had been refuelled with what was described at the time as "ordinary motor spirit" instead of aviation fuel. The aircraft returned to service following repairs by Air Service personnel.

In October 1922, an Air Service detachment was deployed to the former RAF airfield at Fermoy to commence combat operations against Republican forces in the south-west. The F2B Fighter (II) was first deployed to this airfield on October 2, 1922 and at least two more such aircraft (BFVII and BFVIII) are known to have operated from this airfield during the Civil War. In December 1922, a small Air Service detachment was also deployed to the former RAF reserve airfield on the outskirts of Tralee, Co. Kerry, initially equipped with an F2B Fighter (BI). Operating from this airfield, the F2B Fighters carried out reconnaissance flights and other combat missions over the south-west until the detachment was withdrawn to the airfield at Fermoy in October 1923.

Three F2B Fighters of the Air Service were written-off in crashes throughout 1924. The first of these aircraft (BFII) crashed near Baldonnel Aerodrome, killing the pilot, on January 23, 1924, followed by a second (BI) on February 14, 1924. A third F2B Fighter (BFV) crashed at Crumlin, Co. Dublin, on August 6, 1924, following engine failure, but the pilot and observer were not injured. In October 1924, when the Irish Army Air Corps was formed, only three F2B Fighters (BFVI, BFVII and BFVIII) remained in service, being operated by 'B' Flight, No. 1 Squadron. From about 1925 Arabic numbers, without the prefix letters replaced the Roman numerals on these aircraft.

Six Bristol F2B Fighter Mk.IIs were ordered by the Irish Free State Government in 1925, partly to replace the aircraft that had been written-off. Distinguishable from the original batch by their elongated exhaust pipes and revised cowling panels, the first two F2B Fighter Mk.IIs (c/ns 6858 and 6859) were delivered to Baldonnel Aerodrome on October 24, 1925,

Left: An unmarked F2B is returned to its hangar at the end of a flying day. It has always been the policy to hangar all aircraft at the close of the working day unless night flying is required. Of interest are the short lived green white and orange roundels on the wings. (D. MacCarron collection)

followed by the third (c/n 6861) on November 4, 1925. The fourth and fifth F2B Fighter Mk.IIs (c/ns 6863 and 6860) were delivered on November 9 and 10, 1925 respectively, followed by the sixth (c/n 6862) on November 18, 1925. The six F2B Fighter Mk. IIs, which were the first brand new aircraft to be delivered to the Air Corps, were allocated Arabic numerals, without prefix letters, as serial numbers. These aircraft (as Nos. 17 to 22) entered service with 'B' Flight, No. 1 Squadron and over the next five years were used by the Air Corps for advanced flying training and aerial survey flights for the Archaeological Research Commission, and also participated in military exercises held by the Defence Forces.

On September 22, 1925 another of the original F2B Fighters (no.6) was written-off in a crash while participating in Army manoeuvres at the Curragh, Co. Kildare, killing the pilot and observer. Operating from the former RAF airfield at Oranmore in February 1926, three F2B Fighters and two de Havilland DH.9s carried out the first search and rescue mission undertaken by the Air Corps, off the west coast of Ireland. This operation is described fully in section 1.5 on the DH.9. On September 21, 1926, an F2B Fighter Mk. II (No. 17), which was participating in military exercises conducted by the Defence Forces, was written-off in a crash at Hempstown, Co. Wicklow, killing the pilot and observer.

One of the F2B Fighter Mk.IIs (No. 18) had a Rolls Royce Falcon III engine (which had been removed from the Martinsyde Type A Mk.II) installed on June 7, 1928. On August 3, 1928 an F2B Fighter (No.8) was written-off in a crash near Baldonnel Aerodrome, but the crew escaped without injury. Two F2B Fighter Mk. IIs (no. 21 and 20) were withdrawn from use in July 1930 and October 1931 respectively, and the single F2B Fighter (No. 7) still in service was withdrawn from use in April 1934, followed by the remaining three F2B Fighter Mk. IIs (Nos. 18, 19 and 22), in April and May 1935, all of these aircraft being placed in storage at Baldonnel Aerodrome. In June 1935, following a survey of obsolescent aircraft held in storage by the Air Corps, the four aircraft were valued as scrap and sold or destroyed.

Below: On parade! It would appear from this very early photo that not all personnel were issued with the regulation uniforms immediately.

A Rolls Royce Falcon 12 cylinder engine weighing 712lb is being carefully removed from a Bristol Fighter. Great emphasis has been placed technical skills and training within the Corps from the earliest years.
(Air Corps photo via S. Quigley)

Right: The pristine condition of Bristol Fighter No. 18 and the highly polished boots of the ground crew indicate that an inspection or parade of some sort is in the offing.

Below right: No. 18 is undergoing a compass-swinging calibration at Baldonnel, a practice that is still conducted with the modern fleet in the 21st Century.

Colours & Markings

The fuselage and upper surfaces of the wings and tailplanes of the initial batch of eight F2B Fighters had an overall khaki-green matt finish, with a clear dope finish on the undersurfaces of the wings and tailplane. Green, white and orange stripes were displayed chordwise on the upper surfaces of the top wings and under surfaces of the bottom wings, and vertically on both sides of the rudder. Each aircraft's serial number was displayed in white on the upper part of the fuselage centre section. Some aircraft supplied from RAF stocks had green white and orange roundels on the wings but these were quickly replaced with tricolour stripes. The fuselage and wings of the six F2B Fighter Mk. IIs had an overall silver finish, with grey engine cowlings. The tricoloured stripes were displayed in the same positions as on the earlier F2B Fighters. However, the white stripe on the upper wings was slightly wider than the green and orange stripes. Each aircraft's serial number, was displayed in black, on the rear fuselage section, just in front of the tailplane.

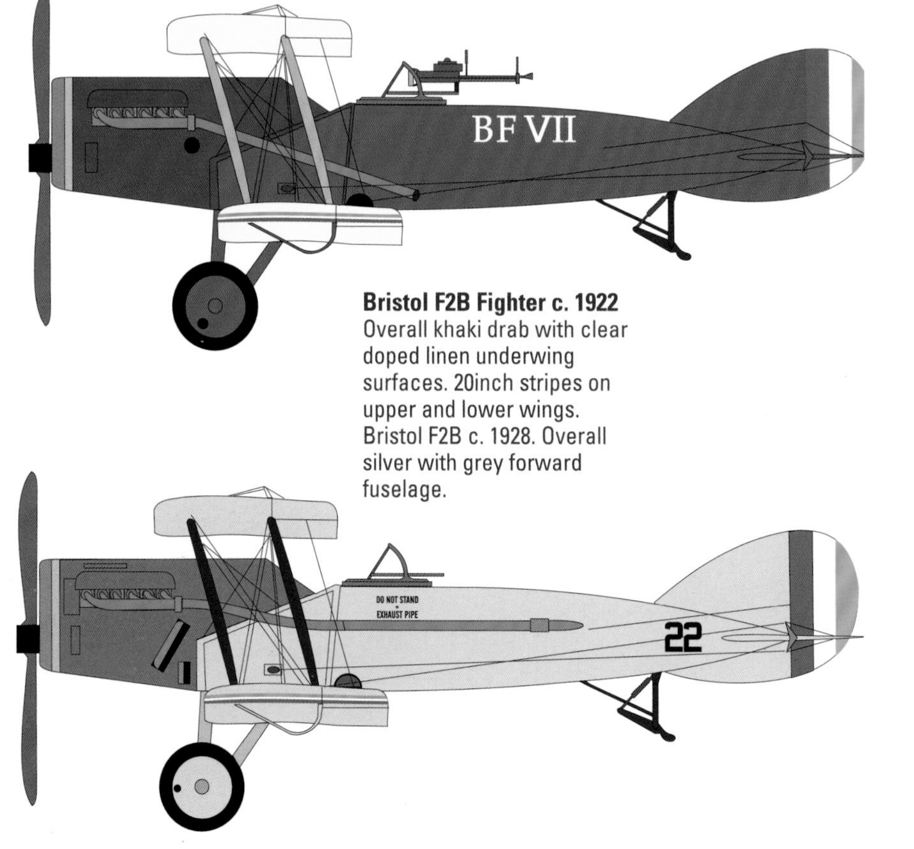

Bristol F2B Fighter c. 1922
Overall khaki drab with clear doped linen underwing surfaces. 20inch stripes on upper and lower wings. Bristol F2B c. 1928. Overall silver with grey forward fuselage.

Left and below: Three photos taken of the authentically restored Bristol Fighter in the Shuttleworth collection indicating how the cockpit and gunners position may have looked like on Bristol Fighters in Air Corps service (P. Hopkins photos)

Right and below: Details of twin Vickers machine guns on mounted on a Bristol Fighter. It's not known if such an arrangement was used on Irish Bristol fighters, the single machine gun mounted on a scarf ring being more commonly seen in photos of the period. (P. Hopkins photo)

Close up of the centrally mounted compass on the F2B. (P. Hopkins photo)

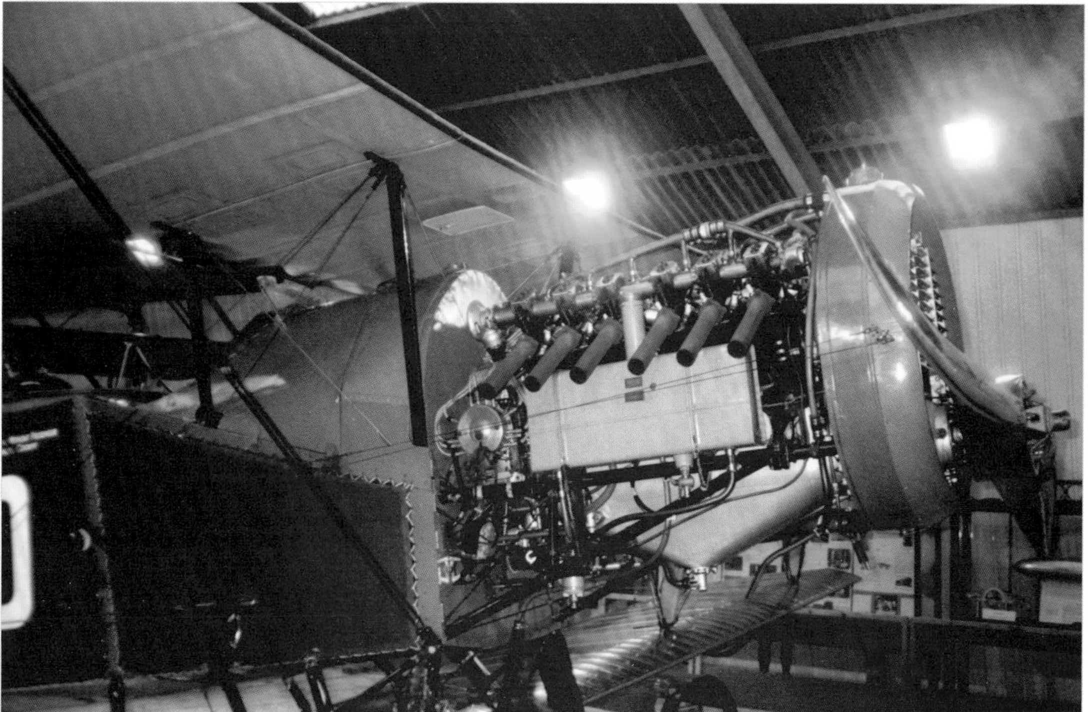

Left and below: details of the Rolls Royce Falcon III engine and propeller fitted to the Bristol fighter
(J. Maxwell photo)

Propeller engaged with a Hucks starter.
(J Maxwell photo)

1.3

Avro 504K (1922 – 1932)

The Avro 504 was initially designed as a fighter, but found its niche as a trainer, becoming the standard elementary training aircraft for the RFC in 1918 and for the RAF in the immediate post-war years. Powered by various rotary engines, large-scale production of the Avro 504K commenced in 1917, by both the parent company and other British aircraft manufacturing companies under sub-contract (including Harland and Wolff Ltd. in Belfast and the Sunbeam Motor Co. Ltd.). In excess of 8,000 Avro 504Ks had been constructed by these companies when production ended in 1926. The Avro 504K was also constructed under licence in Australia, Belgium, Canada, Japan and Russia.

When the First World War ended, the RAF held large stocks of Avro 504Ks surplus to requirements, and many were sold by public auction at Hendon Aerodrome throughout 1919 by the Disposals Board, a British Government agency. All remaining stocks of Avro 504Ks, with various engine types, were purchased from the Disposals Board by Airdisco in 1920, and a number of these aircraft were delivered to civilian operators. About three hundred Avro 504Ks were listed on the British civilian register between 1919 and 1930.

Six Avro 504Ks were delivered to the Irish Air Service between June 1922 and June 1923; five were acquired from Airdisco and one from a civilian operator, the Central Aircraft Co. Ltd. The six Avro 504Ks, which were initially allocated Roman numerals as serial numbers (I to VI), entered service with 'A' Flight, No. 1 Squadron, the flying training unit of the Air Service.

Two of the Avros had interesting histories. Avro 504K No. IV (ex RAF serial E359 was from a batch of 205 (ex-RAF E301-E505) constructed by Harland and Wolff Ltd., Belfast. The aircraft was delivered to the RAF and was subsequently purchased by Airdisco in 1920. When delivered to the Irish Air Service, this Avro 504K became the first and only aircraft manufactured in Ireland to enter Irish military service.

Avro 504K No. VI, the aircraft that was purchased from the Central Aircraft Co. Ltd. (ex-RAF serial D7588) was from a batch of 300 Avro 504Js and 504Ks (ex-RAF serials D7501-D7800) constructed by Avro in 1918. A Certificate of Airworthiness was issued for this aircraft (as G-EADQ) on June 6, 1919, but this had expired in June 1922. Following delivery to the Irish Air Service an Airdisco in-line piston engine was installed in the aircraft, which was then re-designated as an Avro 548. The recruitment of personnel from other units of the National Army was initiated in December 1922, and 13 student pilots commenced elementary flying training on the Avro 504Ks throughout 1923. Following the formation of the Irish Army Air Corps in October 1924, the six Avro 504Ks were operated by 'A' Flight, No. 1 Squadron, which had been retained as the flying training unit. The prefix letter 'A' (for Avro) was also added to the Roman numerals allocated to each of the Avro 504Ks. One of the Avro 504Ks (AII) was written-offin a crash on June 30, 1925.

In 1926, following the recruitment of nine officer cadets and the selection of ten officers from other units of the National Army for a flying training course, the Air Corps was unable to fulfil the resulting increased elementary flying training commitments with the remaining five Avro 504Ks. Four de Havilland D.H.60 Moths were therefore acquired in the same year to supplement the Avro 504Ks for elementary flying training, but three of the Moths were written-off in crashes over the following two years. The Avro 548 (AVI) and an Avro 504K (AI) were also written-off in crashes on September 3, 1926 and March 18, 1927 respectively. The remaining three Avro 504Ks (AIII, AIV and AV), with the sole remaining DH.60 Moth, had continued to fulfil the Air Corps elementary flying training requirements until replaced by Avro 621s in 1930. One of the Avro 504Ks (AV) was withdrawn from use on July 3, 1928, followed by a second (AIII) on June 2, 1931. The last Avro 504K (AIV) was withdrawn from use on May 17, 1932.

Right: As a training type, accidents could be anticipated for the Avro 504K fleet and a minor "prang" is illustrated here. Of note are the silver doped fuselage sides in contrast to the otherwise drab green colour scheme. (D. MacCarron collection)

Colours & Markings

Initially the Avro 504Ks had an overall matt khaki–green finish, with the engine cowlings painted black. The under surfaces were most likely clear doped linen. Green, white and orange stripes, positioned chordwise, were displayed on the upper surfaces of the top wings and the under surfaces of the bottom wings, and vertically on both sides of the rudder. At least one Avro 504 K had a natural metal cowling. Each aircraft's allocated serial number, as Roman numerals, was displayed on each side of the rear section of the fuselage. The Avro 504Ks later had an overall silver dope finish and the prefix letter "A" was also added to the Roman numeral serials.

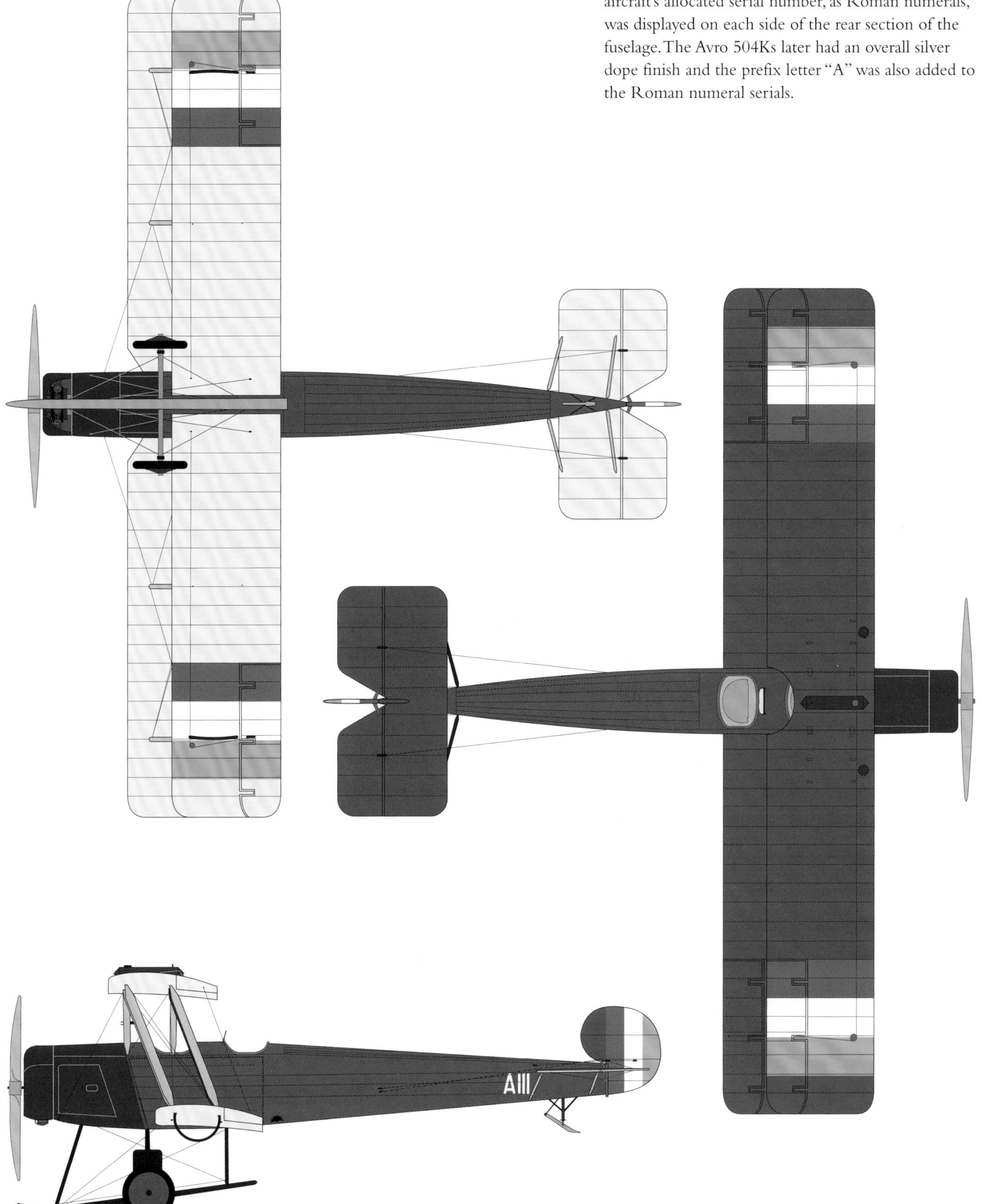

Right: Details of the cockpit and engine of an authentically restored Avro 504K at the Shuttleworth Collection. All of the aircraft in the collection are airworthy and are flown regularly during the summer months. (J. Maxwell photos)

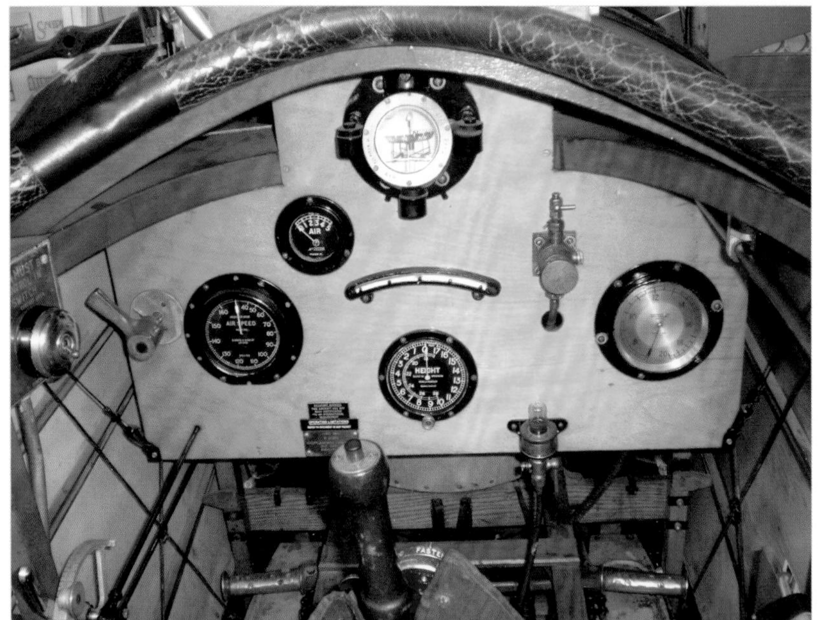

Left: Cadet Wiliam J. Keane, a student pilot, surveys the damage to his Avro 548 No. VI after a landing accident at Baldonnnel. (A.C. Photographic Section)

Left: For almost a generation, the Avro 504K gave countless student military pilots a stable foundation in the practicalities of military flying operations. Note the overall silver dope finish which was introduced across the fleet in the 1920s. (D.MacCarron collection)

Left: Under the watchful eye of a technical NCO, the aircraft technicians remove an Avro504K from its hangar for another hard day's labour. (D.MacCarron collection).

1.4

Royal Aircraft Factory SE.5A (1922)

The Royal Aircraft Factory SE.5a was one of the best combat aircraft to see service in WW1. Powered by a 200-hp Hispano-Suiza engine, the SE.5a entered service with twenty RAF fighter squadrons, but was rapidly withdrawn from operational service throughout 1919 and became surplus to requirements. This was due in no small measure to the unreliability of the Hispano Suiza engine. Notwithstanding these problems, the SE5a was used by RFC aces Ball, Bishop, Mannock and McCudden amongst others. Post war, a number of these aircraft were acquired by Airdisco, and these were subsequently delivered to civilian operators and foreign air forces.

The Irish Air Service acquired a single SE.5a (ex F5282) from Airdisco in August 1922, which was from the final batch of 100 (ex-RAF serial F5249-F5348) constructed by Martinsyde Ltd. The SE.5a was being delivered to Baldonnel Aerodrome on August 14, 1922, accompanied by a Martinsyde F.4 Buzzard, when adverse weather conditions caused both aircraft to divert to Shotwick airfield, south of Liverpool. The Buzzard was delivered to the Air Service on the following day but the SE.5a was not delivered to Baldonnel Aerodrome until early in September due to the aircraft sustaining a damaged tail skid and propeller during the landing at Shotwick and entered service with 'B' Flight, No. 1 Squadron.

With the outbreak of the Civil War in June 1922 an Air Service detachment, equipped with a Bristol F2B Fighter, was deployed to a temporary airstrip on the outskirts of Limerick, for operations against Republican forces in the south-west. The F2B Fighter was damaged in a crash-landing at this airstrip in August and was replaced by the SE.5a. In October 1922, during a patrol flight from this airstrip, the SE.5a force-landed near Mallow, Co. Cork, following engine failure. The pilot, who was unhurt, went to seek assistance to remove the aircraft to safety, but a group of Republican troops arrived and set fire to the SE.5a, which exploded and was destroyed.

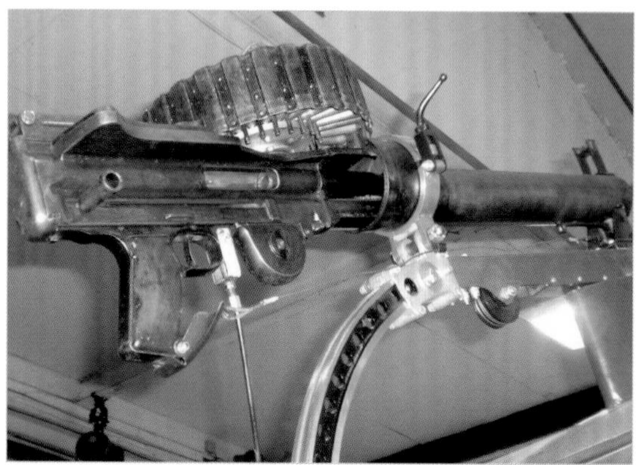

Right: Details of the cockpit and machine gun on a fully airworthy SE5A at the Shuttleworth Collection. Of interest is the spare magazine for the Vickers gun stored in a special container on top of the instrument panel in easy reach of the pilot who had to change magazines in flight! (J. Maxwell & P. Hopkins photos)

Colours & Markings

References on this aircraft are sparse and they differ as to the possible colour scheme used. It is believed that the fuselage and tailfin of the SE.5a had an overall maroon or red finish, with the wings and tailplane painted silver. The red finish on the fuselage could have been unpainted red oxide primer or a variation on the PC 12 finish used on RAF aircraft destined for operations in warmer climes. The national colours were displayed as green, white and orange roundels, on the upper surfaces of the top wings and on the under surfaces of the lower wings. They were also displayed as vertical stripes on both sides of the rudder. Some sources suggest that the roundels were removed and replaced with stripes. Other references state that the aircraft's serial, in white, was displayed only on both sides of the rear fuselage section but this has not been confirmed.

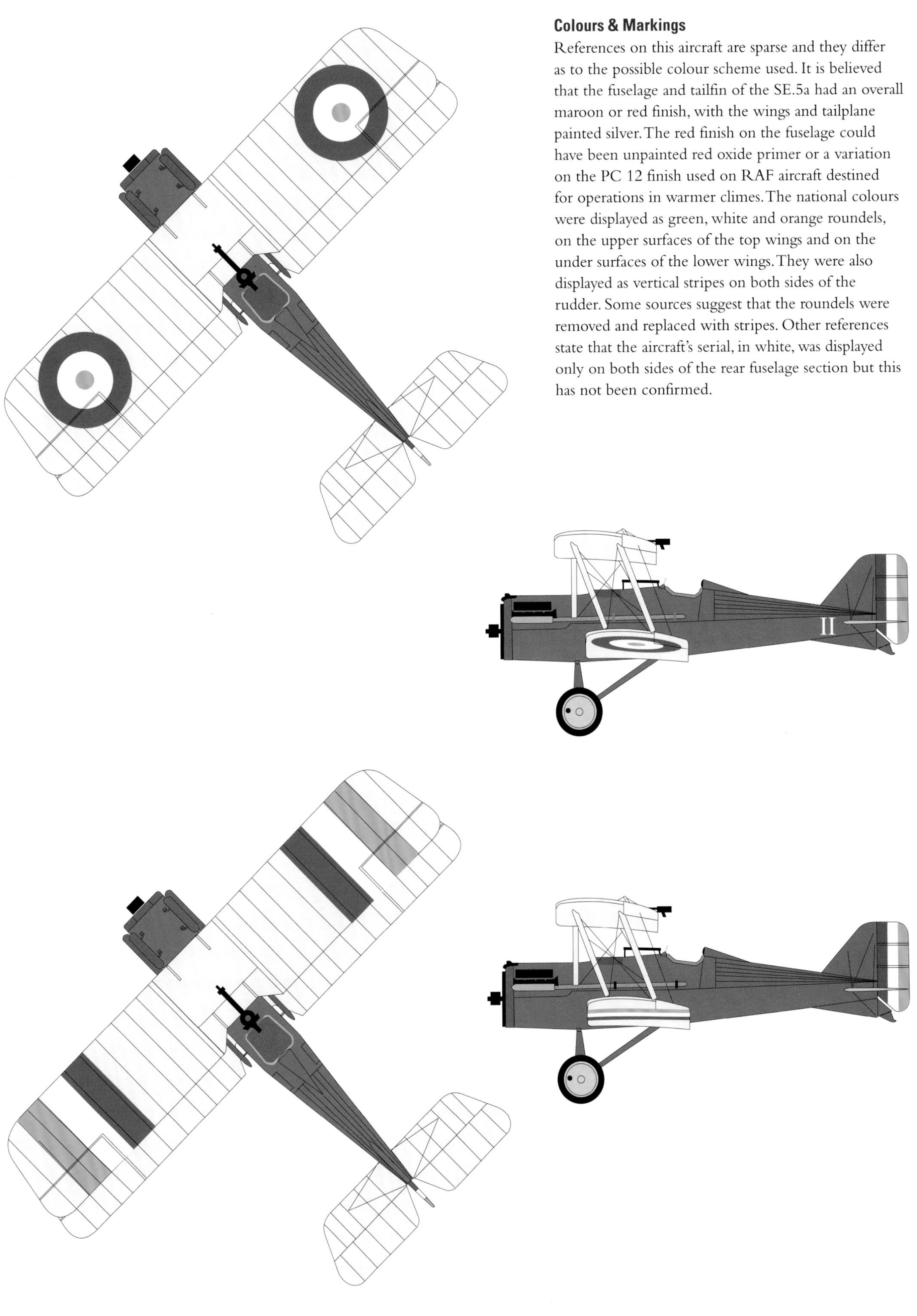

1.5

Airco D.H.9 (1923 – 1934)

Designed for mass production, the D.H.9 was a development of the D.H.4 with a new fuselage placing the pilot and rear gunner in close proximity. On July 26, 1917, the D.H.9 was ordered into large-scale production replacing the production orders for the D.H.4. Powered by a 230-hp Siddeley Puma engine the first production D.H.9 (RAF serial C6051) underwent an extensive flight-testing programme in October 1917. Despite an overall performance that was inferior to that of the D.H.4, large-scale production of the D.H.9 was allowed to continue as cancellation would have lead to severe shortages of aircraft for the front line units. Production ended in 1918 after a total of 3,204 aircraft had been constructed by Airco and twelve other British aircraft manufacturing companies. One of these manufacturers, the Alliance Aeroplane Co. Ltd. (Waring and Gillow Ltd.), constructed a total of 845 D.H.9s, which included a final batch of 345 in 1918 (allocated RAF serials H5541-H5885).

Above: while lacking an occupant in the cockpit, well chocked DH.9 No. DII warms up prior to a mission. (D.MacCarron collection)

Initial deliveries of the D.H.9 to the RFC commenced in December 1917, and 12 squadrons equipped with the aircraft were deployed on combat operations over the Western Front throughout 1918. Due to the unreliability of the Puma engine and the bomber's poor performance above 13,000 feet with a full load of bombs and fuel, these squadrons sustained heavy losses during their combat operations. The D.H.9 also equipped RAF squadrons in the Middle East and was also used for coastal defence patrols, flying training and other duties in the United Kingdom. Following the end of the First World War, the D.H.9 was rapidly withdrawn from use by the RAF and became surplus to requirements, with a large number acquired by Airdisco for disposal. The D.H.9 entered service with at least 13 air forces, and was also constructed under licence in Belgium and Spain in the post-war years. During the Civil War, the Irish Air Service needed an aircraft with sufficient range and speed to provide air support over the entire south-west of Ireland from its southern airfields during combat operations by the National Army against Republican forces. Six Airco D.H.9s were acquired from Airdisco to fulfil this requirement. Delivered between 1st January and 28th February 1923, the six D.H.9s (allocated Roman numerals I to VI as serials) entered service with 'B' Flight, No. 1 Squadron and were the first bomber aircraft to enter service. On January 18, 1923 one of the D.H.9s (IV) was written-off in a crash at Baldonnel Aerodrome, killing the pilot; this was the first fatal aircraft crash to occur in the Irish Air Service.

Operating from the airfields at Fermoy, Co. Cork and Tralee, Co. Kerry until April 1924, the D.H.9s were engaged on reconnaissance flights, dropping propaganda leaflets and patrolling the railway system in the south and south-west regions of Ireland. On June 25, 1923

Left: DH.9 No. 7 in its hangar at Baldonnel. The hangars had been built to Royal Flying Corps specifications between 1916 and 1918. Although not designed for a long life, no less than three of them are in daily use in the 21st century. (C. Bruton photo)

another D.H.9 (I) was destroyed in a crash near Fermoy, killing the observer.

Only four D.H.9s (DII, DIII, DV and DVI) remained in service with 'B' Flight, No. 1 Squadron, following the formation of the Irish Army Air Corps in October 1924. The prefix letter 'D' (for de Havilland) had also at this stage been added to the Roman numeral serials allocated to these aircraft. Over the following six years the D.H.9s were engaged on peacetime duties, which included an aerial survey of the State and a photographic survey of historic sites for the Archaeological Research Commission. The D.H.9s were also used for advanced flying training and participated in the annual military exercises conducted by the Irish Defence Forces during this period.

In February 1926, two D.H.9s participated in the first search and rescue mission by the Air Corps, searching for a missing trawler Cardigan Castle off the west coast of Ireland. Over a four-day period, commencing on February 20, 1926, the two D.H.9s, with three Bristol F2B Fighters, carried out an aerial search over the region, but the trawler was not located due to adverse weather conditions. A contemporary news report appeared in Flight magazine on March 11th 1926 and is reproduced here courtesy of Flight International and the Flight Collection;

> *Capt. Crossley piloted the D.H.9 round Clifden Bay and High Island, and ascertained that there were quite a number of places on the lee shore where a boat could land. They circled down on the island—which is a kind of Atlantic breakwater practically wholly composed of highcliff rock—as close as Capt. Crossley and his observer dared,but they saw no sign of life on the island. It was on a similar island that the crew of the Tenby Cattle, which was also dashed against the rocks and wrecked, were found previously. The weather was very misty and visibility bad, but the aviators, when night was falling, dropped a quantity of food and some first-aid dressings on the island, thusensuring that if any survivors of the wreck should happen to be on the island they would have sufficient food at least to last them for a week. The machines engaged in the work of rescue visited in all a score of islands, but without result. High Island is the island from which the message, written on a piece of board, from four of the survivors was supposed to have been sent out. The search by aeroplanes was instructed by President Cosgrave. When volunteer pilots and observers were called for this hazardous job, every officer present eagerly stepped forward. Although this aerial search failed to bring forth any result, the action taken by the Irish Free State in their effort to trace the English seamen is nevertheless thoroughly appreciated in this country.*

The sentiments expressed by the Flight correspondent in 1926 are as relevant today as they were 80 years ago, as search and rescue became a major and highly publicised role for the Air Corps from the early 1960's with the arrival of the first helicopters.

On February 26, 1926, during its return flight to Baldonnel Aerodrome, one of the D.H.9s (DV) crashed near Oughterard, Co. Galway, and was written-off. In 1929 two D.H.9s, each costing £850 and without engines installed, were acquired from Airdisco as replacements for the three of these aircraft that had crashed. The two D.H.9s were delivered to Baldonnel Aerodrome on April 5, 1929. and (as nos. 7 and 8) entered service with 'B' Flight, No. 1 Squadron. (Arabic numerals were now being allocated as serial numbers to aircraft entering service with the Air Corps.) One of these aircraft (ex-RAF serial H5862) was from the batch of 345 D.H.9s (RAF serials H5541-H5886), constructed by the Alliance Aeroplane Co. Ltd. (Waring and Gillow Ltd.), and the other D.H.9 (ex-RAF serial H9247) was from the batch of 261 (RAF serials H9311-H9412), constructed by Airco.

One of the D.H.9s (DII) was withdrawn from use in February 1930, followed by another (DVI) in April 1931; both aircraft were later scrapped. One of the D.H.9s (no. 8) delivered in 1929 was written-off in an accident on June 10, 1932, and the two D.H.9s (DIII and No. 7) then remaining in service were withdrawn from use in September 1934 and were later scrapped, following a survey by the Air Corps of obsolescent aircraft and aero-engines held in storage in June 1935 that were to be valued as scrap and sold or destroyed.

DH.9 No. 7 in an overall silver colour scheme circa 1926

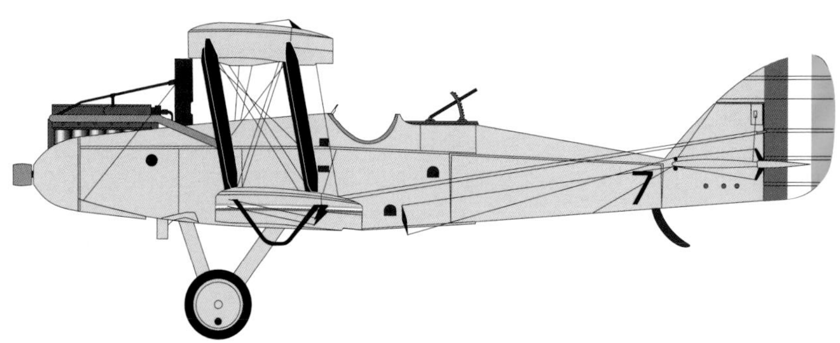

Non standard conversion of DH.9 No.6 to a two seat trainer.

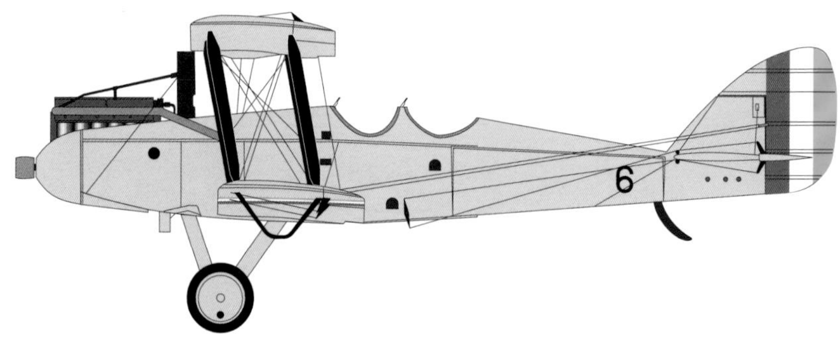

DH.9 DII in the original overall grey scheme with bright red nose cowling.

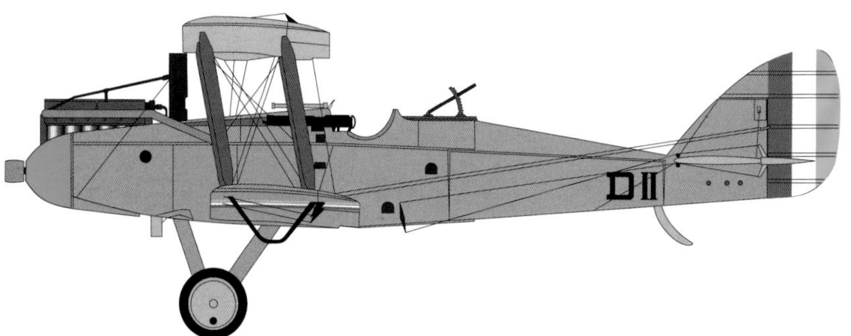

Colours & Markings

The D.H.9s initially had an overall light grey finish, with the front section of the nose painted red. Green, white and orange stripes were displayed chordwise on the upper surfaces of the top wings and the under surfaces of the bottom wings, and vertically on both sides of the rudder. Each aircraft's serial number was displayed in black on both sides of the rear fuselage section, in front of the tailplane. The aircraft were subsequently overall silver.

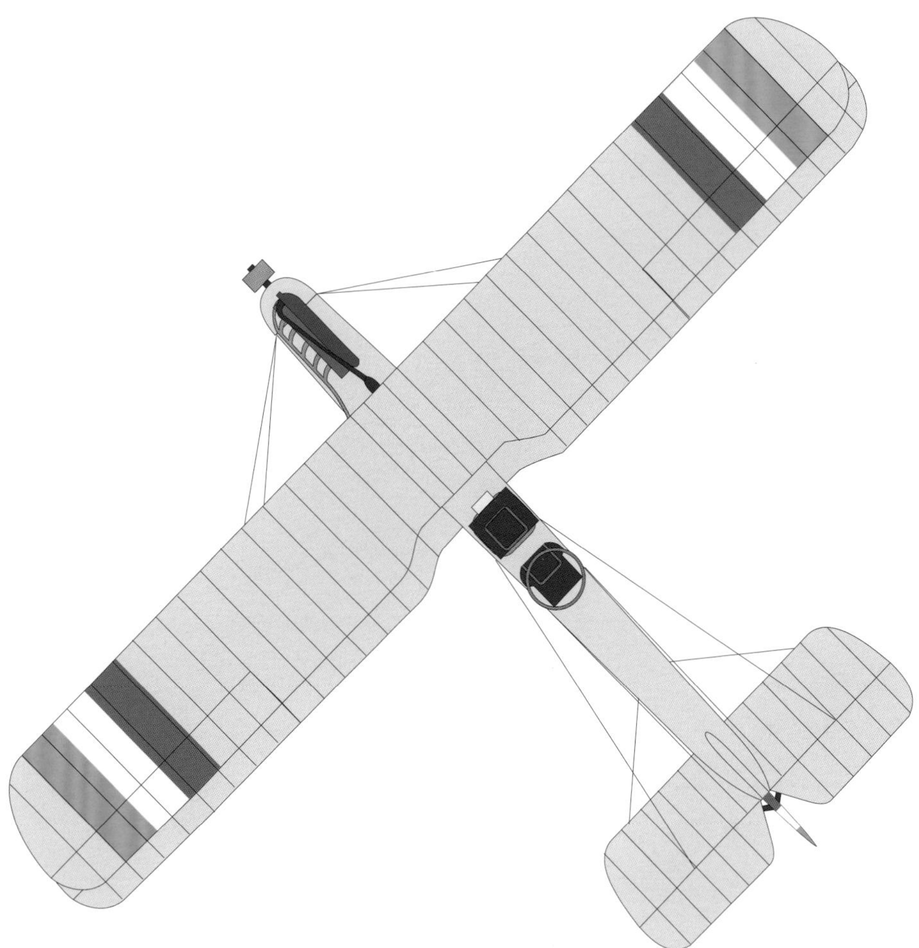

1.6

De Havilland DH.60 Cirrus Moth (1926 – 1935)

In 1924, the de Havilland Aircraft Company initiated the design and construction of a two-seat light aircraft, powered by an inexpensive but reliable engine, to provide economical and safe flying for "owner pilots" and flying clubs. The Airdisco Cirrus, a specially designed 60-hp, four-cylinder piston engine, was selected to power this aircraft. The Cirrus engine was a developed from the Aircraft Disposal Company's 120-hp Airdisco V.8 engine which was largely based on War surplus Renault V.8 engines. The Cirrus engine was an adaptation of this larger engine, but cut in half and fitted with a new crankcase.

Designated DH.60 by the company and later named Moth, the first prototype (c/n 168, registered G-EBKT) flew for the first time on February 22, 1925, powered by a 60-hp Cirrus I engine. The first flight of the second prototype (c/n 169, registered G-EBKU) also occurred in 1925 and production of the Moth commenced in the same year. On December 23, 1925 the first prototype DH.60 Moth arrived at Baldonnel Aerodrome and was evaluated by the Irish Army Air Corps over the following three days.

A total of 20 DH.60 Moths (later known as Cirrus Moths to distinguish them from airframes powered by different engines), which included the two prototypes, was constructed in 1925, followed by a batch of 35 in 1926. Powered by an 85-hp Cirrus II engine, a total of 150 Cirrus Moths was constructed in 1927; these aircraft had an increased payload and cruising speed. Next came the DH.60X in 1928, powered by a 90-hp Cirrus III engine with a revised undercarriage. A total of 403 Cirrus Moths of all versions had been constructed when production of the type ended in September 1926.

In 1926, there was an increase in the Irish Army Air Corps' flying training commitments, following the selection via a competitive Civil Service examination of nine cadets for pilot training. The Air Corps was also concurrently conducting a flying training course for ten officers from other units of the National Army who had been selected for pilot training in the previous two years. As a consequence, more elementary training aircraft were required by the Air Corps and four D.H. 60 Cirrus Moths were ordered from the de Havilland Aircraft Company by the Department of Defence to fulfil this requirement. The four Moths were to be fitted with wider tyres, than the standard type for these aircraft, for landing on soft grass airfields.

The four Cirrus Moths (c/ns 264, 265, 266 and 267) were delivered to Baldonnel Aerodrome on July 12, 1926, and (as nos. 23 to 26) entered service with 'A' Flight, No. 1 Squadron. The Cirrus Moths, all from the batch of 35 constructed in 1926, were the first new aircraft designed and constructed in the post-World War I period to be delivered to the Air Corps. Prior to the delivery flight, the Cirrus Moths had been the subject of a painting by the eminent Irish artist, Sir John Lavery R.A., which was later entitled "The First Flight to Dublin". Some sources have suggested that another two DH.60X Cirrus Moths (c/ns 460 and 461) were ordered for the Air Corps (as nos. 27 and 28) but were later cancelled. The aircraft bearing these c/ns were in any event actually delivered to the Royal Canadian Air Force in 1927.

DH.60s and F2Bs share the flight line at baldonnel on a sunny morning in the late 1920s. (A.C. Photographic Section)

Three Cirrus Moths were written-off in crashes over the following two years; the first (no. 26) on June 29, 1927, followed by the second (no. 24) on June 4, 1928 and the third (no. 23) on July 26, 1928. The remaining CirrusMoth (no. 25), together with two Avro 504Ks and an Avro 621, was used for elementary flying training by 'A' Flight, No. 1 Squadron until six Avro 631 Cadets were delivered in 1932. The aircraft remained in limited service for the next three years and was eventually scrapped in August 1935, following a survey of obsolete aircraft and engines held in storage by the Air Corps.

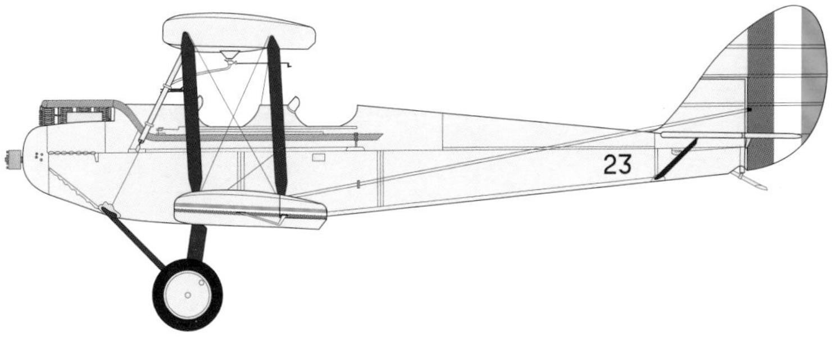

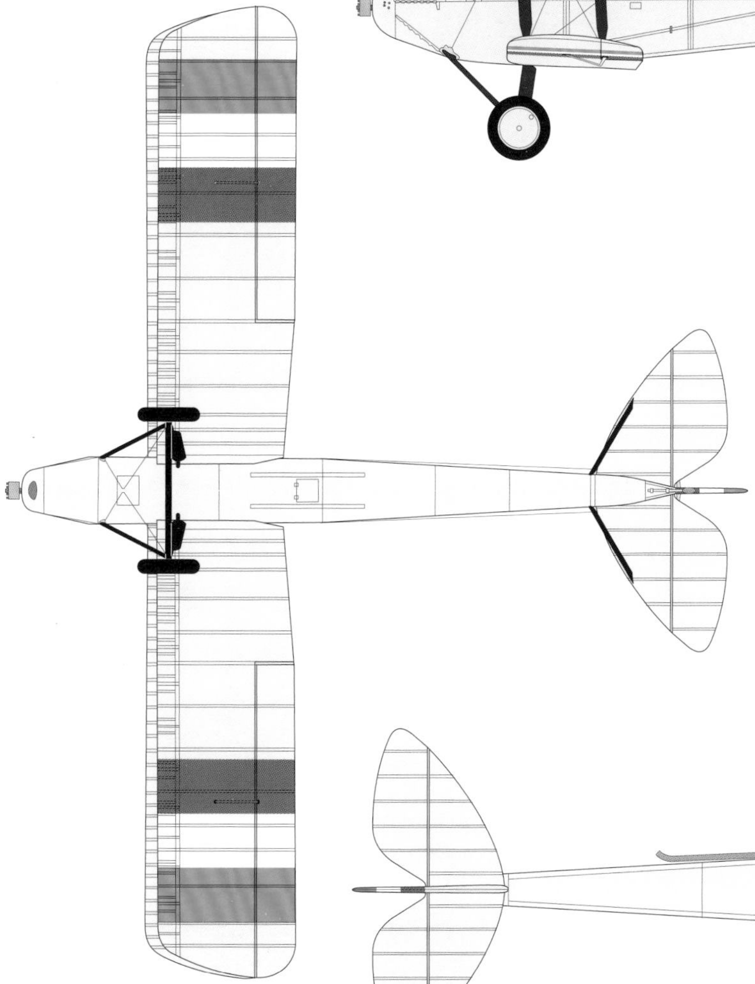

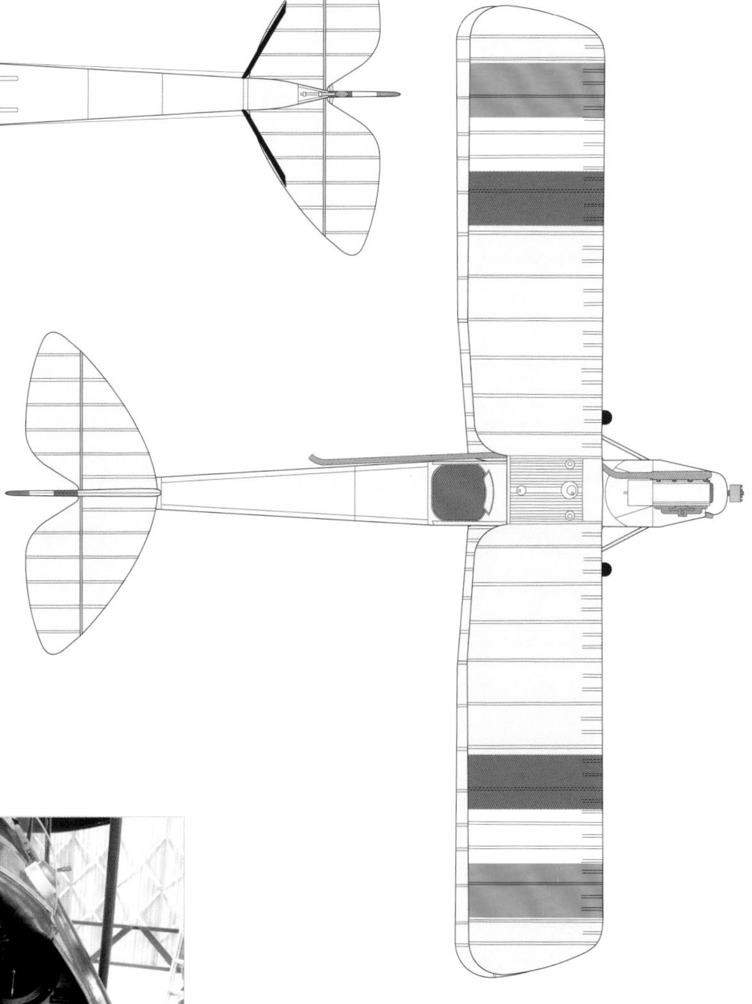

Colours & Markings

The fuselage and wings of the Cirrus Moths had an overall silver finish, with each aircraft's serial number displayed in black on both sides of the rear fuselage, forward of the tailplane. The national colours, in the form of green, white and orange stripes, were displayed chordwise on the upper surfaces of the top wings and the under surfaces of the bottom wings, and as vertical stripes on both sides of the rudder.

Cockpit and engine close-ups of an airworthy DH.60 Cirrus Moth at the Shuttleworth collection.
(J. Maxwell photos)

1.7

Fairey IIIF Mk. II (1928 – 1934)

In 1924 the British Air Ministry issued specifications 19/24 for a three-seat spotter/ reconnaissance aircraft for the FAA, and a two-seat general-purpose aircraft for the RAF. A development of the Fairey IIID, then in service with the RAF and the Fleet Air Arm was submitted by the Fairey Aviation Co. Ltd to fulfil the requirements of this specification designated Fairey IIIF by the company.

The initial versions of this aircraft were powered by a 450 hp Napier Lion VA piston engine but the later Fairey IIIF Mk. II (S1028) flew for the first time on August 18, 1927, powered by a 570-hp Napier Lion XI engine, and thirty-three (S1208-S1227 and S1250-S1262) were ordered for the FAA. Eventually a total of 352 Fairey IIIFs, comprising three variants of the aircraft, was delivered to the FAA. In 1928, to fulfil a requirement for general-purpose aircraft for the Irish Army Air Corps, one Fairey IIIF Mk. II and four Fairey IIIF Mk IVs was ordered by the Department of Defence. The order for the four Fairey IIIF Mk. IVs was later cancelled by the Irish Government due to economic cutbacks. Two of these aircraft (c/ns F969, F970), which were to be diverted from a production batch of twenty-five ordered for the RAF, later entered service with No. 8 Squadron (as J9053 and J9054). The other two Fairey IIIF Mk. IVs (F.1135 and F.1136) were not constructed.

Above: A large aircraft in its day, the Fairey IIIF is inspected by an Air Corps technician and a civilian aircraft inspector prior to its next departure. The underwing bomb racks are noteworthy. (A.C. Photographic Section)

On March 10, 1928 the Fairey IIIF Mk. II (c/n F968), which cost "approximately £5,000", was delivered from the company's factory to Baldonnel Aerodrome, after having been delayed by bad weather. A pair of floats, costing £1,450, was also supplied to convert the Fairey IIIF Mk. II to a seaplane but apparently were never fitted to the aircraft and were scrapped in 1935. This aircraft (ex S1262) was diverted for delivery to the Air Corps from the initial production batch of thirty-three Fairey IIIF Mk. IIs for the FAA. The Fairey IIIF Mk. II entered service with 'B' Flight, No. 1 Squadron, and was used for general-purpose missions, which included crew training, weapons training, aerial photography and mapping surveys. This aircraft was not allocated an Air Corps serial number, but displayed the manufacturer's construction number on the tailfin.

On April 12, 1928, during the initial stage of the first East-West non-stop flight by the Junkers W.33 "Bremen" over the North Atlantic Ocean, this aircraft was escorted to the west coast of Ireland by the Fairey IIIF. On September 13, 1928, during a mapping survey over Co. Cavan, the Fairey IIIF force-landed in a field at a place named Farnham Park, following engine failure caused by a burst oil pipe; there was damage to neither airframe nor crew members. The Fairey IIIF was dismantled and transported by road to Baldonnel Aerodrome and returned to service after re-assembly. The Lion engine installed in the Fairey IIIF underwent a major overhaul by a mechanic from D. Napier & Sons Ltd in April 1930.

On September 10, 1934 the Fairey IIIF crashed at Terenure Road East, in the suburbs of Dublin, and was destroyed by fire. The pilot and observer were killed, but the third member of the crew survived with serious injuries.

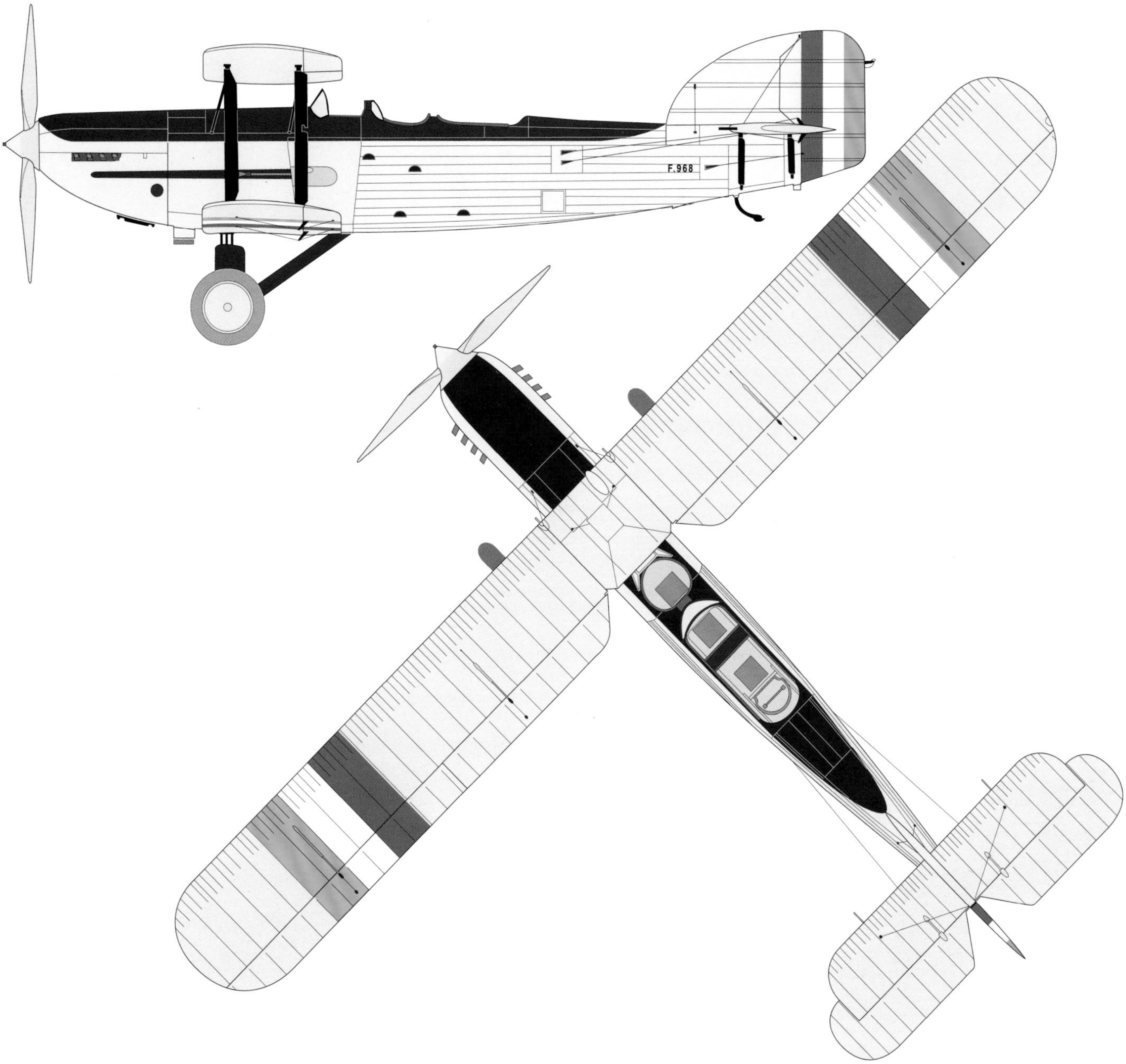

Left: Two general views of the Fairey IIIF in its hangar at Baldonnel. Of note is the small construction number on the rear fuselage and the fact that this IIIF did not have leading edge slats. (A.C. Photographic Section)

Colours & Markings

The Fairey IIIF had an overall silver finish except for the fuselage top decking, which was painted dark admiralty grey or black. The undercarriage and wing struts were painted black. Green, white and orange stripes, positioned chordwise, were displayed on the upper surfaces of the top wings and the under surfaces of the bottom wings, and vertically on the rudder. The aircraft's construction number, in black, was displayed on the both sides of the rear fuselage, in front of the tailplane.

1.8

Vickers Type 193 Vespa IV and Type 208 Vespa V (1930 – 1940)

In 1929, the Irish Army Air Corps had eleven aircraft in service that could be considered capable of carrying out operational missions, but these were reaching the limit of their useful life. The Air Corps required replacement aircraft, and the Department of Defence therefore sought tenders from British aircraft manufacturing companies for suitable types. Vickers put forward its Vespa to fulfil the Air Corps' requirement. This aircraft had been developed as a private venture by Vickers as a replacement for the Bristol F2B. The Vespa did not enter service with the RAF but a Bolivian Government military mission ordered six examples of the type during a visit to the company's factory in 1928.

Four aircraft, designated Type 193 Vespa IVs, were ordered by the Irish Department of Defence in August 1929 for delivery to the Air Corps in 1930, at a cost of £4,500 each. These aircraft were powered by a 492 hp Armstrong Siddeley Jaguar VIc radial engine fitted with a Townend ring cowling. There are photos showing the black painted Townend ring fitted while the aircraft were undergoing pre-delivery trials with Vickers, but it appears that the Townend rings were removed either prior to or just after delivery to the Air Corps. The first Vespa IV flew for the first time on March 25, 1930, followed by the second on March 27, 1930, the third on April 2, 1930 and the fourth on April 7, 1930. The four Vespa IVs were delivered by company pilots to Baldonnel Aerodrome on April 14, 1930 and (as V1, V2, V3 and V4) entered service with 'B' Flight, No. 1 Squadron. The Vespas were the first all-metal aircraft to enter service with the Air Corps, which also at this time introduced parachutes for aircrew.

Designated Type 208 Vespa Vs, four more aircraft were ordered by the Department of Defence in 1930 for delivery in 1931. The Vespa Vs were also powered by Jaguar engines, but these aircraft were not fitted with Townend ring cowlings, and the long exhaust pipes from the engine exhaust collector ring were inclined downwards towards the underside of the centre section of the fuselage, rather than running horizontally. The first Vespa V made its maiden flight on March 25, 1931, followed by the second on March 26, 1931 and the third and fourth on March 30, 1931. The four Vespa Vs were delivered to Baldonnel Aerodrome on April 5, 1931 and (as V5, V6, V7 and V8) entered service with 'B' Flight, No. 1 Squadron.

The Vespas were used for general-purpose duties by the Air Corps, including army co-operation,

Above right: The Vespa's rear gunner was well armed with twin Vickers machine guns, used for self defence, or as illustrated, to bring fire to bear on ground targets. (J. Maxwell collection)

reconnaissance flights, advanced flying training, weapons firing, bombing exercises, aerial surveys and air-to-ground photographic missions for the Defence Forces and Government Departments. Weapons firing and bombing exercises were initially carried out over the air firing range at Kilworth, Co. Cork, and from 1935 onwards at Gormanston Military Camp, Co. Meath. The Vespas also participated in the annual combined exercises conducted by the Defence Forces during this period. Two Vespa IVs were written-off in crashes within a year of their entering service, the first (V4) at the Curragh Military Camp, Co. Kildare, on April 9, 1931, and the second (V3) in the Foxford Mountains, Co. Mayo, on May 18, 1931.

In June of 1932, the Eucharistic Congress (a larger international gathering of Catholic clergy and laypeople) was held in Dublin and units of the Irish Defence Forces, including the Air Corps, participated in the ceremonies to celebrate this event. The huge congregation attending the opening religious services and ceremonies of the Congress in the Phoenix Park, on the outskirts of the city of Dublin, were photographed from the air by a Vespa. This aircraft was also used for low-level aerial photographs of the closing religious ceremony, which was held in the centre of Dublin.
In the same year, the Air Corps received a request from the British Mount Everest Flight Houston

Left: The original Vickers Vespa V1 basks in summer sunshine at Baldonnel. Note the large rear wing spar over which the pilot had to climb in order to enter the cockpit. (A. Peard collection)

Expedition to provide two Vespas for an attempt on the first ever flight over the summit of Mount Everest. To photograph the summit of the mountain, the Everest Expedition required two aircraft powered by air-cooled radial engines driving a large diameter propeller, with a large wing surface area for good high-altitude performance and deep, roomy cockpits to accommodate the pilot, an observer and several cameras. The Air Corps had offered one damaged Vespa to the expedition provided that the Expedition organisers would pay for the repairs. The expedition also required the loan of a Vespa for high altitude crew training which would take place in Britain. Negotiations were continuing on this and the expedition organisers believed they could obtain a second Vespa from the manufacturer to be used on the expedition itself. However this turned out not to be the case as it had been allocated to another customer. Although the Vespas fulfilled most of these requirements, and the response from the Air Corps was positive, the Everest Expedition eventually selected two British experimental aircraft, the Westland PV.3 and PV.6. Powered by the Bristol Pegasus IS3 supercharged radial engine, these aircraft were more efficient at high altitudes and became the first aircraft to fly over the summit of Mount Everest on April 3, 1933. A Vespa powered by this engine and flown by RAF Flt. Lt. Cyril Uwins set a world absolute altitude record of 43,976ft in September 1932.

Four of the Vespas were written-off or badly damaged in crashes and forced landings between August 1932 and September 1933. A Vespa IV (V2) that crashed on August 31, 1932, was not considered worth repairing by the Air Corps and had to be written-off. On August 5, 1933 a Vespa V (V6) was also written-off after going into a spin and crashing during a mock dog fight with three Avro 621 Cadets of the Air Corps during an air display held over the Phoenix Park to celebrate Irish Aviation Day. The pilot was killed in the crash, and the observer, who was seriously injured, later also died. The air display had been organised by the Irish Aviation Club.

A Vespa V (V7), on a flight from Baldonnel Aerodrome to Cork on February 17, 1933, was damaged after a forced-landing near Enniscorthy, Co. Wexford, and had to be dismantled and transported by road to Baldonnel Aerodrome. In September 1933 a Vespa V (V8), which was participating in combined exercises conducted by the Defence Forces, crash-landed at Baldonnel Aerodrome, wrecking its undercarriage. To maintain a flight of four Vespas with No. 1 Squadron, the Department of Defence sanctioned the repair and reconstruction of the two damaged Vespa Vs by the Air Corps; this work commenced in December 1933. The total cost of repairs was £1,500 but, due to delays in the supply of spare parts from Vickers, the two Vespas did not return to service for another two years.

By 1934, only nine operational aircraft remained in service with 'B' Flight, No. 1 Squadron, but two of these were withdrawn from use and another two were written-off in crashes in that year, including a Vespa IV (V1) at Fermoy on July 6, 1934. Four Avro 626s, which were delivered to the Air Corps for advanced flying training in April 1934, were operated by 'B' Flight, No. 1 Squadron until the two repaired Vespas returned to service in 1935. The Vespa Vs returned to service with 'B' Flight, No. 1 Army Co-Operation Squadron, which had been formed

Above: The angular lines of the Vespa were most apparent as it climbed out after take off. (A.C. Photographic Section)

in October 1934, replacing No. 1 Squadron. On July 10, 1935 a Vespa V (V5) was written-off in a crash, and both its airframe and Jaguar engine were used to provide spares for the other Vespas. In the same year, the Jaguar engines from the two Vespa IVs (V1 and V2) were delivered to A.V.Roe & Co. Ltd. for installation in Avro 636s that had been ordered for the Air Corps in December 1934.

On July 15, 1935, in response to a request from the Department of Industry and Commerce, one of the

Vespa Vs (V7) carried out a photographic survey mission over Rineanna, Co. Clare, on the north shore of the Shannon Estuary. The photographs resulting from this mission were later to be used in the planning and laying out of the transatlantic airport at Rineanna, which ultimately became Shannon International Airport.

An unusual role for the Vespa was that of glider tug. In early 1936, Air Corps personnel had constructed a Grunau Baby II glider at a total cost of £84.17.6d from plans supplied by the German parent company. This included £19.15.10d (230 Reichmarks) for parts that were supplied directly from Grunau in Germany. The glider, differing only in one respect from the plans supplied in that the nose cone was made from aluminium instead of wood, had been built under the supervision of Sergeant Johnny Meagher and was used by the Baldonnel Gliding Club. To date the Grunau BabyII and a Dickson Primary Glider trainer constructed around the same time remain the only aircraft to be entirely constructed and flown at Baldonnel. The usual method of getting the glider aloft was to tow it into the air behind a car using a winch mechanism. Using this method the glider could reach an altitude of about 800ft. For an "At home" day held by the Air Corps in June 1936, Lt. D.K. "Dessie" Johnston suggested that the Vespa be used to tow the glider aloft. A quick release tow mechanism was improvised using parachute fittings, the attachment point being the tail skid of the Vespa. For the display, the glider was flown by Lt. Johnston and the Vespa was piloted by Lt. Andy Woods. The glider was released at an altitude of 1800ft and Lt. Johnston entertained the crowd with a series of loops and stall turns. An inspection of the Vespa afterwards revealed that considerable strain had been placed on the attachment points for the tail skid, so the towing of gliders using this method was discontinued. Gliding using a tow car to get airborne continued until 1939 but ceased during the war years. The Grunau Baby II Glider and the Dickson Primary Trainer Glider were sold to a Mr. J.W.P. Benson in 1947 for a total of £35. It was noted on the file relating to the sale that gliding was no longer a part of Air Corps training and that its re-introduction was not contemplated.

In 1937, only two Vespas Vs (V7 and V8) remained in service with the Air Corps, but one of these aircraft (V7) was withdrawn from use following damage to the rear fuselage in a landing accident at Baldonnel on August 17 of that year. Repairing this aircraft was considered to be uneconomical, as production of the Vespa had been terminated by Vickers in 1931 after a total of only fifteen had been constructed. Spare parts would therefore have had to be specially manufactured by the company, and the Air Corps did not have the equipment or machinery to manufacture the required parts. As a result, the crashed Vespa, which had accumulated a total of 465 flying hours, was used as an instructional airframe with the Apprentice School before being scrapped February 1942. A total of 651 flying hours had been accumulated on the aircraft's Jaguar engine, which was used as a spare for the Air Corps' Avro 636s. The remaining Vespa V (no.V8) was written-off in a crash on June 12, 1940.

Right: Glider construction underway in one of the workshops where the technicians are well versed in all aspects of wood and fabric aircraft construction. (A.C. Photographic Section)

Right: the details of the Grunau Baby II glider are explained to Minister Frank Aiken by the Air Corps' O. C. Col. William Delamere. (A.C. Photographic Section)

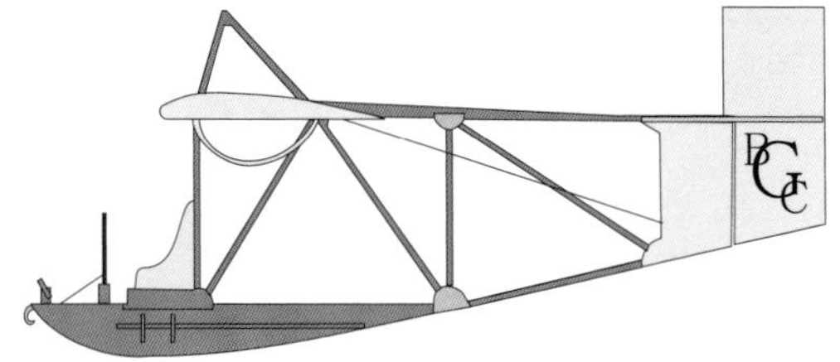

Right: Before flying the Grunau baby, pilots had the opportunity to learn gliding skills on the Dickson Primary Trainer which was also built at Baldonnel. Surviving photos show an indistinct cartoon painted on the upper fin which is not shown in this colour drawing. (J. Maxwell)

Right: The Grunau Baby was a single seat glider and therefore any pilot's first flight was of necessity also a first solo on the type flight!

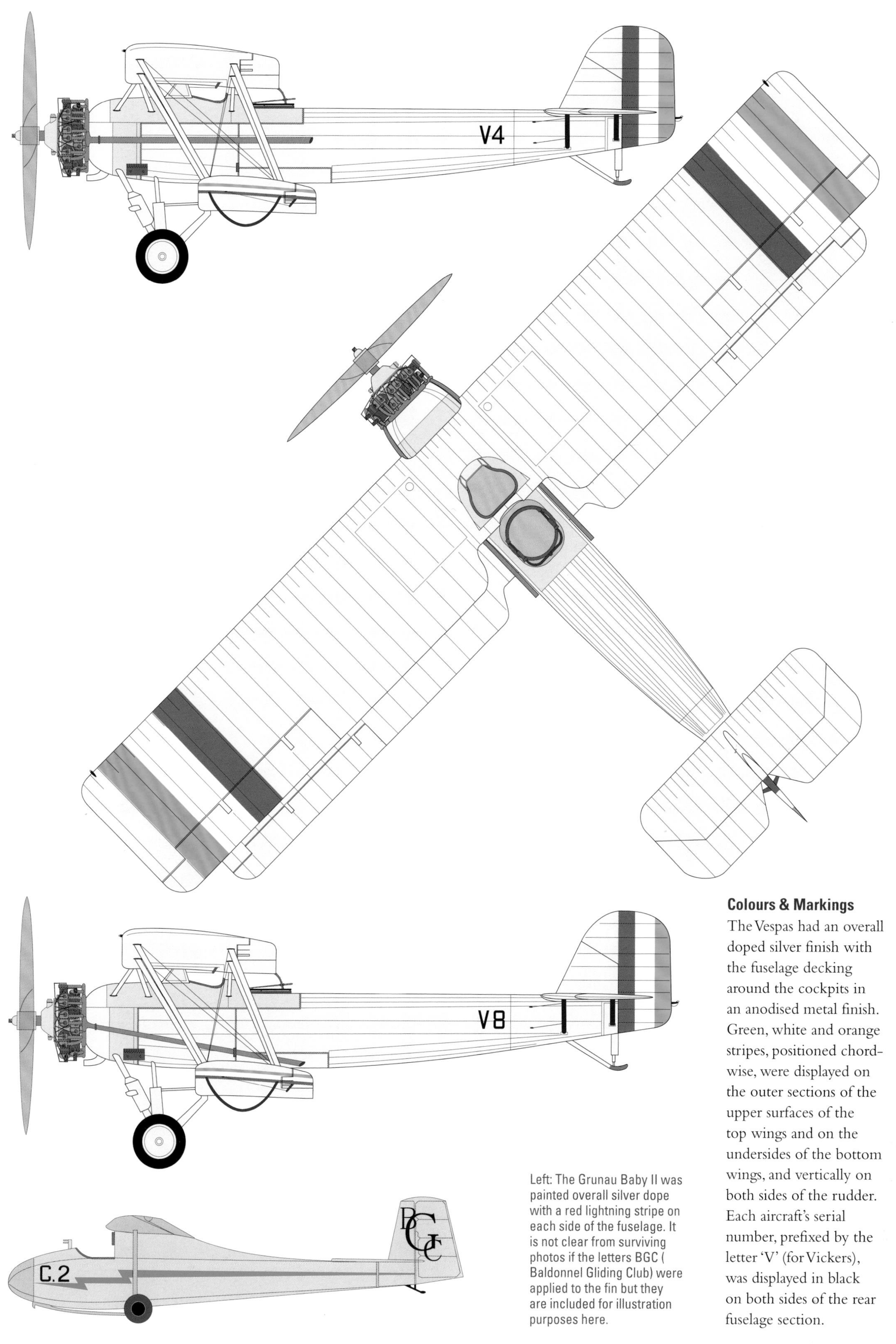

Left: The Grunau Baby II was painted overall silver dope with a red lightning stripe on each side of the fuselage. It is not clear from surviving photos if the letters BGC (Baldonnel Gliding Club) were applied to the fin but they are included for illustration purposes here.

Colours & Markings

The Vespas had an overall doped silver finish with the fuselage decking around the cockpits in an anodised metal finish. Green, white and orange stripes, positioned chordwise, were displayed on the outer sections of the upper surfaces of the top wings and on the undersides of the bottom wings, and vertically on both sides of the rudder. Each aircraft's serial number, prefixed by the letter 'V' (for Vickers), was displayed in black on both sides of the rear fuselage section.

1.9

Avro 621 Trainer (1930 – 1937)

In 1929, there were only three aircraft in service with the Irish Army Air Corps suitable for elementary flying training but these were about to be withdrawn from use in the near future. Three Avro 621 Trainers were therefore ordered by the Department of Defence in the same year as replacements for these aircraft. The first Avro 621 Trainer (c/n 410) was delivered to Baldonnel Aerodrome on March 23, 1930, followed by the second (c/n 411) on April 5, 1930. The third Avro 621 Trainer (c/n 412), which was damaged in a forced landing in Scotland during an initial delivery flight to the Air Corps, had to be returned to the company for repairs, eventually being delivered to Baldonnel Aerodrome on April 17, 1930. The three Avro 621s, which had ailerons fitted only to the lower wings, entered service (as A7, A8 and A9) with 'A' Flight, No. 1 Squadron.

Powered by an uncowled 155-hp Armstrong Siddeley Mongoose IIIA five-cylinder radial engine, the aircraft was underpowered, with a mediocre overall performance. It was subsequently developed into a superb trainer (named Avro 621 Tutor) when powered by a 215-hp Armstrong Siddeley Lynx IV radial engine, and in this form it became the standard elementary training aircraft with the RAF from 1933 to 1939.

The Mongoose-engined Avro 621 Trainer was nicknamed "The Cow" by Air Corps pilots, and two of these aircraft were written-offin crashes in 1930. The first (A7) was destroyed in a crash at Bray Head, Co. Wicklow on November 21, 1930, the pilot and observer surviving with injuries, and the second (A9) was written-off in a crash at Maynooth, Co. Kildare, on November 26, 1930. Operated by the Air Corps Training Schools which replaced 'A' Flight, No. 1 Squadron in October 1934, the third Avro 621 (A8) was withdrawn from use in August 1937 and scrapped.

Far right: Close up of the Mongoose engine installed on a Hawker Tomtit at the Shuttleworth collection. Similar engines powered the Avro 621s in Air Corps service. (J. Maxwell photo)

Far right: Cockpit of an airworthy Avro Tutor of the Shuttleworth Collection. (J. Maxwell photo)

Right: The lack of upper wing ailerons is obvious in this photo of Avro 621 A8 in its hangar. (D. MacCarron collection)

Right: All three Avro 621s are lined up shortly after their arrival in 1930. (A.C. Photographic Section)

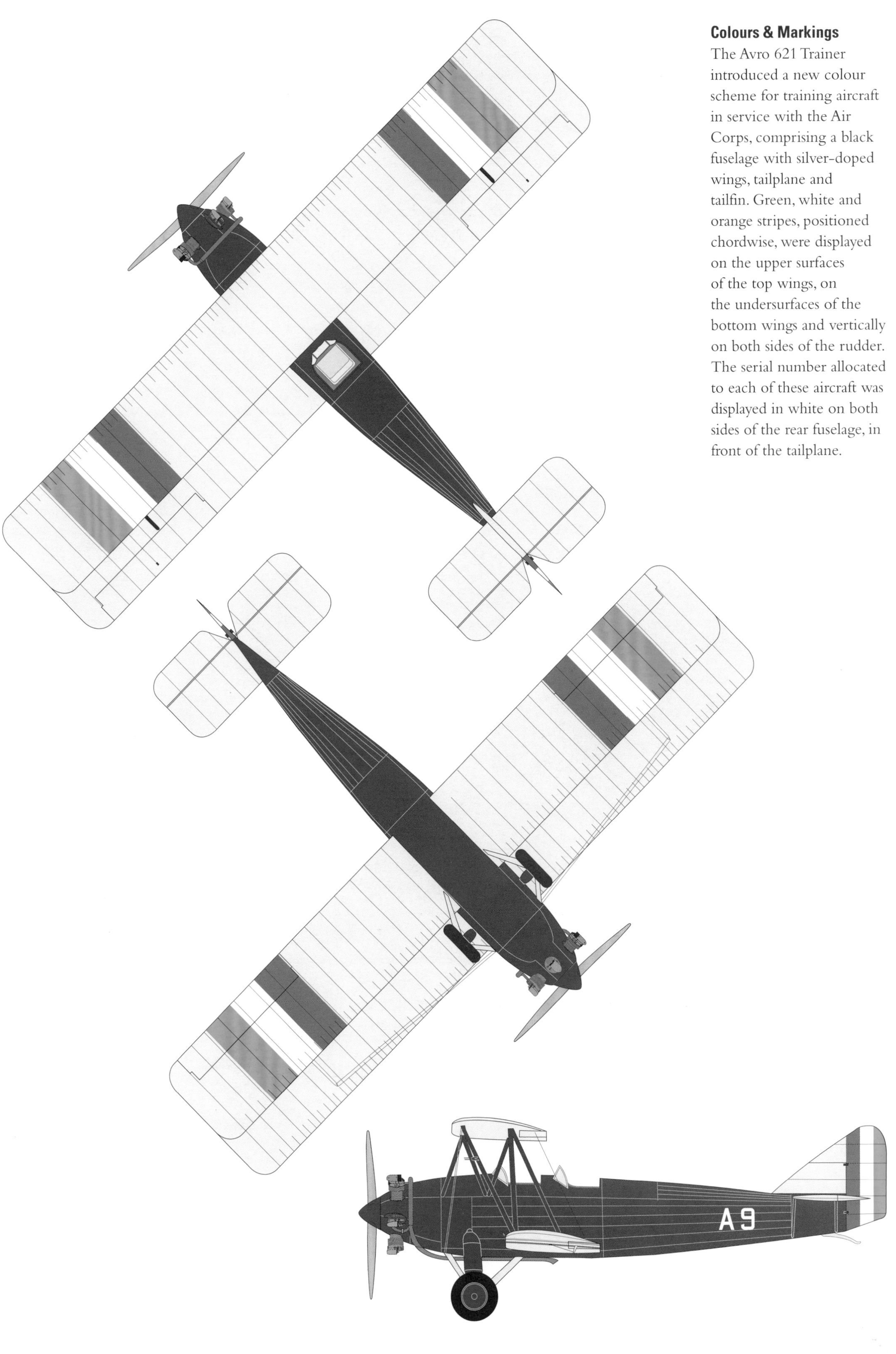

Colours & Markings

The Avro 621 Trainer introduced a new colour scheme for training aircraft in service with the Air Corps, comprising a black fuselage with silver-doped wings, tailplane and tailfin. Green, white and orange stripes, positioned chordwise, were displayed on the upper surfaces of the top wings, on the undersurfaces of the bottom wings and vertically on both sides of the rudder. The serial number allocated to each of these aircraft was displayed in white on both sides of the rear fuselage, in front of the tailplane.

1.10

Avro 631 Cadet (1932 – 1945)

Designated Avro 631, the development of a smaller and lighter version of the Tutor for civilian flying clubs was initiated by A.V.Roe and Co. Ltd. in 1931. Powered by a 135-hp Armstrong Siddeley Genet Major seven-cylinder radial engine, a single prototype (c/n 558, UK civil registration G-ABRS) flew for the first time in October of that year and was issued with a Certificate of Airworthiness in May 1932. Named Cadet, the Avro 631 was a tandem two-seat biplane with a fixed undercarriage, basically similar to the Tutor, but with the control surfaces and wing structures manufactured from wood. A total of 35 Avro 631 Cadets had been built by the company when production ceased in 1934. By 1931, the Irish Army Air Corps had an urgent requirement for an aircraft type that could be used for elementary flying training. 'A' Flight, No. 1 Squadron, had only four aircraft suitable for elementary flying training, of which three were about to be withdrawn from use in the near future. To fulfil this requirement, the Department of Defence ordered six Avro 631 Cadets straight from the drawing board for delivery in 1932. The first six production Cadets (c/ns 581-583 and 584-586) were delivered to the Air Corps in two batches, on March 21, 1932 and April 2, 1932 respectively. Such was the haste with which the aircraft was ordered and delivered the prototype Cadet had not even made its public debut (this occurred at the opening of Skegness Aerodrome in England on May 14th 1932) before the first prodction machines were delivered to the Air Corps; in fact the aircraft had not been issued with Certificates of Airworthiness before delivery. The six Cadets, the first aircraft fitted with wheel brakes acquired by the Air Corps, entered service with 'A' Flight, No. 1 Squadron (as C1 – C6). From October 1934, the Cadets were operated by the Flying Training Schools and were used for elementary flying training by the Air Corps until replaced by the Miles M.14 Magister in 1939.

In June 1932, the Eucharistic Congress was held in Dublin and the ship conveying the Papal Legate was escorted into Dun Laoghaire Harbour, Co. Dublin, by the six Cadets, flying in cruciform formation overhead. This was the first public display of the Avro 631s in Air Corps' service. On August 3, 1933 a Cadet (C3), which was flying in close formation with six other aircraft near Baldonnel Aerodrome during a rehearsal for an air display, touched the wing of the next aircraft in the formation and dived into the ground, killing the pilot. During the air display, which was held two days later over Dublin's Phoenix Park on Irish Aviation Day, a Vickers Vespa V and three Cadets were engaged in a mock dogfight. The Vespa was put into a spin to escape the attacking Cadets, but plunged into the ground, killing the pilot and seriously injuring the observer, who later died.

On September 8, 1934 a seventh Cadet (c/n 730) was delivered to Baldonnel Aerodrome as a replacement

On its return to Baldonnel in 2007 Cadet C7 was greatly admired by all, particularly as it had been restored to airworthy condition. (George Norman photo)

for the crashed aircraft (C3). Fitted with an inverted fuel system, this was the last Cadet constructed by the company and (as C7) entered service with the Flying Training Schools. A second Cadet (C4) was written-off in a crash on June 23, 1937.

On August 14, 1939, the Air Corps deployed a detachment of fifteen aircraft from Baldonnel Aerodrome to Rineanna Aerodrome, the aircraft remaining at this airfield for three days. Comprising Avro Anson Is, Westland Lysander IIs and Cadets, the fifteen aircraft flew in formation over the city of Limerick before landing at Rineanna Aerodrome. Three Cadets also provided an aerobatic display over the city on the same day. On August 30, 1939, the Air Corps again deployed aircraft to Rineanna Aerodrome, including a Cadet for liaison and general support duties. Three Cadets are known to have been operated by this Air Corps detachment at different times throughout 1940.

Most of the Cadets were either withdrawn from use or written off in crashes in 1941 and 1942. The last remaining Cadet (No. 7) was withdrawn from use in August 1945, after accumulating a total of 957 flying hours over the previous eleven years, and was acquired by a civilian pilot in the same month, but was stored following a landing accident in 1946. Although allocated Irish civil registration (EI-AFO and EI-AGO in 1950 and 1954 respectively), the Cadet was never issued with a civilian Certificate of Airworthiness and remained in storage. The Irish civilian registration were cancelled in 1966 and the Cadet was sold in the United Kingdom in 1984, where the aircraft was allocated British civil registration (G-ACFM), which were not taken up. Following limited restoration work, the Cadet was sold to a buyer in New Zealand in May 1991. In 1999, having undergone a complete restoration, the aircraft – which had in the meantime been allotted New Zealand civilian registration marks (ZK-AVR) – flew again in Air Corps colours. This Cadet was purchased by the Irish Government for the Air Corps Museum and flew again at Baldonnel on 29th August 2007 with Brig.Gen. Ralph James, General Officer Commanding the Air Corps, at the controls.

Brig. Gen. James described the Cadet as an absolutely beautiful aircraft to fly, with well-harmonised controls and seemingly much less cockpit noise and slipstream compared to similar aircraft such as the Tiger Moth. The aircraft has relatively small vertical tail surfaces and as a result is limited to operating in about 5 knots of crosswind. This was not really a problem when Baldonnel was a large grass airfield (this was the case up to the 1950's) but today it is only really possible to maintain one section of the airfield with a mowed grass runway. Hence flying in the Cadet is limited to good weather days when the wind direction is favourable. It is truly a unique aircraft and the oldest Air Corps machine still in existence. Had it not been sold into private hands at the end of its service life it may well not have survived, as there was little consideration given to preservation of historic Air Corps aircraft until relatively recent times. Fortunately for the State, Cadet no. 7 has been preserved and it will remain an important piece of Ireland's aviation heritage for the foreseeable future.

Bottom: Fine view of Cadet C7 outside its Museum hangar at Baldonnel. (George Flood photo)

Below: formation flying is an important military flying discipline, as seen in this photo of the original six Cadets cruising at altitude. (A.C. Photographic Section)

Right: Selection of photos showing cockpit and engine details of Cadet C7 at Baldonnel. The controls appear rudimentary by today's standards. (J. Maxwell photos)

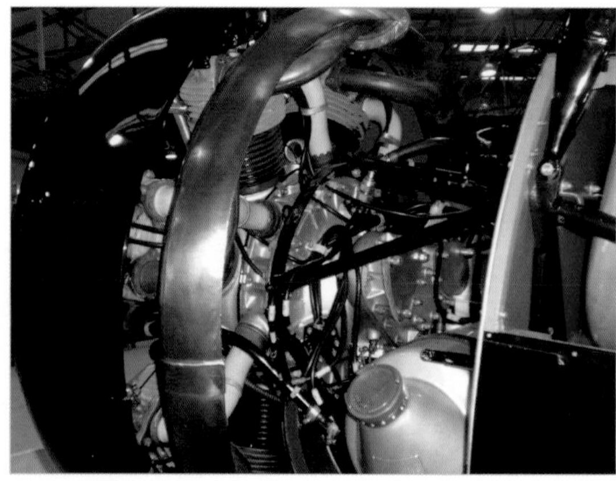

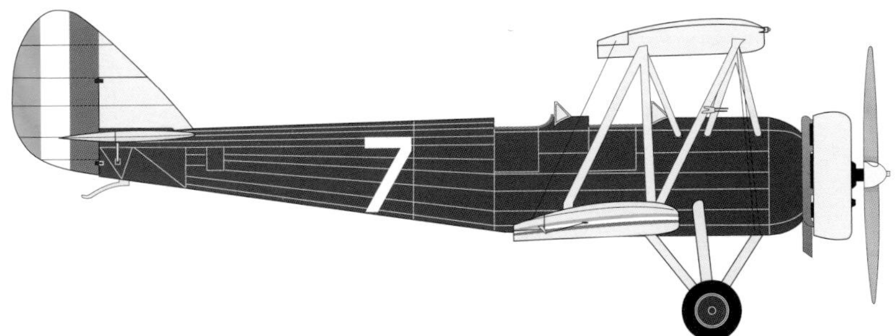

Colours & Markings

On delivery, the Cadets had an overall gloss black fuselage and silver doped wings, tailplane and tailfin, which was the standard paint scheme for Air Corps training aircraft at that time. Green, white and orange stripes, positioned chordwise, were displayed on the upper surfaces of the top wings and on the under surfaces of the lower wings, and as vertical stripes on both sides of the rudder. Initially each aircraft's serial, with the prefix letter 'C', was displayed in white on both sides of the rear fuselage section, in front of the tailplane. From 1938 onwards, the Cadets displayed larger serial numbers, without the prefix letter 'C' (for Cadet), on both sides of the fuselage centre section and on the under surfaces of the lower wings (incidentally, the dropping of this 'C' prefix saw the commencement of the system of allocating serial numbers to Air Corps aircraft that remains in use to the present day). Cadet No. 7 was painted with dark green and dark earth disruptive camouflage on the upper surfaces during World War 2.

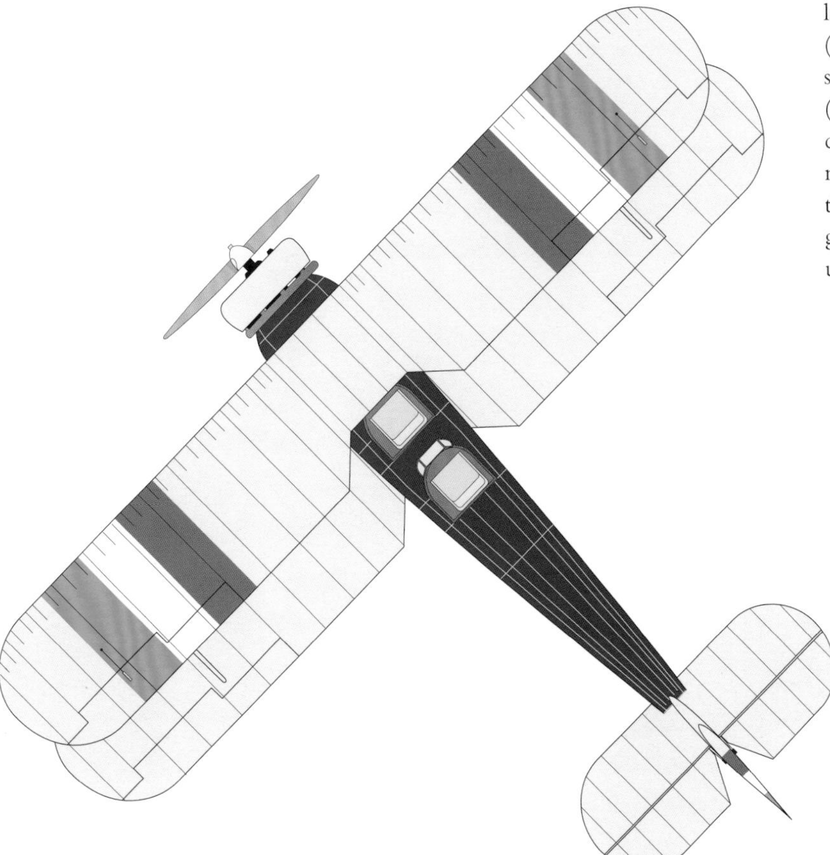

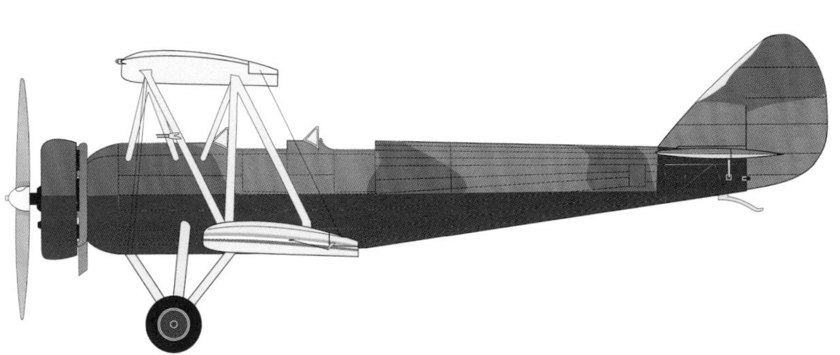

Above: Cadet 7 high over county Kildare in its original colour scheme of black fuselage and silver flying surfaces. Note the silver cowling on the original. All other Avro 631s had black cowlings. (A.C. Photographic Section)

1.11

Avro 626 (1934 – 1941)

Designated Avro 626, a multi-purpose training aircraft developed from the Avro 621 Tutor was designed and constructed by A.V. Roe and Co. Ltd. in 1930, to fulfil the needs of foreign air forces with limited financial resources. The Avro 626 was a two-seat training aircraft, with tandem cockpits, which could also be used for bombing, blind flying, gunnery, night flying, navigation, aerial photography, radio and seaplane instruction, by the use of conversion kits supplied with the aircraft. In addition, the Avro 626 had provision for a third cockpit, behind the standard two, fitted with a steel circular gun mounting for gunnery instruction.

£10,540. The four Avro 626s (as A10 - A13) were initially operated by 'B' Flight, No. 1 Squadron and subsequently (from October 1934) by No. 1 Army Co-Operation Squadron, replacing two Vickers Vespa Vs which were undergoing repairs, having suffered damage in crash landings in the same year. In 1938 the prefix letter "A" (for Avro) was deleted from the Air Corps serial numbers allotted to the Avro 626s.

Over the next five years, the Avro 626s were used for general-purpose duties by No. 1 Army Co-Operation Squadron and for advanced flying training by the Air Corps Training Schools formed in October 1934.

Right: A number of 626's are put through pre-flight inspections, prior to conducting a busy day of flying training. (A.C. Photographic Section)

A batch of four Avro 626s was initially constructed by the company, these aircraft being used for demonstration tours of Europe and South America throughout 1931. Production commenced in the same year and the Avro 626 was eventually delivered to fourteen air forces worldwide, including the RAF and the RNZAF. The Avro 626 was also constructed under licence in Portugal and a total of 178 aircraft had been constructed by the time production ceased in 1939.

In 1933, the Irish Army Air Corps had a need for an advanced training aircraft; in order to fulfil this requirement, four Avro 626s were ordered by the Department of Defence, at a total cost of

The Avro 636s were used by the Training Schools for front and rear gunnery training, bombing, blind flying instruction, navigation, radio and photography, using the conversion kits supplied with these aircraft.

On May 2, 1935, one of the Avro 626s (A13) was destroyed in a crash, killing the pilot, during air-to-ground gunnery exercises at Baldonnel Aerodrome. The remaining three Avro 626s were withdrawn from use between 1939 and 1941: the first (No.10) on April 14, 1939, the second (No. 12) on July 26, 1940 and the third (No. 11) on May 20, 1941. The Apprentice School then used the Avro 626s as instructional airframes before the aircraft were eventually scrapped.

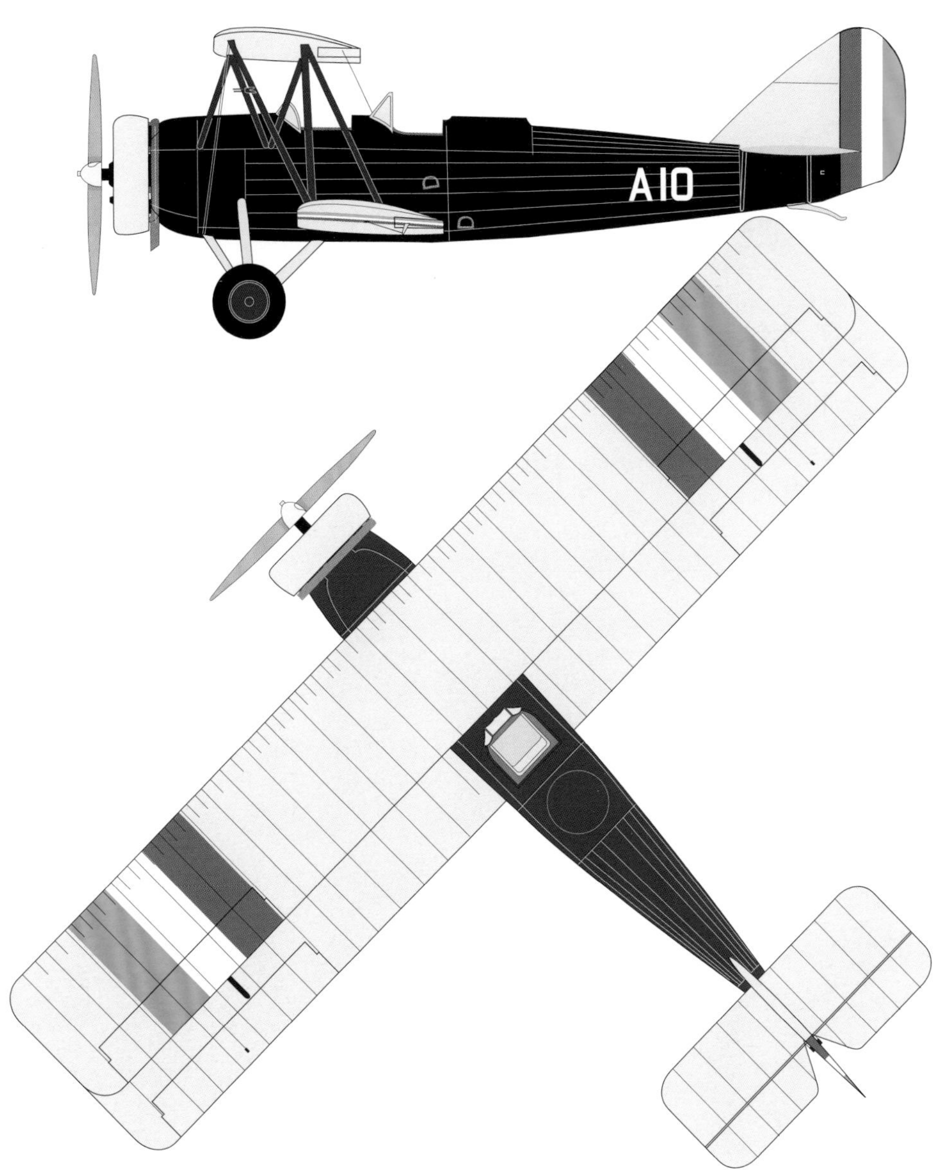

Colours & Markings

The Avro 626s' fuselages were painted black with the wings, tailplanes and tailfins being silver doped, which was the standard colour scheme for all Air Corps training aircraft at that time. Green, white and orange stripes, positioned chordwise, were displayed on the upper surfaces of the top wings, the under surfaces of the bottom wings and vertically, full length, on both sides of the rudder. The serial number allotted to each Avro 626 was displayed in white on both sides of the rear fuselage.

Left: Avro 626 No. A10 carried the then newly-designed two colour boss on the left hand side of the fuselage and the three colour boss on the right hand side during 1934. The two-colour boss was adopted as the new national insignia and gradually appeared on aircraft from 1939. The two-colour boss was superseded by the three-colour boss from 1956.

1.12

Avro 636 (1935 – 1941)

Designated A.W.XVI, two prototypes of a single-seat fighter aircraft, designed and constructed by Sir W. G. Armstrong Whitworth Ltd. in 1930, were submitted to the Air Ministry to fulfil the requirements of Specifications N.21/26 and F.9/26; these specifications were respectively for single-seat fighter aircraft for the FAA and the RAF. The A.W.XVI was unsuccessful in fulfilling both specifications' requirements, but was further developed by the company into the A.W.35 Scimitar powered by a 565-hp. Panther engine, and a prototype (c/n A.W.828) flew for the first time in 1933. The Scimitar (UK civil registration G-ACCD) was submitted as a private venture to fulfil the requirements of Specification F.7/30 for a single-seat fighter aircraft to re-equip RAF fighter squadrons, but the Gloster SS.37 (later named Gladiator) was selected to fulfil this requirement. Four Scimitars were delivered to the Haerens Flyvapen (Norwegian Army Air Force) in 1936, but no further orders for the aircraft were received by the company.

In 1934, a design project for a "fighter trainer", developed from the Scimitar, was initiated by Armstrong Whitworth, but the responsibilty for the design and construction of this aircraft was transferred to A.V. Roe & Co. Ltd. This was because the Armstrong Whitworth A.W.38 Whitley twin-engined bomber aircraft had been ordered into large scale production "straight off the drawing board", and all the company's resources were therefore concentrated on the design and construction of this bomber. The fuselage, undercarriage and tandem dual cockpits of the "fighter trainer" were to be designed and constructed by Avro, but the wings and tailplanes, which were similar to those of the Scimitar, would be supplied by Armstrong Whitworth. Designated Avro 636A, construction of a prototype (c/n 821), which was to be powered by a 420 hp. Armstrong Siddeley Jaguar IV radial engine and used as a demonstration aircraft, commenced in 1934; however, construction was abandoned in 1935.

In December 1934, the Department of Defence ordered four of the "fighter trainers" from Avro to fulfil a requirement of the Irish Army Air Corps for an advanced training aircraft. Designated Avro 667 by the company, but always referred to as Avro 636s by the Air Corps, the four aircraft were to be powered by 460 hp. Armstrong Siddeley Jaguar VIc engines salvaged from the crashed Vickers Vespas in order to keep costs to a minimum.

The Jaguar engines had to be fitted with a propeller of increased diameter, which resulted in the aircraft having to be fitted with a cantilever undercarriage eighteen inches longer than in the original design so as to provide the necessary ground clearance. The pilot's forward view over the engine cowling during landing or taxying was restricted by the lengthened undercarriage , this being the cause of a number of accidents involving broken propellers or bent undercarriages.

The first two Avro 636s (c/ns 863 and 864) were delivered to Baldonnel Aerodrome on October 16, 1935, the remaining two (c/ns 865 and 866) being delivered four days later. The four Avro 636s (as A14 - A17) entered service with the Air Corps Flying Training Schools and were used for advanced flying training over the next five years, including the first Short Service Officer Pilot Course in 1939 These aircraft were also used for weapons training, which included air-to-air and air-to-ground firing exercises over the Air Firing Range at Gormanston Military Camp. In August 1936, despite poor weather conditions, a brilliant aerobatic display by three Avro 636s was the highlight of an "Open Day" airshow organised by the Air Corps at Baldonnel Aerodrome. One of the Avro 636s (no. 16) was written-off in a landing accident at Baldonnel on March 14, 1938. In the same year the prefix letter 'A' was deleted from the serial numbers allocated to the Avro 636s.

The Avro 636s were also operated by No. 1 Army Co-Operation Squadron and later by No. 1 Fighter Squadron, which was formed in 1939. At the outbreak of the Second World War, the three Avro 636s (Nos. 14, 15 and 17), together with Gloster Gladiator Is and Westland Lysander IIs, equipped No. 1 Fighter Squadron. The Avro 636s, which could be flown with the rear cockpit faired over with a removable canvas cover, were operated as single-seat fighter aircraft by the squadron, but were incapable of intercepting or forcing down the majority of Allied or German aircraft that intruded into Irish airspace. At least one of these aircraft (No. 17) was painted in a two-colour disruptive camouflage scheme during this period. On February 9, 1940 an Avro 636 (No.15) was written-off in a crash at Baldonnel Aerodrome following an engine failure. The other two Avro 636s were withdrawn from use in 1941 and were later scrapped.

Colours & Markings

The four Avro 636s were initially finished in the standard colour scheme for Air Corps training aircraft during this period: black fuselages with silver wings, tailplane and tailfin. Green, white and orange stripes, positioned chordwise, were displayed on the upper surfaces of the top wings and under surfaces of the bottom wings, and vertically on both sides of the rudder. Each aircraft's serial number, with the prefix letter 'A' (for Avro), was displayed in white on both sides of the rear fuselage in front of the tailplane. From 1938, when the prefix letter was deleted, each aircraft's serial number was displayed in white on both sides of the fuselage centre section and in black on the undersides of the bottom wings. The three Avro 636s operated by No. 1 Fighter Squadron had the green and orange Celtic boss displayed on the upper surfaces of the top wings and on both sides of the fuselage centre section from 1939 onwards. As already mentioned, at least one (no. 17) was camouflaged in dark earth and dark green paint at the outbreak of the Second World War.

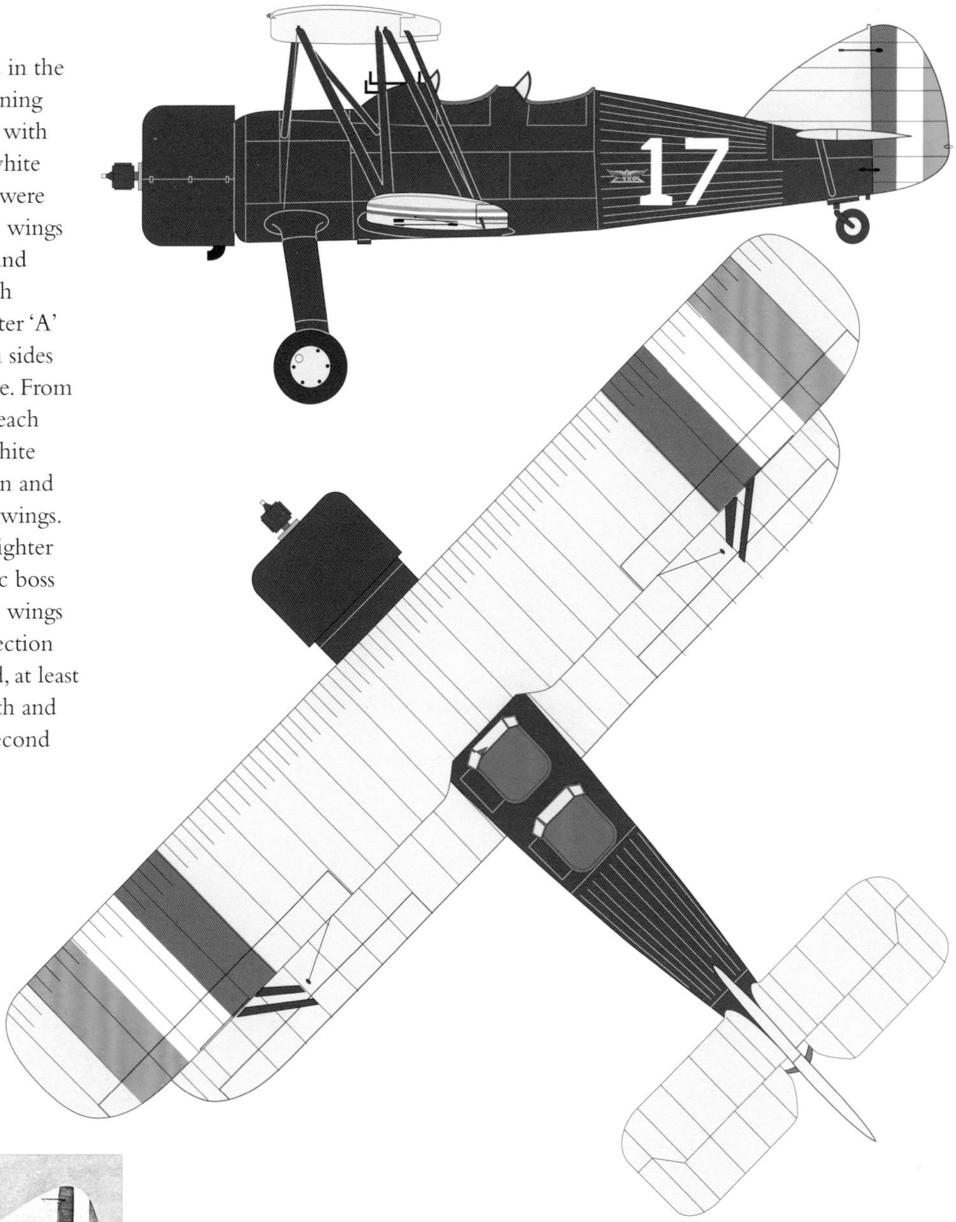

Left: two airborne photos of A14 showing its graceful lines. (reproduced by permission of Aeroplane magazine/www.aeroplanemonthly.com)

The Emergency Period: From Preparations to Aftermath

2.0

The Emergency Period: Preparations to Aftermath (1937 – 1946)

By 1936, only sixteen aircraft were in service with the Air Corps, but over the next three years the force underwent a period of expansion and re-organisation that saw the delivery of modern aircraft. The Air Corps' first twin-engined aircraft (DH 84 Dragon II, used as a target tug), first monoplane aircraft with retractable undercarriage (Avro Anson), first fighter aircraft since 1922 (Gloster Gladiator), first monoplane training aircraft (Miles Magister) and the first – and only – amphibian aircraft (Supermarine Walrus) all entered service during this period. Three new flying units were also formed, No. 1 Reconnaissance and Medium Bombing Squadron in 1937, No. 1 Fighter Squadron in 1938 (replacing No. 1 Army Co-Operation Squadron) and No. 1 Coastal Patrol Squadron in 1939. The green and orange Celtic boss was introduced as the national markings on Air Corps aircraft in 1938 (though it had been designed and trialled on aircraft as early as 1934), being displayed on the upper surfaces of both wings and on both sides of the fuselage.

The Air gunner course of 1943 pose beside a camouflaged Gloster Gladiator. (A.C. Photographic Section)

Following the establishment of the Irish national airline, Aer Lingus Teoranta, the company's first scheduled air service, from Dublin to Bristol, was inaugurated on May 27, 1936, from Baldonnel Aerodrome. Hangar space for the airline's aircraft and other services were provided by the Air Corps until 1940, when all civil air operations were transferred to the recently completed airfield at Collinstown, Co. Dublin, which later became Dublin Airport. A large number of pilots and technicians, having completed their period of service with the Air Corps, would be employed by the national airline in the coming years.

Transatlantic air services from the recently established seaplane base at the port of Foynes, Co. Limerick, commenced in 1939; these services, however, were not run by Aer Lingus, but by Pan Am and BOAC. Construction work on the airfield at Rineanna was also completed in the same year, but transatlantic air services from this airport did not commence until 1945. Air Corps personnel, on secondment to the Department of Industry and Commerce, provided air traffic control services at the Foynes seaplane base and for the airfields at Collinstown and Rineanna for the first ten years of their operation, after which these tasks were taken over by civilian air traffic controllers.

The Second World War See is generally referred to as "the Emergency" in Ireland; use of this term became widespread following the enactment of the Emergency Powers Bill by the Dáil (the Irish parliament) in September 1939, and the declaration of neutrality by the Irish Government. Ireland's stance as a neutral country during Second World War must be seen in the context of the events that preceded the war. As part of The Anglo-Irish Treaty that ended the War of Independence in 1921, 26 of the 32 counties of Ireland became an independent entity, known as the Irish Free State, while the remaining six counties, known as Northern Ireland, remained part of the United Kingdom. This settlement was

Aerial view of Baldonnel in 1938, showing Vespas Cadets and a single Fairey IIIF. (A.C. Photographic Section)

followed by the Irish Civil War that occurred almost immediately between pro- and anti-Treaty factions. Military spending during the Civil War period (which lasted from June 1922 until May 1923) had been enormous, and with ending of the conflict there was a rapid reduction in troop numbers in the National Army and in defence spending generally. This reduced emphasis on defence continued well into the 1930's and was to result in Ireland being ill-prepared for the coming war in Europe.

Following a general election in 1932, the republican Fianna Fáil party, led by Éamon de Valera, formed the government of the Irish Free State. In 1937, de Valera successfully introduced a new constitution, which distanced the new state further from the United Kingdom, and which changed its name to "Ireland" (in Irish, Éire).

De Valera had a good relationship with the then British Prime Minister, Neville Chamberlain, and had been able to gain British recognition of the new constitution. In 1938, De Valera successfully negotiated the return of the so-called Treaty Ports (three Irish ports – the coastal defences at Cork Harbour and Bere Island in Co. Cork, and Lough Swilly in Co. Donegal – that had remained under British jurisdiction after the signing of the Treaty). The major remaining difficulty between the countries was the status of Northern Ireland. The Irish saw it as an integral part of the nation of Ireland, while the British were unwilling to coerce the Unionist majority there into a united Ireland. The status of Northern Ireland effectively created a land border with Britain, and this was one of the factors that exercised Irish defence planners during the Emergency.

In 1940, the United Kingdom was facing the threat of an imminent invasion by German forces, (codenamed Operation Sealion by the Germans). The Germans also had a plan to invade Ireland codenamed Operation Green, which was essentially a diversionary attack to coincide with Operation Sealion. Britain did not wish to see Ireland being invaded by Germany and subsequently used as a base from which to attack Britain from the west. The return of the Treaty Ports to Ireland in 1938 by the previous government galled Winston Churchill, who had become Prime Minister in 1940. In his view, the Royal Navy had been deprived of ports to protect the western approaches, and transit journeys to the Atlantic had been increased by almost 400 miles on a round trip. It was thus tempting for Britain to consider seizing the ports by force by invading Ireland from through Northern Ireland if it was felt at any point that the prevailing circumstances warranted such a move. The UK was reluctant to provide military supplies to Ireland in the lead up to war in Europe for a number of reasons: they needed the weapons for their own use, there was a risk of such supplies being used against them should they need to invade Ireland, and the possibility also existed of their falling into enemy hands following any German invasion of Ireland. The Irish government's view was that Ireland needed to rapidly build up the country's defence forces so that these would act as sufficient deterrent to prevent either side from mounting an invasion. There could be no public agreement for joint military measures with Britain while partition continued. Thus, the problem that presented itself to Irish military planners was a possible invasion by German forces by air and sea on the south and west coasts, or an invasion by Britain from the North.

At a diplomatic level, relations between Britain and Ireland during the war years varied between strained and positively hostile depending on the circumstances prevailing at any particular time. Relations between military men on both the British and Irish sides were, however, more cordial and pragmatic. A secret plan was put in place whereby in the event of invasion by Germany, Ireland would call on Britain for assistance and invite a counter force to come south from Northern Ireland. However De Valera did not altogether trust Churchill to wait for the invitation for the reasons already outlined.

It was against this background of possible invasion from either side that the Irish Army, and by extension the Air Corps, found itself under-equipped to deal with either threat. Military planners came up with a number of scenarios, including a defence of Dublin from invasion by British forces moving south with a defensive line at the Boyne River, and a defence against invasion by German forces in the south of the country with a defensive line at the Blackwater River. Large-scale exercises were conducted in these locations during the war years, and the Air Corps participated in these manoeuvres.

Since the foundation of the State in 1922, the British aircraft manufacturing industry had been the sole supplier of aircraft and ancillary equipment to the Air Corps. However, from 1938 onwards, the delivery of aircraft to the Air Corps from this source was restricted due to an embargo being imposed by the British Government on the export of military aircraft; some aircraft that were actually in the process of being delivered to the Air Corps were even affected by this embargo. In 1939, an Irish military mission visited the United States in an attempt to acquire various types of military equipment, which included combat aircraft for the Air Corps. The American aircraft manufacturing industry could have supplied suitable combat aircraft to the Air Corps. The Seversky Aircraft Company offered to sell the Irish Legation 16 EP-1 Fighter aircraft (EP-1, Export Pursuit, a version of their P-35 fighter) at a cost of $54,975 each with delivery of the first aircraft 75 days after the order being placed and the final aircraft delivery 85 days later. No orders were placed for any aircraft from this source, due to opposition by the Department of Finance on cost grounds and also from officers within the Air Corps itself who were concerned about the potential difficulties in obtaining spare parts from the United States. Notwithstanding the shortages of equipment, the Air Corps introduced a Short Service Officer Pilot scheme in August 1939 and eleven student pilots were recruited, followed by a further twenty in 1940.

On August 30, 1939 an Air Corps detachment comprising aircraft and personnel from No. 1 Reconnaissance and Medium Bombing Squadron and No. 1 Coastal Patrol Squadron was deployed to the airfield at Rineanna and remained there until 1945. Initially the conditions at the airfield were primitive, with no hangars for the aircraft and only basic accommodation for the personnel. Daily coastal patrols off the west, south and south-west coasts, from Lough Swilly, Co. Donegal to Wexford Harbour, were carried out by the aircraft based at this airfield. The coastal patrols had to be curtailed by mid-1940, due to the number of aircraft written-off or damaged in accidents and a shortage of aviation fuel.

In September 1939, at the outbreak of the Second World War, a total of forty aircraft was in service with the Air Corps, comprising twenty-three aircraft capable of carrying out combat operations and seventeen aircraft suitable for flying training and other second-line duties. Approximately the same number of aircraft was in service two years later, following an agreement with the British Government to replace aircraft written-off in crashes or otherwise withdrawn from use from stocks of obsolescent aircraft held in storage by the RAF Only about half of the 40 aircraft in service could be considered suitable for combat operations, but even these were often grounded due to a shortage of spare parts, ammunition and aviation fuel.

In May 1941, diplomatic relations between Britain and Ireland were at a low ebb and the possibility of invasion from the North lead to military exercises being conducted along the Boyne River running through Co. Meath and Co. Louth. As part of these exercises, the Air Corps deployed three Gloster Gladiators to Ballinter House in Co. Meath. Under the command of Lt. Desmond Knowles Johnston, the Gladiators conducted daily reconnaissance sorties in support of the army exercises. As the diplomatic crisis passed the aircraft returned to Baldonnel in August. Interviewed about this deployment many years later the then retired Comdt. Johnston commented that at the time they were under no illusion as to the outcome had an invasion by Britain taken place. With three Hawker Hurricane equipped squadrons s based in the North, the three Gladiators at Bellinter House would have been hopelessly outnumbered. He had no doubt that he and his fellow Air Corps pilots would have given a good account of themselves, but that it would have been an "interesting thirty minutes".

With shortages of aircraft, fuel and spare parts the disbandment of the Air Corps was under consideration towards the end of 1942 with personnel to be deployed to other units of the Defence Forces. This proposed disbandment apparently caused some concern to the British Government, and following consultations, the embargo was raised to enable modern advanced training aircraft and fighter aircraft (in the form of Miles Masters and Hawker Hurricanes) to be supplied to the Air Corps. An RAF officer, Flt. Lt. Don West, was seconded to the Air Corps to conduct conversion courses on these aircraft. The first and only Sergeant Pilot's course was initiated by the Air Corps in 1943, and a total of thirty-one student pilots were recruited under this scheme.

Large-scale military exercises over the countryside north and south of the River Blackwater, in Counties Cork, Tipperary and Waterford, were conducted by the Defence Forces throughout August and September 1942. The Army's 1st "Thunderbolt" Division, known as "Blue Force", was opposed in these military exercises by its 2nd "Spearhead" Division, known as

"Red Force". Detachments of aircraft, known as Air Components, were deployed by the Air Corps to provide air support for both forces during the military exercises. The "Blue Force" was supported by No. 1 Air Component, operating from a temporary airfield at Glenville, Co. Cork, which also included aircraft deployed to Rineanna airfield. Operating from a temporary airfield known as "Rathduff", near Golden, Co. Tipperary, No. 2 Air Component provided air support of the "Red Force". The aircraft operated by the two Air Components were used for observation, reconnaissance, liaison and other missions throughout the military exercises over the forces engaged on these exercises.

Advanced training aircraft in the form of Miles Masters and Hawker Hurricane fighter aircraft from surplus RAF stocks were delivered to the Air Corps throughout 1943. The fighter aircraft were "war weary" after having accumulated a very high number of flying hours over the previous three years, but – due to continued shortages of fuel and spare parts – only a very low number of flying hours was added while these aircraft were in service with the Air Corps. A further batch of fighter aircraft, cannon armed Hurricane Mk IIc's, with minimal RAF service, was delivered in March 1945, apparently to form another fighter squadron; these were the last aircraft delivered to the Air Corps during the "Emergency". In May 1943, following the deployment of No. 1 Fighter Squadron to Rineanna airfield, the detachment from No. 1 Reconnaissance and Medium Bombing Squadron and No. 1 Coastal Patrol Squadron returned to Baldonnel Aerodrome. Both of these squadrons were disbanded in 1944, and their aircraft allocated to General Purpose Flight, which had been formed in the same year. In May 1945, due to the development of Rineanna airfield for post-war transatlantic civil air services, No. 1 Fighter Squadron was deployed to Gormanston Military Camp and operated from this airfield for the next eleven years.

Approximately 200 Allied and German military aircraft either crashed or force-landed in neutral Ireland throughout the "Emergency" period. These aircraft were dismantled and removed from their crash sites by Air Corps salvage parties, with bombs, guns, radio equipment and other items of equipment being brought to Baldonnel Aerodrome. The locations of some of these crash sites were inaccessible to heavy lifting equipment and the crashed aircraft therefore were dismantled and removed from the sites only with extreme difficulty and often in severe weather conditions. Engines, radio equipment and other parts from crashed Allied aircraft were exchanged at the border with Northern Ireland for fuel, ammunition and other items of equipment required by the Defence Forces. Following an agreement with the British Government five British military aircraft that had force-landed in Ireland were acquired for the Air Corps, comprising three Hawker Hurricane fighter aircraft, a Fairey Battle target tug and a Lockheed Hudson medium bomber aircraft.

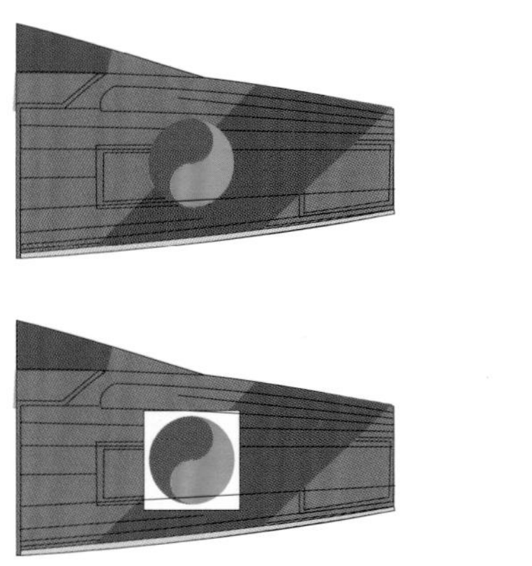

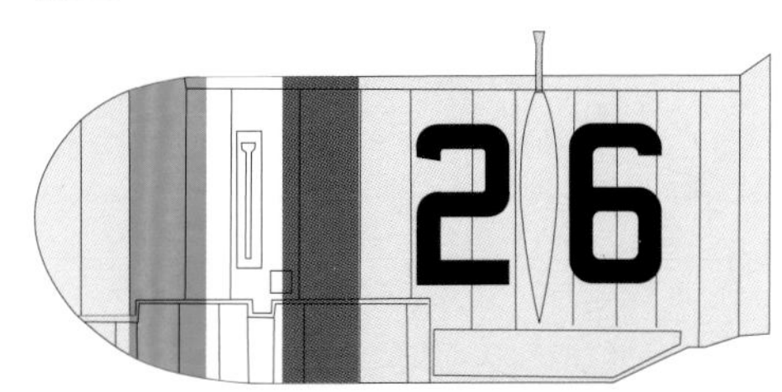

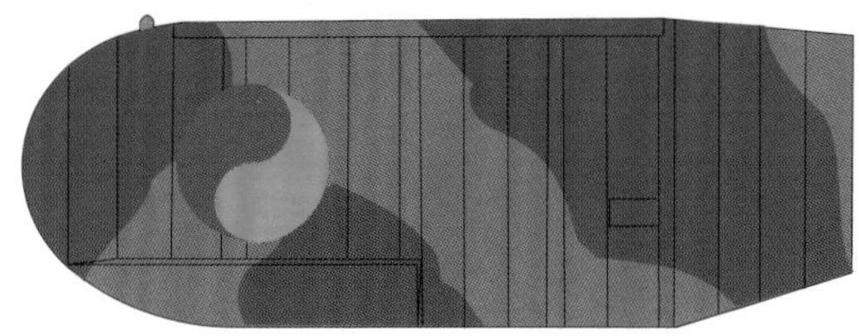

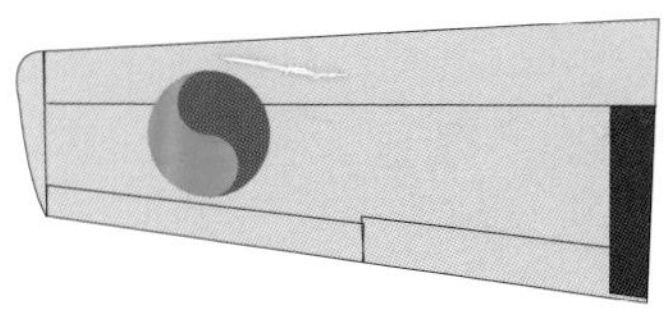

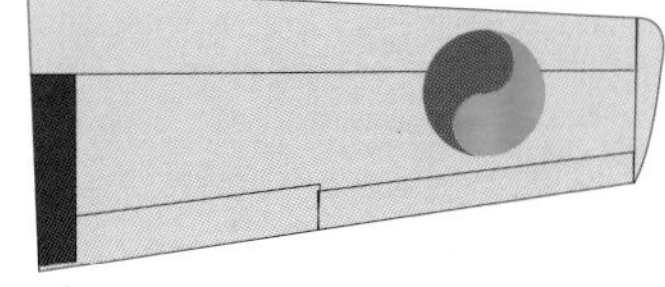

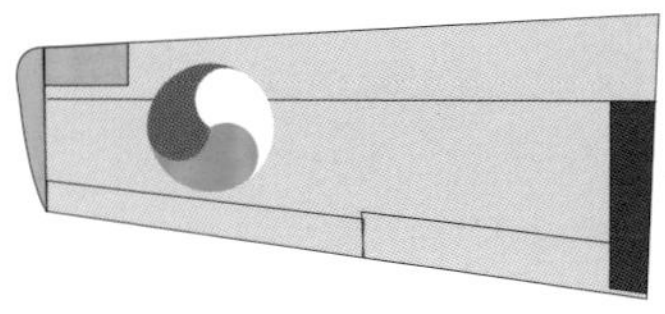

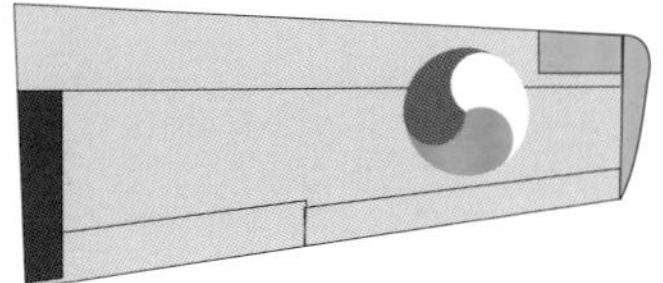

Development of the Irish Air Corps Boss.
From 1922 to 1939 Irish Air corps aircraft could be identified by large tricolours painted above and below the wings. In 1939 a new two colour circular boss was introduced on the fuselage sides and upper wings, though variations of it had been experimented with as far back as 1934. Generally the green portion of the boss faced left on the fuselage sides and on the wings. Following military exercises in 1940 in which ground troops complained of the difficulty of identifying the marking against a camouflaged background a white square was introduced around the fuselage boss. In 1946 a new version was introduced whereby the wing bosses were "handed" so that the green portion was always inboard on the upper wings and faced forward on each fuselage side. This marking was replaced by the three colour boss that was first introduced on the Vampire in 1956 (though versions of this marking had also been experimented with in the 1930s) and has remained in use ever since.

Throughout the "Emergency" the Air Corps was never equipped with a sufficient number of operational aircraft to protect the State's neutrality or provide sufficient air support for the Defence Forces in a combat situation. As stated earlier, this was due to the reluctance of the Department of Finance to sanction the level of expenditure necessary to acquire these aircraft in the pre-war years and to the British Government's arms embargo. A report on the Air Corps issued in 1945 stated that "the Corps was not an effective unit of the Defence Forces during the Emergency".

2.1

De Havilland DH.84 Dragon 2 (1937 – 1941)

In 1932, the de Havilland Aircraft Company received a request from the Iraqi Government to supply a twin-engined military patrol aircraft to the Royal Iraqi Air Force. The British domestic airline, Hillman Airways Ltd., also had a requirement at the time for a twin-engined aircraft capable of carrying six passengers and their luggage from south-east England to Paris. The design and construction of an aircraft to fulfil both of these requirements was initiated by de Havilland in the same year.

Production of this aircraft – known as the DH.84 Dragon – got underway in 1933, with first deliveries of the civil version being to Hillman Airways. Designated D.H.84M, eight examples of the military version were also delivered to the Royal Iraqi Air Force and these were fitted with a modified dorsal fin, longer and more curved than that fitted to the civilian version. The D.H.84M could be armed with machine-guns and was fitted with underwing racks to carry bombs.

Right: The DH.84 was the first twin-engined type to enter Air Corps service in 1937, serving for four years. (D. MacCarron collection)

An improved version with individual framed windows, a strengthened undercarriage with faired struts and an increase in all-up weight by 500 lb was developed by the company in late 1933. Designated Dragon 2, a total of fifty-three had been constructed when production ceased in May 1937. In the previous four years, the Dragon had been delivered to a significant number of British domestic and small foreign airlines. During the Second World War the Dragon was selected by the Royal Australian Air Force (RAAF) to fulfil a requirement for an aircraft to be used for training radio operators and navigators. Production of the Dragon in Australia commenced in 1942, by de Havilland Aircraft (Pty) Ltd., and a total of 87 were constructed for the RAAF.

The prototype Dragon (registered as G-ACAN) visited Baldonnel Aerodrome on April 21, 1933 for a demonstration to the Irish Army Air Corps, followed by a visit by another Dragon (registered G-ACCE) on May 7, 1933, which was used for several trial flights from the aerodrome over the following week. Three years later, the Air Corps needed an aircraft for use as a target tug during anti-aircraft and air-to-air gunnery exercises over the Air Firing Range at Gormanston Military Camp. To fulfil this requirement, the Department of Defence ordered a second-hand Dragon 2 from Airwork Ltd. equipped to Air Corps specifications. This involved the installation of a drogue target-towing winch and cable drum in the fuselage; this winching mechanism was driven by a four-bladed mahogany propeller attached to the starboard side of the fuselage behind the wings. A mounting for an aerial survey camera was installed in the fuselage, together with associated trapdoors, and twin bomb-racks were also fitted to the undersides of the lower wings. A landing light was installed in the aircraft's nose.

The Air Corps' Dragon 2 (c/n 6071, previously on the U.K. civil register as G-ACNI) was one of seven that had been delivered to Jersey Airways Ltd. throughout 1933 and 1934, providing an air service

Left: Another famous DH.84 operating from Baldonnel was Aer lingus'first aircraft "Iolar" flying scheduled services to Bristol in the UK.
(S. Nolan photo)

from the south of England to the Channel Islands. A Certificate of Airworthiness was issued for this Dragon on March 28, 1934, and the aircraft was delivered to Jersey Airways Ltd. in the same month; named "Bonne Nuit Bay", it remained in service with the airline until April 1935.

On March 16, 1937 the Dragon 2 was delivered by an Air Corps crew to Baldonnel Aerodrome and (as DH.18) became the first aircraft to enter service with No. 1 Reconnaissance and Medium Bombing Squadron, which had been formed in the same month. The Dragon was also the first twin-engined aircraft to enter service with the Air Corps. Over the next four years, the Dragon was operated as a target tug over the Air Firing Range at Gormanston Military Camp, towing a drogue-type target during air-to-air gunnery exercises by the Air Corps and ground-to-air firing exercises by anti-aircraft units of the Irish Defence Forces. Photographic assignments for the Defence Forces and Government agencies were also carried out by the Dragon during this period. On December 16, 1941, the Dragon 2 was written-off in a crash at Baldonnel Aerodrome, fortunately without injury to the crew. A ground-locking device on one of the control surfaces had not been removed before take-off, and the aircraft was completely destroyed in the ensuing crash.

In passing it should be mentioned that another DH 84 Dragon was operated from Baldonnel during the 1930's. On May 27, 1936, a daily air service from Baldonnel Aerodrome to Whitechurch Airport, Bristol, using a Dragon 2 (c/n 6067, carrying the Irish civil registration EI-ABI), was inaugurated by the newly formed Irish national airline, Aer Lingus. Leased from a British domestic airline, Olley Air Services, the Dragon 2 was operated by Aer Lingus on this route until 1938. The Dragon 2 was then delivered to a British domestic airline, Great Western and Southern Airlines, which operated the aircraft (with the U.K. civil registration G-ACPY) on an air service from Land's End to the Isles of Scilly, off the south-west coast of England. On June 3, 1941 this Dragon 2 was attacked by a Heinkel He 111H-4 of the Luftwaffe's Kampfgeschwader 28, and crashed into the sea off the Isles of Scilly, killing the crew and passengers.

Left: DH.84 No. 18 has its engines run up before departing for a drogue towing sortie over Gormanston in Co. Meath.
(D. MacCarron collection)

Colours & Markings

The fuselage of the Dragon 2 was initially painted light green, with silver wings and tailplane. Green, white and orange stripes, positioned chordwise, were displayed on the outer edges of the upper surfaces of the top wings and the under surfaces of the bottom wings. The aircraft's serial number was displayed in white on both sides of the rear fuselage section, but the prefix letters "DH" (for de Havilland) were apparently never applied. In 1938, a disruptive camouflage scheme of dark earth and dark green was applied to the upper surfaces of the fuselage, wings and tailplane of the Dragon, with the undersides painted silver. The green and orange Celtic boss, introduced on Air Corps aircraft in the same year, was displayed on the upper surfaces of the top wings and on both sides of mid-fuselage section, with the tri-coloured stripes retained on the under surfaces of the lower wings. The aircraft's serial number, in black, was displayed on both sides of the rear fuselage section. From 1941, the Celtic boss on the fuselage sides was enclosed within a white square.

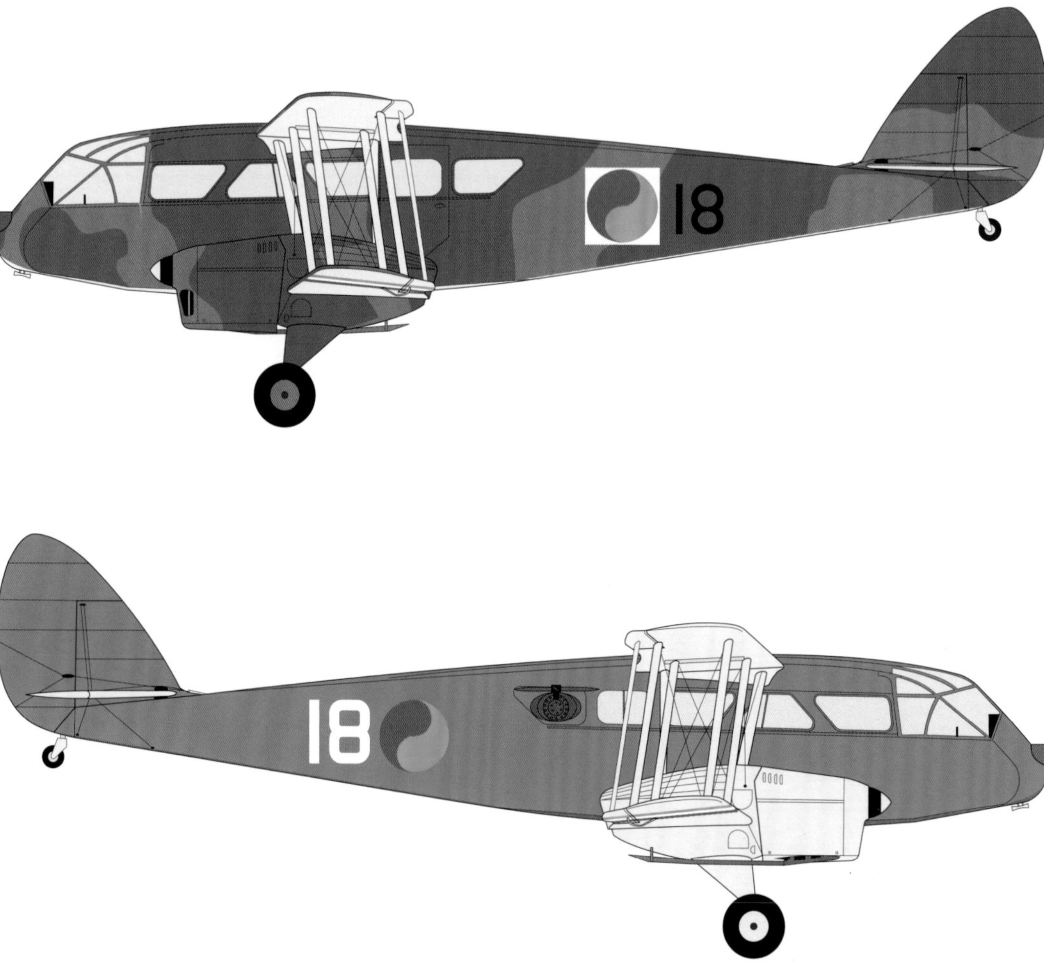

2.2

Avro 652A Anson I (1937 – 1948)

In August 1936, the Department of Defence issued Specification T.M.R.B/10 in order to fulfil a requirement for the Irish Army Air Corps for a twin-engined aircraft to perform a range of tasks (specified as general reconnaissance, long distance and coastal reconnaissance, medium bombing, topographical surveys, coastal fishery patrols, troop transport and aerial ambulance duties). An investigation covering all twin-engined aircraft types manufactured by British and German aircraft companies was conducted by the Department of Defence, but the German firms proved either unable to meet the requirements of the specification, or were not interested in doing so.

Anson No. 22 seen in 1940 painted in wartime camouflage of dark earth, dark green and black. It had originally been painted medium green and silver. (D. MacCarron collection)

Avro, however, submitted a tender, offering to deliver two Anson Is in 1937, at a total cost of £16,561, and this company was eventually selected by the Department of Defence to fulfil this requirement.

The Avro 652 Anson had been designed to fulfil a specification for a coastal reconnaissance aircraft for RAF Coastal Command. It was later used by the RAF and other Commonwealth air forces for training air gunners, navigators and radio operators throughout the Second World War.

Two Anson Is (c/ns 980 and 981) were delivered by Air Corps crews to Baldonnel Aerodrome on March 20, 1937 and as Nos. A19 and A20 (however, there is no evidence that the prefix 'A' was ever applied to the aircraft) entered service with No. 1 Reconnaissance and Medium Bombing Squadron, which had been formed in the same month. Two more Anson Is were ordered by the Department of Defence for the Air Corps in August 1937, for delivery in 1938, at a total cost of £16,381. These Anson Is (c/ns 1033 and 1034) were delivered to Baldonnel Aerodrome on January 19, 1938 and (as A20 and A21) also entered service with No. 1 Reconnaissance and Medium Bombing Squadron. These aircraft had been diverted from a batch of 106 Anson Is ordered for the RAF; these aircraft were allocated the RAF serial numbers K8742-K8847, the machines delivered to the Air Corps being the last two of the batch, K8846 and K8847. The Anson I was the first twin-engined monoplane, and the first aircraft with a retractable undercarriage, to enter service with the Air Corps.

In October 1938, the Department of Defence ordered an additional twelve Anson Is for the Air Corps, all of them to be diverted from a batch of 500 Anson Is then in production for the RAF (and to which the serials N4856-N5385 had been allocated). An initial batch of five Anson Is (the relevant RAF serials being N4863-N4867) were delivered to Baldonnel Aerodrome on February 2, 1939. All displayed their RAF serial numbers on the rear fuselage sides, and

Left: The Anson was the largest aircraft in Irish military service in 1939 and the first twin-engined monoplane with a retractable undercarriage. (A.C. Photographic Section)

carried a disruptive camouflage scheme of dark earth and dark green on the upper surfaces of the fuselage, with tri-coloured stripes, positioned chordwise, on the upper and under surfaces of the wings. The RAF serial numbers were replaced by the Air Corps serial Nos. 41 to 45,. The green and orange Celtic boss replaced the tri-coloured stripes on the upper wing surfaces when each of these Ansons underwent their first major overhaul. These aircraft were also fitted with a steeper sloping windscreen compared to those delivered in 1938, in an attempt to cure leaks that occurred when the aircraft flew through heavy rain.

The other seven Anson I's (RAF serial numbers N5290, N5300, N5320, N5340, N5365, N5380 and N9540), including two fitted with dual controls, were never delivered to the Air Corps due to the British Government having imposed a wartime embargo on the delivery of military aircraft to foreign air forces. In September 1939, these aircraft were being prepared for despatch to the Air Corps by No. 36 Maintenance Unit, RAF, and the allocated Air Corps serial Nos. 46 to 52 had actually been applied, by the time the embargo was imposed. The seven Anson Is were eventually delivered to various training units of the RAF, Royal Canadian Air Force (RCAF) and South African Air Force (SAAF).

Powered by two 350 hp Armstrong Siddeley Cheetah IX radial engines, the Anson normally carried a crew of three, comprising a pilot, navigator/bomb-aimer and radio operator/air gunner. Armament comprised one fixed forward-firing .303 in. Browning machine-gun mounted in the port side of the nose, one .303 in. Vickers machine-gun installed in a manually operated dorsal turret, and up to 360 lb. of bombs.

Nine Ansons, along with the de Havilland D.H.84 Dragon 2, equipped No. 1 Reconnaissance and Medium Bombing Squadron by March 1939.
The first public display of the Ansons occurred on March 17, 1939, when five of these aircraft flew in 'V' formation over the centre of Dublin during the annual St. Patrick's Day parade. Over the following six months, the Ansons were engaged in intensive gunnery and bombing exercises over the Air Firing Range at Gormanston Military Camp. During these exercises, the fin and rudder of one Anson I (No. 43) was accidentally damaged by gunfire at Gormanston, but the aircraft was repaired and returned to service. The Ansons were also used for night flying training, including the simulation of enemy bombers attacking Dublin, during exercises involving anti-aircraft units of the Irish Defence Forces.

On May 18, 1939 an Anson (No. 43) became the first aircraft to land at Rineanna Aerodrome (now Shannon International Airport), Co. Clare, which had been recently completed. Another Anson (No. 41), which became the second aircraft to land at this aerodrome on the same day, had the inscription "JOIN THE VOLUNTEERS" displayed on the undersides of the wings and "VOLUNTEERS" on the underside of the fuselage(formed in 1934, the Volunteers was a reserve force attached to the Defence Forces). A total of 15 Air Corps aircraft, which included the Ansons, flew in formation from Baldonnel Aerodrome to Rineanna Aerodrome on August 14, 1939, remaining there for three days.

On August 30, 1939, an Air Corps detachment was deployed to Rineanna Aerodrome, equipped with four Ansons, two Vickers Supermarine Walrus Is and an Avro Cadet. Operating from this aerodrome, the Ansons and the Walrus Is were detailed to carry out daily coastal patrols, north to Lough Swilly, on the north-west coast, and south to Wexford Harbour, on the south-east coast. An Anson carried out the first

Below: Cockpit of the Avro Anson. (D. Cousins collection)

Right: The Anson proved to be an excellent, if limited coastal patrol aircraft throughout the emergency years. (A.C. Photographic Section)

coastal patrol on the following day, and these patrols were to continue over the next six months, often in appalling weather conditions. The latter contributed to the crashes of three Ansons between September and December 1939.

The first of these crashes occurred on September 8, 1939, when an Anson I (No. 45) was damaged beyond repair, and had to be written-off, following a crash near Dingle, Co. Kerry. Another Anson I (No. 44), which force landed near Nenagh, Co. Tipperary, on October 10, 1939, was dismantled by an Air Corps recovery crew and transported by road to Baldonnel Aerodrome; due to a shortage of spare parts, this Anson did not fly again until June 1945. The third accident happened on December 19, 1939, when an Anson I (No. 43) crash-landed in Galway Bay; the aircraft was towed ashore, but was too badly damaged to be repaired and had to be written-off.

The daily patrols were eventually terminated in 1940, due to the high rate of aircraft attrition and following the formation of the Marine and Coastwatching Service, which provided a more effective surveillance of coastal areas, by day and night, from eighty-three look-out posts sited around the Irish coastline. Occasional patrols were still flown by the Ansons when the Defence Forces required increased surveillance over a particular coastal area. Throughout April 1941, a number of sites adjacent to the Shannon Estuary were surveyed and photographed by the Ansons as possible satellite landing grounds to Rineanna Aerodrome.

In August 1942, during their flight from and to Baldonnel Aerodrome, an Anson escorted the Lockheed Hudson I (No. 91) carrying the Taoiseach (the Irish Prime Minister) and some members of the Cabinet on a visit to the Air Corps detachment and other units of the Defence Forces deployed to Rineanna Aerodrome.

Anson No. 22 was written-off on September 28, 1941, following a crash at Boher, Co. Limerick, and another (No. 42) force-landed at Buttevant, Co. Cork, on August 31, 1942; the latter aircraft was returned to Baldonnel Aerodrome and re-entered service in August 1943 following repairs. Two of the Anson Is (Nos. 20 and 41) were withdrawn from use in November 1943 and January 1944 respectively, cracks and corrosion having been discovered in No. 41, which had accumulated a total of 976 flying hours.

By 1943, only three of the Ansons (Nos. 19, 21 and 42) were in still in service when No. 1 Reconnaissance and Medium Bombing Squadron returned to Baldonnel Aerodrome and was disbanded. The three Ansons were then operated by the General Purpose Flight, which had been formed in the same year, and the Advanced Training School, Air Corps Flying Training Schools. One of the last thre Ansons (No. 21) was written-off in a crash at Rineanna Aerodrome on June 1, 1945, but was replaced by No. 44, which returned to service in the same year after being repaired following its forced landing in 1939. In October 1945, the three Ansons were still in service with the Advanced Training School; two of the aircraft (Nos. 19 and 44) were withdrawn from use in June and July 1946 respectively, with the last Anson (No. 42) being withdrawn from use in March 1948.

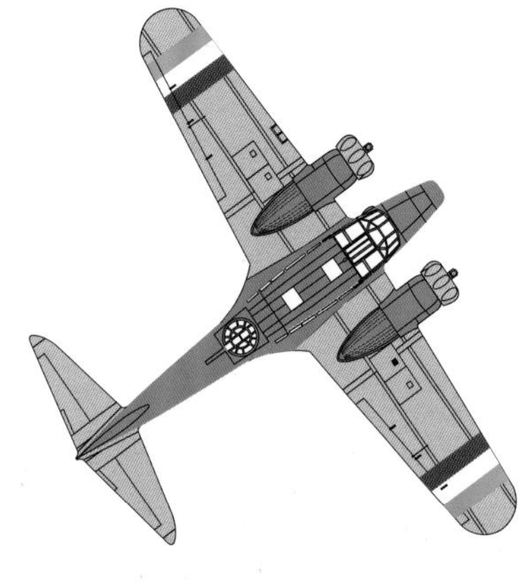

Colours & Markings

The fuselage and engine nacelles of the first four Ansons initially had an overall light green finish with silver-doped wings and tailplane. The cowlings were highly polished metal. Green, white and orange stripes, positioned chordwise, were displayed on the outer sections of the upper and under surfaces of the wings, and vertically on both sides of the rudder. Each aircraft's serial number was displayed in white on both sides of the centre section of the fuselage. The prefix letter 'A' (for Avro) to the serial numbers was apparently never applied to the first four Ansons. In 1938, this paint scheme was replaced by a disruptive camouflage scheme of dark green and dark earth on the upper surfaces of the wings and fuselage with matt black under surfaces. The tricoloured stripes on the fin were removed, and the green and orange Celtic boss replaced the tricoloured stripes on the upper surfaces of the wings, also being displayed on both sides of the centre section of the fuselage. The boss on the fuselage was enclosed in a white square from about 1942 onwards. The serial numbers were displayed in black on both sides of the fuselage, in front of the tailplane.

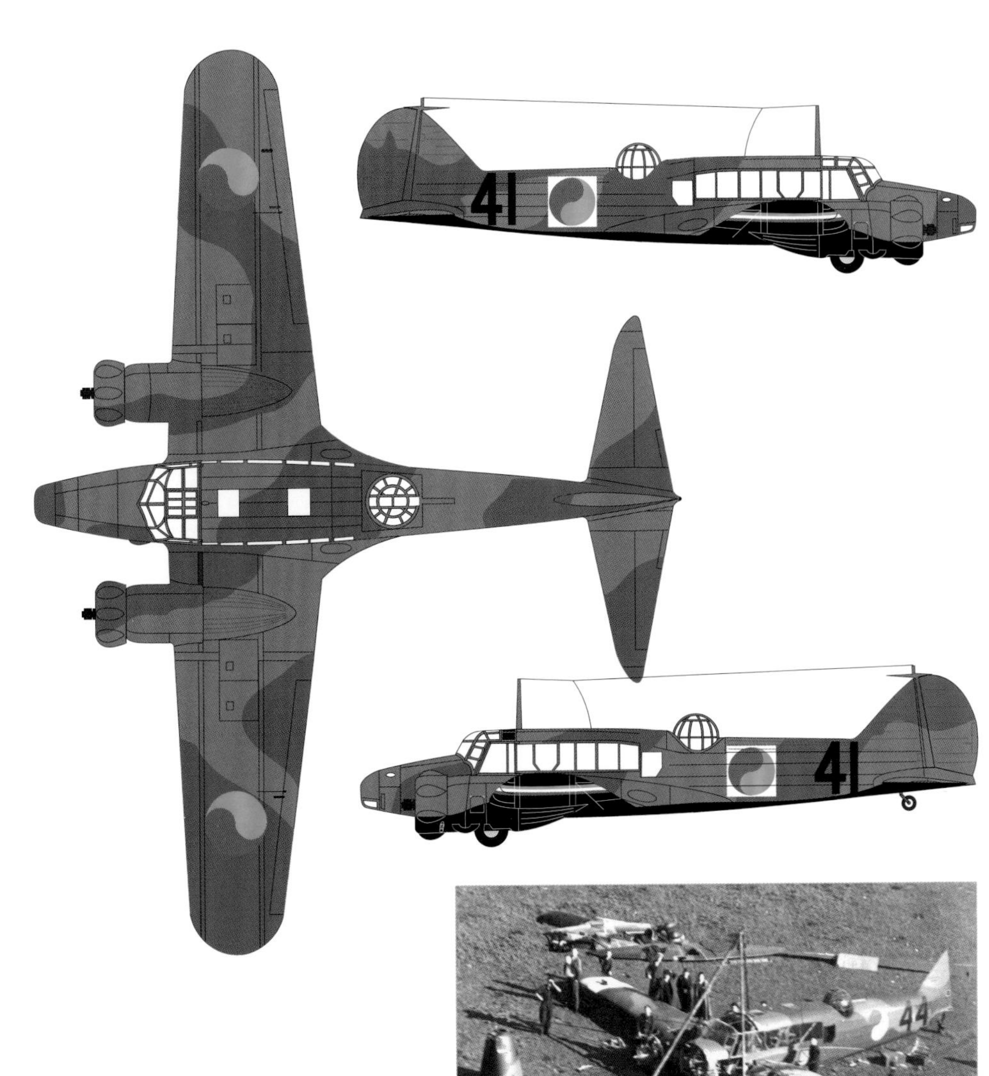

Above: Anson No. 44 seen following a landing accident. It was repaired and returned to full service. Of note are the upper wing stripes in which it was delivered. They were replaced by roundels when the aircraft returned to service following repairs. (A.C. Photographic Section)

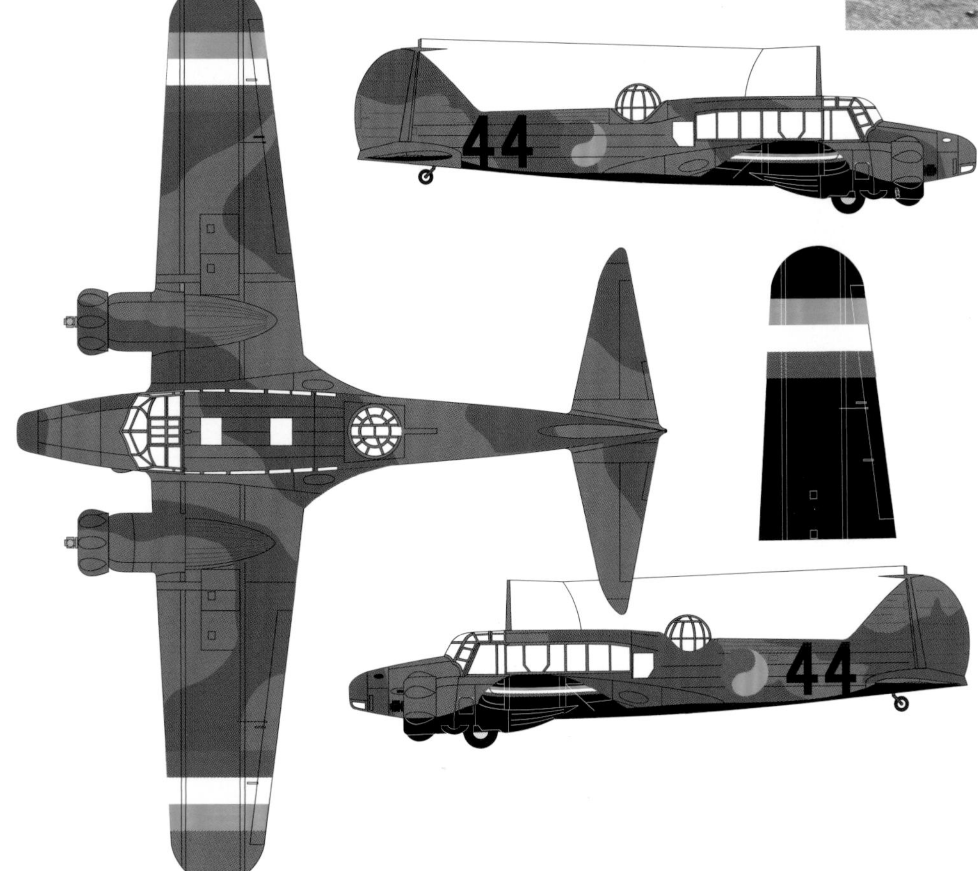

2.3

Gloster Gladiator I (1938 – 1944)

Though judged obsolete by the start of the Second World War, the Gloster Gladiator is most famously associated with the defence of Malta in 1940. The Gladiator was a highly manoeuvrable fighter, though outclassed by the then new monoplane fighters of the late 1930's. The first production version was designated Gladiator I, which was delivered to the RAF from February 1937. The Gladiator I was powered by an 830 hp Bristol Mercury IX nine-cylinder air-cooled radial engine, driving a two-bladed, Watts fixed-pitch wooden propeller The majority of Gladiator Is were armed with four 0.303-in. Colt-Browning machine guns, two of which were mounted in troughs in the sides of the front fuselage and synchronised to fire through the propeller, the other two being fitted beneath the lower wings.

In 1935, the Irish Army Air Corps issued Specification S.S.F.1/10 for a single-seat, single-engine fighter type, and an amount of £22,000 was allocated for the purchase of four such aircraft. This purchase was originally to have been funded out of the 1935/36 Defence Estimates, but the purchase had to be deferred due to over-expenditure in the previous year related to the acquisition of four Avro 636s. In September 1937, the Department of Defence ordered four Gladiator Is from Gloster Aircraft to fulfil the requirement of Specification S.S.F.1/10; the total cost was £27,000, or £6750 for each of the aircraft, which were to be delivered to the Air Corps in 1938. The four Gladiators were to be powered by Mercury VIII engines and supplied to the Air Corps without armament, radio equipment or parachutes. The training of Air Corps mechanics by both Gloster and the Bristol Engine Co. Ltd. to repair and maintain the Gladiators was also included in the overall cost. In October 1937, following further negotiations by the Department of Defence, the company agreed to a reduction of £50 in the cost of each aircraft. The four Gladiator Is were delivered to Baldonnel Aerodrome on March 9, 1938 and (as Nos. 23 to 26) entered service with 'B' Flight, No. 1 Army Co-Operation Squadron.

The Department of Defence subsequently ordered another four Gladiator Is from Gloster Aircraft (which were to have been allocated Nos. 27 to 30), but these aircraft were never delivered to the Air Corps. The non-delivery of these aircraft has been attributed to the company's commitment to large-scale production of the Gladiator for the RAF, the Fleet Air Arm and other air forces. The Department of Defence later also attempted to acquire four Gladiator Is through the British Air Attaché in Dublin, but these aircraft (which were to have been allocated nos. 57 to 60) were never delivered to the Air Corps due to the wartime embargo imposed by the British Government.

Right: Lt. Andy Woods flies Gladiator No. 23 in its pre-emergency colour scheme of medium green fuselage and silver wings. Photo taken by Lt. D.K. Johnston (A. Peard collection)

One of the Gladiators (No. 26) was damaged in a landing accident at Baldonnel Aerodrome on June 2, 1938, and underwent lengthy repairs over the following two years, eventually returning to squadron service in July 1940. Gladiator No. 23 was written-off in a landing accident at Baldonnel Aerodrome on October 23, 1938, without injury to the pilot. When No. 1 Fighter Squadron was formed on January 1, 1939, replacing No. 1 Army Co-Operation Squadron, the two serviceable Gladiators were used

Left: This view of unfortunate Gladiator No. 26 clearly illustrates the under wing gun pods and deployed flaps, indicating a fairly minor, if embarrassing landing accident.
(Air Corps photo via S. Quigley)

by the squadron for an intensive pilot flying training programme throughout that year, which included formation flying, aerobatics, and air-to-air and air-to-ground ground firing exercises at the Air Firing Range at Gormanston Military Camp.

In September 1939, at the outbreak of the Second World War, No. 1 Fighter Squadron was equipped with two Gladiators, two Avro 636s and six Westland Lysander IIs. An offer by the British Government to provide military equipment to the Irish Defence Forces in June 1940, which would have included eight Gladiators and other aircraft, if Ireland had been prepared to enter the war on the allied side, was rejected by the Irish Government.

Throughout the 'Emergency', there was a chronic shortage of spare parts for the aircraft operated by the Air Corps. To enable the Gladiators to remain operational, the Air Corps utilised parts from Mercury VIII engines salvaged from Bristol Blenheim bomber aircraft that had crashed in neutral Ireland. A flight of fighter aircraft to defend Irish airspace against attacks and intrusions by foreign military aircraft was maintained at constant readiness by No. 1 Fighter Squadron each day throughout 1940 and 1941. However, the aircraft at readiness, including the Gladiators, were incapable of intercepting the majority of Allied or German aircraft flying over neutral Ireland, and this practice was therefore discontinued by the Air Corps in 1942. From May to July of 1941, the three Gladiators, operating from a temporary airstrip at Bellinter House, near Navan, Co. Meath, provided support for a brigade of the 2nd Division, Irish Defence Forces, which was monitoring British troop movements in Northern Ireland. These aircraft were airborne for up to eight hours a day, patrolling over neutral Irish territory adjacent to the border, and essential maintenance had to be carried out at night under artificial light. The Gladiators were also used to intercept and shoot down stray balloons, which sometimes drifted over neutral Ireland after becoming detached from one of the many balloon barrages protecting British cities and seaports, as the trailing steel cables attached to these balloons could cause damage to high-tension power lines. Daily flights over Baldonnel Aerodrome were also flown by the Gladiators, to provide weather data and other information for the meteorological service.

Equipped with a mix of Gladiators, Lysanders, Hawker Hinds and Miles Master IIs, No. 1 Fighter Squadron was deployed to Rineanna Aerodrome in May 1943, replacing the two Air Corps units stationed at this airfield. The Gladiators, Hinds and Lysanders were all withdrawn from use following the entry of Hawker Hurricane Is into service with the squadron, deliveries of this type having commenced in July 1943. Two of the Gladiators (Nos. 25 and 26) were withdrawn from use in August and November 1943 respectively and were later scrapped. The remaining Gladiator (No. 24) was written-off in a crash at Celbridge, Co. Kildare, on January 21, 1944.

Although outclassed by more modern fighters, the Gladiator was highly manoeuvrable and could hold its own against more modern types when flown well. Comdt. Dessie Johnston commented on this in the course of an interview in the 1990's, where he compared the flying characteristics of the three fighter types that he had flown in Air Corps service – the Gladiator, Hurricane and Seafire. A highly experienced pilot, he was able to gain the upper hand on several occasions whilst flying Gladiators in mock dogfights against the more modern Hawker Hurricanes that had been added to the Air Corps inventory as the war progressed.

Right: Prior to all departures, the aircraft Captain signed the AF101 form, taking responsibility for the aircraft from the ground crew, a procedure still used today using an updated form. Note the unique line up of all four Gladiators together with an Avro 636 at the end of the row. (D. MacCarron collection)

Right: A front view of Gladiator No. 26's mishap. It flew again after minor repairs. (A.C. Photographic Section)

Right: High over Co. Wicklow Gladiators 24, 25 and 26 display their camouflage finishes while flying in a precise "vic" formation. (A.C. Photographic Section)

Left: Three views of the cockpit of the airworthy Gladiator in the Shuttleworth Collection. Note the padded yellow crash barrier just in front of the instrument panel! (P.Hopkins photos)

Colours & Markings

Initially the fuselages and tailfins of the Gladiators had an overall light green finish, with silver doped wings and tailplanes. Green, white and orange stripes, positioned chordwise, were displayed on the upper surfaces of the top wings, the under surfaces of the bottom wings and vertically on both sides of the tailfin. Each aircraft's serial number was displayed in white on both sides of the centre fuselage section.

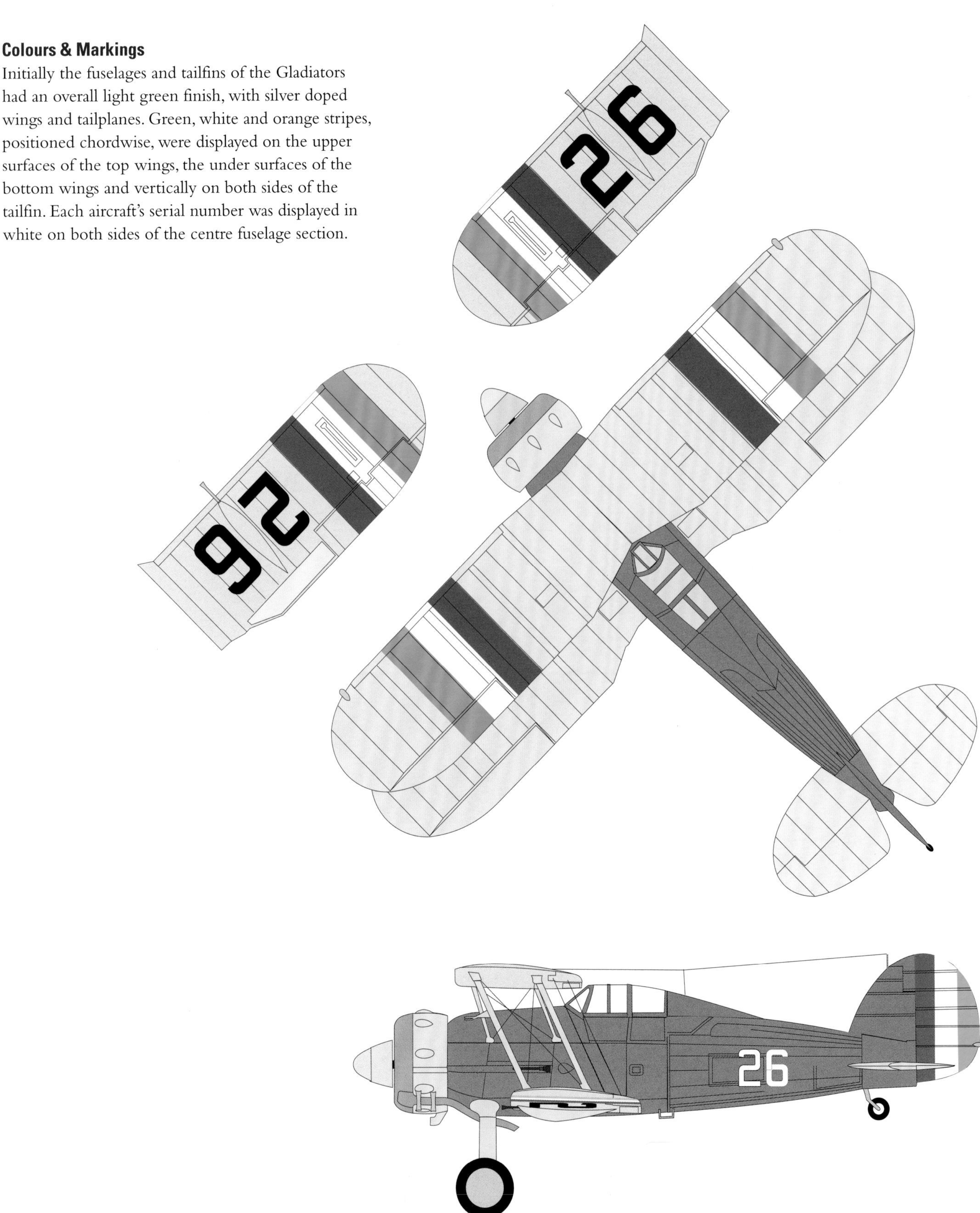

Colours & Markings

In 1939, during routine maintenance, the Gladiator's original paint scheme was replaced by a disruptive camouflage scheme of dark earth and dark green on the upper surfaces of the wings, tailplane and fuselage. The green and orange Celtic boss replaced the tri-coloured stripes on the upper surfaces of the top wings and was also displayed on both sides of the fuselage. The tri-coloured stripes were removed from the tailfin, but were retained on the under surfaces of the wings. Each aircraft's serial number was displayed in black on both sides of the rear fuselage, in front of the tailplane, and on the under surfaces of the bottom wings.

A new crest for No. 1 Fighter Squadron was introduced in 1940. Designed by Lt. Dessie Johnston, it comprised a black panther's head, enclosed in a circle with an orange background, with two parallel scrolls beneath the circle. The inscription "Beag Ach Fiachmar" (Small But Fierce) appeared on the upper scroll, and "No. 1 Fighter Squadron" on the lower scroll. This crest was displayed below the cockpit on the Gladiators.

2.4

Miles M.14a Magister I (1939 – 1952)

In 1937 a programme of expansion and re-equipment, which included the recruitment and training of short-service officer pilots, was initiated by the Irish Army Air Corps. More elementary flying training aircraft were required to enable the Air Corps Training Schools to fulfil the increased training commitments arising from this programme. To meet this requirement, the Department of Defence ordered ten Miles Magister Is in 1938, which had to be diverted by the manufacturer from a batch of fifty aircraft (allocated the RAF serials N5389-N5392 and N5400-N5404) then in production for the RAF.

Magisters that had been struck off charge by the RAF for delivery to other air forces. Flown by Air Corps pilots, the first five of the Air Corps' Magister Is (c/ns 1025-1029) were delivered to Baldonnel Aerodrome on February 22, 1939, followed by the other five (c/ns 1036-1040) on March 8, 1939. The Magisters, which were the first monoplane training aircraft to enter service with the Air Corps, were operated by the Air Corps Training Schools (as Nos. 31 to 40). The spatted undercarriage was retained on these ten Magisters while in service with the Air Corps. In 1940, the Department of Defence attempted to acquire 15 Hawker Hind Is from RAF surplus stocks to be used

Right: a line up of gleaming Miles magister trainers on Baldonnel's grass runways shortly after their arrival in 1939.
(A.C. Photographic Section)

A low-wing monoplane of all-wood construction (the fuselage, wings and tailfin structures were all covered with stressed plywood), the Magister had a metal engine mounting, cowling and struts for its fixed undercarriage. The undercarriage was originally fitted with fairings (or 'spats') covering the wheels, but these were removed by the RAF in wartime service. The Magister, which was the first elementary training aircraft fitted with wing flaps, had two cockpits, in tandem, with dual controls and blind flying equipment was installed in the rear cockpit. A total of 1,280 Magisters had been constructed when production ceased in 1941, which included deliveries of this aircraft to several other air forces. From 1945 to 1947, the manufacturer overhauled and refurbished

for advanced flying and operational training by the Air Corps, but only six of these aircraft could be delivered. Instead of the nine Hinds that could not be delivered, the Air Corps was offered, and accepted, five Magister Is from RAF stocks. The aircraft concerned (ex-RAF serial numbers L6903, N3901, P6414, P6422 and P6440) came from the RAF's No.47 M.U., and were originally delivered to the RAF in 1937 (L6903), 1938 (N3901) and 1939 (P6414, P6422 and P6440). Two of the Magisters (L6903 and N3901) had seen service with the RAF, but the other three had been delivered directly to storage by the manufacturer. The five aircraft were delivered by Air Corps pilots to Baldonnel Aerodrome on June 7, 1940 and (as Nos. 73 to 77) entered service with the Air Corps Training

Magister No. 33 looks a little well-worn in its wartime camouflage. It was often used on the "shuttle" between Baldonnel and the Rineanna detachment in Co. Clare. (D. MacCarron collection)

Schools. These Magister Is were also fitted with the spatted undercarriage when delivered, and these were retained while in service with the Air Corps.

The Magister was the only elementary training aircraft operated by the Air Corps throughout the "Emergency", and was first used by the two batches of trainee pilots recruited under the short-service officer pilot scheme, which commenced in August 1939. The Magister was also used for elementary flying training during the first and only Sergeant Pilot's Course, which commenced in 1943. Thirty-one candidates from enlisted personnel in the Defence Forces were selected for flying training on this course, but only twenty eventually qualified as Sergeant Pilots.

Throughout August and September of 1942, the Irish Defence Forces conducted large-scale military exercises in the south of Ireland, with air support for the opposing divisions provided by Nos. 1 and 2 Air Components, which were deployed by the Air Corps to the region for this purpose. Operating from a temporary airfield at Glenville, Co. Cork, a number of Magisters attached to No.1 Air Component were used for observation, supply and liaison missions during these exercises,

Four of the first batch of Magisters were written-off in crashes, No. 33 on July 1, 1942, No. 35 on September 6, 1942, No. 38 on February 28, 1944 and No. 37 on May 15, 1944. The last of these was the only incident which resulted in loss of life, killing a trainee Sergeant Pilot. One Magister (No. 76) from the second batch was written-off in a crash on October 7, 1941.

From September 1945, eight Magisters were withdrawn from use over the following twelve months, the first (No. 74) in September 1945, followed by three more (nos. 32, 40 and 73) in January, February and March 1946 respectively. Another Magister (No. 31) was damaged beyond repair in a crash on March 2, 1946. Three Magisters (Nos. 39, 75 and 77) were withdrawn from use in August of 1946, and another (No. 36) in September. Some of these Magisters were apparently stored in a field to the south of Naas, Co. Kildare, beside the main road between Dublin and Cork, before eventually being scrapped. The final Magister (No. 34) from the first batch was not withdrawn from use until March 1952.

In 1945, the Department of Defence ordered another 12 Magister Is from Miles Aircraft Ltd. to replace the aircraft that had been written-off or withdrawn from use. Production of the Magister I had ceased in 1941, but aircraft acquired from surplus RAF stocks by the company were overhauled and refurbished for delivery to the Air Corps. These Magister Is were from batches delivered to the RAF in 1938 (their original RAF serials were L8342 and L8352), 1939 (ex-RAF serials N3869 and P6424), 1940 (serials R1826 and R1834), and 1941 (serials T9733, T9803, T9807, V1016, V1089 and V1094), and had been in service with various RAF units before being struck off charge in 1944. The twelve Magisters, which were inspected by Air Corps officers at the company's factory early in 1946, had each accumulated a minimum of 1,000 flying hours.

The first four Magisters from this batch (c/ns 915, 1779, 1827 and 2000) were delivered to Baldonnel Aerodrome on February 1, 1946, followed by three more (c/ns 2040, 2044, 2181 and 2242) three days later. The last three Magisters (c/ns 768, 778, 1835 and 2247) were delivered to the Air Corps on March 9, 1946. The twelve Magister Is (as Nos. 127 to 138) entered service with the Elementary Flying

Left: The Gipsy Major 4-cylinder engine proved to be relatively easy to service once the spare parts arrived from the UK. This engine was photographed when Magister No. 34 was undergoing restoration for display in the Collins Barracks Museum. (J. Maxwell photo)

Right: So successful had the Magister been as a primary trainer, another batch was ordered post war in 1946. Note the lack of spats on the undercarriage and the matt black finish. (A.C. Photographic Section)

Training School, Air Corps Training Schools. Some of the Magisters were also operated by No. 1 Fighter Squadron on liaison and communications duties. On February 7, 1947 one of the Magisters from this batch (No. 133) was written-off in a crash at Gormanston Military Camp, injuring the pilot. Another of these aircraft (No. 137) was damaged after coming into contact with a Miles Martinet (No. 144) on August 4, 1948, but was repaired and returned to service. In February 1949 a Magister force-landed in a football field in the centre of Dublin, following engine failure, but was not damaged and returned to service with the Air Corps.

Withdrawal of the Magisters commenced in 1951, the first (No. 135) in August and the second (No. 128) in November of that year. A further seven Magisters were withdrawn from use in 1952 and the final two (Nos. 130 and 131), which were the last aircraft with open cockpits operated by the Air Corps, were withdrawn from use in January 1953. A total of twenty-seven Magisters were delivered to the Air Corps between 1939 and 1946, the highest number of any aircraft type operated by the Air Corps. An offer of fifty Magisters, which were surplus to RAF requirements, was received by the Air Corps in 1950 to fulfil future elementary training aircraft requirements. This offer was rejected, as the Magister was at that stage considered to be obsolete. One of the Magisters from the first batch (No. 34) was used as an instructional airframe by the Technical Training Squadron for many years before being placed in storage at Casement Aerodrome around 1968. In June 1981, following restoration to static display condition as a class project by Air Corps Apprentices, the Magister was presented to the Irish Aviation Museum at Dublin Airport. Following the closure of this museum, the Magister was returned to Casement Aerodrome and, together with other restored aircraft, was put on display in 1997 during the celebrations to commemorate the 75th anniversary of the formation of the Air Corps. This aircraft is now on display at the National Museum at Collins' Barracks, Dublin.

Far Right: Cockpit of a Miles Magister (J. Maxwell photo)

Right: While a pair of Magisters are undergoing routine maintenance, a Hawker Hind is just visible in the same hangar. (D. Cousins collection)

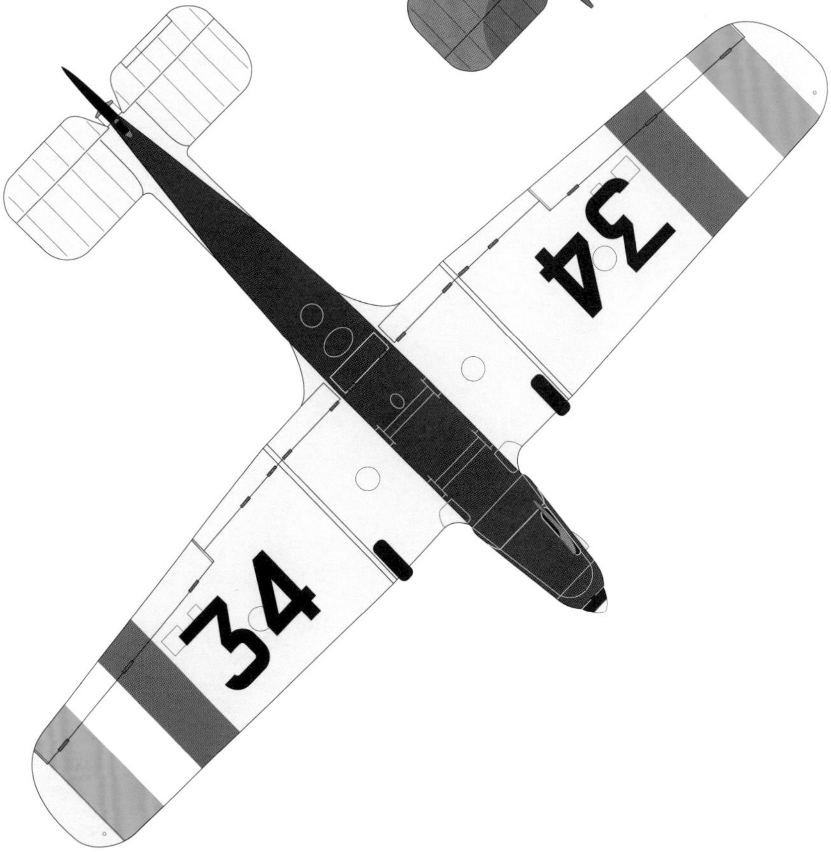

Colours & Markings

The first batch of ten Magisters was delivered in the standard paint scheme for Air Corps training aircraft of that period: overall gloss black fuselage, silver wings and tailfin, with highly polished engine cowling. Green, white and orange stripes, positioned chordwise, were displayed on the outer sections of the upper and under surfaces of both wings, and vertically on both sides of the fin. Each aircraft's serial number was displayed in white on both sides of the fuselage, in front of the tailplane.

The second batch of five Magisters was delivered in the standard RAF disruptive camouflage scheme of dark earth and dark green on the upper surfaces of the wings and tailplane, extending half-way down both sides of the fuselage and engine cowling. The lower section of the fuselage and engine cowling was painted matt black, while the under surfaces of both wings, the tailplane and the wheel 'spats' were painted silver. Green, white and orange stripes were displayed on the upper and under surfaces of both wings, and the orange/green Celtic boss enclosed in a white square was displayed on both sides of the fuselage centre section. Each aircraft's serial number was displayed on both sides of the fuselage behind the Celtic boss in large white numerals, and on the undersides of both wings in black. From about 1940 onwards, this camouflage scheme was also applied to the first batch of Magisters.

The twelve Magisters delivered in 1946 had the fuselage and engine cowlings finished in overall matt black, with silver wings, tailfin and tailplane. The Celtic boss, enclosed in a white square, tri-coloured stripes and aircraft serial numbers were displayed in the same positions as on the second batch of Magisters.

Below: fuel gauge located in the wing of the Magister. (J. Maxwell photo)

2.5

Supermarine Type 236 Walrus I (1939 – 1945)

In 1939 the Department of Defence acquired three Walrus I amphibians to fulfil a requirement by the Irish Army Air Corps for an aircraft to carry out coastal patrol duties.

Three aircraft from a batch of 168 ordered for the Fleet Air Arm (FAA) in 1936 (allocated the FAA serials L2301-L2303) were diverted for delivery to the Air Corps. The first Walrus for the Air Corps (No. N19) flew for the first time on January 10, 1939, followed by the second (N20) a week later, and the third (N18) on February 24, 1939. Following an inspection by the Air Corps the three Walrus Is were accepted for delivery towards the end of February. The registrations were retained as serial numbers for the Walrus Is by the Air Corps, although the prefix letter 'N' was later deleted.

A Walrus at sea, possibly in the Foynes Estuary. Of interest is the upper surface camouflage scheme which was applied in a most economical fashion in order to conserve the paint. (D. Cousins Collection)

On March 3, 1939, the three Walrus Is were flying in formation on their delivery flight to Baldonnel Aerodrome, but became separated after encountering adverse weather conditions over the Irish Sea. One of the aircraft (N20), piloted by Lt. Andy Woods and Lt. D.K. Johnston, returned to Wales. Both pilots were highly experienced at Irish Sea crossings, having ferried many aircraft to and from the UK as members of the Irish Aero Club. They attempted a sea landing near Pembroke, but the conditions were too rough and after landing in a field near the coast, they were billeted by the RAF overnight. The aircraft was delivered to Baldonnel Aerodrome on the following day. The other two Walrus Is reached the south-east coast of Ireland, but one (N18) crash-landed in rough seas off the coast at Ballytrent, Co. Wexford, following engine failure. The upper wing structure was badly damaged, but the Walrus was beached on the shore and secured by the Air Corps crew, with the help of local people. On the following day the aircraft was towed into Wexford Harbour by the Rosslare lifeboat and was later delivered by road to Baldonnel Aerodrome with both wings removed, towed behind a truck. The third Walrus (N19) had to land in the sea off Dun Laoghaire Harbour, due to a dense sea fog which restricted visibility, but was taxied into the harbour and moored to a buoy overnight. The Walrus was delivered to Baldonnel Aerodrome on the following day. The three Walrus Is were the only flying boats or amphibians to enter service with the Air Corps. (An offer in post war years of Supermarine Sea Otters formerly operated by the FAA was declined). The two undamaged Walrus Is (N19 and N20)

Left: Very rare photo of a Walrus about to touch down on a glass surfaced lake. Boat handling drills were taught to all flying boat crew members. (D. Cousins Collection)

entered service with No. 1 Coastal Patrol Squadron, which was formed in 1939, and were initially based at Baldonnel Aerodrome. On August 30, 1939 the two was aircraft were deployed to Rineanna Aerodrome as part of a larger Air Corps detachment assigned to carry out daily patrols off the south and west coasts of Ireland. The first coastal patrol by a Walrus I was flown two days later, but the daily coastal patrols were discontinued in 1940, due to a shortage of aviation fuel and the destruction of three Ansons engaged on these duties in crashes. The Marine and Coastwatching Service took on primary responsibility for day and night surveillance of the coastal regions, but occasional patrols were still carried out by the Walruses or the Ansons over the next three years.

The damaged upper wing of the third Walrus (N18) could not be repaired, and the aircraft was placed in storage at Baldonnel Aerodrome. On September 18, 1940, Walrus N19 was written-off following an accident on the ground at Baldonnel Aerodrome that badly damaged the hull. The upper wing from this machine was fitted to the stored Walrus, which entered service with the Air Corps (as No.18) in 1941. On January 9, 1942 this Walrus took-off on an unauthorised flight from Rineanna Aerodrome and headed east, flown by a young Air Corps officer, with three airmen also on board. The crew apparently intended to become involved in the conflict in Europe but the Walrus was forced to land at an RAF airfield in south-west England, where they were taken into custody and returned to neutral Ireland. The Walrus was later collected by an Air Corps crew and returned to Baldonnel Aerodrome. On September 9, 1942, Walrus No. 20) was written-off in a crash while on detachment to No. 1 Air Component during the military exercises conducted by the Defence Forces in the south of Ireland.

Only one Walrus (No.18) was therefore remained operational when No. 1 Coastal Patrol Squadron was disbanded in 1944 after returning to Baldonnel Aerodrome in the previous year. This Walrus was then operated by the General Purpose Flight before being withdrawn from use on August 2, 1945, at which point it was purchased by Aer Lingus, with a view to using it as a trainer. Allocated the Irish civil registration EI-ACC on August 28, 1945 (which incidentally were not taken up), the Walrus was overhauled by the airline's technicians, but was never used for aircrew training and was placed in storage at Collinstown Airport (later re-named Dublin Airport).

In November, 1946 the Walrus was purchased for £150 by the commander of No. 615 (County of Surrey) Squadron, RAF, to be used as a recruitment aid for the squadron and to provide air experience for ground crew. The Walrus (which carried the UK civil registration G-AIZG) was delivered to the squadron at Biggin Hill, near London, in March 1947, and remained there for about two years before being sold as scrap to a company at Thame airfield in Oxfordshire.

In 1963, the partially scrapped Walrus, without wings, floats or tail unit – was purchased for £5 by the Historic Aircraft Preservation Society, and was delivered to the Royal Navy Engineering School, Arbroath, Scotland, in January 1964. The Walrus was restored –though not to flying condition – by engineering apprentices at the school and, finished in FAA colours (as serial No. L2301), was put on permanent static display at the FAA Museum in Yeovilton on December 6, 1966.

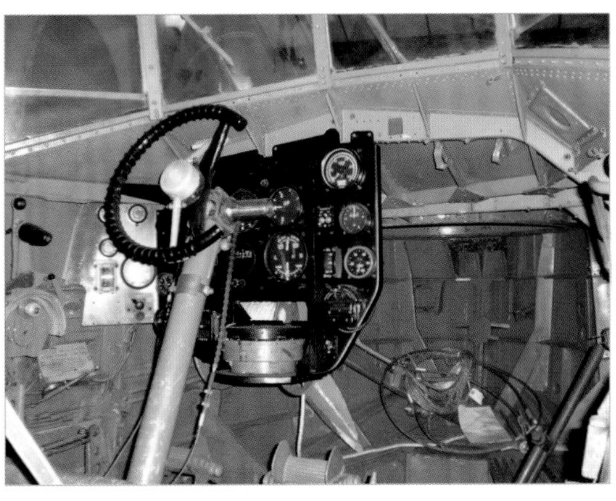

Left: Cockpit of a Walrus (J. Maxwell photo)

Right: Walrus No. 20 on the ground at Fermoy during the Emergency. The type's ability to alight on land or water gave them great flexibility in operation. (D. Cousins Collection)

Right: A pair of technicians on the upper wing of Walrus No. 18 show just how large this amphibian was. The snow on the ground did not seriously hamper flying operations. (D. Cousins Collection)

Left: A Walrus in its original silver finish awaits take off clearance while a Hawker Hind and Miles Magister manoeuvre in front.
(D. Cousins Collection)

Left: The Walrus was a tough bird as evidenced by landing on grass without lowering the undercarriage. Damage was very light!
(Air Corps photo section via S. Quigley)

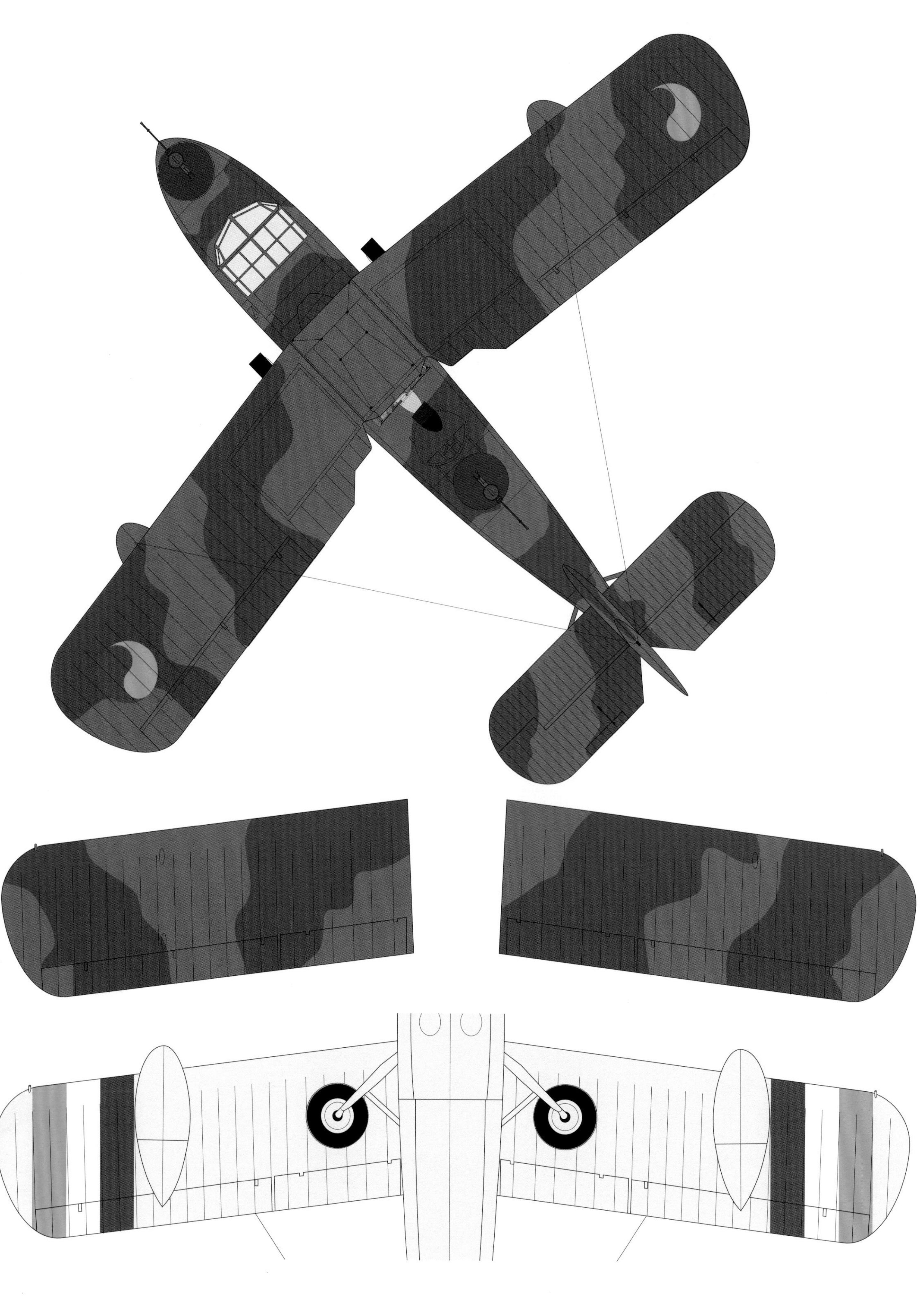

Above: Pilot's seat in a Walrus. No cushions as the pilot normally sat on his parachute. (J. Maxwell photo)

Colours & Markings

The Walrus' initially had an overall silver finish, with black serial numbers displayed on both sides of the rear fuselage section. Green, white and orange stripes were applied chordwise on the upper surfaces of the top wings and on the under surfaces of the lower wings, and vertically on both sides of the rudder. From 1941 onwards, the two remaining aircraft (Nos. 18 and 20) had a disruptive camouflage scheme of dark earth and dark green applied to the upper surfaces of the fuselage and the wings, with the silver finish apparently retained on all under surfaces. The vertical tri-coloured stripes on the fin were removed at this time, but were retained on the wings. At least one of the amphibians (No.18) displayed the green and orange Celtic boss, enclosed in a white square, on both sides of the rear fuselage section.

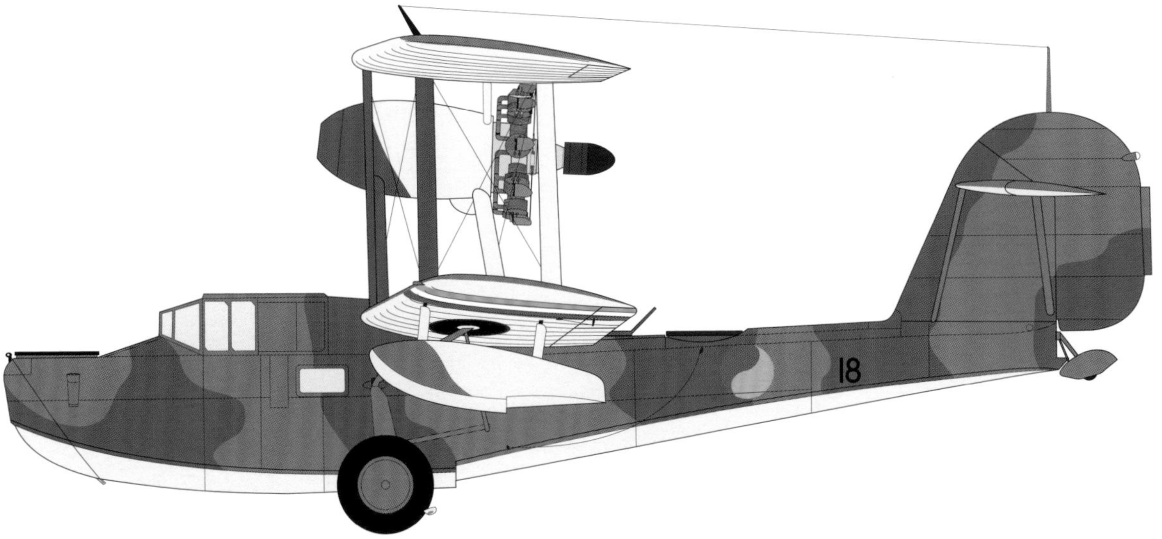

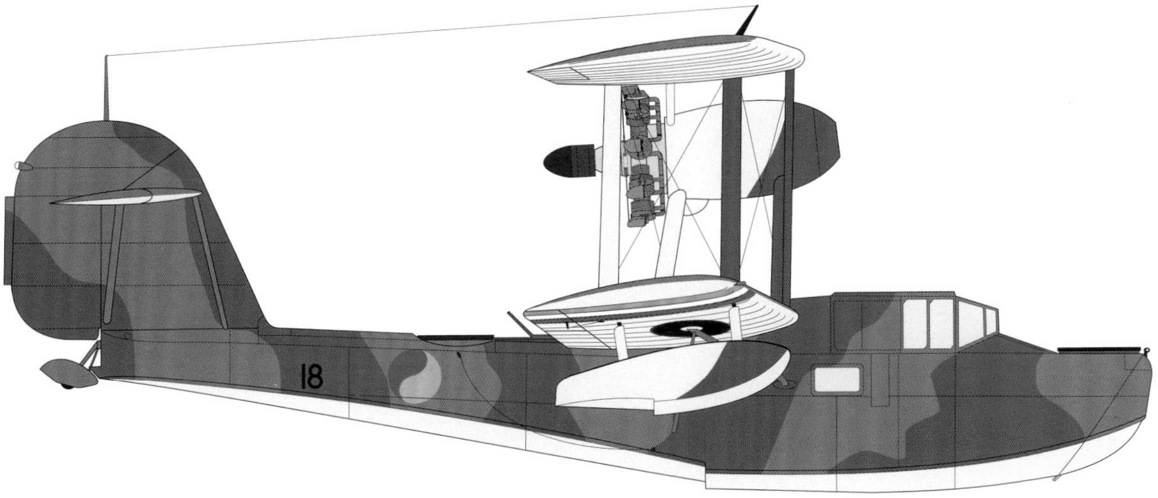

2.6

Westland Lysander II (1939 – 1947)

In 1934 the British Air Ministry issued Specification A.39/34 to fulfil a requirement for a modern single-engined, two-seat, monoplane specifically designed for operations with the army co-operation squadrons of the RAF. Design proposals to fulfil the requirements of this specification were submitted by Westland Aircraft Ltd.; following acceptance of these proposals by the Air Ministry, two prototypes were ordered in 1935.

Named Lysander, an initial production batch of 144 aircraft (to which the RAF serials L4673-L4816 were allocated) was ordered by the Air Ministry in September 1936. Designated Lysander I, the first production aircraft (carrying the RAF serial L4637) flew for the first time in the Spring of 1938, powered by an 890 hp Mercury XII engine. Deliveries of the first Lysander Is commenced in the following month and a total of 169 was delivered to the RAF between 1938 and 1940. The Mercury engine was in great demand at the time for other combat aircraft in large-scale production for the RAF, and was therefore replaced by the Bristol Perseus sleeve-valve radial engine in subsequent production aircraft, which were designated Lysander II. Powered by a 905 hp Perseus XII engine, production of the Lysander II commenced in 1938 but was terminated in June 1940 after 447 had been constructed, most of which were delivered to foreign air forces. When supplies of the Mercury engine became available again later in 1940, production switched to the Lysander III version, which was powered by an 870 hp Mercury XX or XXX engine; deliveries of this version to the RAF commenced in the same year.

In 1938, the Department of Defence ordered six Lysander IIs to fulfil a requirement by the Irish Army Air Corps for a modern aircraft type to be used for army co-operation duties. The overall cost of the six Lysander IIs was £37,500, which included pilot conversion courses on the aircraft and maintenance courses on the airframe for Air Corps technicians, all provided by Westland Aircraft. Technicians also

Right: Capt. D.K. Johnston climbs up into the cockpit of his Lysander before commencing a patrol. Note the practice bomblets on the stub wing.
(A. Peard collection)

underwent courses on the Perseus engine with the Bristol Aeroplane Co., and on the aircraft's propeller by the de Havilland Aircraft Co.; the cost of these courses was also included in the overall amount paid for the aircraft. The 1939/40 Defence Estimates provided for the purchase of the Lysanders, and the embargo imposed by the British Government on the delivery of military equipment to the Air Corps was not applied to these aircraft.

On July 15, 1939 the six Lysander IIs, which were not equipped with radio sets, bomb-sights or aerial cameras, were delivered by Air Corps pilots from the Westland factory to Baldonnel Aerodrome. Initially operated by the Air Corps Training Schools (as Nos. 61 to 66), the Lysanders entered service with No. 1 Fighter Squadron in August 1939. The Air Corps Lysanders carried the standard camouflage applied to the RAF machines, and were the last aircraft delivered to the Air Corps before the outbreak of the Second World War. On August 14, 1939, a formation of fifteen Air Corps aircraft, including the six Lysanders, flew from Baldonnel to Rineanna and remained at the latter location for four days. During this period, a number of demonstration flights by the Lysanders were flown over towns in south-west Ireland.

The F.24 aerial cameras for the Lysanders were delivered in September 1939, and radio equipment was apparently installed in these aircraft by January 1940, evidenced by reports of problems with the send/receive switches on some of the radios in that month. The bombsights for the Lysanders were delivered in March 1940. Flying restrictions were also imposed for a short period in this general timeframe, due to problems with the propeller mechanisms, undercarriage and battery charging equipment. Operating from various airfields throughout the State, the Lysanders participated in a number of army co-operation exercises over the next three years. During this period, the Lysanders appeared in a number of photographs and newsreels issued by the Irish Government for propaganda purposes about the Irish defence forces. Although operated by 'B' Flight, No. 1 Fighter Squadron, the Lysanders were incapable of intercepting or forcing any intruding aircraft that violated Irish airspace throughout the 'Emergency' period. On July 4, 1941, Lysander No. 62 was badly damaged in an accident at Ballybunion, Co. Kerry, and had to be written-off. Nine days later, during army co-operation exercises with the Defence Forces at Edgeworthstown, Co. Longford, another Lysander (No. 65) was written-off following a heavy landing in adverse weather conditions.

Above: The six Lysanders on display at Baldonnel shortly after their delivery flight. (A.C. Photographic Section)

Below: The characteristic heavy rudder pedals of the Lysander. (P. Hopkins photo)

Top: Another view of the six Lysanders shortly before takeoff from Yeovilton on their delivery flight. (AgustaWestland photo)

Combined divisional manoeuvres in the south of Ireland were conducted by the Irish defence forces in the autumn of 1942, with air support for the two participating divisions provided by Air Corps detachments, designated No. 1 Air Component and No. 2 Air Component. From a temporary airfield known as Rathduff, near Golden, Co. Tipperary, the Lysanders were operated by No. 2 Air Component in support of the division knownas Red Force. The Lysanders, and other aircraft, were used for observation, reconnaissance, liaison and other missions during these exercises. On October 2, 1942, during a training flight from Baldonnel Aerodrome to Cork City, Lysander No. 64 was written-off after crash-landing at Castleknock airfield, Co. Dublin, following engine failure.

Right: Lysander cockpit at the Shuttleworth collection. (P. Hopkins photo)

In 1943, the remaining three Lysanders in service with No. 1 Fighter Squadron (Nos. 61, 63 and 66) were replaced by Miles Master Is and Hawker Hurricane Is. During 1943, due to an increase in the number of air-to-air gunnery and ground-to-air firing training exercises, the Air Corps had a requirement for more target tugs. To fulfil this requirement, two of the Lysanders (Nos. 61 and 66) were converted to target tugs in 1944. Over the next two years the Lysander target tugs, in an overall silver finish, were operated by the Advanced Training Flight, Air Corps Flying Training Schools, towing drogue type targets over the Air Firing Range at Gormanston Military Camp during firing exercises by the Defence Forces.

The two Lysander target tugs were withdrawn from use in October 1946 and December 1946 respectively, following the delivery of two Miles Martinet T.T.1 target tugs in the same year. Following its withdrawal from service, the fuselage of Lysander No. 61 was displayed on the forecourt of a garage at Crookstown, Co. Kildare for about twenty years before finally being scrapped. The last remaining Lysander in service with the Air Corps (No. 63) was written-off in a crash on April 15, 1947.

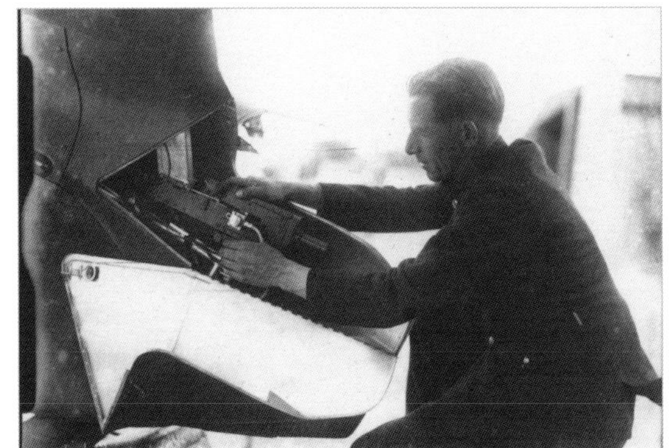

Right: Adjusting the gun in the undercarriage faring. (D. MacCarron collection)

Colours & markings

The Lysanders had been delivered in the RAF disruptive camouflage scheme of that period, with dark earth and dark green on the upper surfaces of the wings, tailplane and fuselage, and the undersides painted light grey. The two-colour Celtic boss was displayed on both sides of the mid-fuselage section and the upper surfaces of both wings, with green, white and orange stripes, positioned chordwise, displayed on the undersides of the wings. The Air Corps serial number was displayed in black on both sides of the rear fuselage section, just in front of the tailplane, while the crest of No. 1 Fighter Squadron was displayed on the front fuselage below the cockpit. In 1944, following their conversion to target tugs, Lysanders Nos. 61 and 66 carried an overall silver finish with the Celtic boss, tri-coloured stripes and serial numbers still displayed in the original positions.

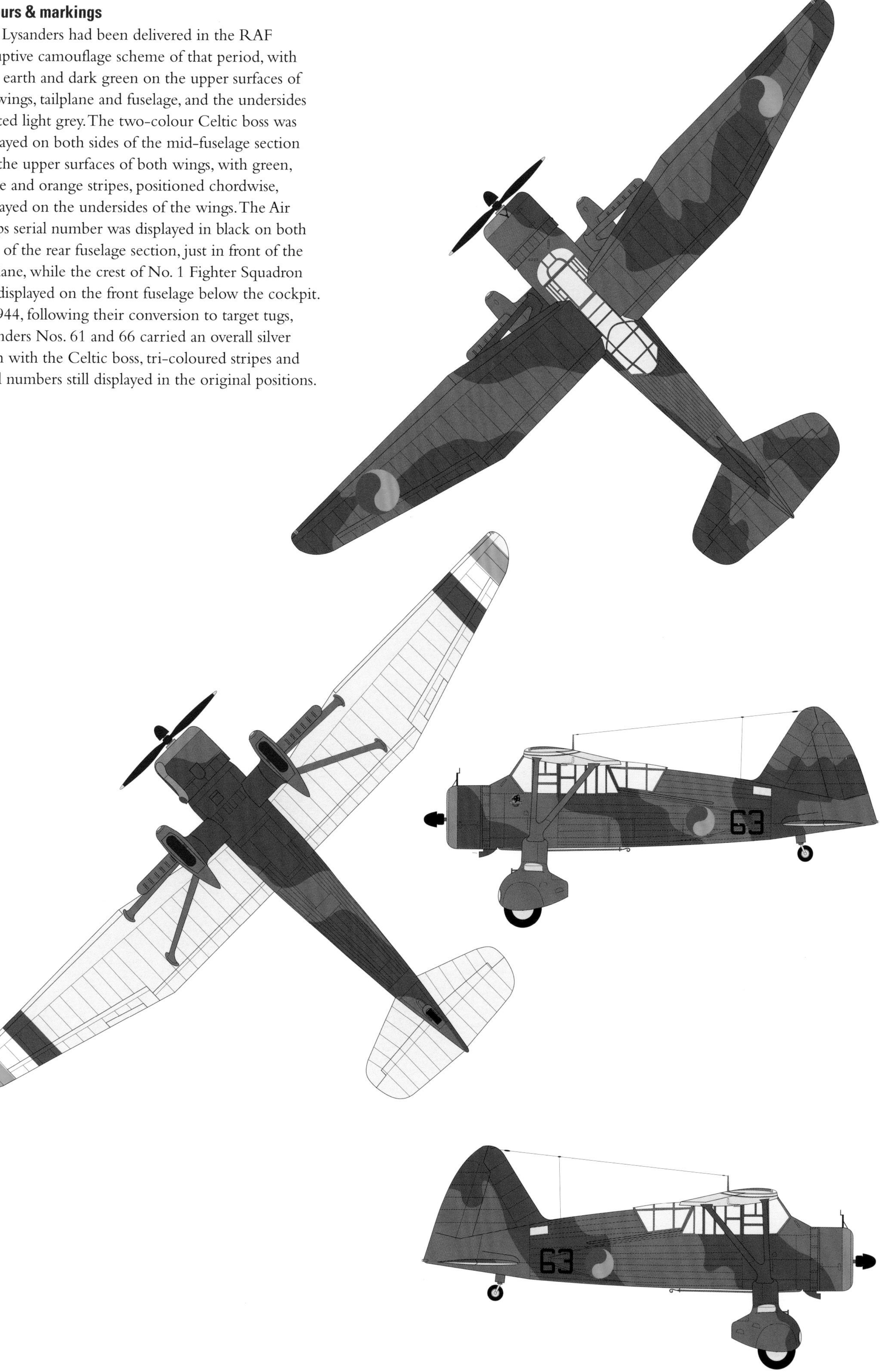

2.7

Hawker Hind I (1940 – 1944)

In 1940, following the recruitment of 31 trainee pilots under the Short Service Officer Pilot scheme, the Irish Army Air Corps had a requirement for an aircraft type, which could be used for advanced flying and operational training duties. To fulfil this requirement, the Department of Defence tried to obtain ten North American Harvard I's but these could not be supplied due to the UK government's embargo on the export of military aircraft that were urgently needed for the fight against Germany. The UK government did, however, agree to the delivery of Hawker Hinds from surplus RAF stocks; the Hind was a development of the Hawker Hart light bomber powered by a Rolls Royce Kestrel V engine. Fifteen were ordered by the Department of Defence, but only six of these aircraft could be delivered to the Air Corps. The total cost of the Hinds was approximately £23,000, which included the Kestrel engines and associated equipment, together with sufficient spares to last an estimated twelve months. The RAF would not give any binding guarantee as to the condition of the Hinds, but each aircraft was said to be good for at least 200 hours before a major overhaul would be necessary. Five Miles Magister Is from RAF stocks were offered to the Air Corps instead of the nine Hinds that could not be delivered, and this offer was accepted.

Six Hind Is held in storage with No. 47 Maintenance Unit at Sealand airfield in Wales (ex-RAF serial numbers K5446, K5559, K6712, K5415, K6755 and K6781) were selected for delivery to the Air Corps; these aircraft were from two batches delivered to the RAF between January 1936 and June 1937. Three of the Hinds (K5415, K6755 and K6781) were configured as combat aircraft, with a single set of controls and carrying full armament and radio equipment. The other three aircraft, however, (K5446, K5559 and K6712)had been converted to trainers by General Aircraft in 1938 and had full dual controls fitted; in addition, some other combat-related equipment had been removed in the course of their conversion. As a consequence, it was specified that the forward-firing armament and bombing equipment were to be re-fitted to these three Hinds before delivery to the Air Corps, and all six aircrfat were to be fitted with full night-flying equipment, including two blind flying hoods. The standard RAF disruptive camouflage scheme was retained on these aircraft, but all RAF markings were removed before delivery to the Air Corps.

The Hinds were flight-tested by Air Corps pilots at Sealand airfield in May 1940, and were delivered to Baldonnel Aerodrome on June 1 of that year following delays due to mechanical faults and bad weather. The six Hind Is (as Nos. 67 to 72) were operated by the Air Corps Flying Training Schools and by No. 1 Fighter Squadron. One of the Hinds (No. 69) was damaged in an accident on June 5, 1940, but was apparently returned to service following repairs, although some sources suggest that this aircraft was withdrawn from use in the same month. On July 27, 1940, during an exercise over the Air Firing

The Hawker Hinds were delivered in 1940 and although obsolete in RAF service, they served with No. 1 Fighter Squadron for about four years. (J. Masterson photo)

Range at Gormanston Military Camp, Hind No. 70 crashed at Laytown, Co. Meath, killing the crew. Operated by 'A' Flight, No. 1 Fighter Squadron, this Hind had accumulated a total of 288 flying hours, comprising 240 hours in service with the RAF and 48 hours in service with the Air Corps. Another Hind (No. 71) was written-off in a crash on September 27, 1940.

Operated by No. 1 Fighter Squadron, the remaining Hinds (Nos. 67. 68, 69 and 72) participated in the combined divisional manoeuvres in the south of Ireland conducted throughout August and September 1942. The Hinds were based at Rathduff airfield in Co. Tipperary throughout these exercises, and were operated by No. 2 Air Component which provided air support for the Irish Army's 2nd "Spearhead" Division, known as "Red Force" for the purposes of these exercises.

Following the delivery of Hawker Hurricane Is and Miles Master IIIs to No. 1 Fighter Squadron in 1943, the four Hinds were withdrawn from use (No. 68 in November 1943, No. 72 in August 1944, No. 67 in October 1944 and No. 69 also at some point in 1944) and later scrapped.

Top: Designed as a bomber, the Hind could carry a useful load, samples of which are seen here on the Hind at the Shuttleworth Collection. (J. Maxwell photo)

Above: Cockpit of the Hind at the Shuttleworth Collection (J. Maxwell photo)

Left: Rear gunners position in the Hind. (P.Hopkins photo)

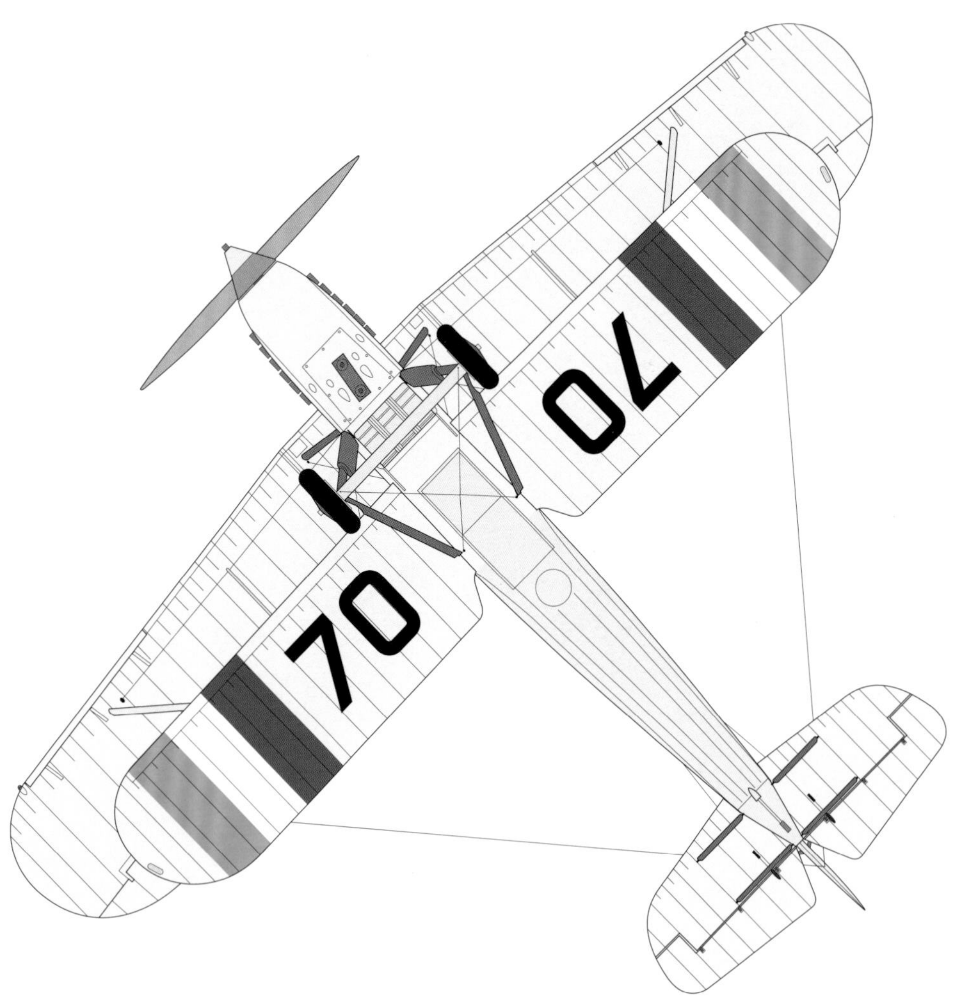

Below: Close up of the single rear Vickers Gun on the Hind. (P.Hopkins photo)

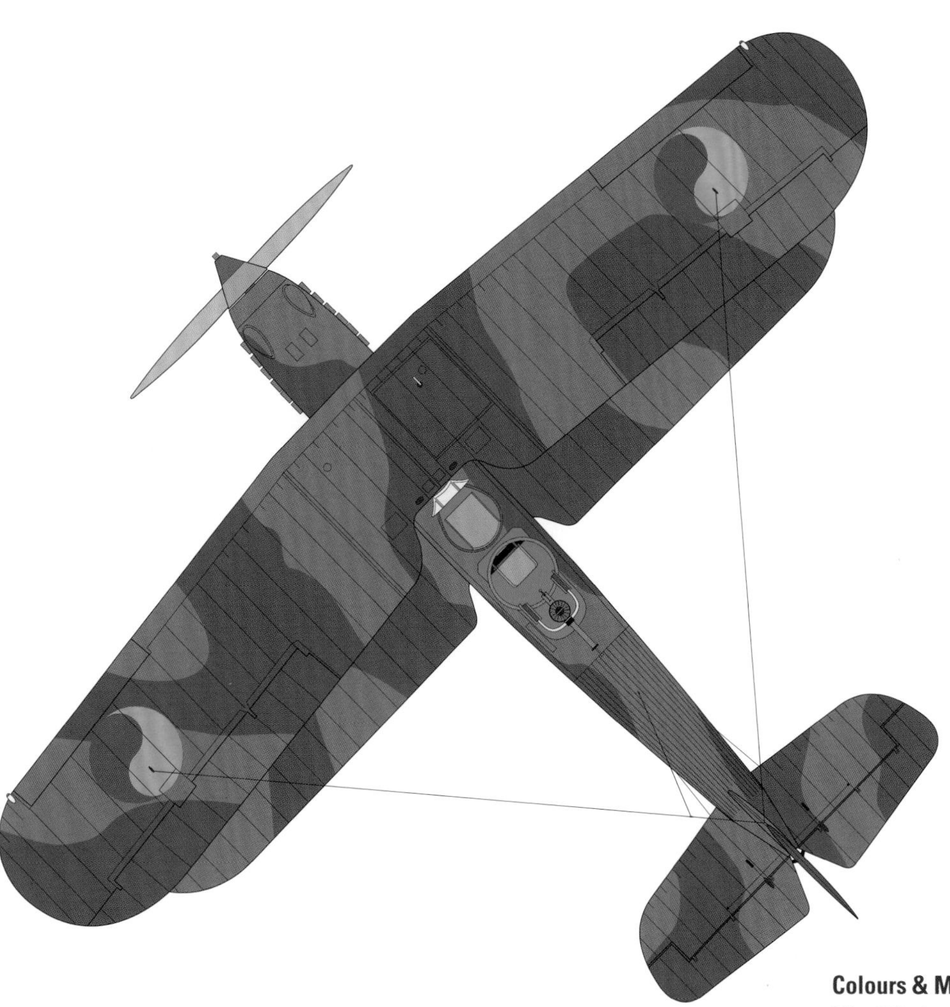

Colours & Markings

The Hinds retained their standard RAF disruptive camouflage scheme of matt dark earth and dark green on the upper surfaces of the wings and fuselage, with the undersides of the wings and fuselage painted silver. The green and orange Celtic boss was displayed on the upper surfaces of the top wings and on both sides of the centre fuselage section, with green, white and orange stripes, positioned chordwise, displayed on the undersides of the lower wings. The Air Corps' serial number was displayed in black on the undersides of the lower wings and on both sides of the fuselage, in front of the tailplane.

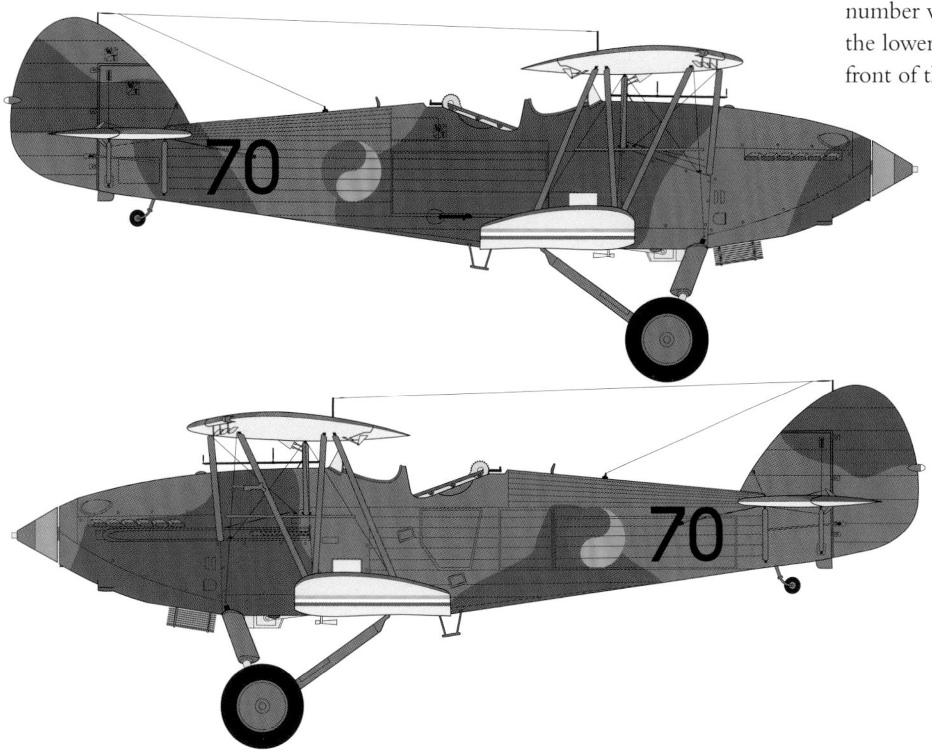

2.8

Hawker Hurricane I, IIa, IIb and IIc (1940 – 1947)

The Hawker Hurricane is perhaps the second most famous British fighter aircraft after the Supermarine Spitfire, despite the fact that it outnumbered its more well-known counterpart during the Battle of Britain in 1940. A number of variants of the Hurricane were acquired by the Air Corps at various stages throughout the war.

Designated Hurricane I, the first production aircraft (with RAF serial L1547) flew for the first time on October 12, 1937, powered by a 1,030 hp Merlin II engine, with deliveries to the RAF commencing in December of the same year. The Air Ministry ordered 1,000 Hurricane Is in November 1938, 500 of which were to be constructed by Gloster Aircraft Ltd., an associate company of Hawker Aircraft Ltd. Hurricane I's were also built in Canada by the Canadian Car and Foundry Co.; these aircraft were given the designation Hurricane X, production of this variant having commenced in 1939. A number of these were also delivered to the RAF. At the outbreak of the Second World War, eighteen RAF fighter squadrons were equipped with the Hurricane I, which had by that time also been delivered to the air forces of Belgium, Finland, Romania, Turkey and Yugoslavia. When production of the Hurricane I ended in early 1941, a total of 3,194 had been constructed by British and Canadian companies.

The next variant, the Hurricane II, was produced in three different sub-variants. The first of these was the Hurricane IIa which, although similar in most other respects to the Hurricane I, was powered by a 1,185 hp Merlin XX engine with a two-stage supercharger, driving a Rotol constant-speed three-bladed propeller; production of this type commenced in September 1940. Next came the Hurricane IIb, which had a strengthened fuselage, was fitted with twelve wing-mounted Browning 0.303-in. machine-guns instead of the eight carried by earlier versions, and had universal attachment points fitted to the undersides of each wing for fuel tanks, bombs or rockets. The final Hurricane II, the IIc, had four 20 mm Hispano or Oerlikon cannon, which had been evaluated and tested on four Hurricane IIs at the Aircraft & Armament Experimental Establishment (A & A.E.E) from February to May 1941. Production of the Hurricane IIc commenced in March 1941, and this variant was operated by the RAF as a fighter-bomber and night-fighter aircraft over the next four years. When production of the Hurricane IIc ended in August 1944, a total of 4,711 had been constructed.

The cockpit canopy pushed back suggests that the pilot of Hurricane No. 93 is enjoying the flight. Having been an RAF aircraft which force-landed in Co. Wexford, it was pressed into service in Baldonnel to become the first of a total of 20 Air Corps Hurricanes. (A.C. Photographic Section).

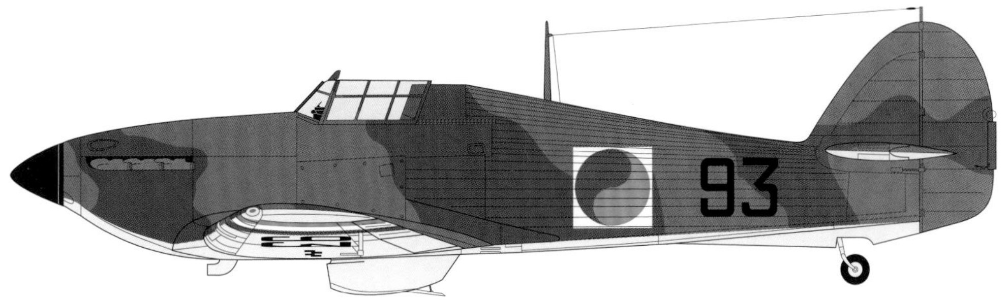

In 1940, the Irish Department of Defence ordered thirteen Hurricane Is for the Irish Army Air Corps, but these aircraft could not be supplied at that time. However, over the next three years, a Hurricane X, a IIa and a IIb did enter service with the Air Corps, all having force-landed in neutral Ireland and subsequently purchased by the Department of Defence.

The first of these aircraft was acquired by the Air Corps when, on September 29, 1940, a Hurricane I and two Hurricane Xs of No. 79 Sqdn, RAFRAF, intercepted and shot down a Heinkel He 111P of the German Luftwaffe's Kampfgeschwader 55, which had been on a bombing mission to Liverpool, over the Irish Sea. Low on fuel after the interception, one of the Hurricane Xs (RAFRAF serial P5178, coded NV-G) force-landed in a field in Co. Wexford, but was not badly damaged and was delivered to Baldonnel Aerodrome after being dismantled by an Air Corps salvage party. Following negotiations with the British Government, this Hurricane, along with three other RAF aircraft that had also force-landed in neutral Ireland, were purchased by the Department of Defence for a total of £10,000; this price included sufficient spare parts to repair each of the aircraft. Following repairs, the Hurricane X (as No. 93) flew again on May 9, 1942 and was operated by the Advanced Training Section, Air Corps Flying Training Schools. This aircraft, which was from a batch of forty Hurricane Xs (RAF serials P5170-P5209) constructed by the Canadian Car and Foundry Corporation, had been delivered to No. 79 Squadron on September 1, 1940. The Hurricane X was the first monoplane fighter aircraft, and the first aircraft capable of exceeding 300 m.p.h. in level flight, to enter service with the Air Corps.

On June 10, 1941, a Hurricane IIa (RAF serial Z2832, coded GZ-M) of No. 32 Sqdn, RAF, intercepted and damaged a Heinkel He 111H-3 of the Luftwaffe's Wekusta 51, which was on a meteorological reconnaissance mission over the Irish Sea. Following the attack, the German aircraft crashed in Co. Wexford, killing all the crew; the Hurricane IIa did not have sufficient fuel to return to its base in Wales and force-landed in a field in Co. Waterford, damaging its undercarriage and propeller. The aircraft was dismantled by an Air Corps salvage party and brought to Baldonnel Aerodrome. This Hurricane had been delivered to No. 32 Squadron in May 1941 and was from a batch of 1,000 Hurricane IIs, constructed by Hawker Aircraft, which were delivered to the RAF between August 1940 and July 1941.

Another Hurricane, this time a IIb variant (RAF serial Z5070,), force-landed in Ireland on August 21st 1941,. This aircraft had become separated from three other Hurricanes in foggy conditions during a delivery flight to an airfield in Scotland. Low on fuel, and thinking that he was over Scotland, the pilot force-landed in Co. Meath, damaging the propeller, air intake, radiator and drop tanks. This aircraft was from a batch of 417 Hurricane IIbs constructed by Gloster Aircraft Co. Ltd. and delivered to the RAF between June and September 1941.

Following negotiations with the British Government, these two Hurricanes were purchased for £7,200 by the Department of Defence, this price including sufficient spares to repair both aircraft, which were to be returned to the RAF when expected deliveries of Hurricane Is to the Air Corps commenced in 1943. Following repairs at Baldonnel Aerodrome, the Hurricane IIb flew again in July 1942 and (as No. 95) was operated by the Advanced Training Section, Air Corps Flying Training Schools. Over the next six months, selected pilots underwent operational conversion courses on this aircraft and on the Hurricane X, which were conducted by an R.A.F pilot, Flt. Lt. Don West, who had been seconded to the Air Corps for this purpose. The Hurricane IIa was also repaired and (as No. 94) flew again in March 1943

A batch of four Hurricane Is (ex-R.A.F serials V6613, V7411, V7540 and Z4037) were collected by Air Corps pilots and delivered to Baldonnel Aerodrome on July 7, 1943 and (as nos. 103-106) entered service with No. 1 Fighter Squadron, which had been deployed to Rineanna Aerodrome in May of that year. On the same day, the Hurricane IIa and IIb (nos. 94 and 95) were returned to the RAF A further seven Hurricane I's entered service with the Air Corps between November 1943 and March 1944, also with No. 1 Fighter Squadron (as nos. 107-114).

The Hurricane Is, which were all from surplus RAF stocks, were "war weary" after intensive operational service with RAF fighter squadrons and training units over the previous three years. Three of the aircraft (ex V6613, V7173 and Z7158) had accumulated over 1,000 flying hours during this period and another(V7411/104) was a Battle of Britain veteran

Above: A line up of Hurricanes at Baldonnel indicates detailed differences in their spinners and in some of the colour schemes. (A.C. Photographic Section)

having been damaged in combat in September 1940 whilst being flown by RAF Flt. Sergeant Hodson who was wounded . This aircraft was repaired and returned to service with 52, 56 and 182/55 Operational Training Units before entering service with the Irish Air Corps.

Operating from Rineanna Aerodrome throughout 1943 and 1944, only an average of 150 flying hours was accumulated by each of the Hurricanes throughout this period, due to mechanical problems, a lack of spare parts (especially tyres) aviation fuel, and the deployment of skilled Air Corps personnel to other units of the Defence Forces. In 1944, the Hurricanes provided a demonstration of aerial firepower against ground targets at the Air Firing Range, Gormanston Military Camp, for staff officers attached to General Headquarters, Irish Defence Forces. Later that year, due to its development for post-war transatlantic airline operations, Rineanna Aerodrome became unsuitable for military air operations and on May 1, 1945 the Hurricanes were flown to the airfield at Gormanston Military Camp, which had been extended and levelled in preparation for the deployment of No. 1 Fighter Squadron to the camp.

Six Hurricane IIc's were delivered to the Air Corps from surplus RAF stocks in 1945, apparently to equip a cadre for the formation of a second fighter squadron. Four of the Hurricane IIcs (ex RAF serials LF541, LF566, LF624 and LF770) were delivered to Baldonnel Aerodrome on March 7, 1945, and the final two (ex RAF serials LF536 and PZ796) were delivered three weeks later. These aircraft were from the final production batches of Hurricane IIcs (RAF serials LF 529-LF 542, LF 559-LG 601 and PZ 791-PZ 835) constructed by Hawker Aircraft, and delivered to the RAF between September 1943 and May 1944. One of the aircraft delivered to the Air Corps (ex RAF serial LF 770) was unarmed, having been operated by No. 1697 Air Despatch Letter Service Flight, RAF, but the four wing-mounted 20 mm cannon were installed before delivery to the Air Corps. These aircraft were the last to be delivered to the Air Corps before the end of the "Emergency" in 1945.

The Hurricane IIc's (as nos. 115-120) entered service with No. 1 Fighter Squadron, replacing the Hurricane Is, which were used for operational training by the Advanced Training Section, Air Corps Flying Training Schools, throughout the remainder of 1945 and 1946, over the course of which period they were gradually withdrawn from use. The first Hurricane I (No. 110) was withdrawn from use in November 1945, following a crash-landing in Co. Wexford, with two more (nos. 103 and 106) following in December 1945 and March 1946 respectively. Hurricane I No. 7 was withdrawn from use in July 1946, followed by another four (nos. 93, 111, 112 and 114) in August, with the last four (nos. 104, 105, 109 and 108) being withdrawn from use over the course of September – November 1946.

As to the Hurricane IIc's, one (No. 115) was withdrawn from use in June 1946, with two more (nos. 119 and 118) following January and March 1947 respectively. In June 1947, Hurricane IIc No. 117 was written-off in a crash and the remaining two aircraft of this type (nos. 116 and 120) were withdrawn from use in November of that year.

Twelve Vickers Supermarine Seafire LF.IIIs were ordered by the Department of Defence in August 1946 to replace the Hurricanes, with deliveries commencing in 1947. The Seafires were to be operated by No. 1 Fighter Squadron, the plans for the formation of a second fighter squadron having apparently been abandoned at this stage, probably due to financial restrictions and to the fact that the war had ended.

Top: The Air Corps Chaplain, Fr William O'Riordan conducts the annual blessing of the fleet ceremony in 1944, a tradition that continues to this day. Note the black spinner of No. 93 at the far right of the picture. (A.C. Photographic Section)

Above: Cockpit detail in an airworthy Sea Hurricane of the Shuttleworth Collection, This aircraft would have differed in minor details from the Air Corps machines. (J. Maxwell photo)

Left: Health & safety regulations were not high on the agenda in the 1940s. Technicians lie on the tail surfaces of Hurricane No. 95 as the engine is run up, risking life and certainly limb in the process! (D. MacCarron collection)

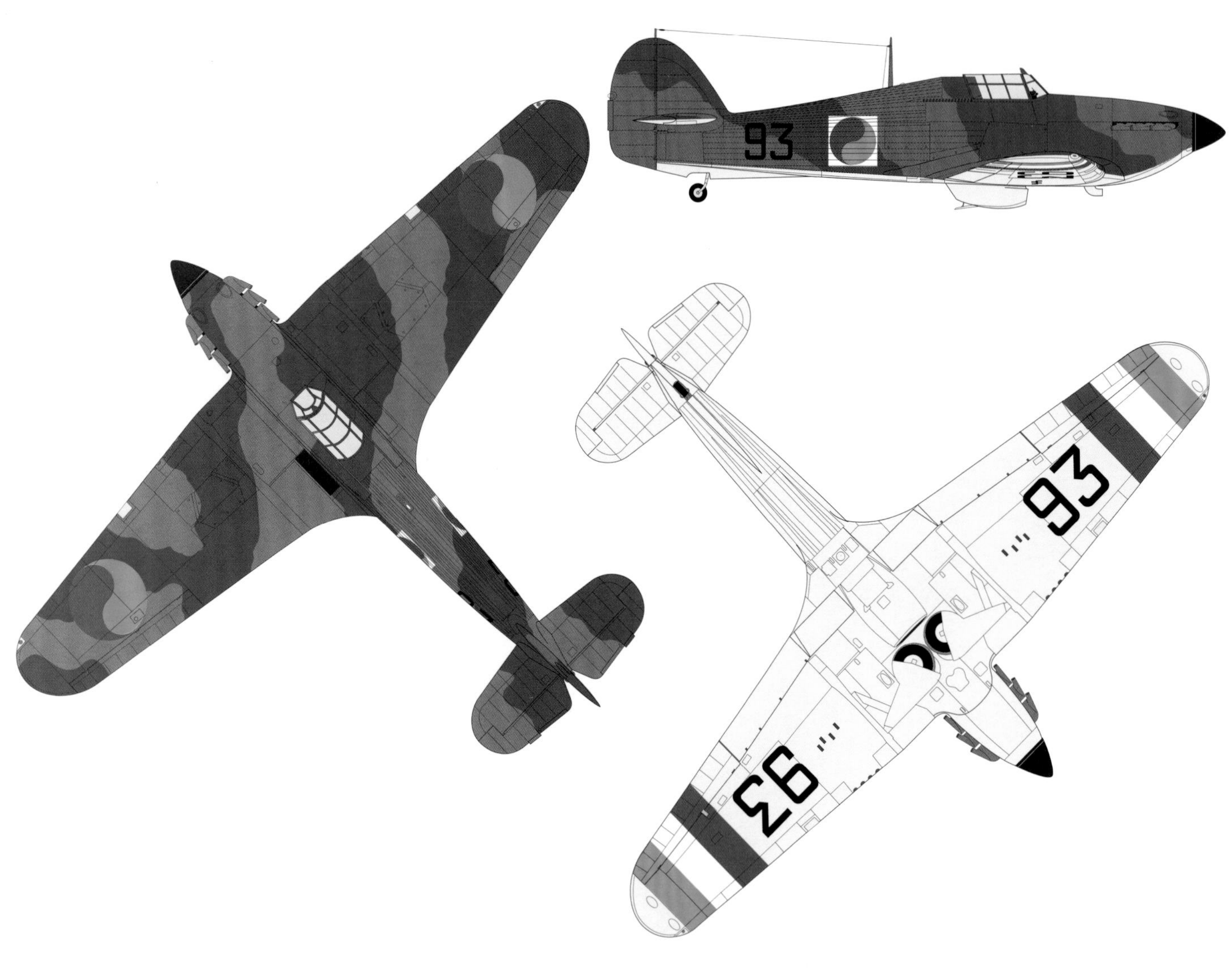

Colours & Markings

The Hurricane X, IIa and IIb had the standard RAF disruptive camouflage scheme of the time of dark earth and dark green on the upper surfaces of the fuselage, wings and tailplanes, which was retained after entering service with the Air Corps, but with a silver-grey or blue grey finish applied to the under surfacesThe green and orange Celtic boss was displayed on the upper surfaces of both wings and on both sides of the fuselage centre section, enclosed in a white square. Green, white and orange stripes, positioned chordwise, were displayed on the outer sections of the under sides of both wings and the serial numberwas displayed in black on both sides of the fuselage, behind the Celtic boss, and on the undersides of both wings.

Some sources claim that the batch of Hurricanes I's delivered in 1943-44 were also painted in the dark green and dark earth upper surfaces scheme similar to the earlier Hurricanes. However, the standard colour scheme for day fighters in RAF service had changed in 1941, with dark earth being replaced by ocean grey with undersurfaces painted medium sea grey. This was because most combats at that stage of the war were taking place at higher altitudes and over the sea, and the dark green/ocean grey/medium sea grey camouflage provided more concealment than the earlier dark green/dark earth/sky combination. It is not clear if the 11 Hurricane Is delivered to the Air Corps in '43-'44 had been repainted by the RAF in the newer scheme or whether it was applied by the Air Corps. However, by 1945 most of the Hurricane I's were in the dark green and ocean grey upper surfaces/medium sea grey lower surfaces scheme. Hurricane X No. 93 was not withdrawn from use until May 1946, and may have retained its original camouflage scheme until the end. The crest of No. 1 Fighter Squadron was displayed on all of the Hurricanes, beneath the exhaust ejector stubs.

The Hurricane IIc's retained the RAF disruptive camouflage scheme of dark green and ocean grey on the upper surfaces of the wings, fuselage and tailplanes, and medium sea grey undersides, which had been introduced in 1941 for fighter aircraft operating over Northern Europe. The two colour Celtic boss, tricolour stripes and serial numbers were displayed in the same positions as on the Hurricane I's.

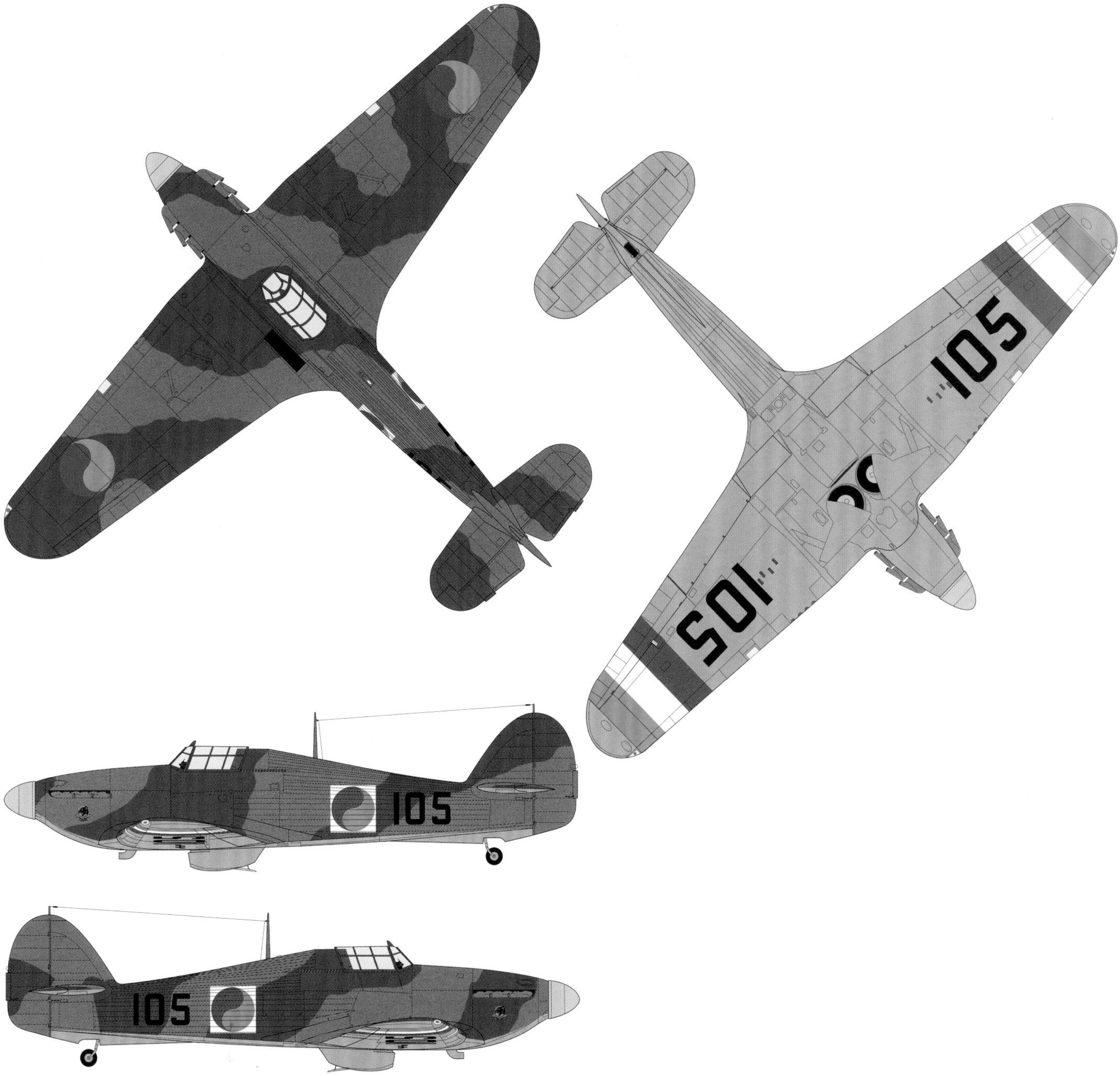

Left: Three Hurricane Mk IIc's head up the east coast in order to unleash their formidable 20mm cannons at the targets moored off the coast at Gormanston Co. Meath. (A.C. Photographic Section)

2.9

Hawker Hector I (1941 – 1943)

The Hawker Hector was a development of the Hawker Hart family of elegant two-seaters, designed in 1935 as a replacement for the Hawker Audax army co-operation aircraft. Because of the demand for Rolls-Royce Kestrel engines for the new Hawker Hind, which was at the time just entering service with the RAF, an alternative power plant was specified for the Hector. This was the Napier Dagger 24-cylinder, H-type, air-cooled engine, the installation of which resulted in the Hector having a blunter, wider nose, by comparison with the pointed, streamlined nose of the Hart. The Hector also had a straight upper wing instead of the Hart's swept-back upper wing, this being required in order to counteract the alteration to the aircraft's centre of gravity resulting from the increased weight of the Dagger engine.

In 1941, a total of 44 aircraft was in service with the Irish Army Air Corps, of which only twenty could be considered in any way suitable for combat operations. Following discussions between representatives of the British and Irish governments about this situation, the UK Air Ministry agreed to allow the export of ten Hawker Hectors, by that time surplus to RAF requirements, to Ireland. Costing £200 each, the aircraft were ordered through the Irish High Commissioner in London. Seven of the Hectors were to be delivered in standard configuration, while three were to be converted to the training role by the RAF prior to delivery; some spares were also included in the contract, along with seven Vickers Mk.V and Lewis Mk.III machine guns, three F.24 Mk.III cameras, and two spare engines.

Ten Hector Is held in storage with various RAF Maintenance Units were selected for delivery to the Air Corps (the RAF serial nos. of the chosen aircraft were K8098, K8102, K8105, K8114, K8115, K8117, K8148, K9697, K9715 and K9725). On May 5, 1941 the aircraft were inspected by Air Corps officers at two RAF airfields in Scotland, Lossiemouth and Kinloss, and nine were flown to the RAF airfield at Newtownards in Co. Down on May 14. The Hectors were subsequently collected by Air Corps pilots and delivered to Baldonnel Aerodrome on May 16, 1941; the tenth aircraft was delivered via the same route twelve days later. The Hectors (as Nos. 78-87) entered service with the Intermediate Training School, Air Corps Flying Training Schools, for advanced flying and operational training. Some of these aircraft were also operated at one time or another by No. 1 Fighter Squadron and No. 1 Reconnaissance and Medium Bombing Squadron. In the event, four of the Hectors rather than three as originally specified(Nos. 80, 82, 84 and 86) were

One of the Air Corps Hawker Hectors photographed shortly after a nose over accident on soft ground. Of note is the heavy Coles Crane in the background, the rear wheels of which have been connected by caterpillar tracks. (D. MacCarron collection)

Left: As with other obsolescent former RAF types, the Hectors proved to be highly valuable for participation in the Army Co-operation role. (A.C. Photographic Section)

actually converted to dual control trainers at Kinloss airfield before delivery to the Air Corps.

On July 21, 1941 one of the Hectors (No. 87) was written-off in a crash. Two others (Nos. 81 and 83) were written-off on September 4, 1941, following a collision on the ground at Gormanston Military Camp. Three additional Hectors were ordered in the same month to replace the three lost to attrition, and these aircraft (ex RAF serials K8130, K8159 and K9761) were delivered to Baldonnel Aerodrome on January 13, 1942, entering service (as Nos. 88-90) with the Intermediate Training School.

Operating from "Rathduff" airfield in Co. Tipperary, the Hectors participated in the major divisional manoeuvres in the south of Ireland conducted by the Defence Forces throughout August and September 1942. The Hectors were operated by No. 2 Air Component, which provided air support for the 2nd "Spearhead" Division, known as "Red Force" for the purposes of the exercises. On August 28, Hector No. 85 was written-off after crash-landing at this airfield when itran out of fuel. Another Hector (No. 88) was withdrawn from use after a further landing accident at the same airfield in September 1942.

Following the delivery of six Miles Master IIIs to the Air Corps in February 1943 for advanced flying and operational training, the remaining Hectors were withdrawn from use throughout that year. Three of the aircraft (Nos. 79, 80 and 84) were withdrawn from use in July, August and September respectively, followed by another four (Nos. 78, 82, 89 and 90) in October. The last remaining Hector in service (No. 86) was withdrawn from use in November 1943. In the same month an offer from the RAF to supply any spare parts required to put the Hectors back into service was declined by the Air Corps, not least because the Napier Dagger engines (each with 24 cylinders, 48 spark plugs and 96 valves) were overly complicated and required a great deal of maintenance.

In 1994 the rear fuselages of two Hector Is that had been in service with the Air Corps were discovered buried in the bank of a stream in a Dublin suburb, and were excavated for eventual restoration.

Below: Hector No. 88 has suffered a nose over accident on landing, a common enough occurrence on soft grass airstrips in Ireland. The heavy weight (1,285 lb (583 kg)) of the 24 cylinder Napier Dagger engine up front probably contributed to the nose over. (A.C. Photographic Section)

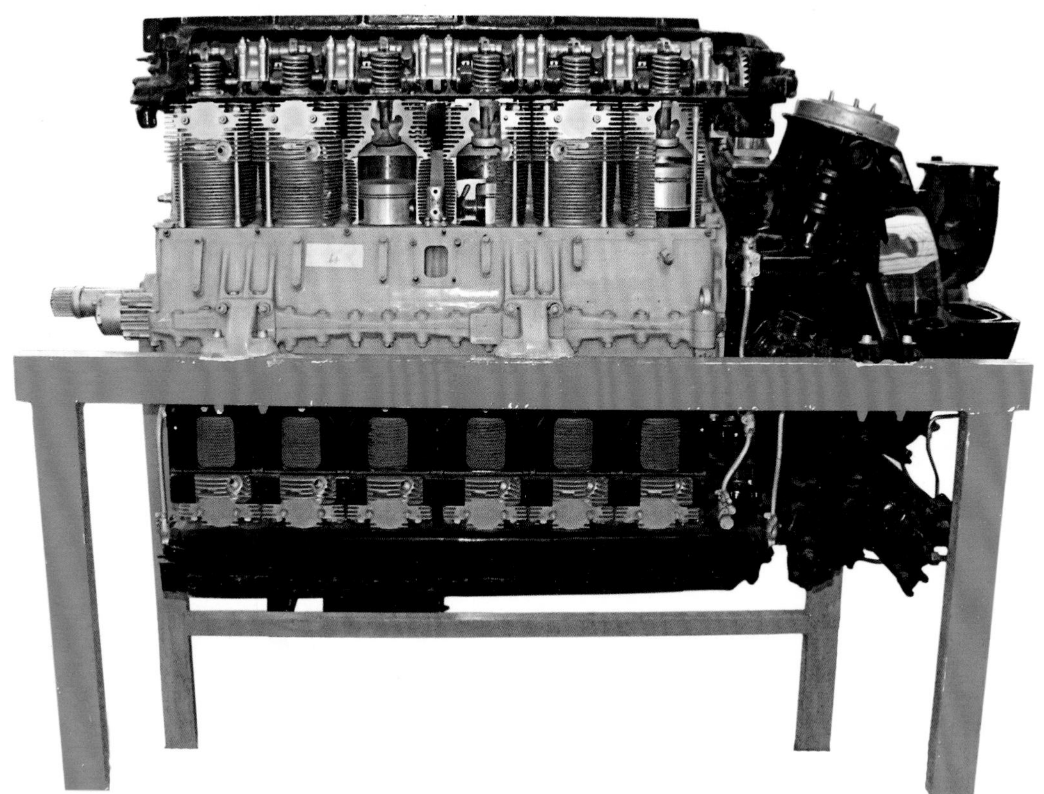

Right: A cutaway Napier Dagger 24 cylinder engine on display at the Air Corps Museum. The engine was smooth running and rotated at up to 4,000 rpm but was prone to cooling problems. (J. Maxwell photo)

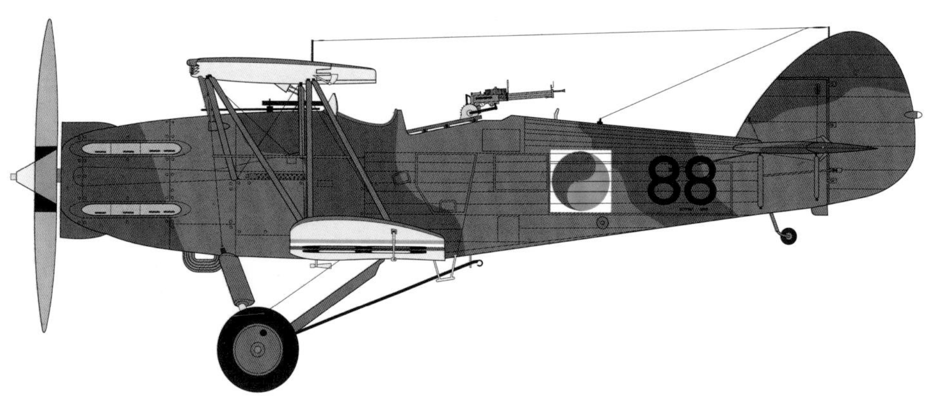

Colours & Markings

The Hector Is retained their standard RAF disruptive camouflage scheme of matt dark earth and dark green on the upper surfaces of the wings, fuselage and tailplane, but the undersides of the wings, fuselage and tailplane were painted silver. The two-colour Celtic boss was displayed on the upper surfaces of the top wings and, enclosed in a white square, on both sides of the rear fuselage. Green, white and orange stripes, positioned chordwise, were displayed on the undersides of the bottom wings. Each aircraft's serial numberwas displayed in black on the undersides of the two lower wings and on both sides of the fuselage, in front of the tailplane.

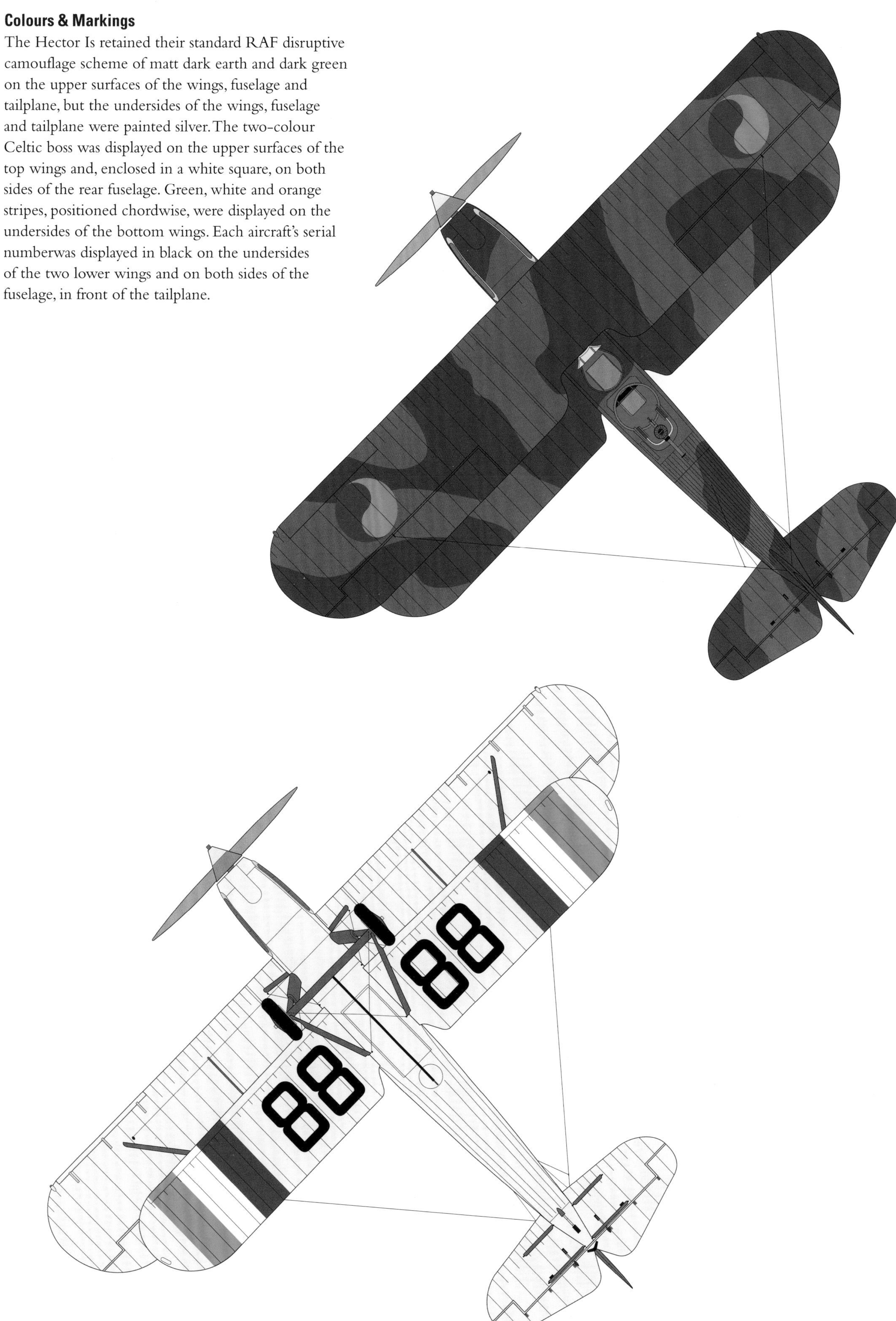

2.10

Lockheed L.214 Hudson I (1941 – 1945)

The Lockheed Hudson was an American-built light bomber and coastal reconnaissance aircraft designed to fulfil an RAF requirement for a twin-engined aircraft that could be used by Coastal Command squadrons

Derived from the company's Lockheed L-14 Super Electra commercial airliner, the Hudson, which was powered by two 1,100 hp Wright GR-1820-G102A Cyclone radial engines, was fitted with more modern equipment than the Avro Anson 1, which was being phased out of frontline service as a land based maritime patrol aircraft. It also had a higher cruising speed, longer range and could carry a heavier bomb load.

Designated Hudson I, deliveries of the aircraft to Nos. 224 and 233 Squadrons of the RAF's Coastal Command commenced in May and August 1939 respectively, both units being fully equipped with the type by the end of that year. Throughout 1940, the Hudsons of No. 233 Squadron, operating from Leuchars in Scotland, were engaged on reconnaissance patrols and combat operations against German shipping and submarines in the North Sea. From December 1940 to August 1941, the squadron was deployed to Aldergrove, near Belfast, providing air cover for Allied shipping convoys and anti-submarine patrols off the north-west and west coasts of Ireland.

At 09.20 hours on Friday, January 24, 1941, a Hudson I from No. 233 Squadron (RAF serial P5123, coded ZS-W) took-off from Aldergrove to provide air cover for a shipping convoy off the north-west coast of Ireland, but the convoy could not be located due to bad weather in the area. The Hudson deviated from its course during the return flight to Aldergrove when its radio became unserviceable, and the navigator was unable to obtain a fix on the aircraft's position due to the weather conditions. About six hours after take-off, the crew sighted land to the east of the aircraft's flight path, which they apparently thought was either Iceland, Norway or Scotland. At 15.50 hours the Hudson was sighted circling over Sligo Bay and the adjacent coastal region, from the Irish Coastwatching Service's look-out post at Roskeeragh Point in Co. Sligo. At 17.10 hours, after the crew had jettisoned the bomb load into Sligo Bay, the Hudson force-landed in a small field at Gark, near Skreen, Co. Sligo. The aircraft landed with the undercarriage retracted, and both propellers were bent on impact with the ground, the underside of the fuselage, the bomb-bay doors and wing flaps also being damaged. The crew were uninjured, but the arrival of the Gardaí and Irish Defence Forces personnel prevented them from destroying the Hudson. The airmen were taken into custody by the Gardaí and were later interned in the Curragh Military Camp, Co. Kildare.

The Hudson was surveyed by an officer from the Irish Army Air Corps, who decided that the damage could be repaired sufficiently to allow the aircraft to be flown out of the field in which it had crash-

Right: Photos of the Air Corps Hudson are rare. After its military service the Hudson took up civil markings as Aer Lingus' EI-ACB although in this photo the "I" is curiously missing. (Liam Byrne/Ronny Vogt collection)

Left: the Hudson is bombed up by ground crew members. Health and safety regulations are of the minimal variety. (A.C. Photographic Section)

landed. An Air Corps salvage party dug a trench under the main wheels to allow the undercarriage to be extended; this enabled the aircraft to be hauled up on to level ground for repairs to be made to the underside of the fuselage. A temporary airstrip was also laid out by the salvage party, which included knocking gaps in some of the stone walls forming boundaries with adjacent fields.

On March 26, 1941, the Hudson was flown out of this temporary airstrip to Baldonnel Aerodrome, piloted by an Aer Lingus pilot Ian Hammond, who was an officer in the Air Corps Reserve. Mr. Hammond had type experience on the Lockheed Model 14 from which the Hudson was developed, two of which had been in service with Aer Lingus (the aircraft concerned were registered EI-ABV and EI-ABW, operated by the airline from June 1939 to May 1940). It was ironic that at a time when the Air Corps was short of modern patrol aircraft, Aer Lingus disposed of the two Lockheed 14's to Guinea Airways.

Following an agreement with the British Government, the Hudson, together with a Fairey Battle T.T.I, a Hawker Hurricane I, and a Miles Master I, (all of which had landed in neutral Ireland,) were purchased by the Department of Defence for a total of £10,000. Spare parts and equipment required for the repairs to the Hudson were supplied by the RAF from Aldergrove airfield, and the aircraft underwent an extensive overhaul at Baldonnel Aerodrome before entering service with the Air Corps. A number of small patches, apparently covering bullet holes, were discovered on the port side of the fuselage during the overhaul, which seemed to indicate that the Hudson had been engaged in combat at some time while in RAF service. Constructed in October 1939, the Hudson (c/n 1812) was from a batch of fifty that had been constructed before December 1939 and delivered to the RAF between March and July of 1940. The Hudson was the first aircraft constructed in the USAto enter service with the Air Corps.

Following completion of all repairs, the Hudson flew again on May 7, 1942 and (as No. 91) was put into service with No. 1 Reconnaissance and Medium Bombing Squadron, based at Rineanna Aerodrome. Assistance with pilot conversion and technical training on the Hudson was provided by personnel from Aer Lingus, who were seconded to the Air Corps for this purpose. In August 1942, the Taoiseach (the Irish Prime Minister), together with some members of the Cabinet, was flown in the Hudson from Baldonnel Aerodrome to Rineanna Aerodrome on a visit to the Air Corps detachment and other units of the Defence Forces stationed at the airfield. During the return flight to Baldonnel Aerodrome, the Hudson flew over the west and north-west regions of the State at the request of the Taoiseach. This was the first time that a Taoiseach had flown in an Air Corps aircraft.

In 1944, following the disbandment of No. 1 Reconnaissance and Medium Bombing Squadron at Baldonnel Aerodrome, the Hudson was operated by the General Purpose Flight until the aircraft was withdrawn from use in 1945. Purchased by Aer Lingus, apparently for crew training and transporting freight, the Hudson was delivered to the airline on August 2, 1945, following the removal of the dorsal gun turret and other military equipment by the Air Corps. However, the Hudson, which was allocated the Irish civil registration EI-ACB, had to be placed in storage by the airline at Dublin Airport when the Department of Industry and Commerce would not issue a Certificate of Airworthiness for the aircraft In May of 1947, the Hudson was purchased by John Mathieu Aviation, a Belgian aviation services operator, and – registered as OO-API – was operated by this company until January 1954. The Hudson was scrapped in the same year.

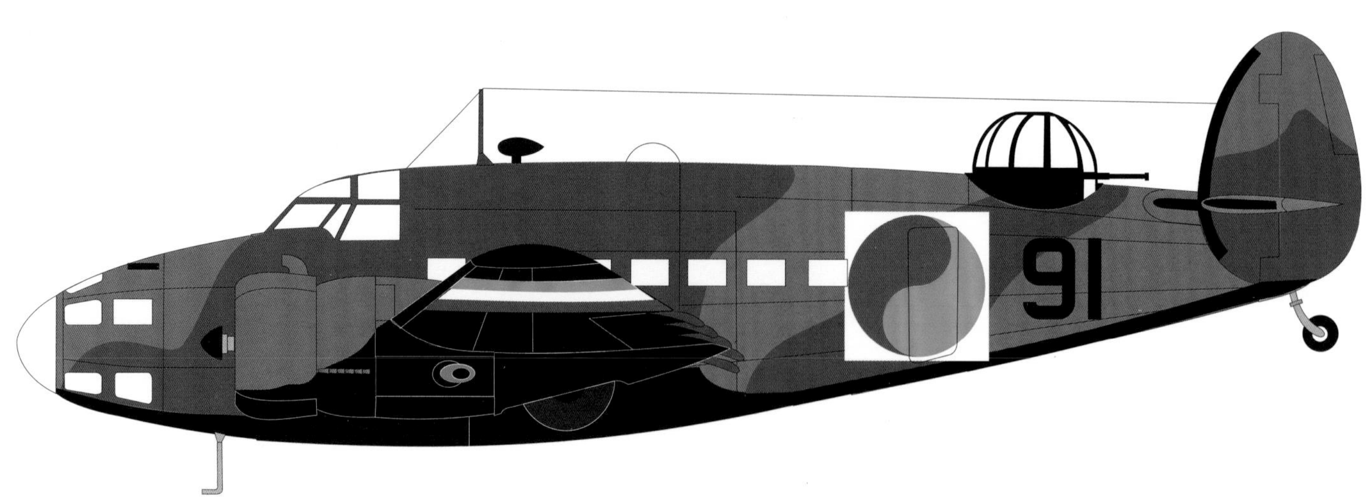

Colours & Markings

The Hudson retained its RAF disruptive camouflage scheme of matt dark earth and dark green on all uppersurfaces, with matt black undersides, while in service with the Air Corps. The RAF roundels were replaced by the green and orange Celtic bosses on the upper surfaces of both wings, and – enclosed in a white square – on both sides of the fuselage. Green, white and orange stripes, positioned chordwise, were applied to the undersurfaces of both wings. The Air Corps serial numberwas displayed in black on both sides of the fuselage, behind the Celtic boss.

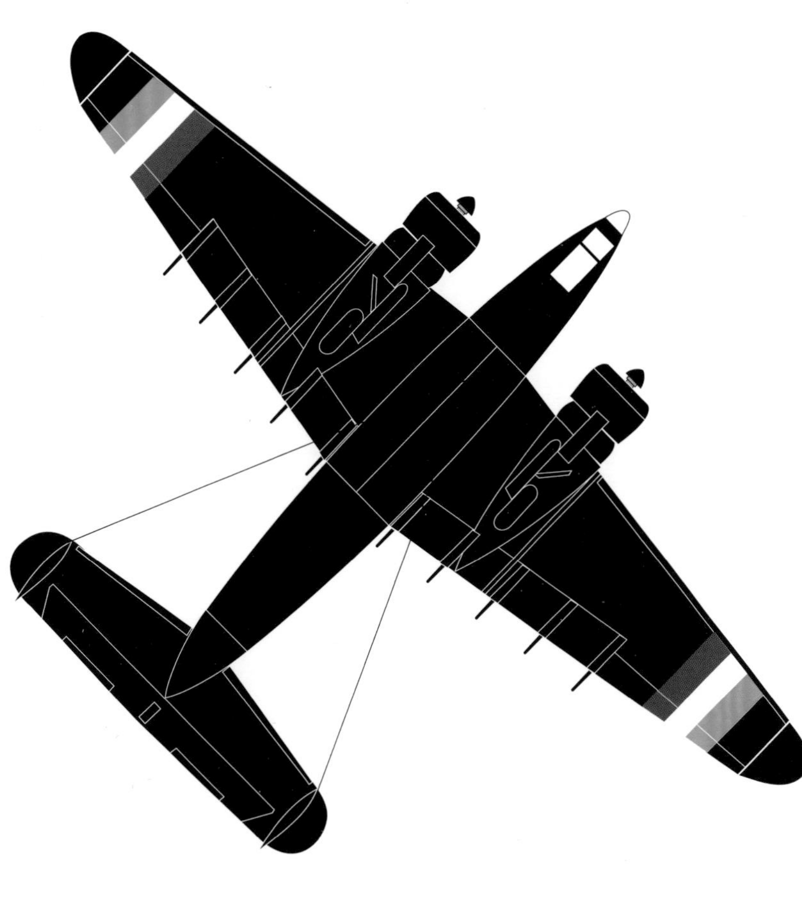

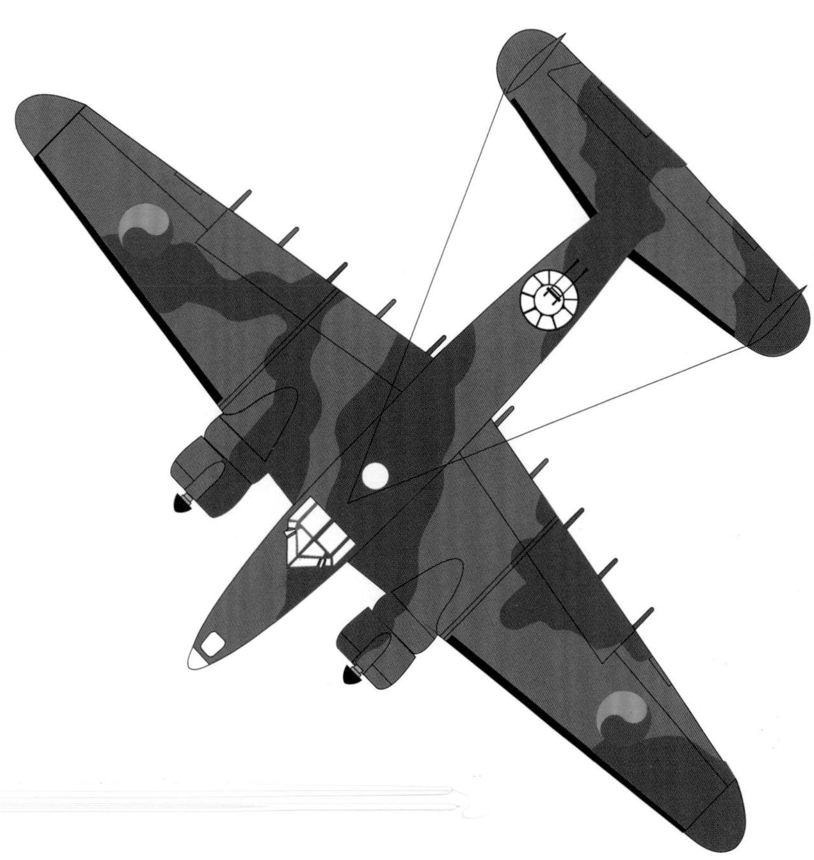

2.11

Fairey Battle T.T.1 (1941 – 1946)

The Fairey Battle was a British single-engined light bomber built by the Fairey Aviation Company in the late 1930s for the Royal Air Force. The Battle was powered by the same Rolls-Royce Merlin engine that conferred contemporary Spitfire and Hurricane fighters with high performance; however, the Battle was a much heavier aircraft with a two-man crew and a 1000lb bomb load. It was a vast improvement on the Hawker Hart and Hawker Hind biplane bombers that preceded it, but by the time it saw action in the Battle of France it was slower than enemy fighters and highly vulnerable to attack.

Following an initial order for 400 Battles in 1936, the Austin Motor Co. had also commenced production at a new 'shadow factory' constructed for this purpose, with deliveries to the RAF commencing in August 1938. Over 1,000 Battles had been delivered to the RAF by the outbreak of the Second World War, equipping 15 Bomber Command squadrons, and the aircraft had also been delivered to six other air forces. In 1940, the Irish Department of Defence attempted to acquire three Battles for the Irish Army Air Corps, but these aircraft could not be supplied by Fairey due to the UK government's embargo on the export of much-needed combat aircraft. When production of the Battle ceased in January 1941, a total of 2,185 had been constructed, 1,156 by Fairey and 1,029 by Austin Motors.

In 1940, the Battle was withdrawn from combat operations by the RAF following heavy losses sustained by the bomber squadrons equipped with this aircraft during the German invasion of France. Production of the Battle continued throughout 1940, but these aircraft were converted to dual-control training aircraft for use in gunnery training and as target tugs, which were operated by RAF training units. The converted Battles were also used for training Allied aircrews in Australia and Canada under the Commonwealth Air Training Plan.

Designated Battle T.T.1. and powered by a 1,030 hp Merlin III or IV engine, the target tug carried sleeve targets in the rear fuselage, or flag targets in a container fitted under the rear fuselage, with both types of target towed by a steel cable operated by a wind driven winch mounted in front of the rear cockpit. The Battle T.T.1 was operated by RAF Bomber and Gunnery Schools, including No. 4 Bomber and Gunnery School, based at West Freugh, near Stranraer, in southwest Scotland. A total of 266 Battle T.T.1s was constructed by Austin Motors, which included the final batch of 66 (which carried the RAF serial numbers V1201-V1250 and V1265-V1280) constructed between August and October 1940.

Right: Battle No. 92 having its engine run up opposite the newly built terminal at Dublin Airport. (D. MacCarron collection)

On April 24, 1941, a Battle T.T.1 (RAF serial number V1222, No. 8) from No.4 Bomber and Gunnery School, flown by a Polish pilot, was on a triangular cross-country navigation exercise over north-west England. The Battle deviated off course and force-landed in a field at Crobally, near Tramore, Co. Waterford, but was not damaged. The pilot had demonstrated considerable skill in landing the aircraft on a field on which substantial obstacles had been placed to prevent just such a landing. Four days later the Battle was flown out of the field to Baldonnel by Air Corps pilot, Lt. D.K. Johnston. Without previous experience on the type, he had trouble with the undercarriage retraction mechanism, and had to make the flight with the undercarriage extended. The engine was also overheating badly on the flight, and cockpit temperatures were very high. Although it was a Battle T.T.1 target tug, this particular aircraft was not equipped with the winching gear, steel cable and other equipment for target towing.

This Battle, along with three other military aircraft that had also force landed in neutral Ireland (i.e., a Miles Master Mk1, a Hurricane Mk1 and a Lockheed Hudson), was purchased for the Air Corps by the Department of Defence at a cost of £500, together with sufficient spares to make it serviceable, by agreement by the UK government. The Battle was from the second last batch of T.T.1s constructed by Austin Motors, and had been delivered to No. 48 Maintenance Unit on August 18, 1940, entering service with No. 4 Bomber and Gunnery School on the following day.

The Battle underwent an extensive overhaul by Air Corps technicians at Baldonnel Aerodrome, but the aircraft's Merlin engine required a complete overhaul, and the aircraft was to remain grounded for two years until a replacement engine became available. Although the suggestion was made that the Battle's engine be replaced by that from Hawker Hurricane I No. 95 for the duration of the overhaul, in the event, authorization for this was never granted. On May 21, 1943 the Battle flew again, powered by a Merlin V engine, which had been delivered to the Air Corps in April of that year.

The Battle was operated as a target tug by the Air Corps, replacing the de Havilland DH.84 Dragon 2 (No. 18) that had been written-off in a crash in December 1941. The winching gear and propeller to drive the winch mechanism were removed from the Dragon and fitted to the Battle after they had been repaired and suitably modified. Due to problems with the supply of steel cables for towing the targets, a hemp rope underwent trials on the Battle as a possible replacement, but these were inconclusive. Operated by the Advanced Training Section, Air Corps Flying Training Schools, the Battle (as No. 92) was used for towing targets over the Air Firing Range, Gormanston Military Camp, during air-to-air firing exercises by the Air Corps and ground-to-air firing exercises by other units of the Defence Forces. A crew of three – pilot, radio operator and winch operator – was carried in the Battle during target towing missions.

On July 13, 1944, the Battle was providing drogue target anti-aircraft practice for units of the Defence Forces at the Air Firing Range when the aircraft's engine caught fire in flight . The Battle made a forced landing on Gormanston airfield, where the fire was quickly extinguished by Defence Forces personnel, preventing serious damage to the aircraft. The Merlin V engine, which had accumulated a total of 71 flying hours, was repaired at a cost of £350 and was apparently installed again in the Battle. In May 1946, the Battle was withdrawn from use and later scrapped.

Left: Rare photo of the Battle at Gormanston. (A. Bedford photo via P. Bedford)

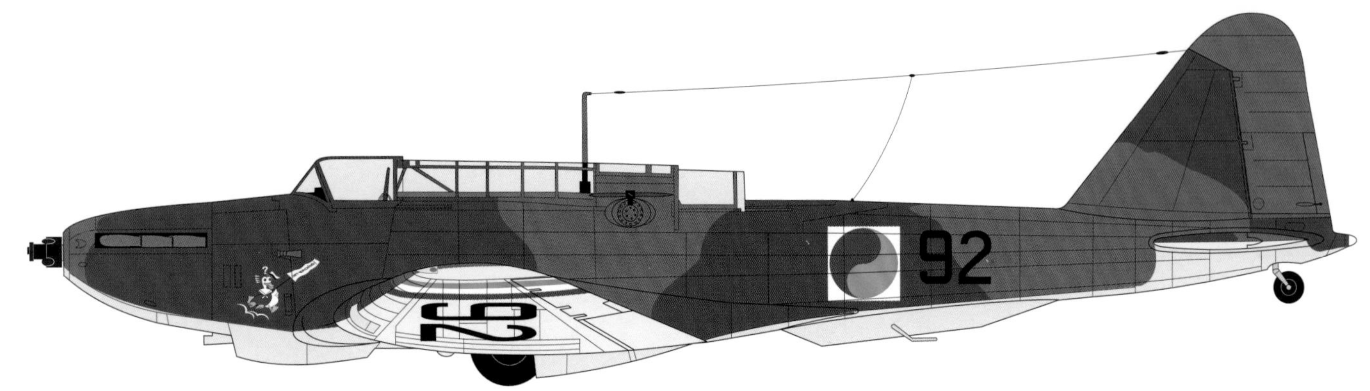
92

Colours & Markings

The standard RAF disruptive camouflage scheme of the period, dark earth and dark green on the upper surfaces of the wings and fuselage, with matt black undersurfaces, was retained on the Battle for a time after entering service with the Air Corps. The RAF roundels were replaced by the green and orange Celtic boss on the upper surfaces of the wing, and – enclosed in a white square – on both sides of the rear fuselage, with green, white and orange stripes, positioned chordwise, on the undersurfaces of the wings. The Air Corps serial number was displayed in black on both sides of the rear fuselage, behind the Celtic boss. At some stage the aircraft was repainted with a lighter colour, possibly silver or light grey, replacing the black on the undersurfaces. The cartoon character 'Donald Duck', towing a drogue target with the words "Get Quacking", was displayed on both sides of the front fuselage, in front of the wing root.

2.12

Miles M.9a Master I, M.19 Master II (1940-1949)

Miles M.25 Martinet T.T.1 (1946 – 1958)

The Miles Master was a two-seat monoplane advanced trainer built for the Royal Air Force and Fleet Air Arm during the Second World War. At the time, the Hawker Hurricane and Supermarine Spitfire were entering service and an advanced training aircraft was required to train pilots to fly these fighters. The Master was a low-wing monoplane with tandem, enclosed cockpits, each having a full set of instruments and flying controls installed. One 0.303 in. Browning or Vickers machine-gun could be installed in the starboard wing, with a camera gun installed in the port wing, and practice bombs could be carried on mountings attached to the underside of the fuselage.

The Miles Master was produced in three main variants based around available engine types. The production Master I, which first flew on 31 March, 1939, used a 715 hp (535 kW) Rolls-Royce Kestrel XXX engine, and an order for 500 of this type was placed by the UK Air Ministry in June 1938; at the time, this was the largest single order for a training aircraft ever placed by the Air Ministry. Production of the Master I ended in April 1941 after 900 had been constructed.

Production of the Kestrel engine had ceased in 1938, which by 1940 resulted in a shortage of these engines for Masters on the production line. The Air Ministry therefore requested that the Kestrel engine be replaced in the Master by the Bristol Mercury radial engine, which was then in large-scale production for the RAF, and of which adequate stocks were apparently available. Production of the Master II, as the Mercury powered version was designated, was about to commence when Miles was notified by the Air Ministry that demand elsewhere for the Mercury meant that these engines could not now be provided for the Master.

The company was then requested to install the 14-cylinder Pratt and Whitney R.1535 S.B. 4-G Twin Wasp Junior engine in the Master. This engine, a supercharged, air-cooled radial then in production in the USA, was readily available in sufficient quantities. Designated M.27 Master III, deliveries of the Pratt and Whitney-powered aircraft to the RAF commencing in March 1941. A total of 602 Master IIIs had been constructed when production ceased in 1942.

In April 1941, sufficient stocks of Mercury engines had finally become available to allow production of the Master II, to which 870 hp Mercury XX or 30 radial engines were fitted. When production of this

Miles Martinet No. 145 awaits its next target towing mission. (A.C. Photographic Section)

Left: Line up of newly arrived Miles Master trainers at Baldonnel, the nearest of which has not yet had its serial number applied to the fuselage.
(A.C. Photographic Section)

variant ceased in 1942 a total of 1,747 Master IIs had been constructed.

In 1941, the UK Air Ministry issued a specification for an aircraft type designed specifically for towing targets during air-to-air and ground-to-air gunnery training exercises by the FAA and the RAF. Miles proposed an aircraft based on the Master II to meet this requirement. Designated Martinet T.T.I, production started late in 1942, with deliveries to RAF training units commencing in early 1943. Production of the Martinet ceased in 1945 after a total of 1,745 had been constructed.

Compared to the Master, the Martinet T.T.1 had a lengthened front fuselage to compensate for the change in the centre of gravity that resulted from the weight of the winching equipment, cable and targets. The pilot and winch operator were accommodated in an enlarged cockpit with a modified canopy. The winching mechanism, which was also housed in the rear of the cockpit, could be powered by an electric motor or a wind-driven propeller, the latter fitted to the port side of the fuselage beneath the cockpit.

The Irish Air Corps' involvement with the Master began on December 21, 1940, when a Miles Master I (N8009) from No. 307 Squadron, RAF, on a flight from Wales to the Isle of Man, deviated from its course in adverse weather conditions and force-landed in a field at Dungooley, Co. Louth, close to the border with Northern Ireland. The aircraft was not damaged, and the pilot decided to take-off again and fly to the nearest RAF airfield over the border, after being informed that that he had landed in neutral Ireland. During the take-off run the aircraft collided with a hidden rock in the field and was badly damaged, but neither of the two airmen on board was injured. The Master was delivered to Baldonnel Aerodrome after being dismantled by an Air Corps salvage party and, together with three other aircraft that had also force-landed in neutral Ireland, was purchased for £10,000 by the Department of Defence following negotiations with the British Government. The Master (as No. 96) underwent repairs at Baldonnel Aerodrome, but had to be permanently grounded after a large crack was discovered in the main wing spar; the machine was subsequently used as an instructional airframe (carrying the code A5) by the Air Corps Apprentice School.

As mentioned previously, by late 1941 consideration was being given to disbanding the Air Corps and deploying its personnel to other units of the Defence Forces, due to the insufficient number of aircraft in service and a lack of spare parts and other equipment. According to military advisers to the British Government at the time, the disbandment of the Air Corps would not be in the UK's interest, and an agreement was reached between the British and Irish governments for the delivery to the Air Corps of modern advanced training and fighter aircraft. Early

Below: Rare shot of Miles Master No. 122 being refueled at Baldonnel.

Above: another view of Martinet 145 showing the wind operated winch on the left side of the fuselage to good effect.
(D. MacCarron collection)

in 1942, as part of this agreement, the Department of Defence ordered six Miles Master IIIs, which were to be delivered from RAF stocks to the Air Corps. An RAF pilot was also to be seconded to the Air Corps as a flying instructor to conduct conversion courses on the Master and Hurricane I (No. 95). On July 3, 1942 a Master III from the RAF's 59 Operational Conversion Unit (with the RAF serial DL670), which was to be used on the conversion courses, was delivered to Baldonnel Aerodrome by Flt. Lt. Don West, the RAF flying instructor. For diplomatic reasons, the Master displayed the British civilian registration G-AGEK on the upper surfaces of the wings and on both sides of the rear fuselage section, with green, white and orange stripes, positioned chordwise, on the undersides of the wings, and was never allocated an Air Corps serial number. The Master was returned to the RAF in November 1942, after a sufficient number of Air Corps pilots had completed the conversion course on this aircraft.

In December 1942, the Department of Defence changed the original order to six Master IIs, as Air Corps maintenance personnel already had experience with the Mercury engine, which also powered the force's Gloster Gladiators. Six Master IIs (ex-RAF serial nos. W9028, AZ741, DL352, DM258, DM260 and DM261) were selected for delivery to the Air Corps, and were ferried to the RAF airfield at Aldergrove in January 1943 from various RAF Maintenance Units in England and Wales,. Each of these aircraft had accumulated only a very small number of flying hours, and had never been in service with any RAF training units. Three of the Masters (W9028, DM258 and DM260) had a single 0.303 in. Browning machine-gun installed in the starboard wing, with a camera gun mounted in the port wing.

On February 10, 1943, five of the Master IIs were delivered by Air Corps pilots to Baldonnel Aerodrome, followed by the sixth two days later. The three Masters with the single machine-gun installed entered service (as Nos. 97-99) with No. 1 Fighter Squadron, which was deployed to Rineanna Aerodrome in May 1943. The other three Masters (as Nos. 100-102) were used for advanced flying training by the Intermediate Training Flight, Air Corps Flying Training Schools. These aircraft were also used for advanced flying training by the first, and only, Sergeant Pilot's Course recruited by the Air Corps, which commenced in November 1943. In 1944, once No. 1 Fighter Squadron had been fully equipped with the Hurricane I, these three Masters also entered service with the Intermediate Training Flight.

A second batch of six Master IIs was ordered by the Department of Defence in 1945; these were again selected from surplus RAF stocks, and flown to the RAF airfield at Long Kesh, Co. Down, in May of that year. Three of the Masters (as Nos. 121-123) were delivered by Air Corps pilots to Baldonnel Aerodrome on May 31, 1945, followed by the others (as Nos. 124-126) on June 15, 1945. All were operated by the Intermediate Training Flight, Air Corps Flying Training Schools.

Three Masters from the first batch were withdrawn from use over the following twelve months, the first (No. 99) on August 25, 1945. This aircraft had accumulated a total of 243 flying hours; following its withdrawal, it was used as a source of spares for the remaining Masters. The second Master (No. 98), which had accumulated a total of 180 flying hours, was withdrawn from use on July 29, 1946 and was used as an instructional airframe by the Apprentice School before being scrapped in 1948. The third Master (No.102) was withdrawn from use on August

8, 1946, after accumulating a total of 273 flying hours and was also used as an instructional airframe by the Apprentice School. Another Master (No. 101) from this batch was written-off in a crash near Baldonnel Aerodrome on August 19, 1946, in which the pilot was unfortunately killed.

In 1947, eight Masters remained in service with the Air Corps, these continuing to be used for advanced flying training. On July 21, 1947, Master II No. 123 from the second batch delivered to the Air Corps was badly damaged in a landing accident at Gormanston Military Camp. This aircraft was placed in storage at Baldonnel Aerodrome, but after being cannibalised for spare parts for the other Masters, it was withdrawn from use in 1948. Four Master IIs (Nos. 97, 100, 121 and 125), which were due a 120 hour inspection and overhaul in September 1948, were grounded for a period around that time by a spares shortage.

On February 3, 1949, during a formation training flight, two Masters (Nos. 121 and 124) collided in mid-air and crashed at Brownstown, Saggart, Co. Dublin, killing both pilots. Another Master (No. 100) was written-off in a crash near Ballymore Eustace, Co. Wicklow, also killing the pilot, on March 23, 1949. The four Masters then remaining in service with the Air Corps (Nos. 97, 122, 125 and 126) were withdrawn from use in September 1949, due to difficulties encountered in obtaining spare parts. The last recorded flight by a Master II in service with the Air Corps (No. 126) occurred on September 16, 1949.

In 1946, the Air Corps had a requirement for a target tug aircraft to replace its Fairey Battle T.T.I and Westland Lysander T.T.IIs, all of which were about to be withdrawn from use. To fulfil this requirement, the Department of Defence ordered two Martinet T.T.1s from the UK Air Ministry, which were to be delivered from surplus RAF stocks. Following discussions with the Department of Defence, the Air Ministry decided that Miles Aircraft Ltd. would supply these aircraft directly to the Air Corps, and two Martinet T.T.1s from RAF stocks (their RAF serials were RG906 and RG907) were returned to the company on March 23, 1946, to be overhauled before delivery to the Air Corps. These aircraft (allocated Nos. 139 and 140) were actually never delivered to the Air Corps, but remained in service with the RAF.

Two Martinet T.T.1s (the previous RAF identities of these machines are unfortunately unknown), costing £2,000 each, were eventually delivered by Miles to Baldonnel Aerodrome on July 7, 1946; although these were new airframes, they were fitted with reconditioned engines. The Martinets (as Nos. 144 and 145) entered service with the Advanced Training Flight, Air Corps Flying Training Schools, but over the next ten years were actually operated by the General Purpose Flight for towing drogue-type targets during air-to-air gunnery practice over the Air Firing Range at Gormanston Military Camp.

Martinets No. 144 was written-off in a crash at Gormanston Military Camp on May 25, 1952, following an aborted take-off. . The propeller, starboard wing and undercarriage of the aircraft were damaged beyond repair, but the remainder was used as a source of spares for the surviving Martinet. The flaps, undercarriage, engine and propeller blades of Martinet No. 145 were damaged in a landing accident at Baldonnel Aerodrome on October 14, 1952. Following repairs by the Technical Wing, which included the installation of a new Mercury engine, this aircraft was returned to service on April 10, 1953. The Martinet was actually fitted with propeller blades that had been salvaged from an RAF Bristol Blenheim that crashed in Ireland during the 'Emergency'. On December 23, 1958, due to a shortage of spare parts, Martinet No. 145 was withdrawn from use, and over the next five years was used as an instructional airframe by the Technical Training Squadron before being scrapped.

Left: Martinet 144 about to take off on a mission. Note the black painted spinner which was not always fitted. (Liam Byrne/Ronny Vogt collection)

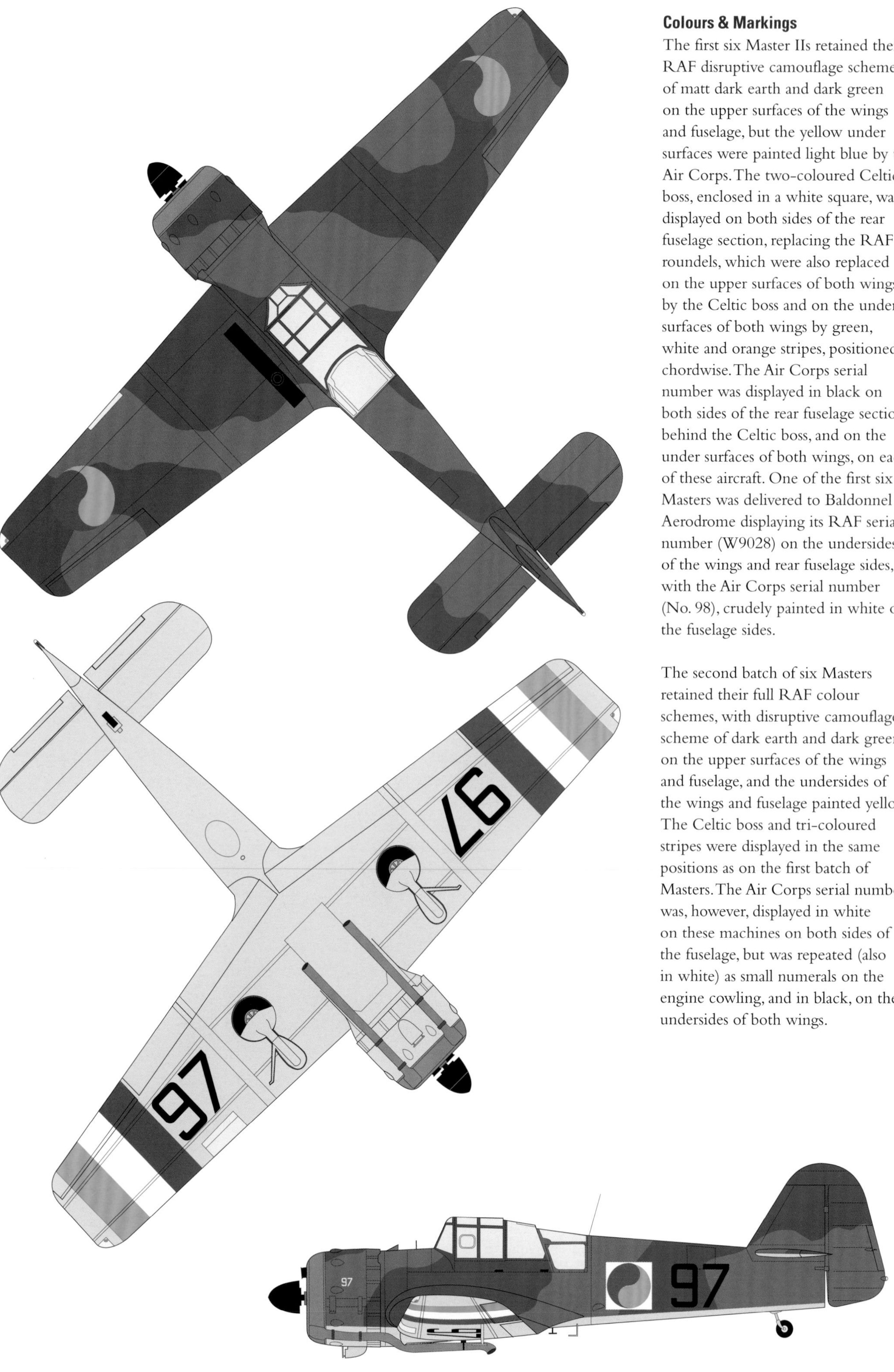

Colours & Markings

The first six Master IIs retained their RAF disruptive camouflage scheme of matt dark earth and dark green on the upper surfaces of the wings and fuselage, but the yellow under surfaces were painted light blue by the Air Corps. The two-coloured Celtic boss, enclosed in a white square, was displayed on both sides of the rear fuselage section, replacing the RAF roundels, which were also replaced on the upper surfaces of both wings by the Celtic boss and on the under surfaces of both wings by green, white and orange stripes, positioned chordwise. The Air Corps serial number was displayed in black on both sides of the rear fuselage section, behind the Celtic boss, and on the under surfaces of both wings, on each of these aircraft. One of the first six Masters was delivered to Baldonnel Aerodrome displaying its RAF serial number (W9028) on the undersides of the wings and rear fuselage sides, with the Air Corps serial number (No. 98), crudely painted in white on the fuselage sides.

The second batch of six Masters retained their full RAF colour schemes, with disruptive camouflage scheme of dark earth and dark green on the upper surfaces of the wings and fuselage, and the undersides of the wings and fuselage painted yellow. The Celtic boss and tri-coloured stripes were displayed in the same positions as on the first batch of Masters. The Air Corps serial number was, however, displayed in white on these machines on both sides of the fuselage, but was repeated (also in white) as small numerals on the engine cowling, and in black, on the undersides of both wings.

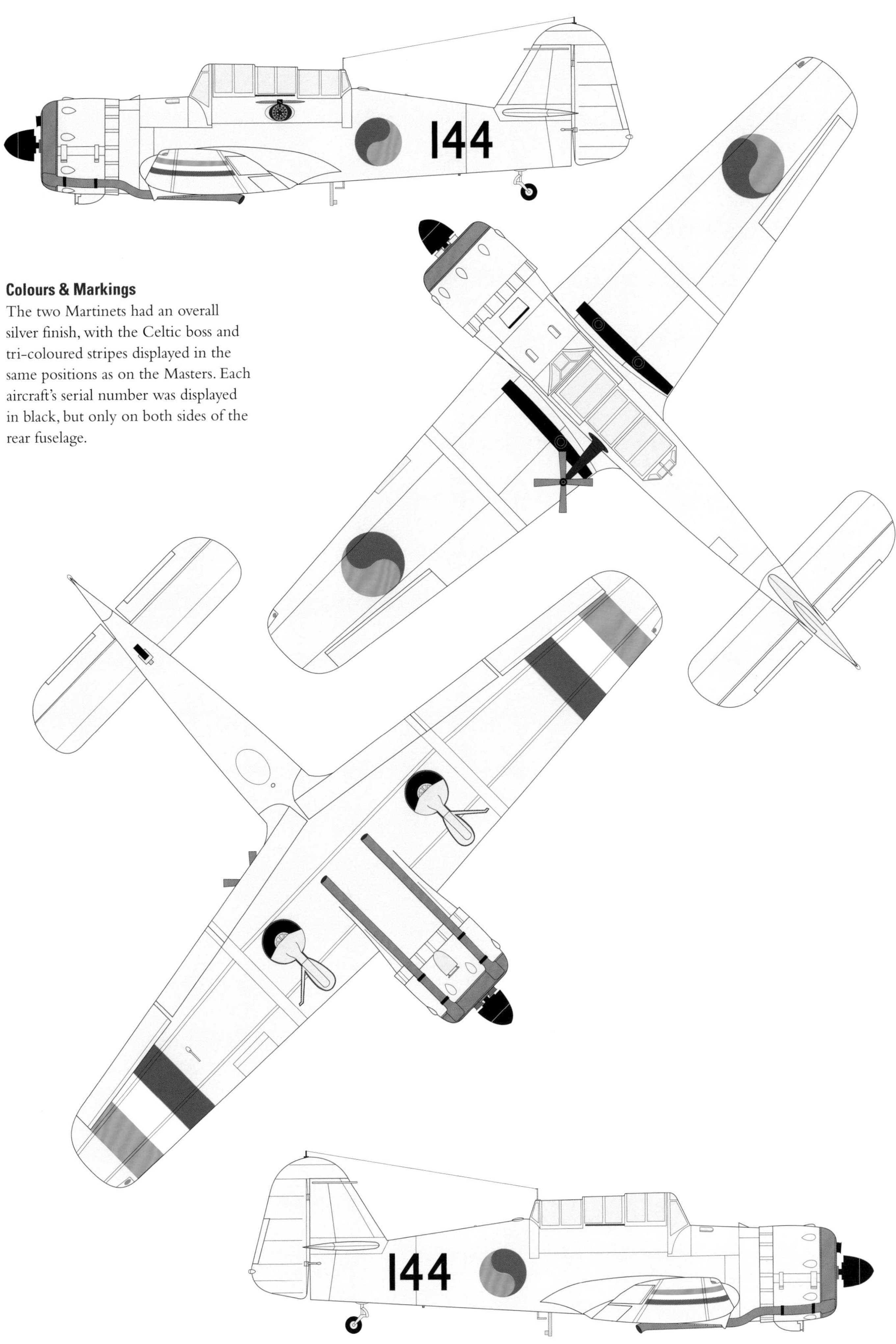

Colours & Markings

The two Martinets had an overall silver finish, with the Celtic boss and tri-coloured stripes displayed in the same positions as on the Masters. Each aircraft's serial number was displayed in black, but only on both sides of the rear fuselage.

New Equipment and New Roles

3.0

New Equipment and New Roles (1946 – 1963)

By 1946, there was a total of 60 aircraft in service with the Air Corps, but within a year the majority of these had been withdrawn from use. However, over the following two years, the Air Corps was re-equipped with fighter aircraft, target tugs, elementary and advanced flying training aircraft from war surplus RAF stocks, which had been refurbished and overhauled before delivery. Three new Avro XIX aircraft for transport and training duties were also delivered to the Air Corps during this period.

The rate of change in aeronautical development was so rapid during the post war years that new technologies in propulsion and aerodynamics rendered even relatively new designs obsolete within a short space of time. In 1948, the Air Corps wrote to a number of British aircraft manufacturers requesting details of both existing and new aircraft, in some cases just for guidance on new developments, in others with a view to replacing existing types operated by the Air Corps. The aircraft for which information was sought included the Supermarine Attacker, Supermarine Seafire 47, Spitfire Tr.9 trainer, Avro Athena basic trainer, Percival Prentice trainer, Boulton Paul Balliol, DH Vampire, DH Mosquito (night fighter and target tug versions), Gloster Meteor MkIV fighter and T.7 trainer. The Spitfire Tr.9 trainer was eventually selected as well as the DH.Vampire T.55 two seat jet trainer, both entering service in the 1950s. Fairey Aviation had offered a two seat trainer version of their Firefly Mk1 and a target tug version, then entering service with a Swedish civil company. Fokker in the Netherlands also offered training aircraft in the form of their S.11 primary trainer and later their S.14 jet trainer but no orders were forthcoming from the Air Corps for these aircraft.

Between 1948 and 1954, a detailed survey of the State's coastline, in which the Air Corps played an important role, was undertaken by the Irish Defence

Below: An unusual vehicle with a Dublin registration plate, a DUKW amphibious truck was operated by a joint Irish/Royal Navy team based at Finner camp in Donegal. Seen here near Finner Camp, the device on the front of the vehicle is an echo sounder for surveying the depth of water inshore. (Denis Gorman photo).

Forces. This coastal survey was required by General Staff H.Q., Irish Defence Forces, as to prepare plans for the defence of the State for which it was essential that up-to-date and accurate information in regard to the suitability of the coasts for landing operations should be available. In October 1948, the Plans and Operations Section, General Staff H.Q., outlined this requirement for detailed and accurate maps of the Irish coastline and plans for a topographical and aerial photographic survey of the coastal regions. A partial survey of the coastal regions of Ireland had been carried out in 1942 but had been limited due to a lack of suitable equipment.

Above: Another activity carried out during the 1950s was mobile GCI radar exercises. Seen here at Dunmore East in 1955 under the command of Air Corps Comdt. D.K. Johnston is the mobile contingent including the AA Mk1 No. 2 radar. (A. Peard collection).

The coastal survey was to include aerial photographic coverage of the coastline and of all possible landing places at low water, accurate measurements of the gradients of all beaches at high and low water, a detailed ground survey and reconnaissance of the coast and adjacent countryside, including approach roads, bridges and potential airstrip sites.

Commanded by an officer from the Corps of Engineers, a survey party was formed, comprising personnel from the Irish Naval Service, Air Corps and the Survey Company, Corps of Engineers. Specialist technical equipment, which was not available to the Irish Armed Forces, had to be provided for the survey party to allow them to fulfill all of the requirements of the coastal survey. Following sanction by the Minister for Defence, a letter was sent to the G.O.C., Northern Ireland District, British Armed Forces, from the Chief of Staff, Irish Defence Forces, requesting assistance with this survey by making available personnel and technical equipment as required, on photographic reconnaissance flights over the north-western coastal areas would also be allowed to land and refuel at military airfields in Northern Ireland. Copies of all typewritten reports about the survey, with vertical and oblique aerial photographs of the more important areas, were also to be provided to the British authorities. Copies of the reports were also sent to the U.S. Naval Attache in London. In the event, a DUKW amphibious truck was and a Sikorsky Hoverfly (the latter being the first helicopter to be operated in the State, albeit with Royal Navy markings) were provided by the British military in support of the survey, with the aerial photography being carried out by the Air Corps using Supermarine Seafires (which had been acquired in 1947) and the Anson XIXs.

Providing assistance for the coastal survey (which was code-named "Operation Sandstone" by the British)

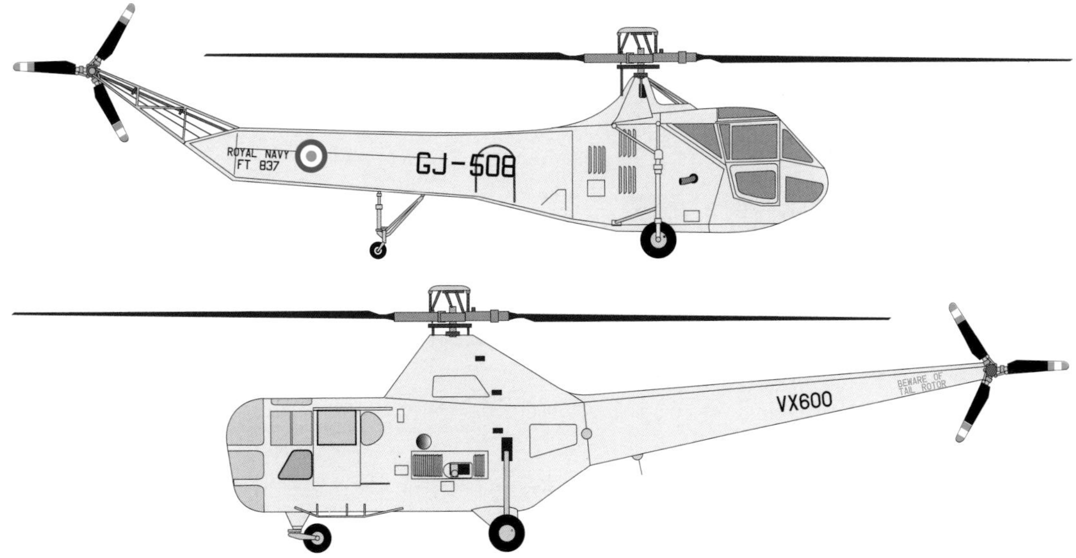

Left: Two drawings of the first military helicopters to operate in Ireland, a Royal Navy Sikorsky Hoverfly which crashed in Youghal and the Westland Dragonfly that replaced it. Both were used during Operation Sandstone.

this request received a positive response. It was agreed that aerial cameras and other technical equipment, together with a helicopter and an amphibious vehicle (DUKW) with echo sounding gear, would be provided by the British military forces for the duration of the survey; technicians familiar with the operation of this equipment would also be seconded as necessary. Air Corps aircraft engaged

was beneficial to Britain and her allies, because at that time it was believed that an invasion of Ireland by Soviet seaborne forces as part of a wider offensive against Western Europe was a possibility. The information from this survey would be invaluable to the Allied forces in formulating plans to counteract and repulse any such invasion. British military personnel involved in this operation were later to

comment warmly on the hospitality and co-operation they received from their Irish counterparts.
During the 1950's the Defence Forces conducted a series of exercises using mobile radar systems. Initially equipped with a WW2 vintage British AA Mk1. No.2 radar system, the exercises involved deploying the radar to coastal headlands around the country with Air Corps aircraft acting as targets for the radar controllers. The exercises were under the command of Capt. D.K. Johnston and as the mobile radar utilized a large number of vehicles for the temporary deployments the operations became known as "Johnston's Flying Circus". Apart from military training the equipment was used on a number of occasions to direct land based aircraft (such as the DH.Chipmunk) in maritime search and rescue operations, in some cases up to 40 miles off the coast. The original AA Mk1. No.2 radar was replaced by a more effective system known as the AA Mk3. No.7, an example of which is on display at the Air Corps Museum. A fixed chain of military radars was never established in Ireland. Commenting on this fact many years after the exercises had been concluded, retired Comdt. Johnston regretted the fact that no radar had been in place on the south east coast at the time of the Aer Lingus Viscount crash in 1968 near Tuskar Rock, Co. Wexford, in which 61 people lost their lives and for which no definitive cause has been found.

To overcome a shortfall in ground technicians in the Air Corps, a 'Direct Entrants Scheme' for training such personnel was introduced in 1949 and this continued for the next fourteen years. A 'Short Service Officer Scheme' for the recruitment of pilots was introduced in 1951, with the initial service commitment being three and a half years, increased to five years in 1960, with the officers remaining in the Reserve for a further seven years. The majority of the officers in the Reserve were employed as pilots by the National Airline, Aer Lingus.

From 1952 onwards, the war-surplus aircraft operated by the Training Schools were replaced by modern elementary and advanced flying training aircraft in the form of De Havilland Chipmunks and Percival Provosts. Modern twin-engined De Havilland Dove aircraft were also acquired, these being used for pilot training, calibration of airport landing aids, aerial photography and transport duties. The construction of concrete runways, and a control tower at Baldonnel Aerodrome commenced in 1954, and this work was completed in June 1956. The first aircraft powered by a turbojet engine to enter service with the Air Corps was the De Havilland Vampire T.55 trainer, three of which were delivered to No. 1 Fighter Squadron in July 1956. The squadron had been redeployed to Baldonnel Aerodrome from

Right: Another view of the DUKW amphibious truck at Finner Camp.
(D. Gorman photo)

The caravan of vehicles required during the mobile radar deployments became known as "Johnston's Flying Circus".
(A. Peard collection)

Left: Two views of the later AA mk.3 No. 7 radar currently on display at the air Corps Museum.
(P.J. Cummins photo)

Gormanston in the same year. The Vampire T.55s were also the first aircraft equipped with ejection seats to enter service with the Air Corps.

With the arrival of the new aircraft, flight training was reorganised within the Air Corps. In 1956, the Basic Flying Training School was formed operating from Gormanston Military Camp, which was re-named Air Corps Station, Gormanston. The Advanced Flying Training School was also formed in the same year, operating from Baldonnel Aerodrome. The Apprentice School was also re-designated the Technical Training Squadron at this time, but reverted to its original name as a component of the Training Wing in 1980.

3.1

Avro XIX (1946 – 1962)

In 1943, the British Government set up a committee, presided over by Lord Brabazon, to recommend the types of aircraft that would be required for post-war civil air transport operations. One of the recommendations of the Brabazon committee was the adaptation of an existing military transport aircraft for civil operations, which was issued as Specification number 19. An Anson XII (with RAF serial MG159) was converted by A.V. Roe and Co. Ltd to fulfil the requirements of this specification; this included the installation of soundproofing in the cabin, and of five oval windows on each side of the cabin and seating for nine passengers. Designated Avro XIX, this aircraft (carrying the UK civil registration G-AGNI) flew again in January 1945. A total of forty-eight Avro XIXs were operated by British domestic airlines in the post-war years.

The Avro XIX was also selected to fulfil an RAF requirement for a light communications aircraft. Designated Anson C.19 Series 1, initial production aircraft had wooden wings and tailplanes, similar to earlier variants of the Anson. Metal wings and tailplanes were fitted to later production aircraft, which were designated Anson C.19 Series 2. Designated Anson T.20 to T.22, variants of this aircraft were also operated by the RAF for training navigators and radio operators, and these remained in service until 1968.

In 1945, the Irish Department of Defence initiated negotiations with Avro to purchase three Avro XIXs for the Irish Army Air Corps, which were to be used for aerial photography and radio and navigational training. These aircraft were to be constructed to Air Corps specifications, which would include dual controls, navigator's and radio operator's stations in the cabin, the installation of an astro-dome in the roof behind the cockpit and fittings for four seats in the rear of the cabin. Provision for the installation of an Eagle IX camera in the floor of the fuselage, with an opening for vertical photography and removable rear windows with wind deflectors for oblique photography, was also included in the specification. A dinghy was also to be installed in these aircraft. The three aircraft were "to be up to date with all modifications applicable to the Mk. XIX with the exception of the metal replacement mainplane and tailplane" fitted to the Avro XIX, Series 2.

Three Avro XIXs with these modifications were ordered by the Department of Defence in February 1946, at a total cost of £34,035, but this price did not include cameras or radio equipment. Three radio transmitters, receivers and "aerial winches" for installation in these aircraft were purchased later for a total cost of £555. Two spare Armstrong Siddeley Cheetah XV engines were also purchased for these aircraft, costing £1,250 each.

Below: Anson XIX, No. 141 on a rare outing from the museum hangar at Baldonnel. (J. Maxwell photo)

Above: Taken in 1972, this photo shows the cockpit of Anson 141 to good effect. (P. Cuniffe photo)

The three aircraft (c/ns 1313, 1314 and 1315) were delivered from the company's factory to Baldonnel on April 10, 1946 by Air Corps pilots, and as Nos. 141-143 entered service with the Advanced Training Flight, Air Corps Flying Training Schools. These were the first new aircraft delivered to the Air Corps following the ending of the "Emergency" in 1945. The Avro XIXs were used for training pilots, navigators and radio operators, but according to contemporary newspaper reports these aircraft were also to be used for "aerial photography . . . passenger service and freight carrying".

From 1948 to 1954, during the large-scale survey of the Irish coastline by the Irish Defence Forces, vertical photographic coverage was provided by the three Avro XIXs, which were by now operated by the General Purpose Flight. The Avro XIXs had to fly straight and level at an altitude of 5,400 feet and at a precise speed, so as to provide detailed and clear photographs of the coastline, but these aircraft had a limited range and had to refuel at adjacent airfields when operating over more remote areas such as Donegal, Kerry and Clare. During the photographic survey of the north-west coast, the Avro XIXs were allowed to refuel at the R.A.F airfield at Ballykelly or the FAA airfield at Eglington, Co. Derry, following an agreement with the British Government. However, problems with the Avro XIXs' Cheetah engines curtailed the participation of these aircraft in the coastal survey, and they were out of service throughout 1951 and 1952 while undergoing major modifications; these modifications included the installation of new navigational equipment and changes to the radios.

On May 8, 1953 one of the Avro XIXs (No. 143) was written-off after ditching in the Shannon Estuary following an engine failure. Another of the machines (No. 142), which was being used for calibrating radar and landing aids at Irish civil airports, had to make an emergency landing at Shannon Airport in 1954 due to an engine fire. The aircraft was not damaged but was finally withdrawn from use following the collapse of its undercarriage during a landing at Baldonnel Aerodrome on January 31, 1958. It was used as an instructional airframe by the Technical Training Squadron until it was scrapped in 1962.

The remaining Avro XIX (No. 141) was withdrawn from use on January 20, 1962 and was used as an instructional airframe by the Technical Training Squadron until 1974. The aircraft was placed in storage at Baldonnel before being delivered to the short-lived Irish Aviation Museum, at Castlemoate House, Dublin Airport, in 1981. The aircraft was returned to Baldonnel on June 11, 1996 and has since undergone a major refurbishment for display in the Air Corps Museum.

Above: Less well known than No. 141, this photo of No. 143 was taken shortly after arrival in 1946. (Air Corps photo section via Con Murphy)

Above: The final member of the trio, No. 142. Note the boss with the green segment facing downward.
(A.C. Photographic Section)

Colours & Markings

The Avro XIXs had an overall painted silver finish with a black anti-glare panel in front of the cockpit; the serial number was displayed in black on both sides of the fuselage in front of the tailplane, and on the underside of the starboard wing. The two colour Celtic boss was carried on both sides of the fuselage and on the upper surfaces of both wings, with tricoloured stripes on the under surfaces of both wings. However, from 1957 onwards, the tricoloured Celtic boss was displayed on the two remaining Avro XIXs (nos. 141 and 142). The Avro XIXs were the first aircraft in service with the Air Corps to display a vertical tricoloured fin flash on the tailfin.

3.2

Vickers Supermarine Seafire LF.III (1947 – 1955)

In 1940, the Royal Navy had a requirement for a single-seat fighter aircraft, with a performance comparable to land-based fighter aircraft, to equip Fleet Air Arm fighter squadrons operating from aircraft carriers. Following a successful series of deck landing trials by a Vickers Supermarine Spitfire Vb that was fitted with an arrester hook under the rear fuselage, the type entered service with the FAA in 1942 as the Seafire 1b.

Compared to the Spitfire Vb, the Spitfire Vc featured a strengthened airframe and the "universal" or "c" wing which had provision to accommodate 4 x 20mm cannon or 2 x 20mm cannon and 4 x 0.303" machine guns. In service, the vast majority were equipped with just two 20mm cannon and the four machine guns. The naval equivalent of this aircraft was the Seafire IIc (fitted with a tailhook ,catapult spools and fuselage strengthening plates) which also entered service in 1942.

Designated Type 358 by the company, the Vickers Supermarine Seafire III was the first variant of this aircraft to be fitted with folding wings (these folded manually in two places, and considerably reduced the overall width of the aircraft), thereby allowing more aircraft to be deployed aboard the Royal Navy's aircraft carriers. The majority of Seafire IIIs were actually constructed as Seafire LF.IIIs for low altitude combat operations, Powered by a Merlin 55M engine driving a four-bladed Rotol propeller, the Seafire LF.III was fitted with a six-stub ejector exhaust to improve the pilot's forward view during take-offs and landings; this replaced the three large exhaust ejector stubs fitted to earlier variants of the aircraft. Equipped with two F24 aerial cameras, the Seafire FR.III was used for photographic reconnaissance missions. From 1943 to 1945 a total of 1,263 Seafire IIIs were constructed by Westland Aircraft Ltd and Cunliffe Owen Ltd. under sub-contract to Vickers Supermarine.

In 1946, the Air Corps had selected the Vickers Supermarine Spitfire IX as a replacement for its Hawker Hurricanes, which were about to be withdrawn, but Vickers Supermarine could not supply these aircraft at that time. The Air Corps then decided to look at the Seafire as an alternative and in this regard a Seafire III visited Baldonnel Aerodrome and Gormanston Military Camp on February 19, 1946, for inspection and flight-testing. The test flights by Irish Air Corps pilots indicated that it was at least 50mph faster in all flight regimes than the Hurricanes then in service with a better rate of climb and no tendencies towards instability. It had a very sensitive elevator when compared to the Hurricane but it was felt that no special training would be needed and that Hurricane pilots would become proficient on the Seafire after a matter of only a few hours familiarisation. At a meeting between Col. W. P. Delamere, officer commanding the Air Corps and representatives of Vickers Supermarine and the British Admiralty on 19 June 1946 the company offered the Air corps 12 Seafire III's at a price of £6,000 each with assurances that none of the aircraft to be supplied had flown from a carrier. Vickers stated that they would repaint the aircraft in any colour scheme required and would apply standard markings and numbers.

Right: Beautiful photo of Seafire No. 157 taken at Weston. Note the mix of exhaust stubs. (J. Masterson photo via S. Nolan)

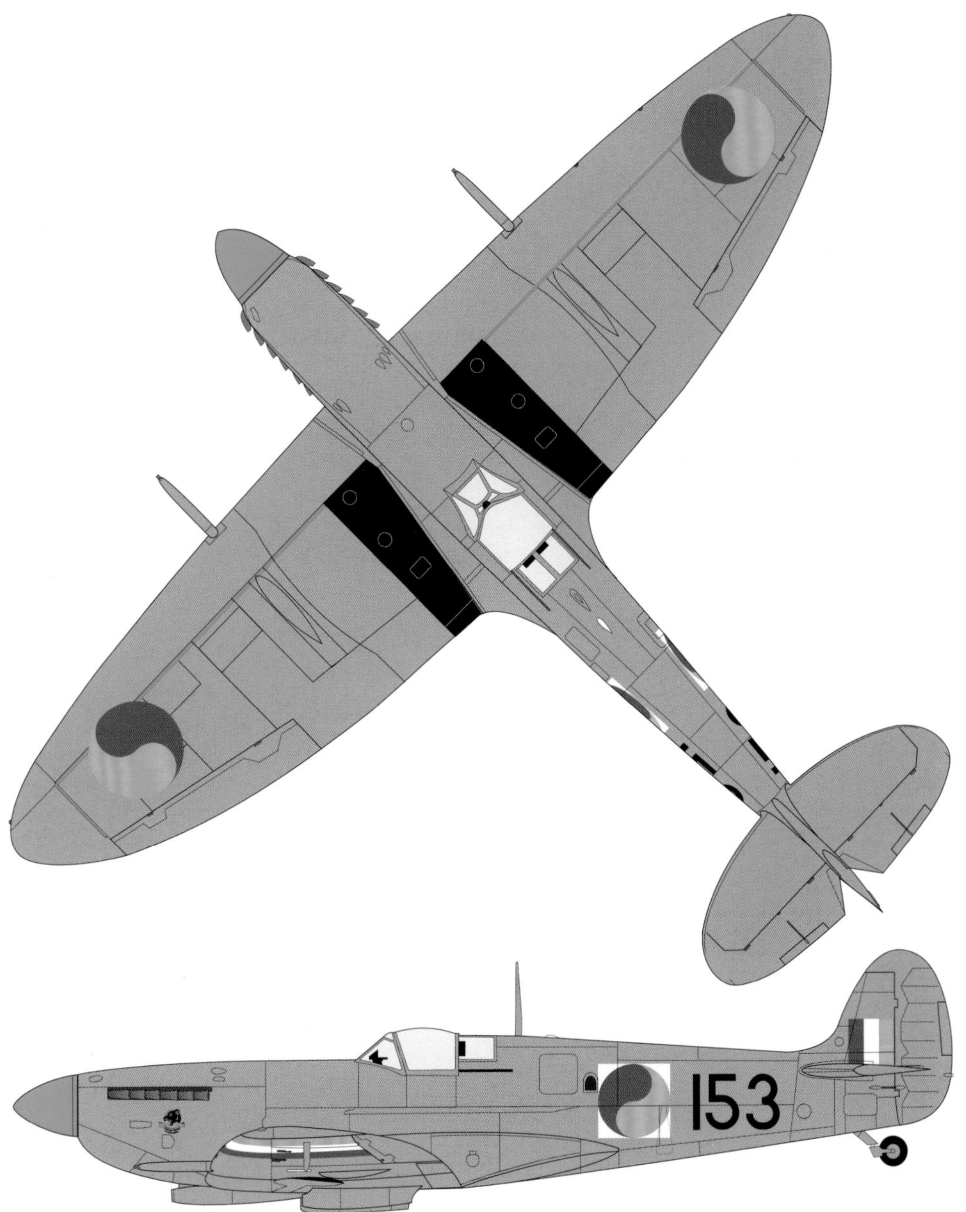

In a letter dated 8 August 1946 Col. Delamere wrote to Vickers enclosing a sample of the colour scheme to be applied to the aircraft and requesting that as the aircraft were to be primarily used as trainers that the wing fold mechanisms be rendered in such a way as to not require maintenance and that all or some of the armour plating be removed to save weight. Following this, 12 'de-navalised' Seafire IIIs were ordered by the Department of Defence on August 31, 1946, at a total cost of £72,000, provision for which was included in the Defence Estimates over the next two years.

Twelve Seafire LFIIIs (R.N. serial numbers PR236, PR302, PR315, PX915, PX924, PX929, PX941, PX948, PX950, PX959, RX168 and RX210) from the Fleet Air Arm's Aircraft Holding Unit at Abbotsinch in Scotland, were selected for delivery to the Air Corps, but one of these (PX959) was written-off in a crash during the delivery flight from the Aircraft Holding Unit and was replaced by Seafire LFIII PX936, while another (PR236) was fitted with the wings from a different aircraft (NF566), which had been written-off in a crash. Although at least seven of the Seafires had been delivered to the British Pacific Fleet in the Far East, and two had actually entered service with FAA. squadrons, a number of the aircraft had only accumulated between three and six flying hours before delivery to the Air Corps. Designated Type 506 by Vickers Supermarine, the twelve Seafire LF.IIIs were refurbished and overhauled by the company before delivery to the Air Corps. The aircraft had their arrester hooks, catapult gear and other naval equipment removed and their folding wings locked in the extended position, although the external longitudinal strengthening plates on the fuselage were retained. Following these modifications, the Seafires were basically similar to late-production Spitfire LF.Vcs, but the name Seafire was retained by the Air Corps. Some of the Browning machine-guns that had been removed from the Westland Lysander IIs operated by the Air Corps, and some of the Hispano cannons from its Hawker Hurricane IIcs, were installed in the Seafires. Cameras for oblique aerial photography could be installed in a compartment in the mid-fuselage section of each of the Seafires, with a small porthole for the camera lens on each side of the fuselage.

Right: Atmospheric shot of two Seafires about to depart on a training flight. (B. Culleton photo)

On January 13, 1947, following an inspection by Air Corps personnel at the Vickers Supermarine factory, the first four Seafire LF.III's were accepted by an official from the Department of Defence. One week later, the Seafires underwent acceptance test flights at the factory by four Air Corps pilots, who subsequently delivered these aircraft to Baldonnel Aerodrome. The Seafires encountered severe weather conditions during the delivery flight on January 24, 1947 and had to divert to an RAF airfield in Wales remaining there for over three weeks. The four aircraft were eventually delivered to Baldonnel Aerodrome on February 17, 1947 and entered service (as nos. 146 – 149) with No. 1 Fighter Squadron, based at Gormanston Military Camp. A second batch of four Seafires (nos. 150 – 153) was delivered to the Air Corps on July 11, 1947 and the last batch of four (nos. 154 – 157) followed on September 29, 1947. The Seafire LF.III was the last single-seat fighter aircraft to enter service with the Air Corps.

In operating the Seafires, No. 1 Fighter Squadron underwent a programme of intensive training over a period of six months, which included air combat tactics, formation flying, photographic reconnaissance and other combat techniques, based on recent wartime experiences of other air forces. The aircraft were also used by the squadron to conduct Fighter Leader and Flight Instructor courses during this period. A number of Seafires were used as target aircraft for the mobile Ground Controlled Interception Radar equipment operated by the Fighter Control Unit during air defence exercises carried out over the next seven years, which were directed and monitored by the Air Squadron, Signal Corps. During this period, the Seafires also participated in a number of military exercises conducted by the Irish Defence Forces, including reconnaissance missions and providing ground support for the opposing forces. The Seafires also participated in the annual commemorations of the 1916 Easter Rising by the Defence Forces during this period, flying in close formation over the military parade in the centre of Dublin.

Two Seafires were written-off in the first two years of Air Corps service, the first (No. 147) in a landing accident at Gormanston airfield on September 15, 1947, without injury to the pilot, and the second (No. 152) in a crash-landing at Mosney, Co. Meath, on September 1, 1949. The latter aircraft was used for training firemen at Dublin Airport by the Airport Fire Service before being scrapped in 1962.

As mentioned in the introduction to this chapter, from 1948 to 1954 the Defence Forces were engaged on a detailed coastal survey of the Irish coastline, which included aerial photography by the Air Corps. Equipped with F.24 cameras installed in the compartment in the mid-fuselage section, the Seafires obtained oblique photographic coverage of the coastline by flying straight and level at an altitude of 800 feet over the sea parallel with the coastline at a precise speed. During the photographic survey of the north-west coast of Ireland from 1950 to 1953, the Seafires were allowed to operate from the RAF airfield at Ballykelly or the FAA airfield at Eglington, following an agreement with the British Government. At least six Seafires (nos. 146, 148, 149, 153, 155 and 157) are known to have landed at these airfields for refuelling and reloading the aerial cameras with film. The Seafires also operated from Shannon International Airport during the photographic survey of the south-west coast of Ireland.

Between 1951 and 1953, another three Seafires were written-off in crashes, the first (No. 154) on May 28, 1951 in the Wicklow Mountains, killing the pilot, the second (No. 151) in Co. Meath, on June 29, 1951, without injury, and the third (No. 148) on May 22, 1953 into the sea off Gormanston, killing the pilot.

The seven Seafires remaining in service were withdrawn from use between 1953 and 1955. The first of these aircraft (No. 157) was used as an instructional airframe by the Technical Training Squadron for the following eight years. In 1961, this Seafire was acquired by the Dublin Technical Institute for use as

Right: Very few colour photos exist of the Seafires. This one was taken after the aircraft had been retired from some years and left on the scrapheap. (G. Skillen photo)

an instructional airframe and was apparently scrapped within the following two years. The remains of a Seafire, identified as this aircraft, were discovered in England in 1995and allocated the British civil registration G-BWEM; parts from this aircraft were eventually used in the reconstruction of a Seafire III. Five Seafires were withdrawn from use throughout 1954, the first (No. 149) in May, followed by another three (nos. 146, 153 and 156) in June and the fifth (No. 155) in August. The remaining Seafire (No. 150) was withdrawn from use in March 1955, and these six aircraft were used as instructional airframes by the Technical Training Squadron over the next five years before being scrapped between 1960 and 1965.

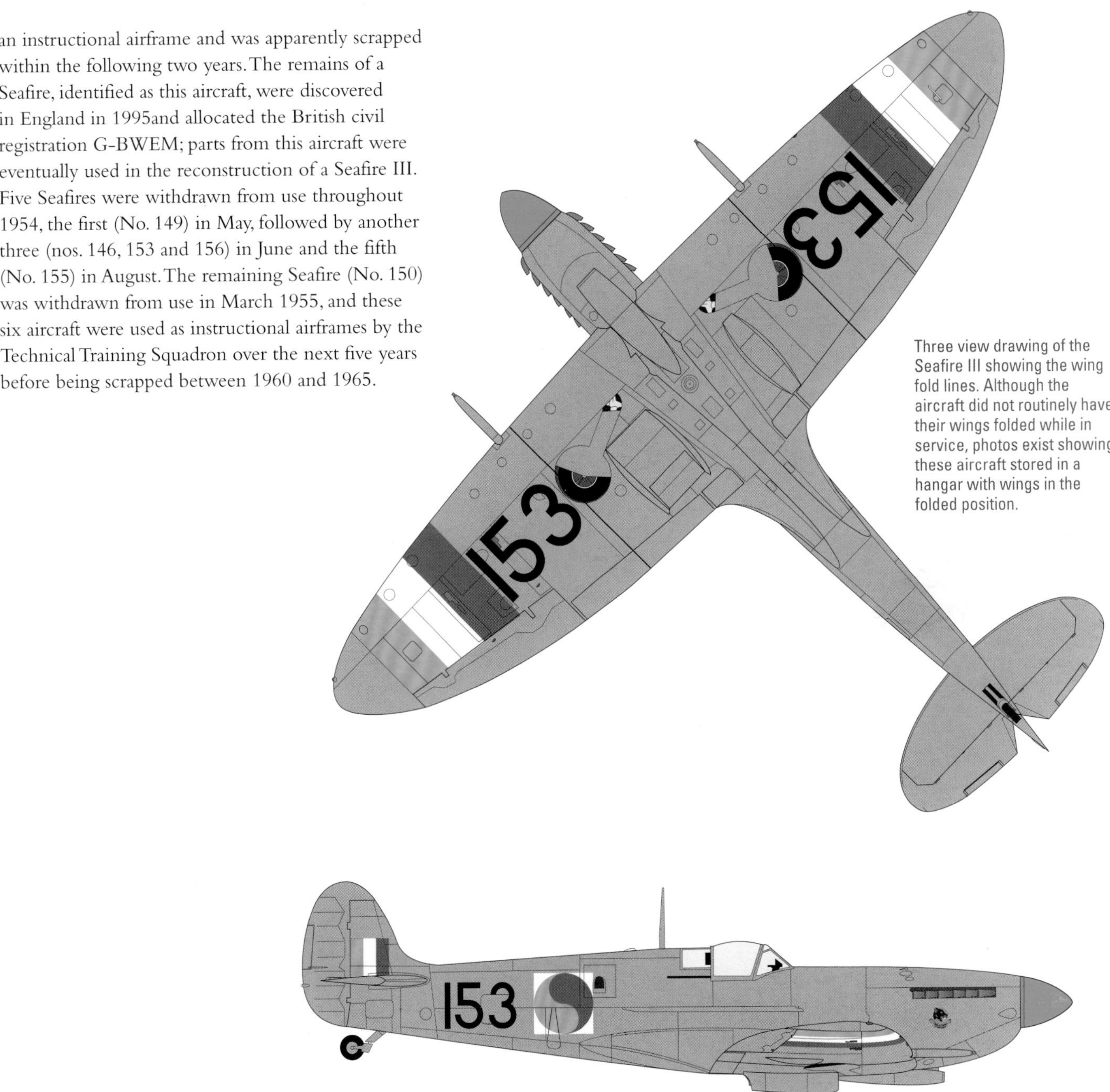

Three view drawing of the Seafire III showing the wing fold lines. Although the aircraft did not routinely have their wings folded while in service, photos exist showing these aircraft stored in a hangar with wings in the folded position.

Colours & Markings

The Seafire LF.IIIs had an overall grey-green finish, with the propeller spinners painted red, although green spinners were used for a time. There has been much debate concerning the exact shade of the grey-green finish as it did not appear to be a standard camouflage colour in use by any other Spitfire or Seafire operator. An examination of surviving parts from a number of Air Corps Seafires by the authors comparing them to modern B.S. standard colour swatches indicates that the colour was B.S. 283 Interior Green. However, samples taken from No.152 (which was kept outdoors for a number of years) showed considerable fading of its finish; in addition, the aircraft are known to have been repainted at some stage during their career with Air Corps, so it is at least possible that a shade other than B.S. 283 may have been used originally.

The green and orange Celtic boss was displayed on the outer sections of the upper surfaces of both wings, and – enclosed in a white square – on both sides of the centre fuselage section. These bosses were "handed" in the sense that the green portion was inboard on both wings and faced forward on either side of the fuselage. Green, white and orange stripes, positioned chordwise, were displayed on the outer sections of the undersides of both wings. Each aircraft's allocated serial number was displayed in black on both sides of the rear fuselage, behind the Celtic boss, and on the undersides of both wings. All of the Seafires were delivered with tricoloured fin flashes, but at least three (nos. 150, 153 and 157) had these removed, probably during routine maintenance. The crest of No. 1 Fighter Squadron was displayed on the engine cowlings of all of the Seafires, under the exhaust ejector stubs.

3.3

Vickers Supermarine Spitfire Tr.9 (1951 – 1961)

After the Second World War, with widespread sales of the Spitfire to newly liberated countries, Vickers Supermarine believed that there was a potential market for a two-seat trainer version of the aircraft. Designated Type 502 by the company, a Spitfire Mk.VIII (ex RAF serial MT818), was re-built as a prototype two-seat training aircraft as a private venture in 1946. The original cockpit was moved forward 13½ inches and a second cockpit, slightly raised, was installed immediately behind, each fitted with a jettisonable sliding hood and with duplicated instruments and controls. The size of the forward fuselage fuel tank was reduced to provide room for the two cockpits, but this was offset by the installation of additional fuel tanks in the wings, replacing the 20-mm cannon. The two 0.303 in. Browning machine guns in both wings were retained, as were underwing attachment points for rocket projectiles or bombs. Designated Spitfire T.8 the prototype flew for the first time on September 6, 1946. Over the next five years, the two seat Spitfire (registered as G-AIDN) was demonstrated to a number of air forces, including a demonstration at Baldonnel for the Air Corps in June 1950. Due to an insufficient number of Spitfire VIIIs being available for conversion, Vickers Supermarine instead acquired twenty Spitfire IXs for conversion to two-seat training aircraft under the company designation Type 509. As the Vickers Supermarine Spitfire Tr.9, 10 of these aircraft were delivered to India, three to Holland, one to Egypt and six to the Air Corps.

The Air Corps' involvement with the type commenced in 1950 when an urgent requirement was identified for an advanced training aircraft to replace its Miles Master IIs, which had been withdrawn from use due to a scarcity of spare parts. Following an evaluation of a number of aircraft types by the Air Corps to fulfil this requirement, which was designated Specification 499/502, the Department of Defence ordered six Spitfire Tr.9's in August 1950, with specialist tools and ground equipment, at a total cost of £71,502. These aircraft were to be delivered to the Air Corps in 1951, and an allocation

Below: Superb shot of the Spitfire Tr.9 resplendent in its original Air Corps colour scheme following restoration in 2005.
(G. Norman photo)

Above: Although the majority of two seat Spitfires still flying are ex-Air Corps aircraft, PT462 isn't one of them. It was restored to flying condition after having been found on a dump in the Gaza Strip in 1984. Seen here flying in formation with No. 161. (G. Norman photo)

of funds to purchase the Spitfire Tr.9's was included in the 1951/52 Defence Estimates. The Air Corps' maintenance personnel already had experience with the Merlin engine, which also powered the Seafire LF.III, the airframe of which was also generally similar to that of the Spitfire Tr.9. The Merlin engines installed in the six Spitfire Tr.9s were overhauled "to give a life of 400 hours" before delivery to the Air Corps.

The first two Spitfire Tr.9s (Nos. 158 and 159) were delivered to Baldonnel by Air Corps pilots on June 5, 1951, followed by two more (Nos. 160 and 161) on June 29, 1951. The last two Spitfire Tr.9s (Nos. 162 and 163) were delivered to the Air Corps on July 30, 1951. One of these aircraft (No.163) was slightly damaged when the undercarriage failed to lock down fully during the landing at Baldonnel Aerodrome, but was repaired by the Air Corps. Each of these aircraft had a previous RAF identity as follows:

No. 158	ex RAF MJ627
No. 159	ex RAF MJ772
No.160	ex RAF MK721
No. 161	ex RAF PV202
No.162	ex RAF ML407
No.163	ex RAF TE308

The six Spitfire Tr.9s entered service with 'B' Flight, Air Corps Flying Training Schools, at Baldonnel and over the following nine years were used for both advanced flying training and weapons training. Commencing in 1953, at least three of the Spitfire trainers (Nos. 158, 159 and 162) were operated by No. 1 Fighter Squadron to replace Seafires that had been written-off in crashes. When the remaining Seafires were withdrawn from use throughout 1954, the Spitfires Tr.9s were operated by the squadron until the first three de Havilland Vampire T.55s were delivered to the Air Corps in 1956. The Spitfire trainers also participated in annual air defence exercises until 1956. On February 15, 1957 one of the Spitfire Tr.9s (No. 160) was written-off in a crash at Baldonnel Aerodrome, but although injured, the pilot survived the incident.

Four of the remaining five Spitfire trainers were withdrawn from use in 1960. The first of these aircraft (No. 159) was withdrawn on January 27 1960, followed by the second (No. 158) in April, having respectively accumulated totals of 1,402 and 1,036 flying hours while in service with the Air Corps. The third aircraft (No. 162) was withdrawn from use on June 28, 1960, having accumulated a total of 762 flying hours since 1951, followed by the fourth (No. 161) in December. The last operational flight by a Spitfire in service with the Air Corps (by No. 163) occurred on September 12, 1961, following which this aircraft was withdrawn from use. Over the following two years, the five Spitfire TR.9s were used as instructional airframes by the Technical Training Squadron at Baldonnel.

Two of the Spitfires (Nos. 158 and 159), were offered for sale by the Department of Defence iand were purchased in 1963 by Film Aviation Services in the United Kingdom and allocated the British civil registrations G-ASOZ and G-AVAV respectively. Both were stored in a dismantled state and in 1968, one of these machines was reassembled (No. 159, fitted with the wings from No. 158) and participated in the making of the film "Battle of Britain", before eventually being sold to a museum in the U.S.A. (with the U.S. civil registration N8R) in 1974. This aircraft is still airworthy and has had the rear cockpit faired over.

No. 158 was sold to a private collector and flew again (with the U.K. civil registration G-BMSB) in November 1993, following a long-term restoration that had commenced in 1977. It is currently still airworthy and located in the United Kingdom.

The other three Spitfire Tr.9s (Nos. 161, 162 and 163) were offered for sale in 1968. No. 161 was bought by the Strathallan Collection but was sold again in 1979 after a period of storage and was allocated the British civil registration G-BHGH in 1980, though this was later cancelled. The aircraft then underwent a long-term restoration (as G-TRIX); this was completed in 1990. The aircraft later crashed on April 8, 2000, killing the new owner Greg McCurragh and instructor Norman Lees. In 2002, Historic Flying Ltd., an aircraft restoration company specialising in rebuilding vintage aircraft, began restoring this aircraft to flying condition with the civil registration G-CCCA. It flew again in 2005 resplendent in the original markings it had worn while in service with the Air Corps. However, this scheme was only carried for a relatively short period, the aircraft currently being painted in Royal Netherlands Air Force markings.

Spitfire Tr.9s Nos. 162 and 163 were purchased by Samuelson Film Services Ltd for the film "Battle of Britain" and were subsequently acquired by the Strathallan Collection. One of the aircraft (No. 163) was sold to Don Plumb, a buyer in Canada. He initially flew the aircraft as a two seater but he later had the rear cockpit faired over. It was sold to Woodson K Woods in the USA (where it was allocated the US registration N92477) in 1975. Mr. Woods restored the second seat position which was still present under the fairing before selling it on to Mr. Bill Greenwood in 1979. It is currently airworthy, registered N308WK and located in Aspen, Colorado.

Following a period of storage at the Strathallan Museum, the remaining Spitfire Tr.9 (No. 162) was sold in 1979 to Nick Grace who undertook a restoration of the aircraft ; this was completed in 1985, following which the British civil registration G-LFIX was allocated. This particular aircraft had originally been built at Castle Bromwich as a Spitfire IX, and – carrying the serial number ML407 – served with six different squadrons of the RAF's 2nd Tactical Air Force, flying a total of 176 operational combat sorties. It was delivered to the RAF's 485 (New

Below: The graceful lines of Spitfire Tr.9 No. 161 are shown to good effect in this shot at Newtonards, Co. Down. (G. Norman photo)

Zealand) Squadron on the April 29, 1944, where it was flown by Flying Officer Johnnie Houlton, DFC, who was credited, whilst flying this aircraft, with the first enemy aircraft shot down by a Spitfire over the Normandy beachhead on D-Day. Post-war, it was converted to the two-seat configuration by Vickers Supermarine and sold to the Air Corps. Nick Grace was killed in a car accident in 1988, but his widow, Carolyn Grace, subsequently learned to fly the aircraft. Registered as G-LFIX, 'The Grace Spitfire', as the aircraft is now known, is painted in its original 485 (New Zealand) Squadron markings as OU-V, and still performs on the air display circuit each year both at public and private shows. The second cockpit now has a standard canopy replacing the large blown canopy associated with the original Tr.9 configuration.

Above: Coming into land with flaps extended, the view for the instructor pilot was always poor but helped somewhat by the blown bubble canopy. (G. Norman photo)

Below: Spitfire Tr. 9 No. 158 anchored to the ground for a full power engine test. A much safer arrangement than that used on the Hurricane shown earlier. (A.C. Photographic Section)

Above and Below:
Contrasting views of the two Spitfire Tr.9 colour schemes used when in Irish Air Corps service.
(Above photo courtecy of G. Norman)

(A.C. Photographic Section)

Colours & Markings

The Spitfire Tr.9s initially had an overall grey-green finish (similar to that of the Seafires) with red propeller spinners. This colour scheme was retained on one of the aircraft (No. 163) until it was withdrawn from use in 1961, but from about 1957 onwards the other Spitfire Tr.9swere repainted in an overall silver finish with the upper section of the engine cowling and the walkways on the wing roots painted black. Initially the green and orange Celtic boss was displayed on the upper surfaces of both wings and on both sides of the rear-fuselage section, with green, white and orange stripes, positioned chordwise, displayed on the outer sections of the undersides of both wings. These markings were replaced by the tri-coloured Celtic boss in the same positions from 1957 onwards. Each aircraft's serial number was displayed in black on both sides of the rear fuselage, behind the Celtic boss.

(Above photos courtecy of G. Norman)

Left: A wet day in Baldonnel. Three Tr.9's on the flight line. (G. Skillen photo)

3.4

De Havilland DHC-1 Chipmunk T.20 and T.22 (1952 – 1980)

In October 1945, de Havilland Aircraft of Canada Ltd., a subsidiary of the British company, initiated design work on an elementary training aircraft to replace the de Havilland Tiger Moth then in widespread service. Designated DHC-1 Chipmunk, production of this elementary training aircraft (which was powered by a 145 h.p. in-line de Havilland Gipsy Major 8 engine and was fully-aerobatic) commenced in 1946, and an initial batch of 158 were constructed between 1946 and 1951. These were delivered to the Royal Canadian Air Force and three other air forces as well as a number of civil operators.

Two Chipmunks were successfully evaluated by the Aeroplane and Armament Experimental Establishment at Boscombe Down in the UK, following which the type was ordered as an ab-initio trainer for the Royal Air Force. The RAF received 735 Chipmunks, designated Chipmunk T.10, which were manufactured in the UK by the parent company The military export version of the Chipmunk T.10, of which 217 were built, was the Chipmunk T. 20; this variant was powered by the de Havilland Gipsy Major 10 Series 2 engine. The Chipmunk T.20 was delivered to 15 air forces worldwide.

The Chipmunk T.21, of which 28 were built, was a civil export version of the Chipmunk T. 20, while the Chipmunk T.22 was a military T.10 converted for civilian use, and in this regard a large number of T.10s were delivered to the flying schools owned by Derby Aviation Ltd. (later to become British Midland Airways), which carried out the modifications required for civil operations. The company was to become one of the main sources for airworthy Chipmunks and spare fuselages, wings and other parts that had been salvaged from aircraft that had crashed or otherwise been withdrawn from use.

A second batch of 60 Chipmunks was constructed in Canada between 1955 and 1956 for delivery to the RCAF Designated Chipmunk T.30, these aircraft were fitted with a one-piece, moulded bubble cockpit canopy, which replaced the metal-framed canopy on earlier production aircraft. When production of the Chipmunk in Canada ceased in 1956, a total of 217 of this version had been constructed. Production of the Chipmunk continued in Portugal until 1961, by which time a total of 1,283 of all variants had been completed in three countries.

From 1950 onwards, the Irish Army Air Corps had a requirement for a modern elementary training aircraft to replace its Miles Magister Is, which were gradually being withdrawn from use. In the same year, an offer from the British Ministry of Defence of fifty ex-RAF Miles Magister Is to fulfil this requirement was rejected by the Air Corps as these aircraft were not equipped with modern instrument flying equipment and were considered to be obsolete. The replacement of the Magisters eventually became so urgent that the 1951/52 Defence Estimates included an allocation of

Right: Two Chipmunks on a rare visit to Cork Airport in September 1964. (G. Desmond photo)

Left: The last airworthy Chipmunk No. 168 photographed in the early eighties over Co. Meath. (R. James collection)

£35,000 for the purchase of new elementary training aircraft for the Air Corps. In 1951, an initial batch of six Chipmunk T.20s was ordered by the Department of Defence, at a total cost of £27,824, for delivery in the following year.

The first batch of three aircraft was delivered to Baldonnel Aerodrome on January 16, 1952, followed by the second on January 31. The six Chipmunk T.20s (as Nos. 164–169) entered service with the Elementary Flying Training Section, Flying Training Schools, thereby allowing – according to a contemporary newspaper report about these aircraft – "all aspects of elementary training [to] be carried out". A second batch of six Chipmunk T.20s was ordered by the Department of Defence in 1952, at a total cost of £32,970, to be delivered later in the same year. These aircraft arrived at Baldonnel Aerodrome on September 26, 1952 having been delivered by Air Corps pilots, and (as Nos. 170-175) also entered service with the Flying Training Schools. The Chipmunk T.20s went on to serve in the elementary flying training role in the Air Corps from 1952 until their eventual retirement in 1980.

The propeller spinner on the Chipmunks operated by the Air Corps was initially fitted with a domed boss which was secured to the hub by a long bolt, but distortion of this bolt caused maintenance problems and the domes were eventually removed from the aircraft. A broad chord rudder was also fitted to the Chipmunks in 1953 or 1954, which was a modification introduced to improve control during climbing manoeuvres and aerobatics. From 1958 onwards, the Chipmunks were also fitted with anti-spin strakes on the rear fuselage, in front of the tailplane, to improve their spin recovery characteristics.

In March 1955, the Chipmunk T.20s were deployed to Gormanston Military Camp and initially taken on charge by No. 1 Fighter Squadron until that unit was deployed to Baldonnel Aerodrome in 1956. In the same year, the Basic Flying Training School was formed, and this unit operated the Chipmunks for the next 17 years from Air Corps Station, Gormanston, as the base had been re-designated in 1956. During this period, a total of 180 trainee Air Corps pilots underwent elementary flying training on the Chipmunk at this airfield. From 1963, an agreement between the Department of Defence, Aer Lingus Teoranta, and the Department of Transport and Power (the government department responsible for the state airline) resulted in over 50 Aer Lingus pilot cadets undergoing training for a commercial pilots licence with the Air Corps over the next ten years, which included elementary flying training on the Chipmunks.

Throughout 1952 and 1953, during the photographic survey of the north-west coast of Ireland, some of the Chipmunks were used for transporting film and photographic equipment to either the RAF airfield at Ballykelly or the FAA airfield at Eglington, for

Below: Line up of newly arrived Chipmunks at Baldonnel. Note the two colour boss as originally applied. (D. MacCarron collection)

Right: Cockpit layout of the Chipmunk on which many Air Corps and for a time , Aer Lingus pilots learned to fly. (J. Maxwell photo)

installation in the Vickers Supermarine Seafire LF.IIIs of No. 1 Fighter Squadron. The Chipmunks were also used as target aircraft for the mobile Ground Controlled Interception Radar of the Fighter Control Unit, operated by the Air Squadron, Signal Corps, during air defence exercises conducted between 1953 and 1956.

Three Air Corps Chipmunks were involved in forced landing incidents caused by engine crankshaft failures due to forging difficulties during manufacture. In the first of these, No. 175 force-landed at Gormanston Military Camp on July 2, 1955, but was returned to service after the crankshaft was replaced by de Havilland. In the second, Chipmunk No. 167 had to be written-off after crash-landing on a golf course, near Clondalkin, Co. Dublin, on September 8, 1959, subsequently being used as an instructional airframe by the Technical Training Squadron until 1968. Finally, No. 168 force-landed at Thomastown, Co. Meath, on October 14, 1960, and was also returned to service after the crankshaft was replaced by the manufacturer. Following these incidents, the crankshafts in the engines of the other Chipmunks were replaced by de Havilland and there were no further failures. Three other Chipmunks operating from Air Corps Station, Gormanston, were written-off in crashes between 1956 and 1963. The first of these involved aircraft No. 165) and happened at Laytown, Co. Meath, north of Gormanston, on June 14, 1956, the aircraft being used afterwards as an instructional airframe by the Technical Training Squadron before being scrapped in 1961. The other two accidents were to Chipmunk T.20s Nos. 175 and 174, which were respectively written-off in crash landings at Gormanston on March 29 and May 23, 1963. Only eight Chipmunks remained in service with the Basic Flying Training School following the accidents detailed above, but this number was insufficient to fulfil the Air Corps' elementary flying training commitments. The Department of Defence therefore acquired two Chipmunk T.22s from Derby Aviation Ltd. One of these aircraft had been rebuilt from the remains of two Chipmunk T.10s that had been in service with the RAF (as WB 561 and WG 320) but were written-off in crashes and purchased as scrap by Derby Aviation; the basic airframe of WB 561was mated with the wings and other parts from WG 320. The second aircraft which had been delivered to the RAF in 1950 (as WB 620) and withdrawn from use in 1953 or 1954, was acquired by Iona Engineering Works Ltd in 1956. Re-designated Chipmunk T.22 following the modifications required for civil flying, this aircraft (with the Irish civil registration EI-AJC) was granted a Certificate of Airworthiness in 1957 and was purchased by Derby Aviation Ltd (and registered in the U.K. as G-ARTP) in September 1964. These two Chipmunk T.22s were delivered to Baldonnel Aerodrome on February 26, 1965 and (as Nos. 199 and 200) entered service with the Basic Flying Training School.

In 1973, the Chipmunks were replaced by Reims (Cessna) FR.172H Rockets, which were to be operated by the Basic Flying Training School based at Air Corps Station, Gormanston; however, very little flying training was carried out using the Cessnas, as they were used mainly in the army co-operation role. The Chipmunks were deployed to Baldonnel Aerodrome and were operated by the Advanced Flying Training School, which at that time became responsible for both elementary and advanced flying training. In 1977, the Chipmunks, together with the Hunting Percival Provosts, were replaced by ten SIAI-Marchetti SF.260WE Warriors in the flying training role.

From 1975, the ten Chipmunks remaining in service with the Air Corps were gradually withdrawn from use over the next six years, commencing with Nos. 170 and 169 in 1975 and 1977 respectively, the latter aircraft being scrapped in 1983. Chipmunk No. 173 was withdrawn from use on December 19, 1978 and placed in storage at Gormanston, until presented to the South East Aviation Museum for static display in July 1985. T.22 No. 199 and T.20 No. 172 were retired in 1979, the former being placed in storage at Gormanston and the latter being used as an instructional airframe by the Technical Training Squadron before being scrapped in 1984. Three more Chipmunk T.22s (Nos. 166, 168 and 171) were withdrawn from use in 1980; one of these aircraft (No. 168) flew again on November 15, 1989, after having been in storage at Gormanston in the interim, and was used for display flying by the Air Corps. The last Chipmunk (No. 164) was retired in October 1981, and was used as an instructional airframe by the Apprentice School Training Wing, before being placed in storage at Baldonnel. This Chipmunk was restored for eventual display in an Irish Air Corps Museum. Sadly, Chipmunk T.22 No. 200 was destroyed in an accident at, Gormanston on April 25, 1980, which killed the crew. This was the only fatal accident that occurred in 30 years of Chipmunk operations by the Air Corps.

Above: The Chipmunk's Gipsy Major 10 engine was relatively easy to maintain. (P. Cunniffe photo)

Left: Note how the seats in the Chipmunk were built into the airframe. (J. Maxwell photo)

Colours & Markings

The Chipmunks all had an overall painted silver finish, with wing root walkways and an anti-glare panel in front of the cockpit painted matt black. Initially, a green and orange Celtic boss was displayed on the upper sides of both wings and on both sides of the fuselage, with green, white and orange stripes, positioned chordwise, carried on the undersides of both wings All of these markings were later replaced by a tri-coloured Celtic boss in the six positions. The Air Corps serial number was displayed in black on both sides of the fuselage, behind the Celtic boss, and on the underside of the starboard wing. Over the years, there was considerable variation in the style of serial numbers applied, ranging from stencil-style to solid black. Day-glo orange was later applied around the engine air intake, the wing tips, the forward section of the tailfin and the tailplane. At least two Chipmunk T.20s (Nos. 164 and 173) displayed the crest of the Basic Flying Training School on both sides of the forward section of the front fuselage; this marking comprised a winged yellow torch, with black stripes and orange and red flames, on a black background, with a yellow scroll underneath bearing a motto in Gaelic, "Onoir, Dilseacht, Buanseasmhacht" (Honour, Diligence, Understanding).

Below: A scrapped Chipmunk showing one of the variations in style in how the serial number was applied. (F. Goodman photo)

3.5

De Havilland (Hawker Siddeley) D.H.104 Dove 4, Dove 5, Dove 7 & Dove 8 (1953 – 1978)

In 1943, the British Civil Aviation Committee on Post-War Transport Aircraft (known as the Brabazon Committee) issued Specification 5B, detailed in Air Ministry Specification 26/43, for a small airliner to replace the de Havilland D.H.89 Rapide on British internal air routes in the post-war years. To fulfil this requirement, the de Havilland Aircraft Co. Ltd. commenced work in 1944 on the design and construction of an all metal, twin-engined, low-wing monoplane, with a retractable undercarriage, to carry eight to eleven passengers.

Designated D.H.104 by the company, the aircraft was powered by two 330 h.p. de Havilland Gipsy Queen 71 supercharged, six-cylinder piston engines, Named Dove, production of the airliner commenced in 1946. The first version, designated Dove Series1, could carry between eight and eleven passengers, depending on the internal layout chosen by the operator. Production of a six-seat executive variant of the aircraft commenced in 1948, this being designated Dove Series 2. Powered by two 380 h.p. Gipsy Queen 70-2 engines, the Dove Series 5 and Series 6 (respectively airliner and executive versions) were basically similar to the initial production variants of the aircraft, but their maximum take-off weight was increased by 300 lb to 8,800 lb, with the payload increased by 20% on stage lengths of 500 miles or less.

Designated Dove Series 4 by the company, production of a light military transport aircraft for the RAF commenced in 1948 to fulfil the requirements of Air Ministry Specification C.13/46. Two crew and seven passengers could be carried in this aircraft which was designated Devon C.1 by the RAF, and as Sea Devon C.20 by the FAA.

Powered by two 400 hp Gipsy Queen 70-3 engines, the Dove Series7 had a solid domed cockpit roof to provide more headroom for the crew, replacing the transparent cockpit roof with a built in direction-finder loop that was fitted to earlier variants of the aircraft. The Dove Series 8 was a five-seat luxury executive aircraft also fitted with the solid domed cockpit roof, with exhaust thrust augmenters fitted to the engines.

During the coastal survey conducted by the Irish Defence Forces between 1948 and 1955, vertical photographic coverage of the Irish coastline was initially carried out by three Avro XIXs operated by the Irish Army Air Corps, However, these aircraft were out of service for long periods throughout 1951 and 1952 due to problems with their engines and other equipment, which delayed work on the survey during this period. To avoid the delays caused by these problems and deficiencies, the Air Corps required a modern aircraft with reliable engines and sufficient range to enable photographic coverage of all Irish coastal regions to be carried out without refuelling. To fulfil this requirement a Dove Series 4 was ordered by the Department of Defence for delivery in 1953.

On February 22, 1953 a Dove Series 4 (c/n 04367) was delivered to Baldonnel and (as No. 176) entered service with the General Purpose Flight. The Dove

Right: The first Dove to enter Air Corps service was No. 176. (P. Cunniffe photo)

Left: Cockpit of the Dove. (Air Corps photo section via S. Quigley)

was the first aircraft fitted with a tricycle undercarriage and reversible-pitch propellers to enter service with the Air Corps. For vertical photography, an aerial camera could be installed in the cabin floor, which had an opening for the lens; a bulged section in the aircraft's forward fuselage window was used for oblique photography. The Dove, which could reach any part of the country without refuelling, was initially used for oblique and vertical photography of the north-west coast of Ireland in July 1953. Photographic surveys of other coastal regions were carried out by this aircraft until the coastal survey was completed two years later. The Dove was also used for testing radio and radar equipment for the Department of Industry and Power, and for advanced, twin-engined pilot training, and transport throughout the State of Government Ministers and officials and high-ranking officers of the Defence Forces. In August 1970, following a heavy landing that cracked the main wing spar, the Dove was withdrawn from use and placed in storage at Baldonnel. The fuselage was delivered to the Civil Defence in Galway for "rescue training" exercises circa 1980, before being transferred to the Civil Defence Headquarters, Phoenix Park, Dublin, in 1983.

Two of the Avro XIXs had been written-off or withdrawn from use following landing accidents by 1958, and the Air Corps needed to replace these aircraft. A Dove Series 5 (c/n 04503) was delivered to Baldonnel Aerodrome on March 24, 1959 to fulfil this requirement, and entered service with the General Purpose Flight as No. 188. On January 27, 1961 this aircraft was written-off in a crash near Shannon International Airport, killing four of those on board.

On July 7, 1961 a Dove Series 7 (c/n 04530) was delivered by Air Corps personnel to Baldonnel as a replacement for the crashed aircraft, and (as No. 194) entered service with the General Purpose Flight. The new aircraft was, according to newspaper reports at the time, fitted "with specialised electronic and photographic equipment . . . to cope with survey work for the Agricultural Institute, harbour development, advance planning of telephone lines, crash surveys and Forestry Commission investigations". Equipped with a de Wilde RC8 Aerial Survey camera installed in the cabin floor, the Dove was used for aerial photographic coverage of cities, industrial regions and other areas of the State for the Ordnance Survey Department, Local Authorities, Government Departments and Agencies. In 1976 and 1977, during a period of good weather with clear skies, the Dove was engaged on a photographic survey of the city of Dublin for the Ordnance Survey Department. This Dove was withdrawn from use in March 1978 and was placed in storage at Baldonnel Aerodrome.

From 1964 onwards, the Department of Transport and Power had a requirement for an aircraft equipped for calibrating navigation aids at Irish airports. To fulfil this requirement a Dove Series 8A (c/n 04525, U.K. registration G-ARSN), which had been placed in storage following its construction in 1961, was purchased in May 1967 from Hawker Siddeley Aviation for £20,000. (In 1963 Hawker Siddeley Aviation had become responsible for the development and production of all de Havilland aircraft types). Operated by the Air Corps, the Dove was originally intended to equip a Flight Checking Unit, which was to be established in 1968; however, this unit was never actually formed. Due to its long period in storage, the Dove required a major overhaul before entering service with the Air Corps, and extra instrumentation and equipment for its calibration role also needed

Above: Dove No. 194 showing off the silver and dayglo colour scheme that was in widespread use on Air Corps aircraft throughout much of the 1960s and 70s. (P. Cunniffe photo)

to be installed. The total cost of this overhaul, and installation of the additional equipment (including a spare engine) came to £82,000. The Dove (with the Irish civil registration EI-ARV) was delivered in September 1967 to a British company, Air Couriers Ltd., for the installation of electronic equipment for radio and radar calibration duties, but all work on the aircraft ceased in November 1968 when this company went into liquidation. Completion of the work on the Dove by another company was estimated to cost over £100,000, and as a consequence the Department of Transport and Power at that stage decided to have the aircraft converted for training air traffic controllers and limited testing of navigational aids, at an overall cost of £87,000.

On December 18, 1970, the Dove Series 8A was delivered to Baldonnel Aerodrome and entered service (as No. 201) with the General Purpose Flight. The Dove was fitted with additional aerials on the fuselage, bulged cabin windows nearest the cockpit and carried the inscription "CALIBRATION" in red over the cabin windows. According to contemporary newspaper reports the Dove was "specially equipped . . . for testing radio and navigational aids at Irish airports", but the aircraft was only used occasionally for the training of radar operators at Irish airports. (The calibration of landing aids continued to be carried out by aircraft of the American Federal Aviation Administration, under contract to the Department of Transport and Power). Over the next seven years, the Dove was used for occasional search and rescue missions, fishery patrols, transport duties and escorting other Air Corps aircraft undergoing maintenance or scheduled overhauls in the United Kingdom or in France. The Dove Series 8a was withdrawn from use in December 1977 and placed in storage at Baldonnel Aerodrome.

In 1980, the Dove Series 7 and Series 8A were advertised for sale and purchased by a British company, Staravia Ltd. The Doves were flown to the company's base at Exeter, England, and placed in open storage (with the U.K. civil registrations G-ARUE and G-ARSN). In October 1983, the Dove Series 7 was sold to a buyer in West Germany and (with German civil registration D-IKER) was issued with a temporary permit to fly for the delivery flight in January 1984. This aircraft was, however, never issued with a Certificate of Airworthiness in Germany and was used as a source of spare parts for another Dove until acquired by a German aviation museum in 1990. The Dove Series 8A was purchased by Aces High Ltd. in January 1983, but two months later this aircraft was delivered to Acme Jewellery Ltd and (with UK registration G-LIDD) underwent a major overhaul throughout the remainder of that year. Following two test flights in 1984 and 1985, this aircraft was again placed in storage at Coventry Airport and advertised for sale. In 1987, the Dove Series 8A was sold to a buyer in Australia and used for charter operations (with the Australian civil registration VH-OBI) by an air charter company, Dove Air.

Colours & Markings

All of the Doves were initially delivered in an overall painted silver finish. Orange dayglo was later applied to the wingtips, nose, front section of the tailfin and the tailplanes of these aircraft.

The Dove Series 4 No. 176 had a green and orange Celtic boss displayed on both sides of the mid-fuselage section and the upper sides of the wings, with tricoloured stripes, positioned chordwise, on the undersides of the wings. However, the tricoloured Celtic boss later replaced these markings in all six positions. The others had the tricoloured Celtic boss displayed on both sides of the mid-fuselage section and on the upper and under sides of both wings.

Left: The final Dove in Air Corps service No. 201 (P. Cunniffe photo)

Left: The same Dove on the day of its arrival at Baldonnel wearing dual civil and military registrations. (George Flood collection)

Left: Former Air Corps Dove No. 201, resplendent in its Australian civiil colour scheme. (S. Nolan collection)

3.6

Hunting Percival P.56 Provost T.51 & Provost T.53 (1954 – 1976)

In September 1948, the British Air Ministry issued Specification T.16/48 in connection with a requirement for a high-performance basic training aircraft to replace the Percival Prentice, then in service with RAF Training Command. In the same year, as a private venture, Percival Aircraft Ltd. had initiated work on designing a basic training aircraft to replace the Prentice, and this was submitted to the Air Ministry for consideration. Powered by the Alvis Leonides engine, the Percival P.56 was selected to fulfil the requirement of Specification T.16/48 and an initial batch of 200 aircraft was ordered by the Air Ministry in May 1951.

Designated Provost T.1, the first production aircraft (WV 419) first flew in January 1953, with deliveries to the RAF commencing in May of that year. The Provost T.1 was the last piston-engined basic training aircraft to enter service with the RAF An export version of this unarmed basic training aircraft, designated Provost T.51, was delivered to a number of foreign air forces and this was similar in most respects to the aircraft in service with the RAF In 1954, Percival Aircraft Ltd. amalgamated with the Hunting Group and was renamed Hunting Percival Aircraft Ltd., which became Hunting Aircraft Ltd. in 1957.

An armed version of the Provost T.1 for the Rhodesian Air Force was designated Provost T.52. This variant had a 0.303-in. machine-gun, with an ammunition bay containing 600 rounds, installed in each wing and a camera gun in the starboard wing root. Bombs and rockets could also be carried on hard points under the wings. The company also constructed another armed variant of the aircraft, designated Provost T.53 and 65 of these were exported to foreign air forces. A total of 451 Provosts of all types had been constructed by the company when production ceased in 1959.

In 1953, the Irish Army Air Corps had a requirement for an advanced flying training aircraft for use by the Flying Training Schools. The number of Vickers Supermarine Spitfire Tr.9s available for the Schools' advanced flying training programmes had been reduced, as some of these aircraft were being used by No. 1 Fighter Squadron to fulfil operational commitments, replacing the Vickers Supermarine Seafires that had been withdrawn from use or written-off in accidents. To fulfil this requirement, the Department of Defence ordered four Provost T.51s, at a total cost of £82,000, which were to be delivered to the Air Corps in 1954; this being the first export order for the aircraft.

The first Provost T.51 (c/n 125) was delivered to Baldonnel Aerodrome on March 6, 1954, followed by the second and third (c/ns 157 and 160) on May

Below: Provost No. 178 running up prior to a training sortie (P. Cunniffe photo)

Provost Cockpit
(J. Maxwell photo)

27, 1954, and the fourth (c/n 179) on July 6, 1954. The four Provosts (as Nos. 177-180) entered service with the Air Corps Flying Training Schools, which were based at Gormanston Military Camp during the construction of concrete runways and a control tower at Baldonnel Aerodrome throughout 1954 and 1955.

In 1954, the Department of Defence ordered four Provost T.53s at a total cost of £85,600, which were to be used for advanced flying and weapons training. The first Provost T.53 (c/n 400) was delivered to the Air Corps on July 21, 1955, followed by the second (c/n 403) on September 20, 1955, and the third and fourth (c/ns 406 and 408) on October 10, 1955. These aircraft (as Nos. 181-184) also entered service with the Air Corps Flying Training Schools, but from 1956 onwards the eight Provosts were operated by the Advanced Flying Training School based at Baldonnel Aerodrome.

Over the next 22 years the Provosts were used by the Air Corps for advanced flying and weapons training by a total of twenty-five "Wings" courses, conducted by the Advanced Flying Training School for Short Service Officers, Young Officers and Regular Cadet Classes. From 1963 to 1973 the Provosts were also used by the Air Corps for advanced flying training for pilot cadets for Aer Lingus. The Provost T.53s, which were also expected to provide air support for the Defence Forces in time of conflict, also participated in a number of military exercises that included simulated ground attacks against the troops engaged on these exercises.

The training syllabus in use at that time required trainees to undergo their basic training on DH Chipmunks followed by advanced training on the Provost. There was a big step up both literally and figuratively from the Chipmunk to the Provost. The Provost cockpit is high off the ground, requiring pilots to climb up on the wings to enter the cockpit. The aircraft was also both very powerful and nose heavy with the big Leonides engine up front. In addition, the Provost was fitted with pneumatic brakes, which, if sharply applied by the unwary, could lead to a nose over and damage to the propeller. In almost every other respect the aircraft was a delight to fly, with well-balanced controls.

Provost T.53 No. 182 was written-off in a crash at Fermoy, Co. Cork, killing the crew of two, on January 3, 1957. A second Provost, this time T.51 No. 179, was also written-off in a crash on Table Mountain, Glenmalure, Co. Wicklow, killing the pilot, on March 5, 1957. The Department of Defence ordered two Provost T.53s as replacements and these aircraft, these machines (c/n 460 and 461) being delivered to Baldonnel Aerodrome on March 23 and April 30, 1960 respectively. These two aircraft, which entered service (as Nos. 189 and 190) with the Advanced Flying Training School, were the last two Provosts constructed by the company.

On April 14, 1962 one of the replacement Provost T.53s (No. 189) crash-landed near Maynooth, Co. Meath, damaging the fuselage. The Air Corps acquired a Provost T.1 (c/n 352) from Hunting Aircraft in August 1963, which was delivered to Baldonnel in July 1964 to provide parts for the reconstruction of the damaged aircraft. The Provost T.1 (ex-RAF, serial number XF846) had been delivered to the RAF in August 1955 and was withdrawn from use

Side by side seating in the Provost greatly assisted instructor pilots to monitor student pilot ability. (J. Maxwell photo)

in February 1960 having accumulated a total of only 8½ flying hours. Using the fuselage and other components from this aircraft, and the wings from the damaged aircraft, the rebuilt aircraft (as No. 189A) flew again on February 21, 1966 and entered service with the Advanced Flying Training School, designated Provost T.53. (The suffix letter 'A' was later deleted from this aircraft's serial number). On May 15, 1969 the reconstructed aircraft was damaged in a collision with a Provost T.51 (No. 178) at Baldonnel Aerodrome and was written-off. Following a period as an instructional airframe by the Technical Training Squadron, this aircraft was then used for fire practice by the Crash Rescue Service at Baldonnel Aerodrome before being scrapped around 1983. In June 1968, a Provost T.51 (No. 180) crash-landed at Castlebaggot, near Baldonnel Aerodrome, following an engine failure, and was written-off.

In 1970, the Air Corps was still operating two Provost T.51s (Nos. 177 and 178) and four Provost T.53s (Nos. 181, 183, 184 and 190), but spare parts for the aircraft and their Alvis Leonides engines were becoming both scarce and expensive; the Provost was also considered to be obsolescent as a training aircraft by this time. A modern training aircraft type was required by the Air Corps, and the SIAI-Marchetti SF.260WE Warrior was eventually selected as a replacement for the Provost, with deliveries commencing in 1977. The Provosts remaining in service at that stage were retired throughout the first six months of 1976, with the last official flight by a Provost T.53 (No. 183) occurring in June of that year.

Above: provost T.53 equipped with rocket rails about to set out on a training sortie. (P. Cunniffe photo)

In 1981, following a period of storage at Baldonnel Aerodrome, the two Provost T.51s (Nos. 177 and 178) were sold to buyers in the United Kingdom (carrying the UK civil registration G-BLIW and G-BKOS). One of the aircraft (G-BLIW) flew again in 1988 in Air Corps markings (as No. 177), and the other (G-BKOS), also in Air Corps markings (as No. 178), flew again in 1989. The latter aircraft, which had accumulated a total of 2,000 flying hours while in service with the Air Corps, was destroyed in a crash at Aldermaston, Berkshire on May 19, 1991.

In 1985, a Provost T.53 (No. 183) was donated to the Irish Aviation Museum following restoration by the Air Corps, but when the museum closed down this aircraft was returned to Baldonnel Aerodrome for eventual display in the Air Corps Museum. Three of the Provost T.53s (Nos. 181, 184 and 189A) were used for fire practice by the Crash Rescue Service at Baldonnel Aerodrome. In 1987, one of these aircraft (No. 184), with the wings from No. 183, was donated to the South East Aviation Museum, Waterford Airport and later moved to the Cavan and Leitrim Railway Museum at Dromod, Co. Leitrim. Provost T.53No. 181 was delivered to the United Kingdom in 1990, in exchange for a damaged Westland Whirlwind HAR. 9, and was used as a spares source for the reconstruction of a Provost T.1. The remaining Provost T.53 (No. 190) was used for a period as an instructional airframe by the Technical Training Squadron, before being placed in open storage with another of these aircraft (No. 189A) at Baldonnel Aerodrome, where both aircraft eventually deteriorated.

Colours & Markings

The Provosts were painted silver overall, with the propeller spinner, an anti-glare panel forward of the cockpit and walkways on the upper surfaces of the wing roots painted in matt black. Dayglo orange markings were later displayed on the wingtips, the spinner, the front section of the tailfin and tailplane. The Air Corps serial numberwas displayed in black on each side of the rear section of the fuselage and on the undersides of the starboard wing. A green and orange Celtic boss was displayed on both sides of the centre section of the fuselage and on the outer sections of the upper surfaces of both wings, with tri-coloured stripes, positioned chordwise, on the undersides of the wings. From about 1957 onwards, these markings were replaced by tri-coloured Celtic bosses in the six positions.

3.7

De Havilland D.H.115 Vampire T.55 (1956 – 1976)

In March 1950 the de Havilland Aircraft Co. Ltd., initiated the design and construction of an advanced training aircraft as a private venture. Designated D.H.115A, the prototype was developed from the Vampire N.F.10 night fighter (itself a derivative of the single seat fighter) and retained the widened fuselage nacelle of this aircraft, with side-by-side seating and dual controls for the instructor and student pilot. The tail booms, tailplane and strengthened wings of the Vampire F.B.5 fighter-bomber were also fitted to the prototype, together with underwing attachments for drop tanks, bombs or rocket projectiles.

Designated Vampire T.11, series production commenced in October 1951 and the first aircraft (with RAF serial WZ414) flew for the first time on January 19, 1952. A total of 526 Vampire T.11s and 73 Vampire T.22s were delivered to the RAF and the Fleet Air Arm respectively. The export version of this aircraft designated Vampire T.55, was also delivered to 20 other air forces worldwide and was also built under licence in Australia, India and Switzerland.

On May 25, 1948, a Gloster Meteor IV (RAF serial RA444, coded A6-B), from No. 257 Squadron, RAF, arrived at Dublin Airport for demonstration to the Irish Army Air Corps. Over the next five days, the Meteor provided flying demonstrations for the Air Corps over Baldonnel Aerodrome, the Curragh Military Camp, Gormanston Military Camp and Dublin Airport. The Meteor was unable to land at Baldonnel Aerodrome or at Gormanston Military Camp as these airfields had only grass runways. At that time the Air Corps did not have a requirement for a fighter aircraft as twelve Vickers Supermarine Seafire LF.IIIs had been delivered to No. 1 Fighter Squadron the previous year.

By 1954, however, the Air Corps did have a requirement for a modern, turbojet- powered fighter aircraft type to replace the Seafire LF.IIIs that had been written-off or withdrawn from use over the previous seven years. To fulfil this requirement, the Department of Defence ordered three Vampire T.55s from de Havilland Aircraft for delivery in 1956. The construction at Baldonnel Aerodrome of concrete

Into the jet age. The Vampire T.55's were the first jet aircraft in Irish Air Corps service. Note the No.1 fighter squadron badge that was first applied to Gloster Gladiators almost twenty years previously. (P. Cunniffe photo)

Extremely rare colour photo of an Irish Vampire in flight. (P. O'Meara photo)

runways and taxiways, and a new control tower, had commenced in the same year at a total cost of £537,850.

On July 21, 1956, three Vampire T.55s (c/ns 15755, 15765 and 15766) were delivered by Air Corps pilots to Baldonnel Aerodrome. These were the first turbojet-powered aircraft to enter service with the Air Corps, and also the first to be equipped with ejection seats. Later that year, the Vampires (as Nos. 185, 186 and 187) entered service with No. 1 Fighter Squadron, which had relocated from Air Corps Station, Gormanston to Baldonnel Aerodrome. Total cost of the three aircraft was £146,000, which were to be "the first of a projected £480,000 fleet of nine de Havilland Vampire Mk. 55 fighters for the Air Corps", according to Dáil debates at the time. However in the event only six Vampires were actually acquired. The first formal appearance of the Vampires occurred on Easter Sunday 1957 during a flypast by two of these aircraft, with three Vickers Supermarine Spitfire Tr.9s over the Defence Forces annual parade in Dublin to commemorate the 1916 Easter Rising. Over the next fifteen years, the Air Corps was usually represented by the Vampires in a fly-past over this parade by the Defence Forces.

In 1960, the Air Corps needed to replace the Vickers Supermarine Spitfire Tr.9s which were about to be withdrawn from use throughout that year. The Vampires acquired in 1956 for the fighter role were also at this stage being used during the later stages of advanced flying training, but once the Spitfires were retired, these three aircraft would be unable to fulfil both the operational commitments of No. 1 Fighter Squadron and these training duties. The Department of Defence therefore ordered three more Vampire T.55s, and funds were allocated in the 1960 Defence Estimates for the acquisition of these aircraft, which were to be delivered in 1961. Interestingly, the unit cost for this second batch of Vampires had fallen from £48,839 to £37,200 each.

Fitted with underwing fuel tanks, the first of the second batch of Vampires (c/n 15815) was delivered to Baldonnel Aerodrome on January 18, 1961, followed by the remaining two (c/ns 15816 and 15817) on March 16, 1961. These were from the final production batch of Vampire T.55s constructed by de Havilland in 1960. The three Vampire T.55s (as Nos. 191, 192 and 193) entered service with 'A' Flight, No. 1 Fighter Squadron.

A further Vampire T.11 (c/n 15563) was delivered to Baldonnel Aerodrome on August 30, 1963 to be used as an instructional airframe by the Technical Training Squadron. This aircraft (ex RAF serial XE977), which was from a batch of 135 Vampire T.11s delivered to the RAF between July 1953 and July 1955, had been in service with No. 8 Flying Training School until struck off charge in July 1963. The Vampire was allocated an Air Corps serial number (No. 198), although this was not displayed while it was in use as an instructional airframe, the aircraft retaining its RAF serial number but with the roundels removed.

The six Vampire T.55s were used by the Air Corps to fulfil the operational requirements of No. 1 Fighter Squadron and for advanced flying training duties during the "Wings" courses for Short Service Officers, Young Officers and Regular Cadet Classes. The current General Officer Commanding the Air Corps, Brig. Gen. Ralph James, recalled his early flights in the Vampire doing "touch and go's" at Baldonnel. Early turbojet engines, such as the Goblin that powered the Vampire, had very long spool-up times compared to modern engines. The throttle had to be opened smoothly while still at 200 feet above the runway in order to have sufficient power for the go around. Nevertheless it was a great aircraft to fly, and pilots got a real push during acceleration sitting almost directly in front of the turbojet engine with just a light wooden structure around them.

From 1957 to 1975, 200 Air Corps pilots are estimated to have completed their advanced flying training on these aircraft. With a fixed armament of two 20mm Hispano cannon (four cannon could be carried but for centre of gravity reasons usually just two were installed in the two seater) and capable of carrying four rocket projectiles on underwing attachments, the Vampires were also used for weapons training exercises over the Air Firing Range, Gormanston. Operated by No. 1 Fighter Squadron, the Vampires were expected to provide air support for the Defence Forces in a combat situation, and were also used as ceremonial escorts for aircraft conveying dignitaries from other countries on official visits to the State.

On May 5, 1961, Vampire T.55 No. 186, with Comdt. J.B. O'Connor as instructor and Cadet Richard McPartland as student pilot on board, was on a training exercise over Co. Cavan. As the exercise included spin recovery, the aircraft was put into this manoeuvre at an altitude of 30,000 feet, but when the instructor attempted the necessary recovery action, the Vampire failed to respond to the controls. As the aircraft passed 10,000 feet, the instructor jettisoned the cockpit canopy and ordered the student pilot to abandon the aircraft. The student pilot ejected from the Vampire and landed safely, but the force of the ejection caused the aircraft to recover from the spin, which allowed the instructor to regain control and return to Baldonnel Aerodrome. This was the first time that an ejection seat was used to evacuate an aircraft operated by the Air Corps.

By 1970, spare parts for the Vampires were becoming both scarce and expensive, and major overhauls of the Goblin engines were costing approximately £16,000 each time. As a consequence, three of the aircraft (Nos. 186, 187 and 193) had been withdrawn from use by 1974, with the others to follow suit over the next two years. During this period, the Air Corps evaluated various aircraft types as potential replacements for the Vampire, which resulted in the eventual selection of the Aérospatiale (Fouga) CM.170-2 Super Magister. On September 11, 1975 the last two Vampires in service with the Air Corps (Nos. 185 and 191) provided an escort during the final stages of the delivery flight of the first two Super Magisters to Baldonnel Aerodrome. The last official flight of an Air Corps Vampire T.55 (No. 191) occurred on March 3, 1976.

Three of the Vampires (Nos. 185, 191 and 192) were apparently used for a short period as instructional airframes by the Technical Training Squadron, while the other three (Nos. 186, 187 and 193) were placed in open storage at Baldonnel Aerodrome. One of the Vampires (No. 185) was presented by the Air Corps to the French aviation museum at Savigny les Beaune the fuselage and tail booms were delivered to the museum on February 3, 1978 in a Transall C.160 of the Armee de l'Air, with the wings following two months later Vampire No. 191 was presented to the Irish Aviation Museum and was restored for static display, but following the closure of the museum in 1986, this aircraft was placed in storage at Air Corps Station, Gormanston. It has been restored once again for eventual display at the Air Corps Museum. A third Vampire (No. 192) was donated to the South-East Aviation Museum in 1987, and after partial restoration the aircraft was placed in storage in a building near New Ross, Co. Wexford. It was subsequently moved to the Cavan & Leitrim Railway Museum in Dromod, Co. Cavan, where it is currently on display. In December 1979, the three remaining Vampires (Nos. 186, 187 and 193) were purchased by buyers in the U.S.A. for restoration, but only one of these aircraft (No. 186), albeit with parts from the other two, was actually deliveredThis Vampire (with the U.S. civil registration N4861K) was apparently used by the U.S. Department of Defence for experiments on the radar reflectively of the aircraft's wooden structure. The remains ofVampires Nos. 187 and 193 remained in open storage at Baldonnel Aerodrome for some time, with the fuselage pod from No. 187 being donated to the South-East Aviation Museum in 1987; this may well have been used in the restoration to static display ofVampire No. 192. The last remaining Vampire T.55 (No. 193) gradually deteriorated to a derelict condition in the Irish weather. The Vampire T.11 delivered as an instructional airframe (as No.

Washing away the fire retardant foam after a minor landing mishap in a Vampire. The aircraft was returned to service within a few days. (P. O'Meara photo)

Vampire No. 187 being towed out to the flight line in March 1970. Note the position of flaps and airbrakes when hydraulic pressure had bled off. (P. Cunniffe photo)

198) was displayed in Air Corps markings outside the Officer's Mess at Baldonnel Aerodrome for a period before undergoing restoration for static display at the National Museum, Collins' Barracks, in Dublin.

Colours & Markings

Initially the first three Vampire T.55s had an overall painted silver finish, but from 1960 onwards orange day-glo was applied to the nose, wing tips, dorsal fairing and forward section of the tailplane; the second batch ofVampire T.55s were finished in the same colours. A tri-coloured Celtic boss (green, white and orange) was displayed on the outsides of the mid-section of the tail booms and outboard on the upper and lower surfaces of both wings. Each aircraft's serial numberwas displayed in black on the outsides of the tail booms, behind the Celtic boss, and on the underside of the starboard wing. The crest of No. 1 Fighter Squadron was displayed on the front section of the fuselage below the cockpit windscreen.

Above: Vampire 185 with the canopy open. The bubble canopy provided a superb view. (P. Cunniffe photo)

Left: A technician makes a last minute adjustment to one of the Vampire's systems on the flight line.
(P. Cunniffe photo)

Refocus & Renewal

4.0

Refocus & Renewal (1963 – 1979)

While many air arms had commenced operating helicopters as early as the 1940's, the Irish Air Corps did not commence rotary wing operations until 1963. As early as 1955, a Bristol Sycamore had been demonstrated to the Irish authorities but no orders were forthcoming at the time. However, severe weather conditions over Ireland throughout December 1962 and January 1963, which combined heavy snowfalls with widespread icing, made the majority of roads and rail lines impassable to all surface traffic, which resulted in the isolation of villages, farmsteads and other residences for long periods. Following a public outcry and political pressure over the lack of rescue facilities during these severe weather conditions, the Irish Government ordered three Aérospatiale Alouette III helicopters for operation by the Air Corps. The arrival into service of the Alouette IIIs significantly enhanced the Air Corps' profile, as the search and rescue (SAR) capabilities of the new machines quickly caught the attention of the Irish public.

The 1970's saw a period of radical change for the Air Corps. All of the aircraft types then in service, other than the Alouette III, were replaced by more modern aircraft. The internal security of the State was under threat following the outbreak of civil strife and terrorism in Northern Ireland, resulting in a significant increase in the number of security operations by the Garda, supported by the Defence Forces. The focus of the Air Corps was to provide air cover during these security operations, and in order to do this, the force was equipped with Reims Cessna FR172H Rocket aircraft for army co-operation and other support duties. More Alouette III helicopters were also acquired during this period to provide air support during security operations, leading to the Helicopter Flight being re-designated the Helicopter Squadron.

During this timeframe, there was a significant increase in the number and variety of the Air Corps' operational commitments but the resignations of experienced pilots and technicians throughout the same period created difficulties in fulfilling these commitments, these included air ambulance, army co-operation, fishery protection, Garda air support, ministerial transport, naval support, SAR missions and a range of other duties assigned by the government. From 1977 onwards, the Irish Naval Service and the Air Corps were engaged in enforcing the protection of maritime resources in the sea areas around the Irish coastline, following the accession of the State to the EEC. in 1973. Two aircraft, Beech Super Kingair 200's powered by twin turboprop engines, were acquired initially for patrol and surveillance flights over the economic zone as an interim measure, but were finally replaced by two purpose-built Casa maritime patrol aircraft in 1994.

Commencing in 1973, a number of Air Corps detachments were deployed to military camps, barracks and civil airports throughout the State for security and search and rescue operations. Equipped with helicopters to provide air support for security operations in the north-west region and areas adjacent to the border with Northern Ireland, Air Corps detachments were deployed to Finner Military Camp and to Monaghan Military Barracks in 1973 and 1979 respectively. By 1975, the Air Corps had identified the need for a larger helicopter capable of transporting troops rapidly near border areas and for use in the SAR role. The then Minister for Defence, Paddy Donegan, had stated that there was an urgent need for a helicopter such as the Aérospatiale Puma or Bell 212 to meet the requirement, but no orders were placed at the time.

The training of pilots was completely revised with the replacement of a syllabus utilising three aircraft (i.e, Chipmunk, Provost and Vampire) by a new one making use of the SIAI-Marchetti SF.260WE Warrior and Fouga CM.170 Magister aircraft that had been purchased to replace the earlier types. Both of the new aircraft types had a secondary counter-insurgency capability when armed with rockets and machine guns.

A BAe-125 executive jet aircraft was acquired by the Department of Defence for the transportation of government ministers and officials during the six-month administration of the Presidency of the EEC by the Irish government that commenced on 1 July, 1979. Operated by the newly formed Ministerial Air Transport Service, this aircraft fulfilled all ministerial travel requirements over the next twelve years., A third Beech Kingair turboprop aircraft was also acquired as a back-up for the transportation of government officials and for twin-engined training, and was the first aircraft flown by an Air Corps crew to cross the Atlantic Ocean. This aircraft type has remained in service for 32 years, and has proved to be an excellent choice for the wide variety of roles that it has had to perform.

Map of Ireland Illustrating some locations relevant to military events from WW2 to the present day.

The "Donegal Corridor" was the narrow strip of airspace through which RAF aircraft based at Castle Archdale could fly over neutral territory to patrol the Atlantic Ocean thus considerably shortening the distance they would otherwise have to travel to reach the patrol area.

4.1

Aérospatiale (Sud Aviation) SE.3160/ SA.316B Alouette III (1963 – 2007)

If any aircraft type can be said to have achieved iconic status with the Irish public, it must surely be the Alouette III helicopter operated by the Air Corps for 44 years. The Alouette III was the first helicopter to enter service with the Air Corps and was very much to the fore in highly publicised operations in Ireland, ranging from search and rescue to air ambulance and disaster relief operations following severe weather.

It had taken quite some time for the capabilities of helicopters in rescue situations to be recognised by the Irish authorities, but the decision to procure the Alouette III was an excellent one, and the aircraft remained in service longer than its intended replacement, the SA 365Fi Dauphin II. As early as January 1955, a Bristol Sycamore helicopter had been demonstrated to the Air Corps; the President of Ireland, Dr. Sean T. O'Kelly and his wife flew over Dublin in this machine. The Sycamore was also demonstrated to the Commissioner for Irish Lights for the resupply of lighthouses and lightships, but no order was placed at the time. Then, following a drowning tragedy on the west coast of Ireland in 1957 in which five people died, a committee was set up to make recommendations to enhance rescue capabilities around the Irish coast in the event of maritime or air disasters. The committee concluded that the occasions on which helicopters would be useful for saving lives would be "rare".

Two further major sea tragedies occurred in 1961, one off the south-east coast and the other off the west coast, after which the Irish Government established a second interdepartmental committee to consider "the advisibility of providing a helicopter sea and air rescue service". The committee's report, which was issued in November 1962, concluded that the expenditure that would be involved in providing a helicopter search and rescue service could not be justified at that time. However, from mid-December 1962 to the end of February 1963, the delivery of essential supplies and the provision of vital services throughout Ireland were immobilised by severe weather conditions. Roads became impassable due to ice, frost and heavy snowfalls across the country, with many villages and residences remaining isolated for several weeks. On January 22, 1963, following adverse press coverage

Below: Alouette 197 ready for the next call out in may 1973. Note the rescue badge to the rear of the entry door. (P. Cunniffe photo)

Left: Very rare photo of Alouette 202 in a short lived experimental colour scheme, a variation on the silver and dayglo scheme used throughout the Air Corps fleet at the time.
(J. Bigley photo)

and widespread public criticism of the Government for not having a helicopter rescue service available during these severe weather conditions, the Minister for Transport and Power announced in the Dáil that "the Government have decided that some helicopters should be acquired . . . for sea and rescue services . . . administered by the Minister for Defence".

The Irish Air Corps quickly conducted an evaluation of a number of helicopter types suitable for search and rescue operations. An allocation of £273,000 was included in the 1963 Defence Estimates "for the purchase . . . of three helicopters", including suitable training courses abroad for pilots. The choice came down to the Westland Whirlwind or the Alouette III. In May, following the selection of the SE.3160 Alouette III to fulfil the Air Corps' requirement, the Department of Defence ordered three of these helicopters, each equipped with a rescue hoist and winch, which were to be delivered during 1963-64. In the same month, four Air Corps pilots were nominated for basic helicopter flying training, to commence on an Alouette II (carrying the French civil registration F-BIRX) of the French commercial helicopter operator Heli Union which arrived in Baldonnel Aerodrome in August. This was the first time since 1922 that the British aircraft manufacturing industry had not been selected to fulfil an Air Corps requirement.

The SE.3160 Alouette III was a development of the earlier Alouette II, with a more powerful turboshaft engine, main rotor blades of increased diameter, a three-bladed tail rotor, tricycle undercarriage, enclosed tail boom and a larger cabin to accommodate the pilot and six passengers. Powered by a 550 s.h.p. Artouste IIIB turboshaft engine, construction of an initial batch of 100 commenced in 1960 and a production Alouette III flew for the first time in July 1961.

On October 30, 1963, the Air Corps accepted its first SE.3160 Alouette III (c/n 1151) at the company's factory in Marignane near Marseilles and crews underwent conversion training there throughout November on this helicopter (which for this purpose temporarily carried the French civil registration F-WDJH). The second Alouette III (c/n 1153, which temporarily carried the French civil registration F-WKQB) was accepted by the Air Corps in the same month. These two Alouette IIIs were delivered to Baldonnel Aerodrome by Air Corps personnel on November 25, 1963 and, as Nos. 195 and 196, entered service with the Helicopter Flight, which had been formed the same year. The third SE.3160 Alouette III (c/n 1194) was delivered to Baldonnel on May 13, 1964 and as No. 197 also entered service with the Helicopter Flight.

The first search and rescue mission by an Air Corps Alouette occurred in December 1963, searching for a French trawler reported missing with an injured crewmember off the west coast of Ireland, although in this instance, the missing vessel was eventually located by another trawler. The first mission resulting in an actual rescue by an Air Corps Alouette occurred on August 8, 1964, when and a man and a boy were rescued from a boat drifting in Dublin Bay following an engine failure. Over the next year, the Helicopter Flight was engaged in the development of helicopter search and rescue techniques, the evaluation and testing of associated equipment and an intensive training programme for aircrew. Aviation fuel storage depots for refuelling the Alouettes during rescue missions were also positioned at a number of secure locations throughout the State, usually at military installations.

Commencing in 1964, search and rescue missions were carried out by the Alouettes all around Ireland and its surrounding coastal sea areas. Fitted with only basic navigation equipment and powered by a single engine, the Alouettes were, however, normally

Left: Heading off on a mission in 1971, the Alouette II would form the mainstay of Air Corps helicopter operations for 43 years.
(P. Cunniffe photo)

limited to daylight search and rescue operations over land and could venture no more than three nautical miles from the coast. On search and rescue operations, the helicopters carried a crew of three, comprising a pilot, winch operator and winchman; these crews were at readiness on a round-the-clock basis, and even though missions were only supposed to be flown between dawn and dusk, in some cases this restriction was overlooked and night missions flown if the need was deemed great enough and the level of risk accceptable. Emergency flotation bags , which could be inflated in the event of ditching following failure of the engine or any other vital components, were fitted to the Alouettes for inshore search and rescue operations. Assisted by voluntary mountain rescue teams, the Alouettes were also used to airlift people injured in mountain accidents to hospital. Between 1976 and 1978, a number of notable mountain rescue missions were carried out by the Alouettes, including a night rescue of two climbers from Muckish Mountain, Co. Donegal, in August 1977. The crews of the two Alouettes that carried out this rescue received awards for their bravery. Over the entire period during which the Alouettes were in service, a total of fourteen crewmen received Distinguished Service Medals in recognition of their bravery and skill whilst operating these machines.

Following an agreement between the Department of Defence, the Department of Health and local Health Authorities, a National Air Ambulance Service to be provided by the Air Corps was established in 1965, and in this regard landing pads for the helicopters engaged on these missions were constructed at the majority of hospitals throughout the State. In the course of their Air Corps service, the Alouettes were used for the majority of the air ambulance missions carried out by the force, and have transported premature babies, patients with serious spinal or head injuries, and serious injuries from accidents or burns to specialised hospitals throughout the State or in Northern Ireland. Organs for transplant, together with medical teams to perform such operations, have also been transported between hospitals by these helicopters.

The first air ambulance mission by an Air Corps Alouette was in fact flown within three months of the type entering service. In February 1964, a seriously ill patient was transported in an Alouette (No. 196) from a hospital in Wexford to a hospital in Dublin. The first air ambulance mission across the border with Northern Ireland occurred on May 3, 1965, when a seriously injured patient was transported from Cork to Belfast. On May 3, 1969, a seriously ill seaman from a weather ship was collected by an Alouette from a Royal Canadian Navy destroyer about sixty nautical miles west of the Irish coast, and transported to hospital.

On Easter Sunday 1966, flying in line astern over the military parade in the centre of Dublin, the three Alouettes participated in the commemoration by the Irish Defence Forces of the 50th anniversary of the 1916 Rising. On July 26, 1966, one of the Alouettes (No. 195) was used to convey President Eamonn de Valera from Cork Airport to Cape Clear Island, off the south-west coast, to open an Language educational facility on the island. This was the first time that a President of the State had flown in an Air Corps helicopter, but since then the Alouettes have been used to transport other Presidents, the Taoiseach (i.e., the prime minister), Cabinet Ministers, foreign Heads of State, members of the Defence Forces General Staff and other distinguished persons to and from locations throughout the State.

The Alouette was proving to be a versatile machine in Air Corps hands, and more roles were gradually assigned to it. The helicopters were used for Army co-operation missions, the frequency of which gradually increased as the internal security situation deteriorated following the outbreak of civil strife and terrorist activities in Northern Ireland. The Alouettes were also used to provide what was described in official documents as "aid to the civil power" from 1969 onwards, which term included air support for the Garda Siochana and during joint Army/Garda security operations. These extra duties created a requirement for another Alouette for the Air Corps, since three helicopters were considered to be the minimum number required to support search and rescue operations. On March 24, 1972an SA.316B Alouette III (c/n 1973) was delivered by Air Corps personnel to Baldonnel Aerodrome and (as No. 202) entered service with the Helicopter Flight. The SA.316B was a further development of the Alouette III, fitted with strengthened main and tail rotor transmissions and powered by an 870 s.h.p. Artouste IIIB turboshaft, de-rated to 570 s.h.p. It flew for the first time on June 27, 1968, with production commencing in 1970. In the same year, Sud Aviation

Right: A sight many an injured hill walker was glad to see, an Alouette approaching with help on board. Taken with a 50mm lens it really was that close! (J. Maxwell photo)

Left: To celebrate 30 years of helicopter operations in 1993 No. 195 received a special commemorative paint scheme. Seen here in April 1994 during a training exercise with Dublin-Wicklow Mountain Rescue Team on Kippure , Co. Wicklow. (J. Maxwell photo)

merged with Nord Aviation and SEREB to form Societé Nationale Industrielle Aérospatiale, otherwise known as Aérospatiale. The first two Alouettes (Nos. 195 and 196), each having accumulated 2,400 flying hours since entering service in 1963, also underwent major overhauls by the manufacturer in France between 1971 and 1973.

From 1970 onwards, there was a substantial increase in the number of air support missions provided by the Alouettes for the security forces, comprising reconnaissance flights, troop transport, command and control, assistance to bomb disposal teams and aerial photography.. From August 1973 onwards, an Alouette was also permanently deployed to Finner Military Camp, Co. Donegal, to provide air support for the Defence Forces and Garda personnel engaged on security operations in the north-west region; the aircraft was also available for search and rescue missions and island relief operations off the north-west coast during stormy weather conditions.

Yet more helicopters were required to enable the Air Corps to fulfil these extra commitments, and the Department of Defence therefore ordered another four SA.316B Alouette IIIs for delivery in 1973 and 1974. The first of these helicopters (c/n 1983) was delivered to Baldonnel Aerodrome on February 4, 1973, followed by the second (c/n 1984) and the third (c/n 2116) on March 29and December 6, 1973 respectively. The three Alouette IIIs entered service with the Helicopter Flight as Nos. 211, 212 and 213. The last SA.316B Alouette III from this batch (c/n 2122), and the last to enter service with the Air Corps (as No. 214), was delivered to Baldonnel Aerodrome on March 25, 1974.

When the Air Corps celebrated ten years of helicopter operations in November 1973, a total of 10,000 flying hours had been accumulated by the six Alouettes in service over that period. The helicopters had carried out 245 search and rescue missions, with 65 people rescued; transported 367 patients to specialist hospitals, including 12 air ambulance flights to hospitals in Belfast and Derry; and carried out over 200 Army co-operation missions. A new crest for the Helicopter Flight was also introduced in November 1973, comprising an ancient Egyptian life symbol enclosed in a circle with the motto in Gaelic "Go Maridis Beo" ("That Others may Live"). In the same year a green, white and orange flag, displayed on both sides of the fuselage and on the undersides of all of the Alouettes, was introduced to facilitate quick identification of the helicopters by the Irish security forces. In November 1974, due to the increase in the number of helicopters in service with the Air Corps, the Helicopter Squadron was formed, replacing the Helicopter Flight.

The eight Alouettes had accumulated a total of 15,000 flying hours without a serious accident up to May 26, 1976, when No. 195 was extensively damaged in a crash-landing at Baldonnel Aerodrome, caused by collective pitch control failure. Following repairs and reconstruction by the maintenance department of Aer Lingus, the Alouette returned to service in August 1978. This helicopter underwent a major overhaul by the Air Corps' Engineering Wing in 1998, after accumulating a total of 8,037 flying hours over the previous 35 years, and was returned to service with the Air Corps. A total of 78 Air Corps pilots had flown this Alouette at some time during this period.

The Alouettes participated in a number of major military exercises conducted by the Defence Forces between 1976 and 1978, being used for logistics support, liaison flights and aerial surveillance for the units engaged on these exercises. During these exercises the Air Corps was also expected to have an Alouette available at all times for search and rescue missions. An Alouette was permanently deployed to

Monaghan Military Barracks from October 1979 onwards, to provide air support for the Defence Forces and Garda personnel during security operations in this region, which is adjacent to the border with Northern Ireland. The Alouettes also participated in the major security operations by the Defence Forces and Garda during the visit of Pope John Paul II to Ireland in September 1979.

Since their delivery in 1963, the Alouette IIIs had also been used for helicopter pilot conversion courses by the Air Corps, but the increasing number of operational missions flown by these aircraft created a requirement for additional machines that could be dedicated to the training role. Two Aérospatiale SA.342L Gazelles were delivered to the Air Corps in 1979 and 1981 to fulfil this requirement, these being used for basic helicopter pilot training, totalling 50 flying hours. Although the Alouette IIIs still had to be used for operational conversion courses, totalling 60 flying hours, the amount of their time devoted to helicopter flying training was considerably reduced overall.

Following a re-organisation of the Air Corps in June 1980, the Helicopter Squadron, comprising a Search and Rescue Flight and a Support Flight, was allocated to the newly-formed No. 1 Support Wing. Subsequently, from 1986 onwards, all helicopters in service with the Air Corps were operated by No. 3 Support Wing, which was formed in that year, and comprised the Army Support Squadron, Naval Support Squadron, Search and Rescue Squadron and the Helicopter School. The Alouette IIIs were operated three of the Wing's units, the exception being the Naval Support Squadron. A further restructuring took place in 2002 and as a result the Alouettes IIIs were subsequently operated by 302 Squadron, No. 3 Operations Wing.

Right: Precise control and total trust between crew members was essential when winching close to cliffs as seen here at Bray Head during a training exercise in 1994. (J. Maxwell photo)

The Alouettes operated by the Air Corps had accumulated a total of 27,800 flying hours by October 1980, and according to Aérospatiale should statistically have all been written-off in accidents, due to the variety of missions and the high number of hours flown by each aircraft. The 1000th air ambulance mission was flown by an Alouette on December 9, 1980, transporting a patient from a hospital in Ballinasloe, Co. Galway, to the National Rehabilitation Centre in Dun Laoghaire, Co. Dublin. In 1981, following an accident to an Alouette III in service with the Koninklijke Luchtmacht (Royal Netherlands Air Force), all Alouettes, including those operated by the Air Corps, were grounded for a short period on the advice of the manufacturer. Fatigue cracks were discovered on the first three Alouettes (Nos. 195, 196 and 197) that had been delivered to the Air Corps, but following a number of modifications, including the fitting of strengthened main and tail rotor transmissions, the three helicopters returned to service, re-designated as SA.316B Alouette IIIs.

In 1980 and 1981, the Alouettes carried out a number of long-range rescue missions over the Atlantic Ocean, off the west coast, which exceeded by a wide margin the limit of three nautical miles for offshore sea rescues. Heavy snowfalls and freezing conditions over the eastern region of Ireland in January 1982 caused a massive disruption to the transportation system throughout the region. Virtually all roads were impassable with villages, residences and farms isolated by snowdrifts. A total of 148 rescue missions over a ten-day period were completed by the Helicopter Squadron, operating the Alouettes and the Aérospatiale SA.330L Puma (No. 232), including delivering food and other supplies to isolated villages and residences, dropping fodder to stranded livestock on farms and transporting seriously ill patients to hospitals. During this period the Alouettes, some with skis attached to the undercarriage for landing on snow or ice, carried out a total of 128 rescue missions and saved 70 lives.

In November 1982, an instructional Alouette III airframe was delivered by Aérospatiale to Baldonnel Aerodrome to fulfil a requirement by the Training Wing's Apprentice School. Constructed from spare parts, with the airframe's metal covering replaced by transparent panels, but without a cockpit frame, engine or rotors, the instructional airframe was not allocated an Air Corps serial number.

When the Air Corps celebrated twenty years of service by the Alouette III in November 1983, a total of 800 search and rescue missions, with 276 lives saved, and 1,400 air ambulance missions, had been carried out by these helicopters. In the same year, following a failure of the tail rotor control system, one of the Alouettes (No. 214) force-landed in field near Longford during an air ambulance mission to Sligo, without injuries to the crew or patient. Following repairs on site the Alouette was able to return to Baldonnel.

A Bristol Sycamore was the first helicopter to be demonstrated to the Air Corps in 1955. It was to be a further eight years before the Alouette entered service. (A.C. Photographic Section)

On August 28, 1987, at a ceremony held at Baldonnel Aerodrome, the Aérospatiale SA.365Fi Dauphin 2 officially replaced the Alouette on search and rescue operations. From November 1963 to February 1987, the Alouettes had carried out a total of 1,000 search and rescue missions, with 314 lives saved. A total of 7,000 flying hours accumulated since entering service was reached in the same year by Alouette III No. 196 during a mountain rescue mission on December 12, 1987; this machine had been delivered in 1963, almost a quarter of a century previously. The Alouettes had to resume search and rescue operations over Ireland's eastern region on September 4, 1989, when one of the Dauphin's was deployed to Shannon International Airport to commence provision of 24 hour search and rescue services off the west coast of Ireland. From 1991 onwards, the majority of search and rescue missions were being carried out by the Dauphin, based at Finner Military Camp in Donegal, or a civilian Sikorsky S-61N, based at Shannon International Airport, replacing the Dauphin originally stationed there.

By November 1993, when the Air Corps celebrated thirty years of operations with the Alouette, the stated primary roles of the type were Army co-operation missions, providing support for Garda security operations and air ambulance missions. The eight Alouettes had by then carried out 1,400 search and rescue missions, saving 400 lives 2,300 air ambulance missions, and over 2,000 security operations; in the course of doing so, the fleet had accumulated 57,411 flying hours. Each of the Alouettes had been completely dismantled and reconstructed at least once, with engines and major components being replaced during major overhauls that lasted six months.

In February 1995, there was severe flooding of farmland around Gort, Co. Galway, following incessant heavy rain over a six-week period. An Alouette was deployed to the area for about two months and was used to drop tonnes of fodder to livestock stranded on the flooded farms. On October 20, 1995, an Alouette (No. 202) crashed into Lough Eske, Co. Donegal, during a low-altitude search for a missing person. The crew were not injured and the helicopter was recovered from the lake but was never returned to service and later formally withdrawn from use.

In December 1997, the Alouette was replaced by the Dauphin for search and rescue operations over the country's eastern region. By this time, the accumulated statistics for the Alouette III fleet since 1963 had reached a total of 1,457 search and rescue missions, assisting 3,077 persons, and 2,597 air ambulance missions. On July 1, 1998 the eastern region Dauphin was replaced by a civilian Sikorsky S-61, which commenced medium-range search and rescue operations over the area, operating from Dublin Airport. The Dauphin thus relieved was to be deployed to Waterford Regional Airport for short-

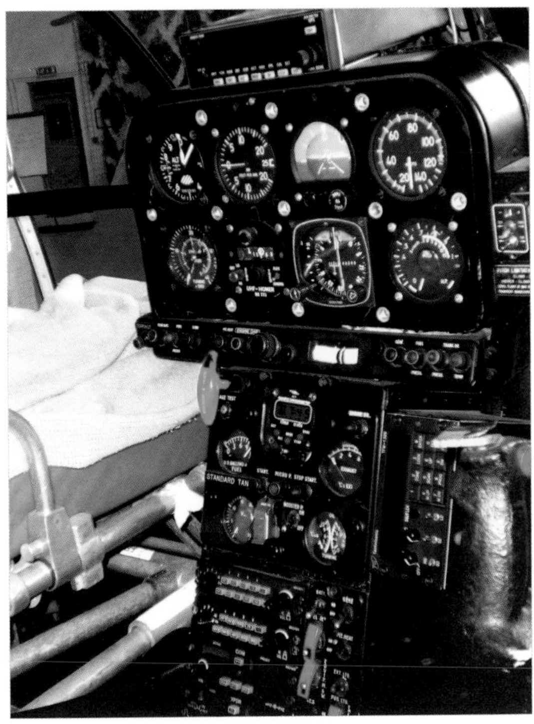
Instrument panel on the Alouette III. Minor upgrades were carried out over the 43 years that the type was in service. (J. Maxwell photo)

range, twenty-four hour search and rescue operations over the south and the south-east, but due to a shortage of trained aircrew, this helicopter would not be deployed for another twelve months.

On July 1, 1998 an Alouette III (No. 214) was deployed to Waterford Regional Airport to commence 'dawn to dusk' search and rescue operations over the south and south-east until the Dauphin became available. Operating from Waterford Regional Airport, known as Air Corps Station, Waterford, a total of 30 search and rescue missions was carried out by the Alouette from July to December of 1998. On the night of July 1, 1999, a Dauphin (No. 248), which had been deployed to the Air Station to replace the Alouette, was destroyed in a crash, resulting in the deaths of the four crew members. The Dauphin was returning to the Air Corps Station in a dense fog after completing a night search and rescue mission over Dungarvan Bay. Due to operational commitments, the Air Corps was unable to replace the crashed helicopter with another Dauphin and an Alouette III (No. 213) was therefore deployed to the Air Corps Station to resume 'dawn to dusk' search and rescue operations on July 2, 1999. On April 22, 2002 the Alouette was replaced by a civilian Sikorsky S-61, under contract to the Irish Coast Guard, for search and rescue operations over the south-east from Waterford Regional Airport. The Alouettes were withdrawn from search and rescue operations in the same year and deployed on army co-operation duties with the Defence Forces.

In their final years of service, the Alouettes were used to provide a fast roping and abseiling capability for the Army Ranger Wing (the Irish Army's special forces unit). They were also used to provide battlefield mobility, moving small numbers of troops during exercises and providing excellent experience in air operations for army units that were about to deploy overseas on UN missions. From 2005 to 2007, two Alouette IIIs were made available for rescue duties for the annual Croagh Patrick mountain pilgrimage which sees many thousands of people climbing the very steep rocky mountain in their bare feet! The Alouettes were used to assist the Irish Mountain Rescue Association teams of volunteers to evacuate casualties down the mountain.

The retirement of the Alouette III from Air Corps service was marked on 21 September 2007 by a synchronised landing by five of the Alouettes, followed by a sixth (Alouette No. 195), thus bringing to an end 44 years of operations by the type. It was a credit to the technicians and maintainers that six of the seven machines still in service were airworthy on their very last day of flight operations, with the non-airworthy example – No. 197 – being used for static display.

Far right: engine details. (J. Maxwell Photo)

Right: The winch was an essential piece of equipment on the Alouette. (J. Maxwell Photo)

Alouette about to take Mountain Rescue personnel on board from a low hover. (J. Maxwell Photo)

Colours & Markings

Initially, the first three Alouette IIIs had an overall silver finish, which was later replaced by an overall light grey finish similar to that applied to the five Alouettes delivered between 1972 and 1974. Dayglo orange panels on the fuselage and tailboom introduced on the first three machines in 1966 was removed when these helicopters were repainted light grey overall.

All of the Alouettes carried their Air Corps serial numbers in black on both sides of the tail boom and, together with their designation and construction number, on the front of the fuselage above the nosewheel. The tri-coloured Celtic boss was carried on both sides of the rear fuselage, with the aircraft's designation and construction number being repeated above and behind this marking on each side. From 1973 onwards, a green, white and orange flag was displayed prominently on both sides of the forward section of the tail boom and the underside of the fuselage. The tail rotor was painted in red and yellow stripes, At least four of the Alouette IIIs (Nos. 195, 196, 197 and 202) had the word 'RESCUE' displayed on the tail boom, which marking was also eventually removed during repainting. Displayed on both entrance doors, the inscription 'HELICOPTER WING' was introduced on these helicopters circa 1998.

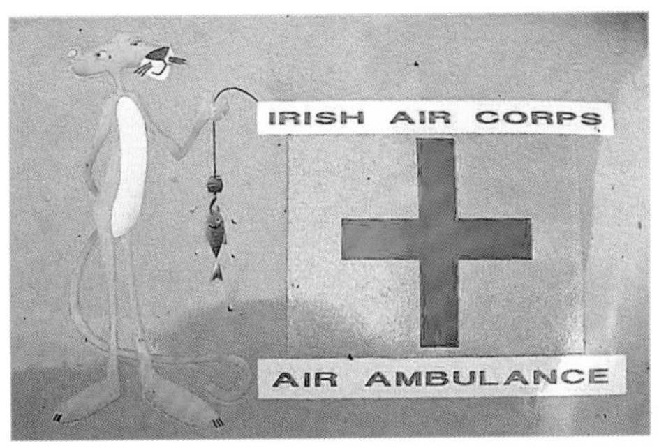

The Pink Panther became the unofficial emblem of the helicopter Search & Rescue Squadron and was painted on helmets, helicopters, lockers etc. Shown here are a few versions of the pink panther that have adorned the Alouette's over the years.

One of the styles of the Search and Rescue badge applied to various helicopters over the years. The scroll reads "Go Mairidís Beo" which translates as "That Others Might Live".

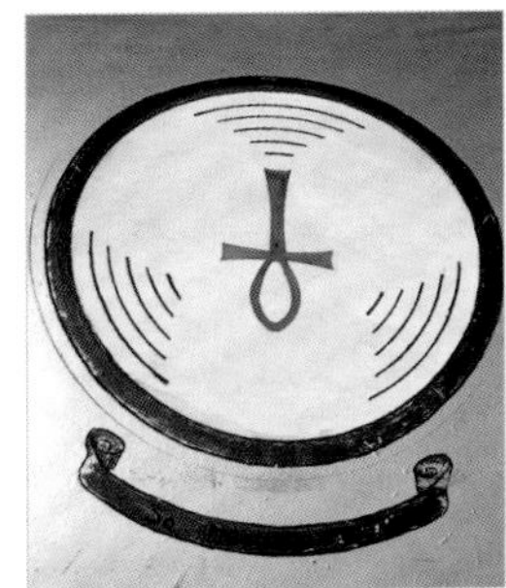

30th anniversary badge applied to all Alouettes except No. 196 during 1997.

Specially commissioned stickers applied to the front of the Alouettes commerorating 25 and 30 years of helicopter operations respectively.

4.2

Reims (Cessna) FR.172H and FR.172K Rocket (1972 – date)

The Cessna 172 is the most successful mass produced light aircraft in history. Designed as a four seat general aviation aircraft, the first production models were delivered in 1956 and the aircraft is still in production as of 2009, with more than 43,000 built to date. The basic airframe configuration has remained almost unchanged since the mid- 1960s, but many updates and refinements have been incorporated over time, resulting in a myriad of different model numbers, detailed descriptions of which are outside the scope of this book. The civil version is marketed under the name Skyhawk, and a military version that was used for elementary flying training by the USAF and eleven other air forces worldwide, is designated T-41 Mescalero.

In February 1960, Cessna acquired a major share in the French aircraft manufacturing company Avions Max Holste, which was re-named Reims Aviation S.A. two years later. Selected models of the Cessna range of light aircraft, including the Model 172, were constructed under licence by Reims Aviation for delivery to customers in Europe and the Middle East.

The prototype of the Reims FR.172E Rocket (c/n 0256), developed by the company from the Model 172, was exhibited at the 1967 Paris Air Show. Powered by the 210-hp. (155kW) Continental IO-360-D 6-cylinder, horizontally-opposed, air-cooled piston engine constructed under licence by Rolls-Royce, this version had a higher cruising speed, increased fuel capacity in the wings,cambered wingtips and other modifications externally and internally.

Following the outbreak of civil strife in Northern Ireland in 1970, the internal security of the Republic of Ireland was also under threat from subversive activities by dissident groups. During this period, the Irish Defence Forces, in support of the Garda Síochana (the Irish police force), became engaged on numerous counter-insurgency operations, but the Air Corps was not equipped with a suitable aircraft type to provide air support for these activities.

The Department of Defence therefore ordered eight FR.172H Rockets, a development of the FR.172E equipped for military service, for delivery in 1972. According to contemporary newspaper reports the eight aircraft, "costing about £20,000 each", were to be used for observation and reconnaissance missions. The aircraft were also to be fitted with the latest navigational aids and radio equipment and could also carry Matra unguided air-to-surface rocket pods.

The first four FR.172H Rockets (c/ns 0343-0346) were delivered by Air Corps pilots to Baldonnel Aerodrome on October 4, 1972, and the remaining four (c/ns 0347-0350) were delivered nine days later. The eight Rockets (as Nos. 203-210) initially entered service with the Advanced Flying Training School, which had undertaken responsibility for the introduction of this aircraft type into service with the Air Corps.

With the arrival of the 'Cessna', as the aircraft has always been referred to in Air Corps service, a new training syllabus was developed to prepare pilots to fly

No. 206 about to take off from a grass strip. Note the 75th anniversary badge that was applied to most of the aircraft in service when the air Corps celebrated its 75th anniversary in 1997. (S. Nolan photo)

Left: Two Reims Cessna FR-172H's flying in close formation near Gormanston. Note the glossy paintwork that replaced the original matt finish in the early 1990s. (A.C. Photographic Section)

army co-operation missions; this included achieving a basic type rating on the aircraft and instrument, night and formation flying training. In this regard, the eight FR.172H Rockets were re-assigned from the Advanced Flying Training School to the Basic Flying Training School and deployed to Air Corps Station Gormanston in 1973, four in January and four in October. As the Air Corps did not at that time have a dedicated army co-operation unit within its structure, this role remained with the Basic Flying Training School. As a consequence of this arrangement, the FR.172Hs were on occasion used to a limited extent for cross country navigation training of pilots in addition to their army co-operation role.

The Cessnas had a strengthened hardpoint under each wing for the attachment of a Matra rocket pod, which could launch twelve 37mm unguided air-to-ground rocket projectiles. Due to a fire at the factory of S.A. Engins Matra in 1972, the pods and rocket projectiles were not delivered until six months after the aircraft had entered service with the Air Corps. The aircraft were also fitted with radio and navigation equipment for both civil and military operations, which included VOR/ILS and ADF receivers for navigation, with VHF twin radio sets to communicate with other aircraft and air traffic control. Over the years, the radio and navigation equipment has been upgraded or replaced with more sophisticated equipment, which has resulted in extra aerials and antennae being fitted to these aircraft for communicating with units of the Defence Forces on the ground. Three of the aircraft (Nos. 205, 208 and 243) also had special radio equipment installed for communicating with the Garda national communications network.
Operating from Air Corps Station Gormanston, the Cessnas were engaged on reconnaissance missions and border patrols along the Republic of Ireland's border with Northern Ireland from 1973 onwards. These aircraft also provided air support for Garda personnel during the transportation of high-profile prisoners or explosives throughout the State and during the delivery of large cash consignments to the commercial banks. Other missions and duties have also been undertaken by the FR.172Hs over the years, including aerial photography, training of air traffic controllers (both military and civil), air ambulance flights, in-shore maritime surveillance patrols, parachute training, target towing, formation flying displays at airshows and transporting Government Ministers and officials. Assistance to Government departments and agencies has also been provided by the aircraft, including aerial surveys to carry out bird, seal and deer counts for the Forestry and Wildlife Services. In 1975 and 1977, the Cessnas were used for air-to-ground firing exercises over the Air Firing Range at Gormanston. Air Firing using these aircraft was later discontinued and the rocket pods withdrawn from use.

The Cessnas are used by the Air Corps for target towing operations over the Air Firing Range at Gormanston during ground-to-air firing exercises by army and naval anti-aircraft units of the Defence Forces, which commenced in 1977. A drogue type target attached to 1,500 metres of steel cable was extended behind the aircraft, operated by a tow winch and a control unit installed in the rear of the Rocket's cabin. An electronically operated Missed Distance Indicator, attached to the towing cable, indicates how close a round had passed by the target drogue, this information being transmitted to a receiver on the ground or on a naval ship. Four FR.172Hs (Nos. 203, 205, 206 and 208) are known to have been used for target towing operations.

The Cessnas were also used by the Defence Forces for parachute training courses, initially from an airstrip at the Curragh Military Camp, which had been

Rare shot of an armed Cessna taking off from Abbeyshrule. (Con Murphy collection)

re-activated for this purpose. The parachute training courses were temporarily suspended by the Air Corps following an accident in the United Kingdom, when a parachutist became entangled in the wheel of a civilian Cessna 172. Following this accident, two of the Air Corps' FR.172Hs (Nos. 206 and 209) were modified by removing the right front seat, the right hand control column and the two rear seats. A special front seat, facing towards the rear, and two lightweight rear seats were fitted to accommodate three parachutists and the pilot in the cabin. The starboard door was also removed and a small platform, mounted on the starboard strut, covered the wheel during parachuting operations. Thus modified, the aircraft were deemed suitable for parachute training, and courses for the Defence Forces re-commenced at Air Corps Station Gormanston in September 1979; over 200 Defence Forces personnel had completed parachute training courses from these aircraft by 1987. These courses by the Defence Forces continued from Clonbullogue airfield, Co. Offaly from 2001 onwards.

In June 1980, following a re-organisation of the structure of the Air Corps, the FR.172Hs were allocated to No. 2 Support Wing, operating from Air Corps Station, Gormanston; this unit was re-designated the Army Co-Operation Squadron in 1986. Following a further structural re-organisation of the Air Corps in 2001, the FR.172Hs were allocated to No. 104 Squadron, No. 1 Operations Wing. In the same year, the aircraft were deployed to Baldonnel Aerodrome when Air Corps Station Gormanston was closed down. Operating from Gormanston, the FR.172Hs had flown a total of 14,000 missions supporting security operations by the Garda and Defence Forces over the previous 28 years.

On April 7, 1981 an FR.172K Rocket (c/n 0671) was delivered to the Baldonnel Aerodrome and (as No. 243) entered service with the Air Corps. This aircraft, which was acquired as a replacement for the first Rocket to be written-off (No. 204), was fitted with wheel spats and tinted glass, and was equipped with "full instrumentation for blind flying", according to contemporary aviation magazine reports. A more streamlined, pointed propeller spinner was also fitted to this aircraft, and was later fitted to the FR.172Hs remaining in service with the Air Corps.

Four Cessnas were written-off in crashes or accidents between 1978 and 2004. The first of these aircraft (No. 204) crashed into the Shannon Estuary during a wildlife survey on September 20, 1978, but both occupants survived without serious injury. On March 1, 1990, following engine failure, No. 207 force-landed in the sea off Air Corps Station Gormanston. The crew was uninjured, but the aircraft had to be written-off due to salt-water corrosion. Following storage in the Apprentice School, this aircraft was delivered to Waterford Regional Airport in August 1998 for fire drill training and evacuation procedures, in exchange for the fuselage of a de Havilland D.H.104 Dove 6 (c/n 04485, ex U.K. civil registration G-ASNG) that had been used at the airport for this type of training. A third FR.172H (No. 209) was written-off following damage to one of its wings, its propeller and undercarriage in a landing accident on November 10, 1993 at Air Corps Station Finner in Donegal. In November 1989, this aircraft had been damaged in a forced landing near Air Corps Station Gormanston, but was repaired and returned to service. The fourth Cessna (No. 243) was written-off in a fatal crash at Clonbullogue, Co. Offaly, on May 6, 2004.

In October 1977, the fuselage of a Cessna 172P (ex U.K. civil registration G-ARLU, c/n 48502) was delivered to Baldonnel Aerodrome from the United Kingdom. This aircraft, which had been damaged beyond repair in a gale in the previous month, was acquired by the Air Corps for use as an instructional airframe by the Apprentice School, but was never allocated an Air Corps serial number.

The remaining Cessnas continue to perform useful roles for the Air Corps and there is no replacement for the type on the horizon, though several aircraft have been put forward by various manufacturers – including Cessna, with its Model 206 Caravan – but so far no orders have been placed. The aircraft is fondly remembered by most Air Corps pilots as the type on which they gained experience following graduation from their basic training.

Number 209 rigged for parachute training with a step on the undercarriage strut. (S. Nolan photo)

To celebrate 25 years of Cessna operations No. 203 was painted in this commemorative colour scheme in 1997. (P.J. Cummins photo)

A Cessna trio heads up the east coast towards their former base at Gormanston. (A.C. Photographic Section)

Right: Details of the 6-cylinder licence built Lycoming engine installed in the Air Corps Cessnas
(J. Maxwell photo)

Right: Drogue towing is just one of the many task carried out by the Cessnas of 104 squadron. A winch is fitted in the rear cabin for the tow cable. Far right photo shows a close up of the Drogue attachment mechanism.
(K. Byrne photos)

Right: instrument panel layout on the Cessna 172. There are a number of variations in the panels across the Cessna fleet including some that still have armament panels for the out of service rockets.
(J. Maxwell photo)

Another view of the Cessna 's engine. They remain the last aircraft to use avgaz in the air Corps inventory. (S. Nolan photo)

Interior trim of Air Corps Cessnas. As always variations exist between different airframes. (J. Maxwell photo)

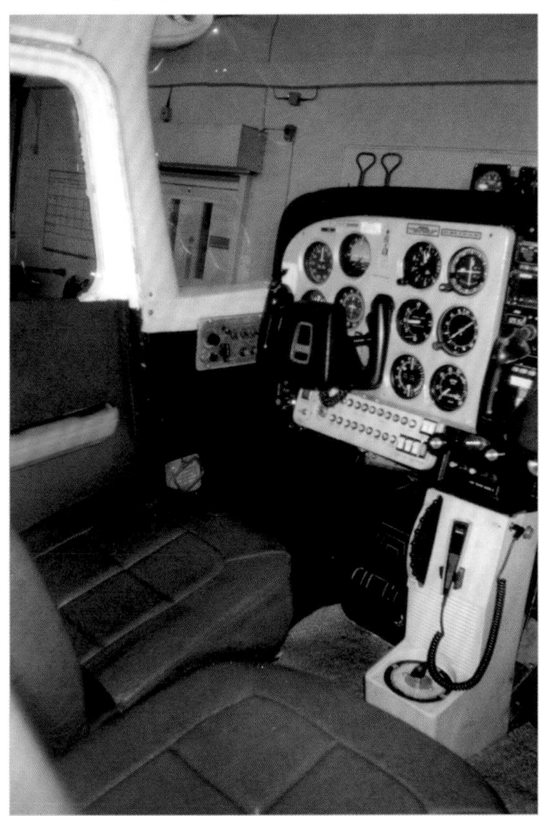

Colours & Markings

The Cessna FR.172Hs were the first aircraft in service with the Air Corps to have an overall matt khaki-green finish. From the early '90's this was changed to a high gloss finish, the paint used being Akzo Nobel 042002; this shade is virtually identical to U.S. Federal Standard FS14079 Forest Green widely used in many military camouflage schemes. The tricolour flag also appeared on the tailfins following the repainting at this time. The Celtic Boss is displayed on both sides of the fuselage centre section and on the upper and lower surfaces of both wings. Each aircraft's serial number is displayed in white on both sides of the fuselage behind the Celtic boss, and on the underside of the port wing. One of the FR.172Hs (No. 203) had a Mickey Mouse cartoon character displayed on the port side of the tailfin for a short period. In 1997, to celebrate the FR.172H's twenty-five years of service with the Air Corps, this aircraft had the upper section of the tailfin painted blue with the lower section painted in green, white and orange stripes. The number "25" was displayed on the blue section, "Cessna FR 172H" on the green stripe, "Reims Rocket" on the orange section, all in white, and "1972-1997", in black, was displayed on the white stripe.

4.3

Aérospatiale (Fouga) CM.170-2 Super Magister (1974 – 1999)

During the late 1940s, it was becoming clear to the operators of the first generation of jet fighters that training on propeller-driven aircraft did not adequately prepare pilots for the very different flying characteristics of jet aircraft, in particular the slow response of the early jet engines to throttle movements, and the lack of propeller drag to reduce speed during descent. Initially, manufacturers provided two-seat training versions of the jet fighters then in service, such as the de Havilland Vampire T.11, but ultimately the consensus at the time was that an altogether new and more cost-effective approach was needed.

In 1948, in response to a requirement issued by the French Ministère de l'Air for a basic trainer, engineers Robert Castello and Pierre Mauboussin, working for the company Etablissements Fouga et Cie came up with a tandem-seat, twin-engine design, the "CM.130R", with the letters 'CM'standing for the designers' names.

Powered by two Turbomeca Palas turbojets with 1.56 kN thrust each, this proposal did not meet the Ministère de l'Air requirements, so Castello and Mauboussin came up with a new design powered by two Turbomeca Marbore turbojets with 3.92 kN thrust each. The new design was designated CM.170R. Named Magister, the first of three prototypes (carrying the French civil registration F-ZWRO) flew for the first time on July 23, 1952. Ten pre-production Magisters were ordered in June 1953. These aircraft, with the three prototypes, were used for manufacturer's trials, flight testing and operational evaluation by the various French flight testing agencies throughout 1954 and 1955. An initial batch of 95 Magisters was ordered in September 1953, with production commencing in 1955, and the first production aircraft flying for the first time on February 29, 1956. Deliveries to the École de l'Air (the Armée de l'Air's training school) commenced in May 1957. A total of 277 CM.170-1 Magisters was delivered to the Armée de l'Air over the next five years. The Magister was to become the standard basic training aircraft with the Armée de l'Air for the next 40 years, and can lay claim to being the first mass produced, purpose built jet trainer in the world. Production and development of the Magister was taken over by a new company, Societé Air Fouga, in September 1956. Two years later this company amalgamated with Etablissements Potez, and was renamed Potez Air-Fouga, which was absorbed into another French company, Sud Aviation, in April 1967. Sud Aviation in turn was absorbed into Aérospatiale, which itself is now part of EADS, the European Aeronautic Defence and Space Company, formed through the merger on July 10, 2000, of DaimlerChrysler Aerospace AG (DASA) of Germany, Aérospatiale-Matra of France, and Construcciones Aeronáuticas SA (CASA) of Spain. A total of 460

Right: Fouga Magisters on the flight line in 1979. Note the equipment trolley using wheels from a long retired aircraft in the background. (J. Bigley photo)

Above: The Fouga Magister was to play a key role in training Air Corps pilots from 1974 until the types retirement in 1999. Note the blind flying hood folded back in the rear cockpit. (P. Cunniffe photo)

CM.170-1 Magisters in were built in France by all of the companies concerned, and a further 469 were also assembled or licence-built in Finland, Germany and Israel.

Following the formation of Aérospatiale in 1970, a number of Magisters that had been withdrawn from use by the Armée de l'Air and other air forces were acquired by the new company. Overhauled and refurbished to 'as new' standard by Aérospatiale, which included the installation of more powerful Marbore VI engines, these aircraft were re-designated as CM.170-2 Super Magisters and offered for sale to interested air forces.

From 1970 onwards, the Irish Air Corps had a requirement for an advanced training aircraft to replace its de Havilland Vampire T.55s, which were about to be withdrawn from use. A number of aircraft types were evaluated by the Air Corps to fulfil this requirement, including the Aermacchi MB.326 and the CM.170 Magister. On March 21, 1974 a CM.170-1 Magister was demonstrated to the Air Corps at Baldonnel Aerodrome and also gave a flying display over the Curragh Military Camp, Co. Kildare. While the aviation press at the time took the view that the MB 326 was likely to be the winner, in April 1974 the Minister for Defence announced that six CM.170-2 Super Magisters had been ordered from Aérospatiale. According to contemporary newspaper reports, the six Magisters were acquired as part of a £1,250,000 package, which included conversion courses for Air Corps pilots and the training of technicians by Aérospatiale.

The first two CM.170-2 Super Magisters (c/ns 357 and 358) were delivered by Air Corps pilots to Baldonnel Aerodrome on August 11, 1975. During the final stage of the delivery flight, the Super Magisters were escorted by the last two Vampire T.55s in service with the Air Corps. The third and fourth Super Magisters (c/ns 359 and 390) were delivered to the Air Corps on February 16, 1976, followed by the fifth and sixth (c/ns 298 and 299) on November 13, 1976. Radio and navigation systems, instrumentation and other equipment to Air Corps specifications, was installed in these aircraft at Dublin Airport by technicians from Aer Lingus. The six Super Magisters (as Nos. 215 to 220) entered service with No. 1 Fighter Squadron; however, from 1980 onwards, following the re-organisation of the structure of the Air Corps, these aircraft were operated by the Light Strike Squadron, No. 1 Support Wing and Advanced Flying Training School, Training Wing.

Three of the aircraft (c/ns 357, 358 and 359) had been delivered to the Austrian Air Force in October 1962, and the fourth (c/n 390) in April 1963, as CM.170-1 Magisters. One ex-Austrian Air Force codes 4D-YL) had been withdrawn from use in October 1971, followed by the other three in 1972 ex-Austrian Air Force codes 4D-YJ, 4D-YK and 4D-YU respectively).

The final two aircraft (c/ns 298 and 299), which had apparently only accumulated a total of six flying hours each, were from the batch of six CM.170-1 Magisters originally destined for delivery to the Katanga Air Force, but placed in storage in 1961. These aircraft have an interesting history. Forty-five CM.170-1 Magisters (c/ns 258-302) were ordered by the Belgian Air Force in 1958 for advanced flying training. Twenty entered service with the Continuation Flying Training School, which operated from Kamina Air Base in the Belgian Congo, but were returned to Belgium following the granting of independence to that colony, which became the Republic of Congo, later re-named Zaire. In June 1960, when the province of Katanga seceded from the Republic of Congo to set up an independent state, a civil war erupted. From the batch of 45 Magisters ordered for the Belgian Air Force, nine (c/ns 294-302) were secretly diverted from this order for delivery to the Katanga Air Force. However only three of these aircraft (c/ns 294-296) were actually delivered, this occurring in February 1961. One of the aircraft was used to attack Irish troops serving with the UN at Jadotville in the Congo. International pressure prevented delivery of the remaining six Magisters, which were placed in storage at an airfield near Brussels. In 1972, these six aircraft were acquired by Aérospatiale for overhaul and refurbishment, and were delivered to the Air Corps and to other air forces.

Right: Line up of all six Fouga Magisters at Baldonnel. They only occasion that all six flew together was on 14th April 1981. (A.C. Photographic Section)

Operated by the Training Wing, the Fougas, as they were always known in the Air Corps, were used for advanced flying training. The training syllabus at the time consisted of 150 hours in the SIAI Marchetti SF.260WE Warrior, followed by 50 hours in the Fouga. For pilots moving onto the Fouga, the key differences lay in the tandem seat layout compared to the side–by–side seating of the Marchetti. As described by Comdt. Paul Whelan, who completed his basic training on the Fouga and subsequently went on to be an instructor and member of the Silver Swallows aerobatic team, the Fouga had a much more "agricultural" and heavier feel to it by comparison with the Marchetti, but it was nonetheless a joy to fly. The tandem seat layout tended to make trainee pilots feel much more isolated than the side-by-side arrangement, so much so that one instructor used to poke trainees with a golf club to ensure that they knew he was still there! It was estimated that a total of 110 student pilots completed their training on the Fougas over their 22 years of service with the Air Corps. The aircraft were also used for type conversion courses for new instructors, totalling 32 flying hours.

Armed with two 7.62 mm machine-guns mounted in the nose with 200 rounds apiece and underwing rocket pods, each containing seven 68 mm rocket projectiles, the Fougas were also used by the Light Strike Squadron for weapons training exercises against targets in the sea, at the Air Firing Range, Gormanston, Co. Meath. Operating these aircraft the squadron also carried out simulated air attacks during military exercises conducted by the Defence Forces and against ships of the Naval Service. Air support for units of the Defence Forces could also be provided by the Fougas in the event of combat operations.

The Fougas were also used as ceremonial escorts for aircraft conveying dignitaries on State visits and for flypasts during other State occasions. The Boeing 747-100 of Aer Lingus that brought Pope John Paul II on an official visit to Ireland in September 1979 was escorted by four Fougas during the final stages of its flight. During official visits to the State by sitting U.S. Presidents in 1984 and 1995, the Fougas carried out fly-pasts over the welcoming ceremonies at Dublin Airport.

In 1987, the six aircraft underwent a complete overhaul by Aérospatiale to extend their service lives for a further ten years. Fitted with 230 litre long-range fuel tanks on each wingtip, two Fougas at a time were delivered to the factory in France for this overhaul. Despite intensive utilisation by the Air Corps, none of the Fougas were written-off in accidents or crashes. One aircraft (No. 215) was damaged when the starboard undercarriage strut collapsed during a landing at Baldonnel Aerodrome on January 15, 1986, but was returned to service with the Light Strike Squadron following repairs by Air Corps technicians. On April 23, 1991, another Fouga (No. 217) force-landed in a field near Whitegate, Co. Cork, because of a fuel shortage, but was not damaged. The aircraft was dismantled by Air Corps technicians and transported by road to Baldonnel Aerodrome, where it was re-assembled and returned to service.

Right: Badges applied to the Fougas as used by the Silver swallows Aerobatic Team. (J. Maxwell photo)

The Fouga Magister had a number of unique features. Unlike modern jet trainers, the rear seat was not raised to allow the instructor in the rear seat to see over the head of the student pilot in the front. The aircraft was instead equipped with a periscope for the instructor, this being useful for seeing the runway on final approach and in ground manoeuvring.

A significant difference between the Fouga and most aircraft was its 'V-tail' or 'Butterfly Tail'. This arrangement saved some weight compared to conventional tail surfaces, but otherwise did not confer any significant performance advantage on the aircraft. The Fouga was not equipped with ejection seats. Instead, each pilot wore a backpack-style parachute, which for semi-automatic operation had the D-ring attached to the aircraft via a static line. Fortunately, no Air Corps pilot ever had to part company from an airborne Fouga. The emergency procedure was to roll the aircraft inverted, jettison the canopies and literally fall out, hoping that the pilot would pass through the gap created by the butterfly tail and that the static line would open the parachute.

Four Fougas flying in box formation participated in an Irish airshow for the first time in 1979, at an event held at Fairyhouse Racecourse, Co. Dublin. Formation aerobatics by three of the aircraft were introduced at an airshow held at Baldonnel Aerodrome in 1986, and four Fougas went on to equip an Air Corps aerobatic display team, the Silver Swallows (the name was derived from the colour of the aircraft and their distinctive V-tail and was chosen by Brig. Gen. Patrick Cranfield), which participated in an airshow held at the same venue in 1987. Two years later, the Silver Swallows, the first aerobatic team to be officially recognised by the Department of Defence since the formation of the Air Corps in 1922, participated in an airshow outside the State for the first time, attending an event held at Newtownards, Co. Down. On July 25, 1990, the team, flying five Super Magisters (Nos. 215, 217, 218, 219 and 220), provided an aerobatic display at an event held at RAF Brawdy, in Wales, and in so doing became the first Air Corps aircraft to participate in an overseas airshow. Due to increased training commitments throughout 1994 and 1995, the Fougas were unavailable for aerobatic team displays at airshows at home or abroad during those years.

In August 1996, the Silver Swallows aerobatic team was re-formed under the leadership of Captain Graeme Martin. The team underwent an intensive training programme to participate in the celebrations marking the 75th Anniversary of the formation of the Air Corps, which were held throughout the following year. All of the training was carried out in the evenings and at weekends, so as to ensure that the aircraft continued to be available for their regular training duties. Training initially consisted of a two ship formation, progressing from high wingovers to full vertical loops. Each member of the team was trained separately with the leader before building up from a two-ship to a three-ship, and ultimately to the full four-ship, formation team. The number two position was occupied by Captain Peter McDonnell, number three was Captain (now Comdt.) Paul Whelan and number four was Lt. Chris Keegan.

In July 1997, the team participated in the special 75th Anniversary airshow at Baldonnel Aerodrome. Later that month the Silver Swallows were awarded the Lockheed-Martin Canestra Trophy for the 'best flying display by an overseas participant' at the prestigious Royal International Air Tattoo, held annually at RAF Fairford in the U.K. This was an extraordinary achievement, considering that they were up against such well-known teams as the Patrouille de France and the Royal Jordanian Falcons flying faster aircraft equipped with smoke generators. The Silver Swallows' routine was performed close to the crowd centre and consisted mainly of vertical manoeuvres requiring sustained 4.5g turns. With the Fouga's relatively long thin wing, the team members worked hard to minimise the visual effect of wing flexing to viewers on the ground. In the following month, the Silver Swallows also participated in airshows in Scotland and Belgium, and the team was disbanded after a final aerobatic display at an airshow held at Shannon International Airport on September 21, 1997.

Two of the Fougas (Nos. 215 and 216) were withdrawn from use on December 19, 1997, and placed in storage at Baldonnel Aerodrome. Two more (Nos. 217 and 218) were withdrawn from use on April 4 and May 23, 1998, respectively. In the same year, No. 219 was grounded for a 300 flying hours inspection, but did not fly again. The last Fouga in service with the Air Corps, No. 220, was withdrawn from use on June 11, 1999.

Following their withdrawal from service the Fougas were placed in storage at Baldonnel Aerodrome before being donated to various institutions and agencies in Ireland and Europe. No. 215 was overhauled and repainted for display beside the passenger terminal at Baldonnel Aerodrome. In November 2004 this aircraft was transferred to the Dublin Institute of Technology, Bolton St., for use as an instructional airframe. No. 216 was donated to Cork Institute of Technology but remained in storage outdoors at Cork Airport. In December 2005 this aircraft was returned to Baldonnel Aerodrome to be overhauled and repainted for eventual static display at the Irish Air Corps

Below: The sharp end of the Fouga, which could be armed with machine guns and rocket pods. (G. Norman photo)

Right: No ejector seats were fitted to the Fouga.
(J. Maxwell photo)

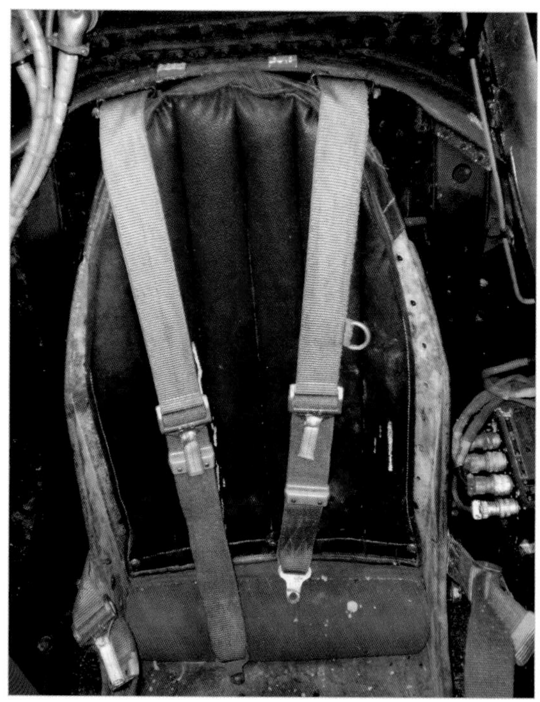

Museum. No. 217 was donated by the Air Corps to the Austrian Air Force historic aircraft collection and was collected by a Lockheed C-130K Hercules of that air force in March 2005. No.219 was retained in the Air Corps Museum.

Finally, mention should be made of the Fouga Magister instructional airframe used by the Air Corps Apprentice School. On September 9, 1975, a CM.170-1 Magister (c/n 79) that had been presented to the Air Corps by the Armée de l'Air was delivered in a Nord Noratlas. The aircraft (coded 3-KE in Armée de l'Air service) had been written-off after the undersides of the fuselage of had been damaged in a forced landing on November 13, 1974, having served with several units of the Armée de l'Air with the Air Attaché at the French Embassy in Stockholm in Sweden. The Armée de l'Air markings were retained on the Magister after delivery to the Air Corps, and the allocated Air Corps serial number (No. 221) was never displayed on this aircraft. It was eventually dismantled and placed in storage at Baldonnel Aerodrome.

Right Cockpit details of the Fouga.
(A. Smith photos)

Colours & Markings

The Fouga Magisters had an overall painted silver finish (not natural metal), with day-glo red on the nose, the outer sections of the wingtip fuel tanks and in a band painted around the rear fuselage section. The tri-coloured Celtic boss was displayed on both sides of the fuselage centre section, and on the outer sections of the upper and under surfaces of both wings. Each aircraft's serial number was displayed in black on both sides of the front fuselage section, on the underside of the starboard wing, and in smaller numerals on the rear fuselage section and on the front of both wingtip fuel tanks. The aircraft had a black anti-glare panel in front of the cockpit, with red and white stripes on the VOR antennae mounted on both sides of the nose.

The aircraft also had two decorative badges on either side of the nose during the 1997 display season. One badge was the Silver Swallows' crest and the other was a light strike squadron badge.

Right: Spectacular photo of the Fouga in its element. (D. Corcoran photo)

4.4

Siai-Marchetti SF.260WE Warrior (1977 – 2006)

Designed by Stelio Frati, a freelance Italian aircraft designer, the SF.260 was an elegant, high performance three-seat trainer, and the only Italian-built fixed wing aircraft to see service with the Air Corps. The prototype was designated the F.250 (it was powered by a 250 hp Lycoming engine) and first flew on July 15, 1964. Production aircraft, all built by SIAI Marchetti, had a 260 hp Lycoming engine and were designated SF.260, this model flying for the first time in 1966.

Initially designed as a sporting and touring aircraft, development of the aircraft for military elementary and intermediate flying training was undertaken by SIAI-Marchetti, which included structural strengthening of the fuselage, wings and undercarriage. The prototype (c/n 3-79, registered I-SJAV) flew for the first time on October 10, 1970 and was designated SF.260MX. All of the modifications introduced on this prototype were incorporated in all subsequent civil and military variants of the aircraft, which were designated SF.260D (civil) and SF.260M (military). Powered by the same engine, a light tactical support aircraft retaining the same training capability was developed from the SF.260M, the prototype (registered I-SJAV) flying for the first time in May 1972. This variant was designated SF.260W Warrior, and was fitted with two NATO standard underwing pylons to carry gun pods, rocket pods, bombs, camera pods or jettisonable auxiliary fuel tanks.

The prototype of another military variant of this aircraft, which retained the same training and tactical support capabilities but was powered by a 350 shp Allison 250-B17C turboprop engine, flew for the first time on April 8, 1981; this version was designated SF.260TP. The three military variants of the SF.260 have at the time of writing been delivered to the air forces of 22 countries worldwide.

From the mid 1970s, the Irish Air Corps had a requirement for an aircraft type to replace the de Havilland Chipmunk and the Hunting Percival Provost for basic and advanced flying training. A number of aircraft types was evaluated by the Air Corps to fulfil this requirement, including the Saab MFI.17 Supporter, the Scottish Aviation Bulldog and the SF.260W Warrior.

On April 4, 1976, the Department of Defence ordered ten SF.260WE Warriors (The suffix letter 'E' denoted 'Éire'). According to a statement from the Department of Defence at the time, the Warriors, were "the best buy for flying, technical and economic reasons", and would be used for "initial training up to jet training stage" which would include "primary pilot schooling, aerobatics and formation flying, air firing, operational

Right: The Warrior lives up to its name unleashing a salvo of rockets over the firing range at Gormanston. (A.C. Photographic Section)

Left: View of Marchetti 222 showing the large underwing serial on the right wing. (S. Nolan photo)

training of pilots, and…for basic and refresher courses for instructors".

On March 4, 1977 the first four SF.260WE Warriors (c/ns 24-01/289-292) were delivered to Baldonnel Aerodrome by Air Corps pilots, who had completed a conversion course on this aircraft at the company's factory. The remaining six Warriors (c/ns 24-05/293-298) were delivered to the Air Corps on April 16, 1977. The Warriors (as Nos. 222-231) entered service with the Basic and Advanced Flying Training Schools. In 1980, following a re-organisation of the structure of the Air Corps, the Warriors were allocated to the Basic Flying Training School, Training Wing, which was re-designated as the Flight Training School, Air Corps College, in 2001.

The cockpit of the Warrior, which was fitted with dual controls, could accommodate an instructor and student pilot in the front, seated side-by-side, with another person in the rear seat, and the aircraft were used for basic and intermediate flying training by the Air Corps; the Warriors were also used for instructor training courses. A total of 150 flying hours was accumulated by a student pilot on the Warrior, including aerobatics, instrument, formation and night flying, navigation and weapons training. Thereafter, students would progress onto the Fouga Magister for another 50 hours of flying training before graduating. Weapon pylons under the Warriors' wings could carry Matra gun pods containing 7.62mm general purpose machine-guns, or Matra rocket pods containing six 68mm rocket projectiles, and thus armed, the aircraft were used for weapons training exercises over the Air Firing Range at Gormanston Military Camp.

The "Marchettis", as the aircraft were colloquially known in Air Corps service, also had a little publicised reconnaissance role and could be equipped with Vinten Reconnaissance Pods containing cameras for air-to-ground photographic missions, including infra-red photography. A full range of communications and navigation equipment, to Air Corps specifications, was installed in the Warriors, comprising dual VHF/AM radios, automatic direction finder, an IFF ("identification friend or foe") transponder, distance measuring equipment (DME) and VHF/AM radio for communications with other units of the Defence Forces. A total of 101 student pilots had completed "Wings" courses on the Warriors by 1997, with 64 Air Corps pilots also qualifying as instructors on the aircraft in the same period. With relatively small, laminar flow wings that resulted in a high wing loading, the SF.260WE took considerable skill to fly accurately, and as such was an ideal trainer aircraft.

On March 3, 1977 the fuselage of a SF.260MC (c/n 11-09) was delivered to Baldonnel Aerodrome to be used as an instructional airframe (as No. 233) by the Technical Training Squadron (re-named the Apprentice School, Training Wing in 1980). This aircraft (ex Italian civil registration I-SJAS) had been in service with the Zaire Air Force (as AT 109).

On January 24, 1978 one of the Warriors (No. 224) was written-off in a landing accident at Baldonnel

Left: Little publicised Vicon reconnaissance pod mounted on the right wing pylon of a Marchetti. (P.J. Cummins photo)

Aerodrome, and a replacement was ordered by the Department of Defence. The replacement aircraft SF.260WE (c/n 24-11/373) was delivered to Baldonnel Aerodrome on April 2, 1979 and entered service with the Training Wing as No. 235, but was written-off in a fatal flying accident at Dunboyne, Co. Meath, on February 10, 1982. A third Warrior (No. 223) was written-off in a fatal crash on December 13, 1990 at Edenburt, near Virginia, Co. Cavan, followed by a fourth (No. 228) in a crash at Clondalkin, Co. Dublin, on August 23, 1993, although in this instance the crew escaped without injury. In 1989, one of the Warriors (No. 230) was damaged in an accident at Baldonnel Aerodrome but was returned to service following repairs by the Air Corps. Warrior No. 227, which had been damaged in a forced landing at Clane, Co. Kildare, on February 21, 1991, was transported to Italy in the Air Corps' CASA CN.235 in October of the same year and underwent repairs by the manufacturer before returning to service with the Training Wing. Towards the end of their service with the Air Corps, the service's engineers took on the task of redesigning the instrument panel to replace instruments for which spares were becoming scarce, and to improve the cockpit ergonomics.

On June 3, 1991, three SF.260Ds (c/ns 707, 770 and 772), which had been leased by the Air Corps from Skylane Flight Management Ltd. were delivered from the USA to Baldonnel Aerodrome to enable pilot training commitments to be fulfilled in view of the Warriors lost to attrition. The three aircraft, which had been evaluated for the 'Enhanced Flight Screener' programme being introduced by the USAF at that time were leased at a fixed charge per flying hour up to 180 hours. Operating from Air Corps Station Gormanston, the three SF.260Ds were not allocated Air Corps serial numbers but retained their U.S. civil registrations (i.e., N402FD, N405FD and N407FD), and were used by the Basic Flying Training School to provide initial elementary flying training for student pilots. From May 1992, the SF.260Ds were operated again by the Air Corps, under the same leasing terms, before returning to the USA in November of that year. The SF.260Ds were lighter than the W version, and the Air Corps' instructor pilots therefore tended to prefer them for their aerobatic qualities over the heavier Warriors.

In 2004, eight Pilatus PC-9M Turboprop trainers entered service with the Air Corps to replace both the Marchettis and the Fouga Magisters. For a time, the Marchettis were kept in operational storage until six of them were sold by tender in 2006 to Airpower Aviation Resources based in Los Angeles The six aircraft were dismantled in late 2006 and crated for shipment to Los Angeles; following their arrival they entered the U.S. civil register on 15 May 2007. The seventh aircraft, SF.260WE No. 231, was retained by the Air Corps for eventual display in its museum.

Colours & Markings

The SF.260WE Warriors were initially painted matt olive green overall, which was replaced by a high-gloss finish from 1993 onwards. The paint used was Akzo Nobel green 042002, which is virtually identical to the U.S. Federal Standard FS14079 Forest Green shade used on many U.S. military aircraft. The Warriors had a black anti-glare panel in front of the cockpit and day-glo red was applied to the outer sections of the wing-tips, the upper tip of the tailfin, the tips of the tailplane, the fuselage nose and the propeller spinner. The tri-coloured Celtic boss was displayed on both sides of the fuselage mid-section and on the outer sections of the upper and undersurfaces of both wings. The Air Corps serial number allocated to each Warrior was displayed in white on both sides of the rear fuselage section, behind the Celtic boss, and on the underside of

Right: Three leased SF.260's were used in the early 1990s to cover a shortfall in available aircraft for pilot training. They retained their US registrations during the period of the lease. (M. Nason photo via R. James)

the starboard wing. From about 1993 onwards, a green, white and orange fin flash was displayed on the upper section of both sides of each Warrior's tailfin. Various animal and bird characters – mostly from television and film cartoons – have also been displayed on the tailfins of the Warriors. The animal characters comprised 'Barney' (No. 222), 'Pluto' (No. 227), and 'Goofy' (No. 230), 'Sylvester' (No.228), 'Bugs Bunny' (No. 229) 'Pepé le Peu' (No. 226) and 'Road Runner' (No. 225). Other characters comprised a crane smoking a cigar (No. 231) and an eagle (No. 226), while No. 230 displayed a cartoon character depicting a pre-historic man carrying a club. A devil character painted in red was also displayed on the tailfin of another of these aircraft (No. 225). No official sanction was ever received in relation to the display of these cartoon characters.

Under the hood, the 260hp Lycoming engine that powers the Marchetti.
(J. Maxwell photo)

The three SF.260Ds had an overall white finish with a black anti-glare panel in front of the cockpit, their U.S. civil registrations being displayed in black on both sides of the mid-fuselage section behind the cockpit.

The cockpit was redesigned by Air Corps engineers. A comparison of the two types is shown here.
(J. Maxwell & S. Nolan photos)

Left: Gun pods (shown here), rocket pods and camera systems could be carried by the Marchetti in Air Corps service.
(J. Maxwell photo)

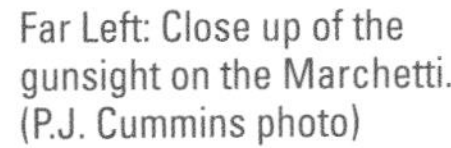

Far Left: Close up of the gunsight on the Marchetti.
(P.J. Cummins photo)

Left: Just of the many cartoon characters that have adorned the tailfins of the Marchettis during their service.
(S. Nolan photo)

4.5

Beechcraft Super King Air 200 (1977 – date)

The Beechcraft company of Wichita, Kansas has developed a highly successful range of light commercial aircraft since its inception in 1932. Many of these light twin engine aircraft found favour with air forces worldwide and the company has engaged in a process of continuous development of its various product lines. The Kingair was a pressurised and turboprop powered development of the earlier Queen Air range. In the 1970's Beech produced a further development of the Kingair with a fuselage extension and a new T tail configuration as compared to its progenitor. Powered by the highly reliable Pratt & Whitney Canada PT6A-41 engines developing 850shp(649kW) this version was marketed as the Beech Super Kingair 200 and became a bestseller. The military version for the US armed forces was known as the beech C-12 Huron and this too has been developed into a multitude of special mission variants. The type has subsequently been developed into the Beech King Air 350, which remains in production at the time of writing. More than 6,600 aircraft of the King Air line have been delivered to date, and these are operated by corporate, commercial, military and special mission operators in more than 94 countries.

In 1973, following the accession of the Republic of Ireland to the European Economic Community (EEC), a 170-nautical mile economic zone was established over the sea areas around the Irish coastline, which was extended to 200 nautical miles four years later, covering an area of 132,000 square miles (341,880 square kilometres). On April 1, 1977, the Irish Government assumed responsibility for the protection of the maritime resources in the extended economic zone, which was to be monitored by aircraft of the Irish Air Corps and ships of the Irish Naval Service. To fulfil this operational commitment, the Air Corps required an aircraft powered by two turboprop engines, with the range and endurance for sustained maritime operations, which also had the latest communications and navigation equipment installed. A number of such types were evaluated by the Air Corps, including the Britten Norman Defender, Shorts Skyvan, Hawker Siddeley HS 748 Coastguarder, GAF Nomad, Cessna Titan, Swearingen Merlin, Cessna 404, Dornier Do-28D Skyservant, Fokker F.27 Maritime and the Beech Super King Air 200. At that time there were two de Havilland Doves in service with the Air Corps, operated by the General Purpose Flight, which were not suitable for sustained maritime surveillance operations and were almost at the end of their operational lives.

In March 1977, the Minister for Defence announced in the Dáil (the Irish parliament) that a Beechcraft Super King Air 200 "for fishery protection and surveillance around the coast" had been leased from United Beech of Scandinavia, the U.S. company's

Right: Atmospheric shot of King Air No. 234 in front of the old terminal at Dublin Airport. (J. Bigley photo)

Tucked in tight beside the Learjet 45 from which this shot was taken using a 50mm lens, King Air No.240 has clocked up over 16,000 flight hours since entering service in 1980.
(K. Byrne photo)

Swedish agency, which had responsibility for marketing the aircraft in Europe. The Super King Air 200 was to be leased for a period of three years, commencing in April, with Beechcraft providing initial flight training on the type for four Air Corps pilots in the USA. On March 10, 1977, a Super King Air 200 (c/n BB-208) was delivered to Baldonnel Aerodrome; this aircraft was practically new, having flown for the first time only in December 1976 and accumulating a total of just 57 flying hours in the interim. The Super King Air 200, which carried a Swedish civil registration (SE-GRR) and was finished in a blue and white colour scheme, underwent intensive trials and evaluation by the Air Corps throughout March. Operated by the General Purpose Flight, the Super King Air 200 (as No. 232) commenced regular fishery protection and surveillance flights in April over the sea areas off the south and west coasts of Ireland. This aircraft was also used for crew conversion training, instrument training and SAR missions. The Swedish civil registration was replaced with the Irish civil registration EI-BCY. The Super King Air 200 was the first aircraft type powered by turboprop engines, and only the second U.S.-manufactured aircraft, to enter service with the Air Corps, the first having been the Lockheed Hudson many years previously!

It would not have been possible for the Air Corps to adequately carry out its maritime surveillance role with just one aircraft, so a second Super King Air 200 (c/n BB-376) was leased from United Beech of Scandinavia; this aircraft was delivered to Baldonnel Aerodrome on July 12, 1978, and (as No. 234) entered service with the General Purpose Flight. This Super King Air 200 (ex-U.S. civil registration N4914M) had an overall white finish with a black and orange cheatline, was allocated the Irish civil registration EI-BFJ, but this were not displayed on the aircraft. In December 1979, in a move that was described at the time as an interim measure, the two Super King Air 200s were purchased outright by the Department of Defence to fulfil the requirement for maritime patrol aircraft; it was intended that the aircraft would be operated by the Air Corps in this role for no more than five years. From June 1980 onwards, following the restructuring of the Air Corps, these two Super King Air 200s were operated by the Maritime Squadron, No. 1 Support Wing.

A third Super King Air 200 was acquired by the Air Corps in 1980 from the Beechcraft Aircraft Corporation. On May 7, this aircraft (c/n BB-672) was flown by Comdt. Mick Hipwell and Capt. Paddy O'Shea from the company's factory in the United States to Baldonnel Aerodrome; this was the first transatlantic flight by an Air Corps aircraft and crew. The Super King Air 200 (as No. 240) entered service with the Transport and Training Squadron, No. 1 Support Wing, This aircraft was used for a wide variety of tasks, such as pilot conversion training, transport of Government Ministers and officials (for which the aircraft was operated by the Ministerial Air Transport Service. and emergency air ambulance missions, including the transport of seriously ill patients, medical teams and human organs for transplant operations to British and Irish hospitals. This Super King Air 200 has never been used in the maritime role, but its acquisition allowed the other two Super King Air 200s to be used solely for maritime surveillance and SAR operations. From 2001, Super King Air 200 No. 240 was operated by 102 Squadron, No. 1 Operations Wing.

Flying from Baldonnel, the Super King Air 200s of the Maritime Squadron were normally engaged on

Right: Normally kept in pristine condition, King Air NO. 240 is seen here at Waterford Airport following a long flight. Note the pattern of exhaust staining on the wings due to the wash from the propellers.
(D. Leahy photo)

Dáily surveillance flights over the sea areas of the economic zone. On these flights, which could last for up to four hours at an altitude below 5,000 feet, and cover an area of about 10,000 square miles, the Super King Air 200s normally carried a crew of four, comprising a pilot, co-pilot and two observers. Ships detected on the aircraft's Bendix radar and suspected of illegal fishing or other prohibited activities were investigated by the patrolling Super King Air 200, which would descend to an altitude of about 200 feet for this purpose. Using a hand-held Hasselblad camera, one of the observers would photograph the ship concerned through a cabin window in the rear fuselage.

If requested to do so by the Marine and Rescue Co-Ordination Centre at Shannon International Airport, the two King Air 200s also carried out SAR missions over the sea areas around the Irish coastline. In later years, the Super King Air 200s were also used to fly 'top cover' for Air Corps helicopters engaged on SAR missions, providing navigation "fixes" and course information for the helicopter crews. The Super King Air 200s also relayed radio communications to and from shore bases during low-level SAR operations by the helicopters over the sea.

Below: The cockpit of the King Air 200. Since the retirement of the Fouga Magisters in 1999, most of the twin engine training has been carried out on the King Air.

These two Super King Air 200s were involved in a number of dramatic SAR operations over the sea areas off the south and west coast of Ireland. In 1979, during the Fastnet Yacht Race, a violent storm scattered most of the participating yachts over the Atlantic Ocean, south and west of the Irish coastline. The Super King Air 200s participated in the international sea search that took place after the storm had abated, and were responsible for locating a total of sixty of the lost yachts. Following the mid-air explosion and subsequent crash of a Boeing 747 of Air India in 1985, which occurred about 100 miles south-west of Ireland, the King Air 200s participated in the international search by helicopters, aircraft and shipping for survivors, bodies and wreckage from the airliner. Radio messages from the helicopters and ships engaged on this search were also relayed by the King Air 200s to shore-based rescue centres.

Due to fatigue limits on the airframes and salt-water corrosion caused by low level flights over the ocean, the two Super King Air 200s of the Maritime Squadron were nearing the end of their operational lives by 1989. The safety limit for these aircraft when engaged on maritime operations was considered by the manufacturer (and therefore also by the Air Corps) to be 5,000 flying hours. As a consequence, one of the Super King Air 200s (No. 232), which had accumulated a total of 5,322 flying hours, had to be withdrawn from maritime operations in May 1990. This aircraft was subsequently used occasionally by the Air Corps for pilot conversion and transport missions until acquired by American Sales Aircraft International (as N60MK) and delivered to the USA in January 1992 The other Super King Air 200

Left: King Air 200 just after takeoff from Waterford Airport clearing showing the underwing registrations. (P.J. Cummins photo)

(No. 234) was withdrawn from maritime operations in 1991, after accumulating a total of 5,229 flying hours. In November 1991, this aircraft was according to newspaper reports, purchased by Gannt Aviation for $500,000, and (having been allocated the U.S. civil registration N409GA) was delivered to the USA.

In April 2003, Super King Air No. 240 was flown to Greenley Island in Newfoundland to commemorate the 75th anniversary of the first east to west crossing of the Atlantic Ocean made by the Junkers W33 Bremen, crewed by Herman Kohl, Baron von Hunefeld and Col. James Fitzmaurice, who acted as navigator. The Bremen had taken off from Baldonnel on its historic flight. The Kingair was flown by the General Officer Commanding the Air Corps, Brig. Gen. Ralph James, who was accompanied by Col. Gerry O'Sullivan, Capt. Eamonn Murphy and Sgt. Anthony Cronin, together with Ronan Lee, a journalist from RTE, the Irish national radio and television broadcaster. The flight was uneventful in the sense that all of the sophisticated navigation and other systems worked as advertised. Brig. Gen James commented later that it put into stark contrast the enormity of the achievement of the early pioneers on the Bremen, who at great risk to themselves had flown the Atlantic and landed in a desolate wilderness without any of the modern aids to navigation that had been developed over the intervening 75 years.
The Super King Air 200 has proved to be one of the most cost effective and versatile aircraft ever purchased by the Air Corps. The type has now been in service for 32 years, and continues to play an invaluable part in twin-engine training for pilots progressing onto the Learjet 45 or Casa CN 235 maritime patrol aircraft, in addition to the other roles already outlined.

Left: Three photos showing variations in livery worn by No. 234 during its service life with the Air Corps. (J. Bigley and S. Nolan photos)

Right: A pair of shots showing off the clean lines of King Air No. 240. Often used in the past as a backup to the Gulfstream GIV for transporting VIPs around Europe, this role has now been taken over by the faster Learjet 45 from which these photos were taken. (K. Byrne photo)

Right: Two photos showing the two liveries worn by No. 234 when in Air Corps service. (J. Bigley photos)

Left: King air No. 240 is towed out of the hangar for another mission. (G. Norman photo)

Left: King Air No. 234 undergoing maintenance in 1987. (J. Maxwell photo)

Colours & Markings

The first Super King Air 200 (No. 232) initially had a white finish on the upper surfaces of the fuselage, wings and engine nacelles, with the undersides in blue, the two colours separated by a white/red/ white cheatline, on the fuselage and engine nacelles. In 1983, this paint scheme was replaced by an overall high visibility white finish, with dayglo red stripes on the rear fuselage, wings and nacelles. The Celtic boss was displayed on both sides of the rear fuselage, in front of the dayglo red stripes, and on the upper and under surfaces of both wings. A 'swept' tricoloured fin flash was also displayed on both sides of the tailfin. The aircraft's serial numberwas displayed in black on both sides of the lower section of the tailfin and on the undersides of both wings. The inscription 'MARITIME' was carried over the cabin windows.

The second aircraft, No. 234, was delivered in an overall white finish, with the rudder fin painted blue and orange, and a similar coloured cheatline extending along the centre of the fuselage from the nose to the rear fuselage section; a similar cheatline was also displayed on the engine nacelles. A high visibility paint scheme, similar to the other Super King Air 200 but with slight differences in the dayglo red striping on the rear fuselage, replaced the original paint scheme in 1983. The Celtic boss and fin flash were displayed in the same positions on this aircraft as on No. 232, but with the inscription 'MARITIME SQUADRON' carried over the cabin windows. The dayglo red faded quickly to various shades of orange on both aircraft in the harsh, salt-laden environment over the Atlantic.

Super King Air 200 No. 240 originally had an overall white finish with a green, white and orange cheatline on the fuselage sides, and on the engine nacelles. The Celtic boss bisects the cheatline on both sides of the rear fuselage, and is also displayed on both wings, with the serial number and the fin flash in the same positions as on the other Super King Air 200s. The titles Irish Air Corps - Aer Chor na hÉireann were applied above the cabin widows. This aircraft was repainted in 2003 with a new curved cheatline, and the name Fitz was applied under the cockpit windows in honour of Col. James Fitzmaurice who had flown on the first east-west crossing of the Atlantic in 1928.

4.6

British Aerospace BAe 125-600 and BAe 125-700 (1979 – 1992)

The accession of the Republic of Ireland to the European Economic Community (EEC) in 1973 was expected to bring a substantial increase in attendance by government ministers at meetings and other engagements throughout Europe. On December 12, 1972, a decision was therefore taken by the Irish Government to purchase an executive jet to facilitate travel to such meetings and engagements by ministers and senior civil servants Use of scheduled airline services was considered to be both time-consuming and inconvenient for the majority of ministerial travel requirements, and the de Havilland Doves operated by the Irish Air Corps at that time were unsuitable for ministerial flights and also approaching obsolescence. A modern executive-type aircraft, powered by turbojet engines and operated by the Air Corps, was considered to be the most cost-effective solution, and would also provide the necessary security and flexibility required for ministerial flights. However, in March 1973, following a change of government, the decision to purchase an executive jet aircraft for ministerial flights was rescinded.

Six years later, the Presidency of the EEC passed to the Irish government for the period from 1 July to 31 December 1979. During this time, there would be a substantial increase in the number of ministerial flights and an executive-type aircraft was required to fulfil these travel commitments; the capability of flying from Dublin to Athens – the most distant EEC capital city from Dublin – without refuelling was deemed to be necessary when choosing the aircraft type. A detailed evaluation of all available executive aircraft was undertaken by the Department of Defence, which included demonstrations by a Dassault Falcon 20 and a British Aerospace BAe 125-700 at Baldonnel Aerodrome in January 1979. The BAe 125-700 was eventually selected to fulfil the Irish government's requirement, being considered the most cost-effective solution, having a lower purchase price, lower operating costs, greater ease of maintenance and better reliability than its rivals.

The BAe 125 had been developed by De Havilland Aircraft Ltd. as a medium-sized executive aircraft. Initially designated DH.125, it was renamed the HS.125 after de Havilland Aircraft Ltd. became a division of Hawker Siddeley Aircraft in 1963. When the latter company merged with the British Aircraft Corporation to form British Aerospace in 1977, the name changed to BAe 125. The aircraft was developed through a series of versions, the most notable of which are as follows:

Right: BAe 125-700 No. 238 on the flight line in 1980. (P. Cunniffe photo)

- DH.125 Series 1 with Rolls Royce Viper 520 turbojet engines and with six cabin windows per side. The Series 1a were aircraft destined for the US market and the Series 1b were aircraft marketed elsewhere.
- DH.125 Series 2 with Rolls Royce Viper 522 turbojet engines and five cabin windows per side.
- HS.125 Dominie T.1, a high speed navigation trainer for the RAF based on the DH. 125 Series 1b.
- HS.125 Series 3 with upgraded Rolls Royce Viper engines and an increase in gross weight to 21,500lbs.
- HS.124-400 with a gross weight of 23,300lbs.
- HS.126-600 with a 3ft 1in fuselage stretch over the earlier variants and powered by Rolls Royce Viper 601 engines. The gross weight had been increased to 25,000lbs.
- HS.125-700 with the same fuselage and wings as the - 600 series but powered by Garret TFE321 turbofan engines resulting in vastly better fuel consumption compared to the Viper powered variants.

In May 1979, the Department of Defence ordered a BAe 125-700 from British Aerospace for delivery in February 1980. Pending the arrival of this aircraft, a BAe 125-600B (c/n 25256) was leased from the company in the same month, with conversion courses on the aircraft for Air Corps crews and technicians commencing at the same time. The leased aircraft was one of the two HS.125-600 prototypes (U.K. civil registration G-AYBH) and had been used as a demonstration aircraft by Hawker Siddeley Aviation Ltd. until 1974, before being leased in turn to the Civil Aviation Authority, Philippine Airways and Jet Aire over the following four years. The Air Corps pilots who initially trained to fly the aircraft in 1979 were Comdt. Mick Hipwell (OC General Purpose (GP) Flight, Comdt. Kevin Hogan (OC Photo Section), Capt. Ralph James and Capt. John Goss (both GP Flight).

The leased BAe 125-600B was delivered to Baldonnel Aerodrome on June 1, 1979 and (as No. 236) entered service with the Air Corps. Following an intensive programme of crew training and route proving flights to destinations in Europe, the first official ministerial flight occurred on June 15, 1979, from Dublin to Brussels. Two days later, the Taoiseach (i.e., the Prime Minister), with other Government Ministers and officials, was flown in the aircraft to Strasbourg, where he addressed the European Parliament as President of the EEC On November 27, 1979 No 236 was taking-off from Baldonnel Aerodrome to return to British Aerospace for a routine maintenance inspection, but had to abort the take-off after colliding with a flock of birds. The aircraft was damaged beyond repair after the undercarriage collapsed when, after running off the runway, it crossed a trench that had been dug for the installation of new approach/threshold lighting. The crew were not injured in the crash and the aircraft was returned to British Aerospace by surface transport in January 1980.

The crashed aircraft was replaced by another leased BAe 125-600B (c/n 256015), which had flown for the first time in 1973, and had been in service with two civil operators, one in the United Kingdom and the other in Kuwait, before being returned to British Aerospace in 1979. The aircraft was delivered to Baldonnel Aerodrome on December 6, 1979, and entered service as No. 239. Over the next two months the replacement BAe 125-600B was used for ministerial flights and for crew training by the Air Corps, before being returned to British Aerospace on February 28, 1980.

On February 13, 1980 the Air Corps' own BAe 125-700 (c/n 257082) was delivered to Baldonnel Aerodrome and entered service as No. 238. The cost of this aircraft was quoted at £2,500,000, according to contemporary newspaper reports. From June 1980 onwards, the BAe 125-700 was operated by the Ministerial Air Transport Service (MATS) Transport and Training Squadron, No. 1 Support Wing. The aircraft was only to be used for official flights by the president, government ministers and officials of the public service, with each flight authorised by the Department of the Taoiseach (i.e., the prime minister's office), according to a set of guidelines formulated by the government. Despite the publication of these guidelines, there was at the time almost constant criticism by the opposition parties and in the national press about the utilisation of the BAe 125-700 (which became known universally as the 'Government Jet'.

The BAe 125-700, which had the latest navigation and communications equipment installed, was capable of non-stop flights to all destinations within the EEC and fulfilled all ministerial travel requirements over the next twelve years. Due to intensive utilisation by the Air Corps meeting ministerial travel and crew training commitments, the total number of flying

The underside of the BAe 125-700 taken at an airshow at Faireyhouse Race course in the early 1980s. (J. Byrne photo)

BAe-125-600 No. 239 replaced the earlier leased No. 236 which was damaged in an abortive takeoff at Baldonnel. Note the Viper turbojet engines in slim nacelles compared to the turbofans on the BAe125-700.

hours accumulated annually by this aircraft was often the highest for any BAe 125 worldwide. A record total of 750 flying hours was accumulated by the aircraft in 1983, which included a total of 103 hours in one month. The BAe 125-700 was also used for emergency air ambulance flights, which included transporting seriously ill patients, medical teams and human organs to hospitals at home and abroad.

From January to June 1990, the Presidency of the EEC was to be administered by the Irish government. The EEC had undergone a major expansion since 1973, becoming increasingly involved in worldwide political and economic developments, and there was expected to be a significant increase in the number of ministerial flights to destinations in Europe and throughout the world. To enable MATS to fulfil these global travel commitments, the Irish Government leased a Gulfstream III (Air Corps serial No. 249) for the duration of the Presidency,. over the course of which there was intensive utilisation of the BAe 125-700, the Gulfstream III and the Super King Air 200, transporting Ministers and officials throughout Europe and farther afield.

A total of 123 flying hours was accumulated by the BAe 125-700 in March 1990, the highest number of hours accumulated in a month since entering service with the Air Corps. In July 1990, the aircraft underwent a major overhaul prior to being offered for sale by the Irish Government, but the tenders received were unacceptable and the aircraft continued to be operated by MATS, visiting 14 countries and landing at 49 airports throughout that year. The BAe 125-700 completed ten years of service with the Air Corps in the same year, having landed at 130 airports in 22 countries during this period. In 1991, during the Gulf War, the BAe 125-700 was used by M.A.T.S. to convey the Minister for Foreign Affairs to a number of Middle Eastern countries on various diplomatic missions in the region. The lease on the Gulfstream III had been extended in 1990, but this aircraft was not the property of the Irish government and would therefore have incurred prohibitive insurance costs to provide 'war risk' cover for these ministerial flights.

A Gulfstream IV (Air Corps serial No. 251) was delivered to the Air Corps in December 1991 as a replacement for both the BAe 125-700 and the Gulfstream III. The BAe 125-700 was withdrawn from use in October 1992 following a 'pre-sale' survey in the United Kingdom, and was eventually sold in Mexico. On December 2, 1992, the aircraft (carrying the civil registration XA-TCB) departed Baldonnel Aerodrome on a delivery flight to that country. A total of 8,173 flying hours had been accumulated by the BAe 125-700 over its twelve years of service with the Air Corps.

Colours & Markings

The first BAe 125-600B (No. 236) had an overall gloss white paint scheme with a green, white and orange cheatline extending from the nose to the rear fuselage. The tri-coloured Celtic boss was displayed on the front section of the fuselage, behind the entrance door, and on the upper and undersurfaces of both wings. A swept tri-coloured fin flash was displayed on both sides of the tailfin. The Air Corps serial numberwas displayed in black on the tailfin beneath the fin flash, and on the underside of both wings. The replacement BAe 125-600B (No. 239) had a similar paint scheme, but with a black cheatline extending from the nose to the rear fuselage. The engine pods on both of these aircraft were unpainted.

The BAe 125-700B (No. 238) also had an overall gloss white finish, with a tri-coloured cheatline extending from the nose over the two engine pods to the rear of the fuselage. The tri-coloured Celtic boss, outlined in green, was displayed on the upper and under surfaces of both wings, and on both sides of the front fuselage, with a tri-coloured swept fin flash appearing on the tailfin. The Air Corps serial number was also displayed in the same positions as on the previous two aircraft. The inscription 'IRISH AIR CORPS – AER CHÓR na h-ÉIREANN was displayed over the windows on both sides of the fuselage of this aircraft.

Above: BAe-125-700 at Dublin Airport. (S. Nolan Collection)

Below: The ill-fated No. 236 which was damaged in a take-off accident, fortunately without injury to the crew.

4.7

Aérospatiale (SA.342L) Gazelle (1979 – 2005)

Sleek, swift, and highly manoeuvrable, the Gazelle was designed to fulfil a French army requirement for a light observation helicopter. In 1964, Sud Aviation was engaged on large-scale production of the Alouette II and III, but realised that a replacement for these helicopters would eventually be required. Initially designated X-300, but later re-designated SA.340 by the company, preliminary design work was started by Sud Aviation in 1964, and in the same year the company entered into an agreement with the German helicopter manufacturing company, Bolkow Entwicklungen AG, to develop a glass fibre rotor blade and associated rigid-rotor system. Construction of a prototype helicopter commenced in 1966.

The first prototype SA.340 (c/n 001, carrying the French civil registration F-WOFH) flew for the first time on April 6, 1967, fitted with the standard main and tail rotors from the Alouette II. The second prototype SA.340 (c/n 002, registered F-ZWRA) made its first flight on April 12, 1968, fitted with a rigid main rotor and a so-called fenestron, a multi-bladed tail rotor mounted in a duct in the fin. Both of these features were major innovations in helicopter design; the rigid rotor design eliminated drag and flap hinges in the rotor head, reduced vibration and simplified maintenance, while the fenestron resulted in improved ground safety and reduced drag. The SA.340 was selected as one of three helicopters (the Puma and the Lynx being the others) for a joint production programme by British and French helicopter manufacturing companies. Production of the SA.340 was to be undertaken by Westland Aircraft Ltd., to fulfil a requirement by the British army for a light observation helicopter.

Designated SA.341 by the company, and named Gazelle in July 1969, the first of four pre-production helicopters (c/n 01, registered F-ZWRH) flew for the first time on August 2, 1968, fitted with a semi-articulated rotor head retaining flapping hinges, following problems encountered with the rigid rotor system on the prototypes. The first flights of the other three pre-production SA.341s (c/n 02 F-ZWRL, c/n 03 F-ZWRI and c/n 04

Lt. Col. Jim Lynott lands Gazelle No. 241 at Renmore Barracks in Galway. (K. Byrne photo)

Left: Gazelle No. 237 at Baldonnel in May 1980. Note the aerodynamic fairings on the skids which were often removed and the Rescue Squadron badge on the engine cowling.
(P. Cunniffe photo)

F-ZWRK) occurred in the same year, with the third pre-production SA.341 being delivered to Westland Aircraft in the U.K. in August. Designated Gazelle AH.1, this SA.341 was used as a prototype for the development of a light observation helicopter to fulfil the British army's requirement.

Sud Aviation was merged with Nord Aviation and SEREB in 1970 to form a new company, Aérospatiale, which – together with Westland Aircraft – commenced production of the SA.341. Powered by a 590 shp Astazou IIIA turboshaft engine, production Gazelles, by comparison with the pre-production machines, had a lengthened cabin, with two rear access doors, and an enlarged tail unit. Deliveries of the Gazelle to the Aviation Légère de l'Armée de Terre (ie, the air component of the French army) commenced in 1973, followed by deliveries to the British army, the Fleet Air Arm and the RAF, which commenced in February 1974. Production of the Gazelle by Westland Aviation ceased in March 1984, after a total of 294 had been constructed.

Further civil and military variants of the Gazelle were developed by Aérospatiale, powered by uprated Astazou XIVM engines and fitted with an improved fenestron, providing for an increase in take-off weight and an overall improvement in performance, and these were designated SA.342J and SA.342L, respectively. The Gazelle in all its variants proved to be highly successful, being delivered to over 25 air forces and built under licence in both Egypt and the former Yugoslavia.

In 1978, the Irish Air Corps had a requirement for three training helicopters, which could be used both for basic flying training and pilot conversion courses. Due to a substantial increase in the number of operational commitments that the Aérospatiale SA.316B Alouette III had to fulfil, there were restrictions on the availability of these helicopters for basic conversion courses and continuity training. There was also a requirement for a helicopter equipped for I.F.R. operations (i.e., instrument flight rules – basically, bad weather or night operations) and with an autopilot installed, which could be used during the initial stages of conversion courses for pilots selected to fly a leased Aérospatiale SA.330 Puma that was to be delivered to the Air Corps in the near future. Several helicopter types were evaluated by the Air Corps to fulfil these requirements, including an SA.342M Gazelle (with the French civil registration F-WXFI), which was demonstrated at Baldonnel on April 2, 1979.

A single SA.342L Gazelle was ordered by the Department of Defence in August 1979, costing £650,000; this aircraft was intended to be used mainly for training duties. Three Air Corps pilots, who would subsequently deliver the helicopter to Baldonnel Aerodrome, underwent a conversion course on the Gazelle at the Aérospatiale flying training school . The company also conducted a three-week maintenance course on the Gazelle for Air Corps technicians, which was followed by a one-week course on the Astazou engine with Turbomeca.

The SA.342L Gazelle (c/n 1772) was delivered by an Air Corps crew to Baldonnel Aerodrome on December 30, 1979 and (as No. 237) entered service with the Helicopter Squadron. From June 1980 onwards, the Gazelle was operated by the Basic Flying Training School, Training Wing. The equipment fit on the Gazelle was a major step up from that on the Alouette III. It had a stability augmentation system which provided for a degree of 'hands off' flying, and it also had a sophisticated navigation suite with VOR/DME, automatic direction finder and instrument landing systems.

How do you move a helicopter that doesn't have wheels? With a specialised ground handling trolley.
(J. Maxwell photo)

Right: Following service with the Air Corps, Gazelle No. 241 was sold to a private buyer and is now on the Hungarian register as HA-LFQ. (Simon Thomas photo)

A second SA.342L Gazelle (c/n 1854), which had been ordered by the Department of Defence in June 1980, was delivered to Baldonnel Aerodrome on January 14, 1981, and (as No. 241) also entered service with the Basic Flying Training School, Training Wing. This Gazelle was equipped with an autopilot and an improved stability augmentation system. Initially the Gazelles were used for I.F.R. training for pilots on conversion courses, each totalling 20 flying hours, to fly the leased Aérospatiale SA.330J Puma. Both Gazelles were later modified with an autopilot system that would more closely resemble the system fitted to the SA365 Dauphin helicopters acquired by the Air Corps in 1986. The third Gazelle was not acquired by the Air Corps, due to a lack of available funds in the poor economic circumstances that prevailed in the mid-1980s.

From 1987 onwards, the Gazelles were operated by the Helicopter School, one of the elements of No. 3 Support Wing, which at that time was responsible for all helicopter operations within the Air Corps. After qualifying on fixed wing aircraft, student pilots selected to fly helicopters then underwent a basic helicopter conversion course on the Gazelle, totalling 50 flying hours, and operational training was completed on the Aérospatiale SA.316B Alouette III, totalling 60 flying hours. The Gazelles were used from 1986 onwards for the initial stages of pilot conversion courses for the Aérospatiale SA.365 Dauphin 2. For a short period, the Gazelles were used for basic instrument flying training at night during continuation training for pilots flying the Aérospatiale AS.355N Ecureuil of the Garda Air Support Unit. The Gazelles were also used for air ambulance duties and for the transportation of Government Ministers and officials and other dignitaries.

On April 18, 1987, Gazelle No. 241 crash-landed on marshy ground during a training flight, following an engine failure, but skilful piloting prevented damage to the helicopter or injury to the crew. The engine from the other Gazelle (no. 237) was installed in this helicopter, which was then flown back to Baldonnel Aerodrome on the same day. On August 16, 2002, following another engine failure, Gazelle No. 237 was written-off after crash-landing in a field near Baldonnel Aerodrome, but happily without injury to the two crew members. The remaining Gazelle (i.e., No. 241) was withdrawn from use on December 31, 2005, having accumulated a total of 5,240 flying hours in Air Corps service. It was subsequently sold to a private owner and is now based in the UK with the Hungarian registration HA-LFQ.

Right: Cockpit of the Gazelle which was upgraded on several occasions and used to train pilots going on to the larger Dauphin helicopter. (S. Nolan photo)

Bottom right: The complex engine and ancillary equipment on the Gazelle. (J. Maxwell photo)

Opposite page
Top: Photographed in 1981 with a specially tinted canopy for use in night flying training. (P. Cunniffe photo)

Middle: Nice contrast between the colour schemes on 237 and 241. (A.C. Photographic Section)

Bottom: For overwater flights the Gazelle could be equipped with emergency flotation gear attached to the skids. (J. Bigley photo)

Colours & Markings

The first Gazelle (No. 237) was delivered in an overall light grey finish (Aerodur grey c21/100) with the nose, fin tip and underside of the cabin painted red, which had been applied in error by the manufacturer instead of the dayglo orange specified. A small tri-coloured fin flash was displayed on both sides of the fin and the tri-coloured Celtic boss was displayed on both sides of the forward section of the tail boom. The Air Corps serial number was displayed in black on both sides of the rear section of the fuselage.

The second Gazelle (No. 241) also had an overall light grey finish, but with the correct dayglo orange shade specified by the Air Corps on the of the fin tip, nose and underside of the cabin. The dayglo orange, which had a tendency to fade quickly, was later replaced by bright red "non-dayglo" paint during a major overhaul. The Celtic boss and serial number were displayed in the same positions as on the first Gazelle. Initially the fin flash was not displayed on this helicopter's fin, but was later applied following a repaint after a major overhaul. The Helicopter Squadron crest, with the motto "Go Maridis Beo" ("That Others May Live"), was displayed on both sides of the gearbox cowlings of the two Gazelles for a short period, but was later removed. In 2001, Gazelle No. 241 had a commemorative pink panther badge applied beneath the rear cabin window to mark its participation at the Royal International Air Tattoo. This badge remained in-situ until the aircraft was retired from service.

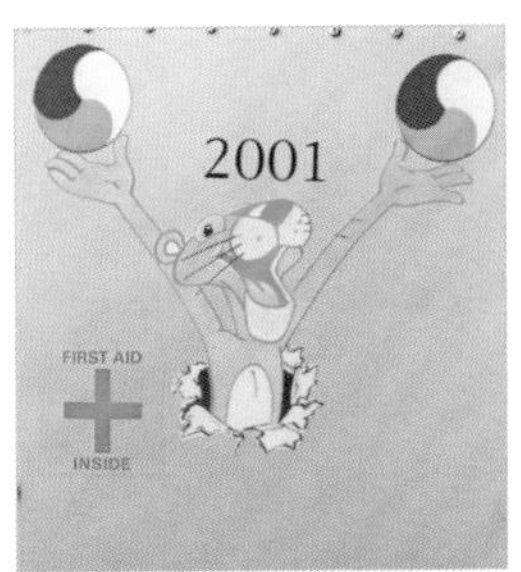

Expansion

5.0

Expansion (1980 – 2000)

In June 1980, due to increased operational commitments, a re-organisation of the Air Corp took place resulting in the formation of five distinct Wings for administration, engineering, operations and training duties. The Training Wing, comprising Basic Flying Training School, Apprentice School and the General Training Depot, was responsible for the training of pilots, technicians and other Air Corps personnel. Equipped with operational aircraft, No. 1 Support Wing initially comprised Light Strike Squadron, Maritime Squadron, Helicopter Squadron, Transport and Training Squadron. Based at Air Corps Station, Gormanston, No. 2 Support Wing comprised Army Co-Operation Squadron flying the Cessnas. The Administration and Engineering Wings were not equipped with aircraft.

The early 1980s saw an intensification of the civil strife in Northern Ireland that had started ten years earlier. Policing the border was a major concern in order to prevent terrorists carrying out cross border attacks in the North. There had been a long held requirement for larger troop transport helicopters to enable rapid deployment of troops along the border. This requirement was partially met by a relatively short lease of an Aérospatiale SA 330 Puma helicopter in 1981. However the lease was curtailed due to the dire economic circumstances facing the country at that time. The use of an advanced twin engine helicopter gave the Air Corps an immense boost in capability over the single engine Alouettes that had been in service since 1963. As soon as circumstances permitted the Air Corps ordered five brand new state of the art Dauphin helicopters, the first of these being delivered in 1986. Two of these were equipped to operate from the Naval Service ship L.E. Eithne thus adding an additional role to the Air Corps' range of operational requirements.

A further re-organisation took place in 1986 with the disbandment of No.2 Support Wing and the consolidation of No. 3 Support Wing, which comprised Search and Rescue Squadron, Naval Support Squadron, Army Support Squadron and Helicopter Squadron, operating all the helicopters in service with the Air Corps.

Named the "Silver Swallows", the first official Air Corps aerobatic team was formed during this period, participating in air shows throughout Ireland and Europe until disbandment in 1997.

An Air Corps detachment was deployed to Shannon International Airport in 1989 and to Waterford Regional Airport in 1998, providing search and rescue services over the south-west and south-east regions until replaced by civilian helicopters in 1991 and 2002 respectively. On July 1, 1999, while returning from a search and rescue mission, a Dauphin helicopter crashed near Waterford Airport, killing the crew of four. This was the first fatal crash in thirty seven years of helicopter operations by the Air Corps.

During 1994, a distinctive blue uniform was introduced for Air Corps personnel, replacing the standard green uniform worn by all units of the Defence Forces since 1922. Flight training for female Air Corps personnel commenced in 1996, with the first female pilot qualifying in 1998.

Whilst the Air Corps had a long history in providing support to the Gardai, a dedicated Garda Air Support Unit was formed in 1997, equipped with a single Aérospatiale SA 355N helicopter and a fixed-wing Britten-Norman Defender 4000 aircraft which were allocated Air Corps serial numbers. Although the crews assigned to these aircraft are Garda personnel, the pilots are provided by the Air Corps.

During this period several major infrastructural projects were undertaken at Baldonnel including the upgrading of accommodation, hangar refurbishment, upgrading of the fuel storage facility and the construction of a new Garda Air Support Building.

In 1998, a review of the Air Corps and Naval Service was undertaken by a firm of consultants, Price Waterhouse, and a report was later presented to the Minister of Defence. The report had been commissioned as part of the Efficiency Audit Group, EAG, which was established by the Government in April 1988 to examine the workings and practices of each Government Department with a view to recommending improved and alternative policies and methods which reduce costs and improve efficiency. This report recommended a reduction in the number of Air Corps personnel and a re-equipment programme, which included acquiring new helicopters, training aircraft and more maritime patrol aircraft, though not all of the recommendations were carried out in full.

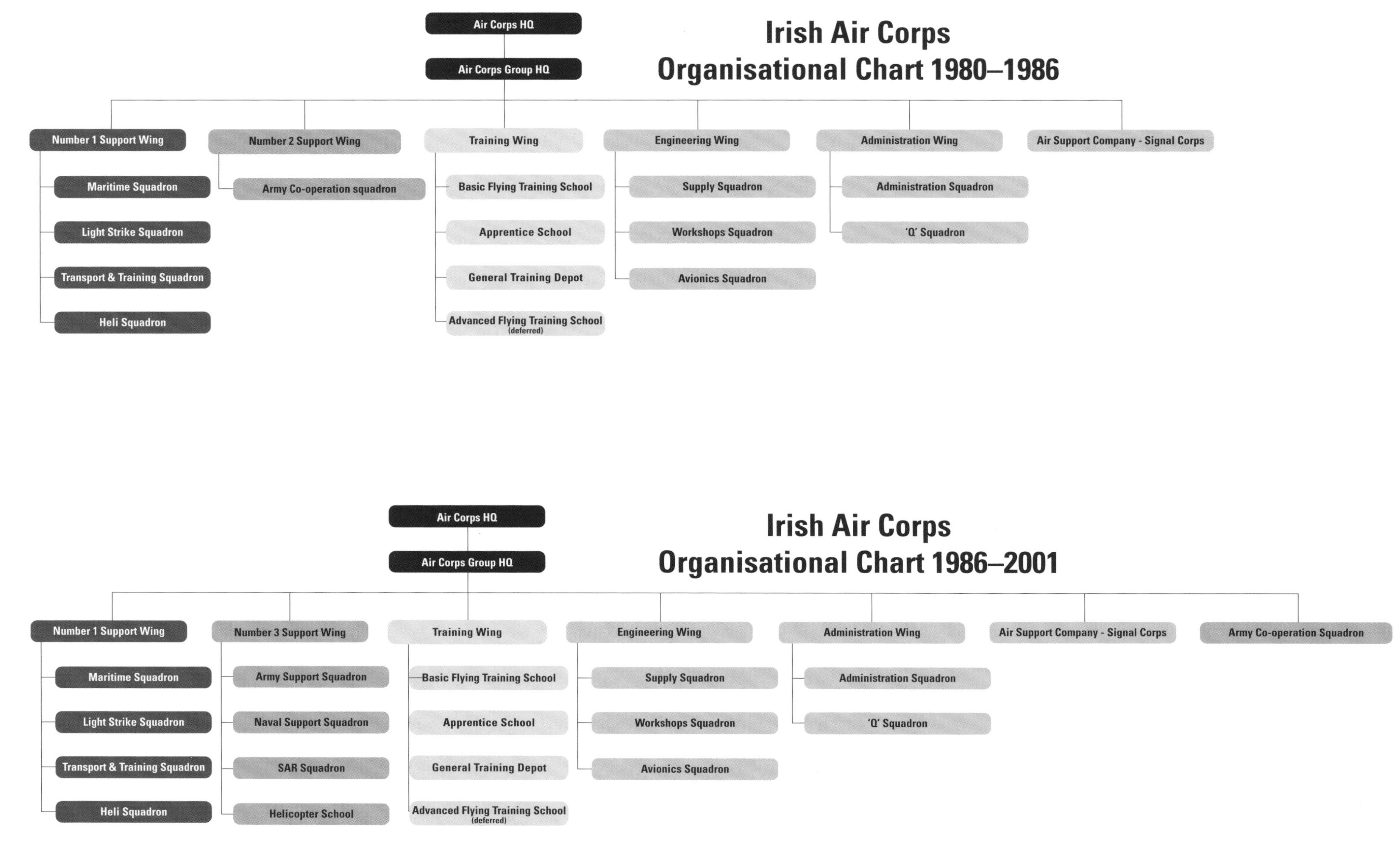
Irish Air Corps
Organisational Chart 1980–1986
Air Corps HQ
Air Corps Group HQ
Number 1 Support Wing
Maritime Squadron
Light Strike Squadron
Transport & Training Squadron
Heli Squadron
Number 2 Support Wing
Army Co-operation squadron
Training Wing
Basic Flying Training School
Apprentice School
General Training Depot
Advanced Flying Training School (deferred)
Engineering Wing
Supply Squadron
Workshops Squadron
Avionics Squadron
Administration Wing
Administration Squadron
'Q' Squadron
Air Support Company - Signal Corps
Irish Air Corps
Organisational Chart 1986–2001
Air Corps HQ
Air Corps Group HQ
Number 1 Support Wing
Maritime Squadron
Light Strike Squadron
Transport & Training Squadron
Heli Squadron
Number 3 Support Wing
Army Support Squadron
Naval Support Squadron
SAR Squadron
Helicopter School
Training Wing
Basic Flying Training School
Apprentice School
General Training Depot
Advanced Flying Training School (deferred)
Engineering Wing
Supply Squadron
Workshops Squadron
Avionics Squadron
Administration Wing
Administration Squadron
'Q' Squadron
Air Support Company - Signal Corps
Army Co-operation Squadron

5.1

Aérospatiale SA.330L Puma (1981 – 1983)

Thundering along barely fifty feet above the Military Road that winds its way through the Wicklow Mountains south of Dublin, the Air Corps' dark green SA330L Puma was a most impressive and unexpected sight in the autumn of 1981 for hill walkers more used to seeing the smaller Alouette III helicopters operating in this area. It was a sight that was to be short lived, however, as the big machine was to remain in service for just over 18 months. It nevertheless had a tremendous impact on operations during that time, and it was to be more than twenty years before the Air Corps would once again operate helicopters with similar load-carrying capabilities.

The Aérospatiale SA330 Puma was originally developed to fulfil a 1962 French Army requirement for an all-weather transport helicopter. The type was also selected to fulfil an RAF requirement for a tactical transport helicopter, and co-production of the type by AeAérospatiale and Westland was covered under the 1968 agreement that included the joint production of both the Lynx and Gazelle helicopters. The SA330 Puma was an export success and proved to have excellent growth potential, ultimately leading to the development of the AS 332 Super Puma, variants of which are still in production in 2009.

From 1975 onwards, the Irish Air Corps had a requirement for medium lift helicopters for the rapid deployment of troops to reinforce units of the Irish Defence Forces and the Garda Siochána engaged on security operations. The Irish authorities had been impressed by the apparent ease with which the RAF managed to move large numbers of British Army personnel rapidly around border areas using their Wessex and Puma helicopters. There was also a requirement for a medium-range, all-weather helicopter to carry out SAR missions off the west coast of Ireland. Over the next five years, a number of helicopters were evaluated by the Air Corps to fulfil this requirement, including the Bell 212 and the Aérospatiale SA.330 Puma. In 1979, three SA.330 Pumas were leased from the BundesGrenschutz (i.e., the West German Border Police) for security operations by the Garda Siochána during the visit of Pope John Paul II to Ireland. These machines were flown by German pilots, but Irish Air Corps personnel served as navigators during these operations and were able to witness at first hand the capabilities that these large machines had to offer.

Also in 1979, a SA.330J Puma (carrying the French civil registration F-BRQK) was demonstrated to the Air Corps at Casement Aerodrome. Originally constructed as an SA.330F Puma (c/n 1240) fitted with metal rotor blades, this helicopter had been delivered to the Ethiopian Air Force (in the service of which it carried the serial number 850) in December 1973. The aircraft was used as a personal transport

Right: Puma No. 242 seen at Cork Airport in September 1981. (G. Desmond photo)

The Puma was the first helicopter in Air Corps service equipped with weather radar. (L. Whelan photo)

by the Emperor Hailie Selassie and was returned to Aérospatiale in 1976. Re-designated as SA.330L after the metal rotor blades were replaced by wide chord composite rotor blades, and powered by two Turmo IVc engines, the helicopter was used by the company for demonstration purposes over the next three years. Emergency flotation bags were also permanently fitted to the SA.330L, these being carried on the lower section of the front fuselage and on the sides of the main undercarriage fairings. A weather radar was also fitted in a nose-mounted radome.

In 1981, this aircraft was leased from Aérospatiale by the Department of Defence for a period of two years, at a cost of £500,000 per annum. It was intended that it would be used for operational evaluation by the Air Corps pending the subsequent purchase of a similar helicopter. Four Air Corps pilots underwent a conversion course on the helicopter at the company's factory in France, and the Puma (as No. 242) was delivered to Baldonnel on July 22, 1981 becoming the first twin-engined helicopter to enter service with the Air Corps. During the final stages of the delivery flight the Puma was escorted by two Aérospatiale SA.342L Gazelles and a SIAI-Marchetti SF.260 Warrior of the Air Corps. The Puma, which was also the largest aircraft in service with the Air Corps at the time, was initially operated by the Advanced Flying Training School, Training Wing, for pilot conversion courses. The Puma then entered service with the Helicopter Squadron, No. 1 Support Wing.

Twenty troops could be transported in the Puma, seated on canvas seats running down the centre of the spacious cabin, with rapid disembarkation being possible through the large cabin doors. Equipped with HF, UHF and VHF radios for communications, ADF, VOR/DME, ILS and TACAN navigation aids and the nose-mounted weather radar, the Puma could also carry out long-range, all-weather air-sea rescue missions by day or night. Some of the canvas seating was removed when the helicopter was used for SAR missions, and a winch was fitted over the starboard cabin door. Eight airline style seats, facing forward, could also be fitted inside the cabin for transporting government ministers or other dignitaries. The Puma was also used occasionally for air ambulance missions.

The Puma provided a massive boost in capability compared to the Alouette IIIs that were in service at the time. Not only could it carry significantly heavier loads over longer distances, but the big cabin provided plenty of room for winch crew to render assistance to those that they had rescued; furthermore, the big doors made winching easier, as

Compared to the Puma helicopters in RAF service at the time, Puma 242 was equipped with enlarged wheel sponsons containing large fuel tanks and integrally mounted flotation gear. (L. Whelan photo)

Right: the Puma was a major advance over the Alouette III that was then in service with the Air Corps as evidenced by the radio and navigation equipment installed in the cockpit. (L. Whelan photo)

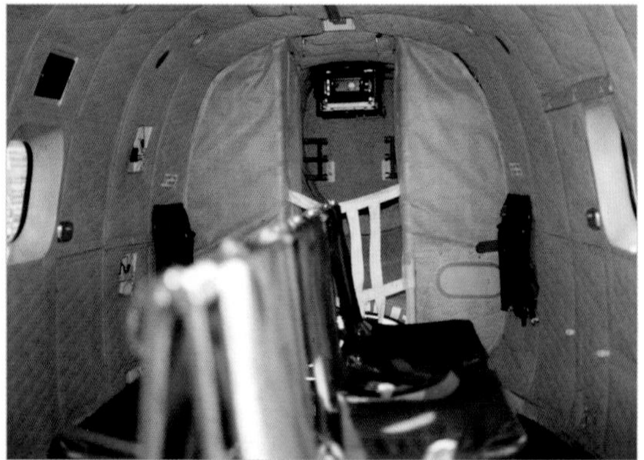

Right: Two views looking fore and aft from the centre of the capacious cabin with troop seats running down the centre of the cabin. (L. Whelan photos)

the crew could stand at full height at the door rather than half crouching as required in the Alouette.

In January 1982, throughout the eastern region of Ireland, many villages, residences and farms were isolated by heavy snowfalls and freezing weather conditions, making the roads impassable and immobilising surface transport. Throughout this period of adverse weather, the Helicopter Squadron airlifted food and other supplies to these isolated communities and inhabitants, dropped fodder to stranded livestock on farms and transported seriously ill or injured patients to hospital. Over a period of ten days, a total of 148 rescue missions was carried out by the helicopters operated by the Squadron, which included twenty rescue missions by the Puma, saving twenty-eight lives, and nineteen fodder drops to stranded farm livestock by this helicopter. Foodstuffs and essential supplies were also delivered by the Puma to Tory Island, off the north-west coast, which had been isolated from the mainland by stormy seas. In addition, the Puma carried out a search for survivors from a French trawler that had sunk off the south-east coast during this period. The first air-sea rescue mission by the Puma occurred on September 21, 1982, when an injured fisherman was airlifted to hospital from a Spanish trawler in the Atlantic Ocean.

In January 1983, the lease on the Puma was terminated by the Department of Defence, although it was not due to expire for another six months. The Puma, which had accumulated a total of 800 flying hours since entering service with the Air Corps, was due a major overhaul at an estimated cost of £100,000. Flown by an Air Corps crew, the Puma was returned to the Aérospatiale factory in the south of France on February 27, 1983. Plans by the Department of Defence to acquire an SA.332 Super Puma for the Air Corps were also abandoned, due to strict curbs on expenditure imposed by the government at the time. This particular Puma remains in use today for experimental test programmes with the Centre d'Essais en Vol (CEV) in France carrying the civil registration F-ZLAT.

Below: The Puma was fitted with composite rotor blades, a new innovation at the time. (L. Whelan photo)

Left: Puma 242 seen at Baldonnel in August 1981. Note the large sponsons with orange warnings for the ground crew not to walk on them! (P. Cunniffe photo)

Colours and Markings

The Puma had an overall dark khaki green finish with the main cabin doors outlined by thin orange stripes. The helicopter's serial number was displayed in white on both sides of the rear section of the fuselage, over the main undercarriage fairings. The Celtic boss was displayed on both sides of the centre section of the tail boom, and the national flag was displayed on both sides of the engine cowling, just above and in front of the main cabin doors. The inscription "DANGER", in black on a yellow background, was displayed on both sides of the rear of the tail boom.

Below: Following its return to France in 1983, the Puma joined the French test and evaluation centre (CEV) where it photographed in 2007.
(Jean-Paul Gilbert photo)

5.2

Aérospatiale SA.365Fi Dauphin 2 (1986 – 2006)

The Aérospatiale SA 360 Dauphin was a single-engine utility helicopter developed as a replacement for Aérospatiale's Alouette III in the early 1970s. However, the new helicopter was not a great success and production was cancelled after a relatively small number of them had been built. A twin-engine derivative, the Dauphin 2 went on to become one of Europe's most successful helicopter types and derivatives remain in production at the time of writing.

The prototype SA.365N Dauphin 2, (c/n 5100, F-WZJD) flew for the first time on March 31, 1979, powered by two 660 shp Turbomeca Arriel 1C turboshaft engines. Production of the SA.365N commenced in 1980, following orders from the U.S. Coast Guard (designated HH-65A Dolphin) and some civil operators An agreement was also negotiated by Aérospatiale for licence production of the Dauphin 2 in China, as the Harbin Z-9 Haitun. Designated SA.365F, a naval variant was developed initially for the Royal Saudi Naval Force, powered by two 700 shp Arriel 1M turboshaft engines.

From about 1980 onwards, due to increased SAR commitments the Irish Air Corps had a requirement for a modern helicopter, which would replace the Aérospatiale SA.316B Alouette III. Formulated by an Alouette III Replacement Board, this requirement was for a short-range, twin-engined helicopter, equipped with the latest navigation, radar and flight control systems, which would be capable of carrying out maritime SAR missions in adverse weather conditions, by day and night. The Irish Naval Service also had a requirement for a helicopter to operate from the Helicopter Patrol Vessel, L.E. Eithne, due to enter service in 1984, to be used for fishery protection and maritime surveillance duties.

In December 1982, following an evaluation of various helicopter types, which included the Westland W.G.13 Lynx, the Department of Defence announced that five Dauphin 2s had been ordered to fulfil these requirements. Apparently the original intention was to acquire ten Dauphin 2s, but the Department of Finance would only provide sufficient funds to acquire five of these helicopters for the Air Corps. The five Dauphin 2s were to be equipped for SAR operations, with computerised navigation and automatic flight control systems installed and two of the helicopters would also be specially equipped for shipborne operations. These Dauphin 2s would also be the first helicopters in the world to have a five screen electronic flight instrumentation system or EFIS installed in the cockpit, which provided a dual multi-mode display for the pilot and co-pilot. A fenestron tail rotor, similar to the Aérospatiale SA.342 Gazelle, was also fitted to the Dauphin 2s, with the main rotor blades and parts of the fuselage

Right: Dauphin 245 over a choppy sea. Rescues have been carried out in conditions where waves as high as 40ft created difficulty in maintaining an automatic hover height. (Air Corps photo section via Bernie Murran)

constructed from composite materials. The first two Dauphin 2s were to be delivered to the Air Corps in December 1984, followed by the third in June 1985, with the fourth and fifth to be delivered in January and February 1986. However, due to problems with the development and integration of the avionics systems installed in the helicopter, deliveries of these helicopters was delayed by eighteen months.

Designated SA.365Fi, (the small i being used to designate the helicopter as a sub-variant with a unique equipment fit as specified by the Air Corps) the first Dauphin 2 (c/n 6124) for the Air Corps flew for the first time on September 19, 1984. This helicopter, together with a company owned Dauphin 2, was used for testing and development of the avionics systems and both helicopters were also used for deck landing trials on the L.E. Eithne in February 1985, off the north-west coast of France. The second Dauphin 2 (c/n 6168), which flew for the first time in 1985 was displayed in the Aérospatiale helicopter enclosure (as H114) at the Paris Air Salon in the same year. The first two Dauphin 2s were each fitted with crashproof fuel tanks, a modified undercarriage and a hydraulically operated harpoon to secure the helicopter to the flight-deck of the L.E. Eithne during naval operations. In May 1986, following an intensive test programme and flight certification of the two Dauphin 2s (as F-ZKBZ and F-ZKBJ), a number of Air Corps pilots commenced a basic conversion course on these helicopters at the French company's factory, totalling 10 hours, prior to delivery to Baldonnel. Fifty technicians also underwent a maintenance training programme on the helicopter at the company factory.

On June 25, 1986 the first and third Dauphin 2s (as Nos. 244 and 246) were delivered by Air Corps pilots to Baldonnel. The helicopters were escorted on the final stages of the flight by an Alouette III and two SIAI-Marchetti SF.260WE Warriors. The second Dauphin 2 (as No. 245) was delivered to the Air Corps on July 18, 1986, followed by the fourth (as No. 247) on August 28, 1986 and the fifth (as No. 248) on December 19, 1986. The five Dauphin 2s entered service with SAR Squadron, No. 3 Support Wing, which had been formed in the same year, but two of the helicopters (Nos. 244 and 245) were also operated by Naval Support Squadron. Partially financed by the EEC the total cost of the five helicopters was IR£20m according to contemporary news reports.

Throughout 1986 and 1987 the Air Corps conducted an intensive training programme for pilots and aircrew assigned to the Dauphin 2s, which had been formulated before the helicopters were delivered. This programme concentrated on training pilots and aircrew for daylight maritime SAR missions, emergency procedures and supporting the security forces. The two Dauphin 2s (Nos. 244 and 245) of the Naval Squadron were also engaged on operational training on the L.E. Eithne throughout October and November 1986.

Above: equally useful on land or sea, a Dauphin deposits a mountain rescue team member on a hill top in Wicklow. (M. Farrell photo)

The Dauphin 2 (generally referred to as just the Dauphin in Air Corps service) carried a crew of four, comprising a pilot, co-pilot, winch operator and winchman, for SAR operations and could accommodate up to five rescued persons. A rescue hoist was fitted over the starboard side of the cabin and the helicopter was also equipped with a flotation system for emergency landings on the sea, comprising inflatable pontoons fitted into the fuselage, on both sides of the nose, with sealed rear compartments. They were also used for air ambulance missions by day or night and for the transportation of the President, members of the Cabinet, Government officials or visiting dignitaries throughout the State, carrying up to eight passengers and two pilots on these flights. A blue carpet was fitted on the floor and padded seats, covered with a blue material, were installed in the Dauphins for these flights. To fulfil the Air Corps commitments of providing "Aid to the Civil Power", the Dauphins were also used for the transportation of high-security prisoners and were used to provide air support for the security forces during operations against terrorists and criminals.

Dauphin 245 was taking off to search for a missing climber near Diamond Hill in Connemara in August 1992. (J. Maxwell photo)

In January 1987 during severe weather conditions, which included heavy snowfalls, a Dauphin (No. 248), with skis attached to the extended undercarriage, was used for air evacuation, rescue and air ambulance missions throughout the State,. The first maritime SAR mission by a Dauphin occurred on March 10, 1987, when an injured fisherman was winched off a Spanish trawler in the Atlantic Ocean, eighty miles off the west coast of Ireland. A total of eight SAR missions had been carried out by these helicopters between March and August of that year when the Dauphin officially replaced the Alouette III on SAR operations, at a ceremony held at Baldonnel on August 28, 1987. A Dauphin also participated for the first time in a joint SAR exercise with a Westland Sea King of the RAF and a lifeboat of the RNLI in the following month. A total of 1600 flying hours was accumulated by the Dauphins throughout 1987, comprising training flights, totalling 1175 flying hours, and forty SAR and fifteen air ambulance missions, totalling 425 flying hours.

In 1987 the Air Corps also initiated a training programme for pilots and aircrew assigned to the Dauphin to enable SAR operations to be carried out by night, including instrument flying procedures, navigation exercises, automatic transition to the hover over water and winching exercises. The resignation of a number of pilots and technicians to take up employment in civil aviation, who had qualified on the helicopter, caused serious disruption to the training programme. The number of Dauphins, personnel and time available for night flying training was also restricted by the requirement to maintain one of the helicopters at permanent readiness for SAR missions and guarantee availability all year round. Three Dauphins had to be available to fulfil this requirement: one at permanent readiness for SAR missions, one on stand-by in the event of the primary helicopter developing an unscheduled fault and one on routine maintenance.

Throughout 1988 there was widespread criticism in the national news media and by opposition parties in the Dáil and about the inability of the Dauphin to carry out SAR operations by night, the helicopter's inadequate range and limited cabin accommodation for rescued persons, in comparison with the Sea King. These criticisms ignored the fact that the Dauphin was a short-range helicopter, acquired as a replacement for the Alouette III and for shipborne operations, which limited the size and capabilities of the helicopter to fulfil all these requirements. In favourable weather conditions the Dauphin was capable of carrying out SAR missions up to 140 nautical miles from the last refuelling point, which was reduced to approximately 110 nautical miles in adverse weather conditions and 70 nautical miles by night. The Dauphin could also be refuelled from the L.E. Eithne, while hovering close to the vessel, with a consequent increase in range for maritime SAR missions.

In April 1988, in a reply to a question in the Dail, it was revealed that the total annual cost of maintaining a Dauphin at permanent readiness was £3.85 million, which included the salaries of Air Corps aircrews, technicians, administrative and support services. Despite these difficulties and commitments, a number of pilots and aircrew were qualified for night SAR missions on the Dauphin in the that year, with the first night rescue mission occurring on July 29, 1988, when three fishermen were winched to safety from their boat, which had run aground on a sandbank in Rossport Harbour, Co. Mayo. Commencing in October 1988, the Air Corps also deployed Dauphins to Shannon Airport for intensive day and night training exercises over the Atlantic Ocean to enable crews to gain experience for maritime SAR operations off the west coast. A total of 78 SAR missions were conducted by the Dauphins in 1988, including two night rescue missions, resulting in the saving of 41 lives.

Left: Two of the Dauphins (244 and 245) were equipped to operate from the Navy's L.E. Eithne. Note the harpoon for deck landing on the underside of the fuselage.
(J. McFarland photo)

In 1988 a campaign for a SAR helicopter base on the west coast of Ireland was initiated by a lobby group known as the West Coast Search and Rescue Action Committee. A base on the west coast would result in a considerable reduction in the response times by the Dauphins for SAR missions over the Atlantic Ocean. In a report submitted by this group to the Irish Government, the following proposals were included: the SAR Squadron should be deployed to Shannon International Airport; a Dauphin should be stationed at Finner Army Camp, Co. Donegal, for SAR operations off the north-west coast; a medium range helicopter should be acquired for the Air Corps, or operated by a private company under contract, to carry out maritime SAR missions beyond the range of the Dauphin. In response to these proposals the Irish Government established a Review Group on Air/Sea Rescue Services early in 1989, which issued an interim report in May of that year. This report included a recommendation that a Dauphin should be deployed to Shannon International Airport in September, to provide a twenty-four hour SAR service for the west coast region. In March 1990 the Review Group issued its final report, which recommended that "two medium range helicopters be purchased for the Air Corps", but in the interim "a private contract to provide a medium range SAR service should be negotiated as a matter of urgency". The report also recommended that the Dauphin should be deployed to Finner Military Camp to provide a short range twenty-four hour SAR service for the north-west region, when the medium range helicopter commenced operations from Shannon Airport.

Seven crew members were rescued by a Dauphin from a beached ship at night, off Arklow, Co. Wicklow, in March 1989. In the same year the Dauphins carried out a total of 105 SAR missions, with sixty-six lives saved, which included eighteen SAR missions by night. This was the highest number of SAR missions carried out by the Air Corps since 1964, when the Helicopter Flight first commenced SAR operations.

On September 4, 1989 a detachment from SAR Squadron, equipped with a Dauphin, was deployed to Shannon Airport, to provide a twenty-four hour, short range SAR service for the west coast region. Operating from the airport, designated Air Corps Station, Shannon, the Dauphin carried out twenty-seven SAR missions over the next four months.
In 1990 the Dauphins completed the first full year of SAR operations from the Air Corps Station, comprising a total of ninety-five SAR missions, including twenty-two missions conducted by night, resulting in forty-eight lives saved. During this period

Left: Spectacular view of a Dauphin over Dublin in May 2006.
(A.C. Photographic Section)

Above: Instrument panel on the Dauphin. This was the first Electronic Flight Instrumentation System installed on an Air Corps helicopter. (S. Nolan photo)

an injured seaman was rescued by a Dauphin from a ship about 150 miles north-west of Shannon Airport, after the helicopter had refuelled at sea from the L.E. Eithne. Thirty-five air ambulance and organ transplant missions were also carried out by the Dauphins in the same year including five night flights.

On the night of April 4/5, 1991, a Dauphin and an RAF Sea King winched sixty-six people off a French factory ship that had grounded on rocks at the entrance to Galway Bay. In November 1991 the crews of both helicopters jointly received an award from the Shipwrecked Mariners Society of London for their bravery during this dramatic rescue. Throughout 1991 the Dauphins carried out a total of eighty SAR missions, which included seventeen by night, and ten air ambulance missions. Operating a Sikorsky S-61N helicopter from Shannon Airport, a commercial helicopter operator (Irish Helicopters Ltd.) commenced a twenty-four hour medium range SAR service for the west coast region on July 15, 1991, under contract to the Department of the Marine. On the same day the Dauphin was deployed to Finner Military Camp, which was designated Air Corps Station, Finner.

Over the four years ending December 31, 1990, the two Dauphins of Naval Squadron had only accumulated a total of 100 flying hours on shipborne operations, due to the Air Corps intensive helicopter training programme and SAR commitments. In November 1991 the Comptroller and Auditor General issued a report, which criticised the Department of Defence for having "no coherent operational programme put in place for the use of the Dauphins for fishery protection duties". The report concluded, "that the benefits expected in enhanced fishery protection which should have been derived from the acquisition of the Eithne and the Dauphins, had not materialised". Operating from the L.E. Eithne in December 1991, a Dauphin participated for the first time in the detention of two foreign trawlers that were illegally fishing in Irish territorial waters, off the south-west coast. A total of 446 deck landings and on the L.E. Eithne were carried out by the Dauphins of Naval Squadron in 1992, an increase of 300 per cent over the previous year.

Following the deployment of the Dauphin to the west coast the Air Corps could only provide a daylight SAR service for the east coast region, operating the Alouette III from Baldonnel. In November 1995, following the death of a fisherman when a trawler sank at night off Howth Harbour, Co. Dublin, a Marine Emergency Review Group was set up by the Minister for the Marine to review the marine SAR services available on the east coast. The Air Corps was also requested by the Minister to evaluate the feasibility of providing a "twenty-four hour air and sea rescue service" for the east coast region. Commencing in December 1995, the Air Corps provided a twenty-four SAR service for the region, operating an Alouette III by day and a Dauphin by night, from Baldonnel.

In March 1996 the Review Group issued an interim report, with a recommendation that "as a short-term solution . . . the best probability for immediate SAR coverage on the east coast would be provided by the Air Corps' existing SA.365F Dauphin fleet". The final report of the Review Group was submitted to the Minister for the Marine in June 1996, recomennding the leasing of a medium range, multi-engined helicopter by the Irish Government to provide a twenty-four, all-weather SAR service for the east coast region. A Sikorsky S-61N, operated by a commercial helicopter operator (CHC Helicopters Ltd.) on lease to the Government, commenced medium-range SAR operations from Dublin Airport on July 1, 1998.

In November 1996 the Ministers for Defence and for the Marine had also announced that a twenty-four hour SAR service for the south and south-east regions would be provided by the Air Corps. The location of the Marine Rescue Helicopter Service for this region would be Waterford Regional Airport, which was announced in December 1997, and a Dauphin was to be deployed to the airport on July 1, 1998, when the leased medium range helicopter commenced SAR operations from Dublin Airport. However, due to a shortage of qualified pilots, the Air Corps was unable to provide a Dauphin on this date, but a "dawn to dusk" SAR service for the region was provided by an Alouette III, which was deployed to the airport on the same date. A Dauphin was to be deployed within a year to provide a twenty-four hour

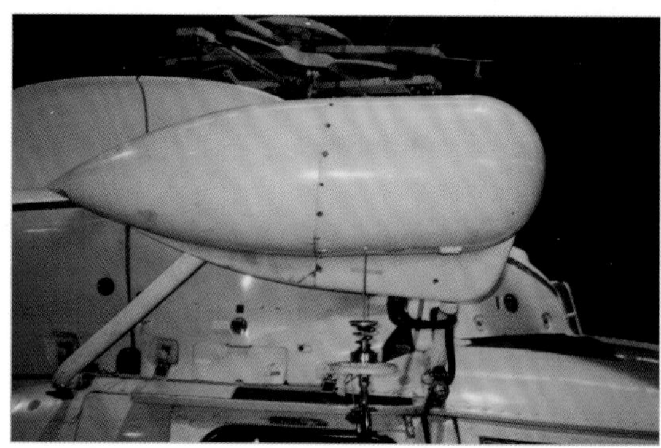

Right: The winch which is so vital in virtually all rescue operations is housed in an aerodynamic fairing above the starboard cabin door. (J. Maxwell photo)

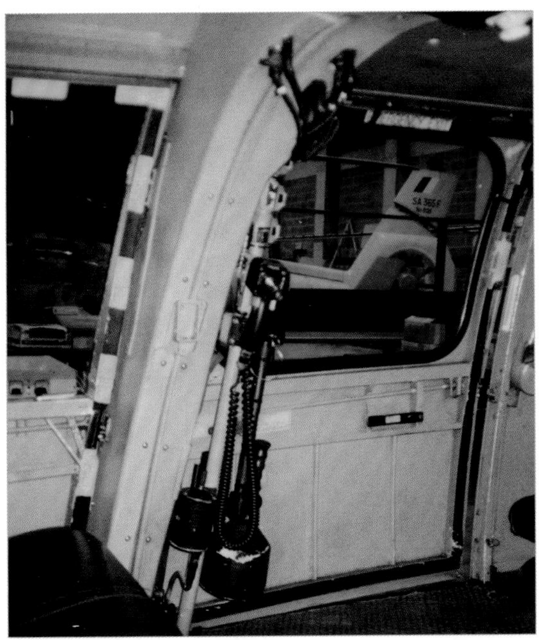

Left: Interior view of the winch operator's position. The winch operator has controls for the winch, searchlight and can also have limited control of the helicopter's position. (J. Maxwell photo)

SAR service from the airport, which was designated Air Corps Station, Waterford.

On July 1, 1999 a Dauphin (No. 248) was deployed to Air Corps Station, Waterford, to commence a twenty-four hour SAR service for the south and south-east regions. On the same night the Dauphin carried out the first SAR mission from the airport, searching for a small boat lost in fog in Dungarvan Bay, which was located by the helicopter and taken in tow by a lifeboat. Visibility at the airport was restricted by dense fog and the Dauphin was unable to land, despite making three attempts. Running low on fuel, the helicopter then attempted to land on Tramore Strand, south of the airport but crashed into nearby sand dunes, resulting in the deaths of Capt. Dave O'Flaherty, Capt. Mick Baker, Sgt. Paddy Mooney and Cpl. Neil Byrne. This was the first fatal accident to have occurred in thirty-six years of helicopter operations by the Air Corps. The Dauphin which crashed had accumulated a total of 4,562 flying hours since 1986 and had flown 450 SAR missions, with 150 lives saved. The loss of the crew was keenly felt throughout the tight knit Air Corps community and the investigation into the crash lead to a major revision of flight safety procedures at all levels in the organisation. The bravery and sacrifice of the crew was officially recognised in 2008 with the posthumous award of Distinguished Service Medals to the four men.

Due to other operational commitments, the retirements of qualified pilots and a shortage of qualified technicians, the Air Corps was unable to deploy another Dauphin to Waterford Airport for SAR operations. Operating from Air Corps Station, Finner, the Dauphin continued to provide a SAR service for the north-west region. From 2001 the Dauphins were operated by 301 Squadron, No. 3 Operations Wing. A total of 71 SAR missions, with 36 lives saved, were carried out by the Dauphins in 2002. Operated by Air Corps crews, a leased S-61N was to provide a twenty-four hour all-weather medium-range SAR service for the for the north-west region, based at Sligo Airport, commencing in 2003.

The S-61N (No. 257) commenced SAR operations in July, replacing the Dauphin, but the lease on the helicopter was cancelled by the Minister for Defence in December 2003 as a result of crewing difficulties. The Dauphin was again deployed to Sligo Airport until October 11, 2004, when replaced by an S-61N, operated by a civilian helicopter operator, under contract to the Irish Coastguard Service, to provide an SAR service for the north-west region.

From December 2003 onwards a number of modern type helicopters were evaluated by the Air Corps, to fulfil a requirement for a light utility helicopter and also to replace the Dauphins, which by then required major overhauls and upgrading to remain in service. The Dauphins had undergone major overhauls between 1993 and 1995, costing approximately €5 million. Further overhauls was considered to be too expensive as spare parts for these helicopters were becoming scarce as a result of these helicopters having been equipped originally with a unique hybrid EFIS system.

On May 7, 2003 the first Dauphin (No. 244) was withdrawn from use, having accumulated a total of 5,400 flying hours. The second Dauphin (No. 245) was placed in temporary storage in 2004 and was withdrawn from use on April 21, 2005, having accumulated a total of 5,950 flying hours. One of the remaining two Dauphins (No. 246) was withdrawn from use on December 20, 2005, followed by the other (No. 247) on February 27, 2006, each having accumulated 6,000 and 5,510 flying hours, respectively. The Dauphin (No. 247) had accumulated a further six flying hours carrying out three ambulance missions in 2006. The Dauphins were purchased by Rotor Leasing Inc. in the USA and were delivered by sea in containers in 2006. Rotor Leasing overhauled Dauphin No. 247 and repainted it in an attractive camouflage scheme of sand and light green. It was intended that the helicopters would be sold on to private collectors but in the event they were sold to a dealer in South America for eventual use by the Chilean Navy.

Left: the complex rotor head on the Dauphin. (J. Maxwell photo)

Colours & Markings

The Dauphins had an overall light grey finish with the underside of the fuselage painted red and the engine compartment painted white. Medium blue stripes separated the overall light grey finish of the fuselage from the red undersurfaces and the white finish of the engine compartment. The top surface of the engine compartment, stabiliser fins, the underside and top section of the tail, were also painted red. The helicopter's serial numbers displayed on both sides of the rear fuselage, the helicopter's designation and construction number displayed on the tail, and the nose radar housing were are all painted black.

The Celtic boss was displayed on both sides of the rear fuselage, in front of the serial number and a tri-coloured fin flash was displayed on both sides of the upper section of the tail. The St. Brendan crest, a Celtic cross on a white sail with a small star on a blue background, was displayed on the sides of the entrance doors. From 2000 onwards the name of a member of the crew of the crashed Dauphin (No. 248) was inscribed on the gearbox housing of the other four helicopters as follows: (Capt.) Dave O'Flaherty (No. 244); (Capt.) Mike Baker (No. 245); (Sgt.) Paddy Mooney (No. 246) and (Cpl.) Neil Byrne (No. 247).

Right: The rotor blades could be folded on all five Dauphins. It was normally only necessary to do this for the two Dauphins that could operate aboard ship. Hence this rare photo of a Dauphin with folded blades at Baldonnel. The tailfin could also be folded down for storage but this was never done.
(K. Byrne photo)

Right: A Dauphin on board the L.E. Eithne. Operating off the west coast in large Atlantic sea swells called for skilful piloting and co-ordination among all crew members.
(A.C. Photographic Section)

Hovering into wind, a simulated casualty is winched on board the Dauphin strapped to a narrow stretcher. (J. Maxwell photo)

Dauphin 247 in cowboy country. Following retirement from Air Corps service the four remaining Dauphins were sold to a company in the US which repainted No. 247 in this attractive camouflage scheme. It was demonstrated at various trade shows thoughout the US. (C. Bateman photo)

All four Dauphins were subsequently sold to a South American company which refurbished them prior to their entry into service with the Chilean Navy in March 2009. (William Olave Solis photo)

5.3

Gulfstream Aerospace Gulfstream III and IV-SP (1990 – date)

Two of the most reliable aircraft ever to enter service with the Air Corps, the Gulfstream III and IV were developed from a line of executive aircraft designed by Grumman Aircraft Engineering Corporation. In October 1978 the assets of Grumman American Aviation were acquired by American Jet Industries and development and production of the Gulfstream III was undertaken by a new company, Gulfstream American Corporation.

Powered by two 11,400 lb.s.t. Rolls-Royce RB.163 Spey turbofan engines, the first production Gulfstream III (c/n 300, N300GA) flew for the first time early in 1980. Following Type Certification by the Federal Aviation Administration in September 1980, deliveries of the Gulfstream III commenced before the end of the year, with the majority of these aircraft operated as executive aircraft by major business corporations. The Gulfstream III has also entered service with a number of air forces worldwide, including the USAF, US Navy, US Marines and the US Army. Production of the Gulfstream III ended in September 1986 after 202 had been constructed.

In March 1983 a design programme for a larger, more advanced executive aircraft, with a structurally re-designed supercritical wing and increased fuel capacity, was initiated by the company, which had been re-named Gulfstream Aerospace Corporation in November 1982. Designated G.1159C Gulfstream IV, production commenced in 1986, with the first deliveries in 1987 and over 300 had been delivered worldwide to business corporations and several air forces by the end of 1996.

Powered by two 12,420 lb.s.t. Rolls-Royce Tay 610-8 turbofan engines, the Gulfstream IV had a lengthened fuselage, which allowed the inclusion of a sixth window on both sides of the spacious cabin, and a cockpit equipped with advanced electronic flight instruments and flight management systems. Extra fuel capacity in the more aerodynamically efficient wings, which are fitted with winglets, also increased

Below: Gulfstream GIV in flight with a PC-9 keeping pace.
(A.C. Photographic Section)

Right: The Gulfstream GIII seen at a snowy Dublin airport in 1991. (Con Murphy photo)

the aircraft's maximum range to almost 5,000 miles. In September 1992 the Gulfstream IV-SP went into production, which had an increased take-off weight and payload with more advanced avionics equipment installed in the cockpit.

From January to June 1990 the Presidency of the EEC was to be administered by the Irish Government, which would result in a significant increase in the number of worldwide flights by Government Ministers and officials during this period. To enable Ministers to fulfil the worldwide commitments of the EEC the Irish Government issued a requirement in November 1989 for a long-range executive aircraft, to be leased for six months, commencing in January 1990. This was a very tight time frame and the response to the tender included companies offering a Boeing 727, an early model Canadair Challenger, and the Gulfstream GIII.

Following an evaluation of the various executive aircraft types, the Gulfstream III was selected to fulfil this requirement, which would be leased for the six months from Gulfstream Aerospace at an overall cost of IR£1.3.million, according to a Dail statement. Gulfstream initially offered airframe N303GA but this had been damaged in an accident when operated by the Ivory Coast government and was rejected by the Air Corps/Dept of Defence acceptance team. The Gulfstream III that was subsequently leased (c/n 413) had been constructed in 1983 (as N357GA) and was delivered to the US company, Joseph E. Seagram & Sons, (as N77SW) in January 1984. Four years later the Gulfstream III was acquired by the Federal Aviation Administration and was operated by this US Government agency (as N1) until May 1989. The aircraft was then acquired by the Metlife Credit Corporation (as N8266M) and was returned to Gulfstream Aerospace in September 1989.

In December 1989 a number of Air Corps pilots underwent ground school courses and conversion courses on the Gulfstream III at the Flight Safety Inc training centre in Savannah, Georgia which were included in the overall cost of the lease.

Following a non-stop transatlantic ferry flight of 3,300 miles from Savannah, flown by Comdt. Con Murphy and Captain Gerry Webb accompanied by Gulfstream training captain, Karl Neumaier, the Gulfstream III was delivered to Casement Aerodrome on January 4, 1990 and (as No. 249) entered service with the Ministerial Air Transport Service (MATS), Transport and Training Squadron, No. 1 Support Group. A crew of four, comprising two pilots, a flight engineer and a flight attendant and up to twelve passengers, could be accommodated on the Gulfstream III. Although primarily acquired for transporting Government Ministers engaged on EEC business, the Gulfstream III was also used for conveying the President and the Taoiseach on State visits to other countries.

The first long-range ministerial flight by the Gulfstream III, from Dublin to Washington, D.C. was flown less than a week after its arrival in Ireland, on January 10, 1990. (This was the only occasion on which the GIII made a non-stop east to west crossing of the Atlantic as the required fuel reserve could only just be met by the GIII in favourable weather conditions).

Within weeks of the GIII entering service, the aircraft became the first Air Corps aircraft to complete a round the world flight, conveying the Minister for Foreign Affairs to several countries on EEC business. This was a challenge considering the aircraft's newness and the Air Corps' lack of trans-global operational experience. Commencing on February 7, 1990 the Gulfstream III initially flew over the Atlantic Ocean

Formerly operated by the FederalAviation Administration in the US, the GIII was operated in this US government colour scheme during its service with the Air Corps.
(P. Cunniffe photo)

from Baldonnel to Ottawa (6hrs 40 min flying time) and continued the flight over Canada to Anchorage (Alaska) two days later. On the following day the Gulfstream III became the first Air Corps aircraft to fly over the Pacific Ocean, refuelling at Sapporo (Northern Japan) before flying on to Brunei in a total flight time of 15hrs 20mins. After a 2 day stop in Brunei, the aircraft made the short flight along the coast of North Borneo to Kuching, the capital of the Malaysian state of Sarawak. The following day, the crew flew a training detail to Kuala Lumpar and Singapore (Seletar) returning to Kuching that evening. For the return home, the Gulfstream III flew westwards to Dubai via Bombay for refuelling, becoming the first Air Corps aircraft to visit the Indian sub-continent. Next morning saw the aircraft flying from Dubai to Rome, arriving back at Baldonnel on February 18, 1990, having flown a total of 25,000 miles during the previous eleven days in 50 hours and 10 minutes flying time. The crew for this historic journey were Comdt. Con Murphy, Captain Gerry Webb, Captain Dave Gohery, Stewardess Cpl. Ruth Murphy and Gulfstream engineer John Stark.

The 6 month lease of the Gulfstream III was deemed to have been very successful with the aircraft giving excellent reliability during its ministerial flights, transporting Government Ministers and officials on EEC business throughout the EU as well as further afield to Oman, Kenya, Namibia, Sao Tome, the US, Canada and Mexico. The lease on the aircraft was extended for a further sixty days when the British Aerospace BAe 125-700 underwent a major overhaul in July and August 1990. In August, following the release of Brian Keenan, an Irish citizen who had been held hostage in the Lebanon, the Gulfstream III was used to fly him from Damascus to Dublin. The lease on the Gulfstream III was again extended in September 1990 and continued "on a pro-rata basis" until terminated on March 6, 1992, when the aircraft was returned to Gulfstream Aerospace. The Gulfstream III had accumulated a total of 1,777 flying hours while in service with the Air Corps, which included 929 flying hours in the first year of operations.

In June 1990 the Irish Government placed advertisements in trade journals requesting tenders for "an executive jet aircraft . . . capable of undertaking journeys of up to 3,500 nautical miles" to replace the Gulfstream III and the BAe 125-700, which was about to be withdrawn from use. A technical and economic evaluation of various executive aircraft was initiated by the Air Corps with the assistance of the Dept of Transport and Aer Lingus in September to fulfil this requirement and the choice eventually centred on the Gulfstream GIV and the Dassault Falcon 900. Part of the technical evaluation included checking the capability to fly non-stop from Baldonnel to Washington DC. Both manufacturers offered demonstration flights and so on 2nd October 1990 Falcon 900 HB-IAD flew the route non-stop in 8hr 45minutes and on 13th October 1990 Gulfstream GIV N400GA completed the same flight in 7hrs 45 minutes. However, it was not just a question of pure speed. Whichever aircraft was chosen would have to complete the journey with sufficient fuel reserves for safety and meet defined payload capability with additional communication and navigation equipment installed. Neither aircraft quite met the specification and so Gulfstream came back with a proposal to supply a GIV but to remanufacture it at a later date to bring it up to the new GIV-SP standard then under development.

On March 25, 1991 the order was placed with Gulfstream Aerospace Corporation for a new Gulfstream IV aircraft by the Department of Defence. A Gulfstream IV (c/n 1160), which had flown for the first time on February 26, 1991, was selected by the company to fulfil this order and was delivered in April to the Gulfstream Aerospace completion facility in Long Beach, California for the installation of communications and navigation equipment, to Air Corps specifications. The interior layout for 14 passengers was also fitted out at the facility, which included Irish materials, a colour scheme and other equipment selected by the Office of Public Works.

Throughout October and November 1991 the Gulfstream IV underwent an extensive acceptance and flight test programme in Long Beach under the Air Corps project team of Comdt Con Murphy and engineers Lt Col Ultan Lyons, Comdt. Tom Moloney and Mr Dave Shaw. The Gulfstream IV, under its temporary US registration N17584 was then flown back to Savannah for painting before final delivery to Department of Defence officials on 19th December 1991.

On December 20, 1991, the Gulfstream IV was delivered non-stop from Wilmington, Delawere to Baldonnel and (as No. 251) entered service with the Transport and Training Squadron, replacing the Gulfstream GIII. The first ministerial flight was on 15th February 1992 although the Taoiseach Charles Haughey had flown on the aircraft the previous week when he accompanied a crew training flight to Kirkwall in the Orkney Islands on 8th February 1992. A total of 584 flying hours was accumulated by the Gulfstream IV in 1992, including 169 flights for the MATS.

Between July and September 1994 this aircraft underwent an upgrading to Gulfstream IV-SP standard by the company in the USA. The first round the world flight by the Gulfstream IV was completed over fourteen days, commencing on September 14, 1994, when the Taoiseach visited Australia and New Zealand. The Gulfstream IV flew eastwards from Baldonnel to Irkutsk, Siberia, and after refuelling, flew on to Hong Kong, before landing in Perth, Australia. On the return journey from New Zealand the Gulfstream IV flew north-eastwards to Hawaii, then on to Edmonton, Canada before crossing the Atlantic Ocean to arrive back at Casement Aerodrome on September 28, 1994. A total of 670 flying hours was accumulated by the Gulfstream IV in 1994, including 114 MATS flights.

The expenditure incurred in acquiring the Gulfstream IV resulted in widespread criticism in the national newspapers and by the Opposition parties in the Dáil. On February 20, 1992, in response to this criticism, the Minister for Defence informed the Dáil that the aircraft "was being acquired on the basis of a ten-year lease . . . and the leasing cost would amount to about two million pounds per annum". It was also revealed that the aircraft operated by the MATS are used for official duties by the President, Taoiseach, members of the Government and authorised officials of the public service, with each flight authorised by the Department of the Taoiseach. Throughout September and October 1994 there was further criticism in the national newspapers and by Opposition politicians about the operating costs and utilisation of the Gulfstream IV. In January 1995 the Government established a special committee, which reviewed "the cost-effectiveness, efficiency, security and flexibility . . . and the use of . . ." the aircraft operated by the MATS. Details about the operating costs and the utilisation of the Gulfstream IV for ministerial flights was provided in the Dáil and in public statements from the Government but the criticism of the aircraft's utilisation and expenditure by politicians and newspapers was to continue into the future.

From July to December 1996 the Presidency of the EU was administered by the Irish Government, which resulted in a significant increase in the number of ministerial flights throughout Europe and to other countries worldwide. During this period there was intensive utilisation of the Gulfstream IV by Government Ministers engaged on EU business and by the President, Taoiseach and Tanaiste on official visits to foreign countries. In the same year the Gulfstream IV completed five years of service with the Air Corps, having visited sixty countries in five continents, flown over all the major oceans of the world and landed in twenty states of the USA during this period. A total of 1,180 flying hours was accumulated by the Gulfstream IV and Beechcraft Super King Air 200 throughout 1996, incorporating 261 MATS flights.

On January 20, 1999, during an official visit by the Taoiseach to Palestine, the Gulfstream IV became the first executive aircraft, operated by a foreign government, to land at Gaza airport. A second round-the-world flight was completed by the Gulfstream IV between January 30 and February 12, 1999, when the Tanaiste visited Japan, New Zealand and Australia. On the return flight the Gulfstream IV refuelled in Western Samoa before crossing the Pacific Ocean to reach Honolulu for an overnight stop. On the following day the Gulfstream IV flew on to Edmonton, Canada, to refuel before crossing the Atlantic Ocean to land at Casement Aerodrome. The Gulfstream IV was also used by the President during official visits to Central American countries, Mexico, USA and the United Kingdom. Between July and September 1999 the Gulfstream IV underwent a major overhaul in the USA by Gulfstream Aerospace and in November conveyed the Taoiseach on visits to Hungary, Slovenia and Kosovo, on behalf of the

The Gulfstream GIII makes a short stop at Dublin Airport to pick up passengers. (S. Nolan collection)

The GIV seen at altitude trailing contrails. It can fly at altitudes up to 45,000 ft. (A.C. Photographic Section)

European Union. A total of 598 flying hours was accumulated by the Gulfstream IV in 1999, which included 111 flights by MATS.

In November 2000 a wing leading edge on the Gulfstream IV was damaged by a tractor engaged on towing operations at Baldonnel. The aircraft was out of service for two weeks while awaiting a new leading edge, which had to be manufactured by Gulfstream Aerospace. In the same year the Gulfstream IV accumulated a total of 786 flying hours, which included 140 flights by MATS.

Two ministerial flights by the Gulfstream IV had to be aborted in February 2001 due to a fault in the aircraft's nosewheel steering, which was repaired by an aircraft maintenance company in Switzerland. The Gulfstream IV completed a third round-the-world flight of 17,286 nautical miles over ten days, commencing on March 4, 2001, during visits by the Tanaiste to the USA and Japan to promote investments in Ireland. In June 2001, during a routine maintenance inspection of the Gulfstream IV, serious corrosion was discovered in the tail section. The aircraft was out of service for about three months while the tail section underwent repairs. There was no hangar at Baldonnel to completely accommodate the Gulfstream IV, due to height of the tail section and the rear fuselage had to remain exposed to the elements, which apparently lead to the corrosion. The Gulfstream IV completed ten years of service with the Air Corps in the same year, having accumulated over 7,200 flying hours in that period, which was one of the highest number of flying hours for this aircraft type. Total cost of operating the Gulfstream IV over the ten years was €44.06 million, which included lease costs, with the final lease instalment paid in December 2001. A total of 510 and 336 flying hours was accumulated by the Gulfstream IV on ministerial flights in 2001 and 2002 respectively. Since then the Gulfstream GIV has continued to give excellent service to the Air Corps. The interior was recently refitted though no changes were made to any aircraft systems or flight equipment. It is highly reliable and can cruise at altitudes well above the normal air traffic. It is cost effective and continues to be used on ministerial air transport missions throughout Europe and the world.

Colours and Markings

The Gulfstream III was delivered to the Air Corps with a white finish on the upper fuselage section, tailfin, tailplane, engine nacelles and the wing surfaces. The lower fuselage section and undersides had an overall blue finish, separated from the upper fuselage section by a gold cheatline running along the fuselage. This paint scheme had been retained since the aircraft had been in service with the Federal Aviation Administration. The tri-coloured Celtic boss was displayed on both sides of the front fuselage section, aft of the entrance door, and on the mid-section of the upper surfaces of both wings, with a tri-coloured fin flash displayed on both sides of the upper section of the tailfin. The aircraft's serial number, in black, was displayed on both sides of the lower section of the tailfin and on the undersides of both wings. The inscription, IRISH AIR CORPS – AER CHÓR NA h-ÉIREANN, in black, was displayed above the windows on both sides of the fuselage. The titles and Irish script were painted in Baldonnel some time

The comprehensively equipped cockpit of the GIV. (Con Murphy collection)

after its arrival. The Gulfstream IV has an overall gloss white finish with a green cheatline running along the mid-section of the fuselage and on both winglets. The tri-coloured Celtic boss is displayed on both engine nacelles and on the upper and under surfaces of both wings. A tri-coloured "swept" fin flash is also displayed on both sides of the upper section of the rudder.

The aircraft's serial number, in green, is displayed on the engine nacelles and on the undersides of both wings. A large gold harp is displayed on both sides of the tailfin with a small gold harp on the port side of the fuselage, aft of the entrance door.

Below: Clearly showing the official emblem of State on the fin, GIV No. 251 takes off on another mission from Dublin Airport.
(P. Cunniffe photo)

5.4

CASA CN.235-100 and CASA CN.235MP (1991 – date)

In October 1979 the Spanish and Indonesian aircraft manufacturing companies, CASA and IPTN entered into an agreement to collaborate on the development of a new regional commercial transport aircraft. A joint company, Airtech, was established in 1980 to undertake the development and production of the aircraft, with the financial costs, design work and production to be shared equally between the two parent companies. Designated CN.235, one prototype was to be constructed by each company.

The Spanish prototype (ECT-100) flew for the first time on November 11, 1983, followed by the Indonesian prototype (PX-XNC) on December 30, 1983. Over the next three years the two prototypes underwent an intensive flight programme, which included visits by the Spanish prototype to Dublin and Shannon Airports in February 1986 during icing trials. The first production CN.235 flew for the first time on August 19, 1986, following orders for the aircraft by Indonesian and Spanish regional airlines. However, the civil version was not a sales success. The development of a basic military transport aircraft, designated CN.235M, was undertaken by AirTech and four of these aircraft were delivered to the Royal Saudi Air Force between December 1986 and April 1987. Over 200 of these aircraft had been delivered by 1998 to a number of air forces worldwide, including fifty CN.235Ms for the Turkish Air Force, which had been constructed under licence in Turkey.

Designated CN.235MPA, the development of a maritime patrol variant was initiated by IPTN in 1986 to fulfil a requirement for the Indonesian Air Force. Commencing in 1990, a maritime patrol variant was also developed by CASA, which is significantly different from the aircraft developed by IPTN and is named the CN.235MP Persuader, The prototype CN.235 (ECT-100) was used by CASA for testing and development of equipment and the various systems that were to be installed in the maritime patrol aircraft.

Below: The Casa CN235 is currently the largest aircraft type operated by the Air Corps. (A.C. Photographic Section)

Right: The first Casa CN.235 in Air Corps service was leased while the two that been ordered were under construction in Spain. Seen here at Waterford in a high visibility colour scheme, it was not equipped with specialised maritime surveillance equipment. (D. Leahy photo)

Powered by two 1,750 shp General Electric CT7-9C turboprop engines, the CN.235MP is a high-wing monoplane with a pressurised fuselage and a rear ramp that can be opened in flight to drop life rafts, emergency rations or various markers during SAR operations. The aircraft as first delivered, was equipped with an advanced search radar system, the Litton APS 504(V5), housed in a large radome attached to the underside of the front fuselage section and is used for surveillance, SAR, weather detection and beacon interrogation, and can detect small objects down to one square metre in size in all weather and sea conditions. A Forward Looking Infra-Red (FLIR) sensor using thermal imagery, housed in a rotating ball-shaped mount under the nose, can detect and classify surface contacts on the sea at night and in adverse weather conditions during SAR operations. Three navigation systems are installed in the CN.235MP to maintain a constant and accurate track of the aircraft's position. A 70mm Agiflite stabilised camera was also installed in the aircraft, operated through two removable bubble-shaped windows on both sides of the fuselage, and was integrated with the aircraft's navigation systems, with each image annotated with the date, time, latitude and longitude during exposure. A full range of airborne and marine communications equipment is also installed in the CN.235MP.

By 1989 the Irish Air Corps had a requirement for a maritime surveillance aircraft to replace the two Beechcraft Super King Air 200s, which were about to be withdrawn from use in the near future as they had reached their safe time limits for operating in a maritime environment. In September 1989 the Department of Defence invited tenders from aircraft manufacturing companies to fulfil this requirement. A Maritime Aircraft Evaluation Board was established at the same time, which evaluated a total of 13 aircraft types over the next eight months and recommended the procurement of two CASA CN.235MPs, in a report issued in May 1990. Among the types submitted for consideration were the DH Canada Dash 8, a specialised martime patrol version of the Kingair, the Dassault Falcon/Gaurdian, the Fokker F.27, the Saab 340, the HS-748, the Casa 212 and the Casa CN.235. Two CN.235MPs were ordered by the Department of Defence in April 1991, for manufacture in Spain and delivery in 1994, at a total coast of €55.3 million, according to contemporary newspaper reports. Half of this amount was to be provided from EU funds, on condition that 90% of the flying hours would be accumulated by these aircraft on maritime surveillance operations over the Irish sector of the European Economic Zone.

The two Super King Air 200s were withdrawn from use in 1990 and 1991 and an interim aircraft for maritime surveillance operations was required by the Air Corps until the two CN.235MPs could be delivered. To fulfil this requirement the Department of Defence acquired a CN.235M-100 (c/n C019) from CASA in April 1991, having been used by the company (as EC-330) for demonstration flights and trials. This aircraft, which was returned to the company when the two CN.235MPs were delivered, was not specifically equipped for maritime surveillance operations but the weather radar equipment installed in the nose was capable of locating shipping in the maritime patrol area.

Below: instrument panel on Casa No. 250 (S. Nolan photo)

Casa No. 250 photographed outside a hangar at Dublin Airport. The underside was sprayed silver. (S.Nolan photo)

The precise position and identification of shipping would be determined by an observer/photographer operating the installed navigation equipment in the aircraft. Throughout May 1991 a number of Air Corps flight crews and maintenance technicians underwent a training programme on the CN.235M-100 at the company factory in Spain.

The CN.235M-100, which is the largest aircraft to enter service with the Air Corps to date, was delivered to Casement Aerodrome on June 6, 1991 and entered service (as No. 250) with Maritime Squadron, No. 1 Support Wing. The first maritime surveillance mission by the CN.235M-100 occurred on June 7, 1991 and a total of 426 flying hours was accumulated by the aircraft in the following six months, including 100 maritime surveillance missions. On these missions the CN.235M-100 normally carried a crew of five: pilot (captain), co-pilot, flight engineer, sensor operator and observer/photographer. A total of 830 flying hours was accumulated by the CN.235M-100 in 1992, including 1547 sightings of fishing trawlers logged during 152 maritime surveillance missions over the European Economic Zone.

The CN.235M-100 also participated in thirteen SAR operations during this period, which included searching, detecting and guiding other ships or rescue helicopters to the distress area. Top cover during the SAR operations was also provided by the CN.235M-100, relaying radio communications from the helicopters or ships to shore-based rescue agencies. The first SAR mission by the CN.235M-100 occurred on July 1, 1991, in response to a distress call from a Spanish trawler, which had a seriously ill crew member on board, 150 miles off the west coast of Ireland. The CN.235M-100 located the trawler and flew top-cover as the seaman was winched off the trawler by a Dauphin and flown to a hospital in Galway.

Air ambulance missions were also conducted by the CN.235M-100, including the transportation of human donor organs and seriously ill patients to hospitals in the State or abroad, often with medical personnel in attendance. On the night of September 23, 1994 the CN.235M-100 was damaged in a landing accident at Baldonnel, during an air ambulance mission transporting donor organs from Cork to Dublin. The aircraft returned to service following repairs by Air Corps technicians. A total of 57 air ambulance missions were flown by the CN.235M-100 in the first four years of service with the Air Corps.

The CN.235M-100 was also used for parachute training courses by the Defence Forces and as a general transport by the Air Corps. In October 1991 a SIAI-Marchetti SF.260 Warrior (No. 227), which had been damaged in a forced landing, was delivered in the CN.235M-100 to the company factory in Italy, to be repaired. The CN.235M-100 No. 250, which had accumulated a total of 3,142 flying hours while in service with the Air Corps, was returned to the company on January 16, 1995, following the delivery of the two CN.235MPs. The Department of Defence had not accepted an offer from CASA to acquire the CN.235M-100 for $2m. It was later purchased by the Chilean Government for $5m.

The two CN.235MPs (c/ns 085 and 094) were delivered to Casement Aerodrome on December 8, 1994 and (as Nos. 252 and 253) entered service with Maritime Squadron, No. 1 Support Wing. Officially designated CN.235-100M/IR-01, these were the first maritime patrol variants of this aircraft to be delivered to any air force worldwide. On the following day one of the CN.235MPs (No. 252), with a company test pilot and airborne radar instructor on board, carried out the first maritime surveillance mission off the west coast of Ireland. The other CN.235MP (No. 253) was returned to the company factory on December 10, 1994 for fitting out to be completed before returning to service on January 28, 1995. To operate the advanced radar and navigation systems installed in these aircraft an Airborne Operators Course for Air Corps personnel had been conducted throughout 1994. The first phase of this course, which lasted for twelve weeks, was held at Baldonnel and the final phase, over eight weeks, was provided by Provincial Airlines at St. Johns Airport, Newfoundland. A number of Air Corps crews also underwent a period of intensive training, from December 1994 to February 1995, to attain operational capability on the CN.235MP.

The maritime areas of the Irish sector of the European Economic Zone, which cover approximately 132,000 square miles, is regularly patrolled by the Irish Naval Service and the CN.235MPs of the Air Corps. On a maritime surveillance mission, usually lasting between six and nine hours, the CN.235MP normally carries a crew of six, comprising a pilot (aircraft commander), co-pilot, two airborne radar operators, a photographer/observer and a technician/observer. Reports of all shipping sighted during a patrol, with other observations, are transmitted to the Irish Naval Service's Operations Centre.

Left: Instrument panel on the Casa CN.235 No. 252 specifically built for the Air Corps. Note the additional equipment by comparison with that on the previous page. (S. Nolan photo)

Life-saving equipment carried by the CN.235MP on SAR missions includes a liferaft and emergency rations, which can be air-dropped over the rescue area through the open rear ramp door. Smoke, dye or illumination markers can also be launched from the CN.235MP to enable helicopters or other shipping to locate a ship in distress or any survivors. The aircraft's sophisticated radar equipment is also used to accurately guide helicopters or other shipping to the rescue area and the CN.235MP can also provide top-cover to co-ordinate and provide a communications link with shore-based rescue agencies during these operations. The CN.235MPs are also used for air ambulance missions and parachute jumps by Defence Forces personnel.

The CN.235MPs accumulated more flying hours in the first six months of maritime surveillance operations, with almost three times more sightings of shipping, than the two Super King Air 200s could achieve in twelve months. A total of 1,700 flying hours was accumulated by the CN.235MPs in 1995, including 237 maritime surveillance patrols, with over 6,000 sightings of shipping. Two Air Corps pilots had each accumulated a total of 1,000 flying hours on these aircraft by 1998. A total of 10,000 flying hours was accumulated by the CN.235M-100 and the two CN.235MPs between June 1991 and May 1999, including 270,000 sightings of shipping during maritime surveillance operations. On May 28, 1999 this achievement was celebrated at a ceremony at Baldonnel, attended by maritime aircraft and crews from the air forces of France, Portugal and Spain. From 2001 following re-organisation of the Air Corps structure the CN.235MPs were operated by 101 Squadron, No.1 Operations Wing.

After thirteen years of service the two aircraft received a major upgrade costing €12.5 million with the first (No.252) completed in December 2007 and the second (No. 253) in July 2008. The upgrade was known as FITS, Fully Integrated Tactical System and it included the replacement of the original search radar with a Telephonix "Ocean Eye" AN/APS-143C(V)3 radar and a new forward looking infra red system together with new operator consoles and a rearrangement of internal equipment and seating. The AgiFlite camera was replaced by a Nikon D2X connected to the navigation system so that latitude/longitude information can be stored with the image for later use.

Apart from the tasks of maritime patrol and SAR mentioned above one of the more unusual tasks carried out by the CASA aircraft crews is that of reporting on the Whale population off the west coast of Ireland. In 2007 a pod of nine sperm whales was spotted on the surface over 100 miles off the Mullet peninsula at the edge of the continental shelf during a routine patrol. This is an area where little cetacean monitoring is undertaken so the news of such an encounter was most welcome to the Irish Whale and Dolphin group who are dedicated to the conservation and better understanding of whales, dolphins and porpoise in Irish waters.

Left: Comparison of the FLIR systems used by the Casa. The one on the left was replaced by the system on the right during an upgrade in 2008. (J. Maxwell photo)

Right: Old and new radar operators stations following the FITS upgrade carried out on both CASA's. (S. Nolan photos)

Right: Ramp open in preparation for a rescue drop of survival equipment. It's believed that this has only been carried out on two live operations. (A.C. Photographic Section)

Far right: For marking positions on other wise featureless seas, smoke markers can be dropped from a chute within the cabin. It's angled rearwards to take advantage of the slipstream effect. (S. Nolan photo)

Right: a view of the rescue equipment that can be dropped to vessels in difficulty. (J. Maxwell photo)

Colours & Markings

The wings, tailplane, upper surfaces of the fuselage, and engine nacelles of the CN.235M had an overall white finish, with the undersides of the fuselage and engine nacelles painted silver. Day-glo red stripes, slanted towards the rear of the aircraft, were displayed on the forward fuselage section, on the rear fuselage section in front of the tailplane, the engine nacelles and on the tips of the wings and tailplane. The inscription "MARITIME" was displayed on both sides of the front fuselage section, under the cockpit, with the inscription "AER CHÓR na h-ÉIREANN" displayed on both sides of the rear fuselage section, in front of the day-glo red stripes. The tri-coloured Celtic boss was displayed on both sides of the rear fuselage and on the upper and under surfaces of both wings, with a tricoloured fin flash displayed on both sides of the upper section of the tailfin. The Air Corps serial number, in black, was displayed on both sides of the tailfin and on the undersides of the port wing.

The fuselage and wings of the CN.235MPs are finished in an overall medium blue FS 15177, with a light blue FS15450 cheatline extending from the nose along the fuselage sides and across the rear ramp door. The inscription "MARITIME" is also displayed under the cockpit, on the lower section of both sides of the front fuselage. The inscription "IRISH AIR CORPS" is displayed on the upper section of both sides of the fuselage, over the entrance doors, behind the cockpit, and "AER CHOR NA h-EIREANN" is displayed on both sides of the tailplane fillet. The serial number, in black, Celtic boss and tricoloured fin flash are displayed in the same positions as on the CN.235M.

Above: The search radar housed in a large under fuselage radome is shown to good effect in this view of Casa No. 252. (J. Maxwell photo)

The Air Corps Pipe Band so often seen on parades around the country, are an integral part of Air Corps ceremonial life. Seen here, having been flown in by a CASA No. 250 to a Families Day in this pre 1994 photo. (R. James collection)

5.5

Eurocopter (Aérospatiale) AS.355N Twin Ecureuil (1997 – 2007)

The Air Corps had a long history in providing support to the Garda Síochána. Indeed, one of the earliest recorded missions in support of the police took place on 23rd June 1936 when Lt. D.K. Johnston took off in Avro 636 (A15) to carry out a search following a bank robbery in Finglas, Co. Dublin. During the troubles in Northern Ireland the Air Corps provided aerial support for cash and commercial explosive escorts near border areas using Reims Cessna FR-172 aircraft equipped with radios capable of operating on Garda frequencies. It was becoming clear from experience in Britain and elsewhere that a dedicated full time air support service could be extremely useful in routine policing duties.

In 1996 the Irish Government established an Inter-Departmental Technical Group to formulate specifications for a helicopter and a fixed-wing aircraft to equip the new Garda Air Support Unit (GASU), which was to be formed in January 1997. The AS.355N Twin Ecureuil was selected by the Group to equip the GASU, following a thorough evaluation of tenders for various helicopter types used for police support operations in other countries. On December 12, 1996 the Minister for Justice announced that a contract had been awarded to Eurocopter International to supply a single AS.355N, which would be delivered in 1997, at a cost of IR£3m, according to newspaper reports. The Irish Air Corps was to provide the pilots and routine maintenance when the helicopter entered service with the GASU. The Air Corps also carried out tasks with GASU Observers using the Alouette III helicopter until the delivery of the AS.355N.

The AS.355N Ecureuil 2 had its origins in the single engine AS.350 Ecureuil (Squirrel) which was designed and constructed by Aérospatiale as a follow up to their highly successful Alouette II, but with reduced noise and vibration levels together with lower operating and maintenance costs. It utilised a composite three-bladed main rotor, with a glass fibre hub known as Starflex, which requires virtually no maintenance. A twin engine variant was developed under the designation AS.355 with the first prototype flying on 3rd October 1979. A production model known as the AS355 N Ecureuil 2 is powered by two Turbomeca Arrius 1A engines and is equipped with a Full Authority Digital Engine Control (FADEC) system for better single engine performance. This variant is marketed as the TwinStar in the United States

The AS.355N Ecureuil 2 (c/n 5633) for the GASU was initially delivered to McAlpine Helicopters Ltd,

Right: The Garda AS.355N was a regular sight over Dublin where it had a positive impact in law enforcement. (A.C. Photographic Section)

Left: The Garda helicopters operate throughout the country. AS.355N No. 255 was photographed on the helipad at Fanad Head lighthouse, Co. Donegal. (T. Mansfield photo)

Oxford (as G-BXEV) on April 24, 1997 for the installation of specialist equipment required for police support operations. Maintenance training for technicians and initial pilot conversion courses on the helicopter was also provided by the company for Air Corps personnel over the next three months. On August 22, 1997 the Twin Ecureuil (as No. 255) was delivered by an Air Corps and Garda crew to Baldonnel.

Over the next two weeks the helicopter was used by the GASU to achieve operational status in time for a ceremony to mark the occasion of the GASU functioning with its own equipment on September 9, 1997 at which the then Minister for Justice, John O'Donohoe was present. (The unit itself had been officially launched earlier that year by the previous Minister for Justice, Nora Owen). In the first year of operation the Twin Ecureuil accumulated a total of 1,211 flying hours, comprising 2,730 operational support missions and was directly responsible for sixty-four arrests by the Gardai.

The Twin Ecureuil was at constant readiness to provide aerial surveillance round the clock during Garda operations against the majority of criminal activities. The terms of reference for the deployment of the Garda air assets state that they may be deployed if there is an immediate threat to life, to incidents of a criminal or terrorist nature, to incidents where there is an immediate threat of serious public disorder, tasks leading to the prevention or detection of crime, evidence gathering, intelligence gathering, photographic tasks and traffic management and monitoring. Operational control of the air assets remains with the Department of Justice, Equality and Law Reform.

The Twin Ecureuil normally carried a crew of three, an Air Corps pilot and two Garda observers. Dual video recorders were used for viewing and recording images from a 3-chip daylight camera and a FLIR (Forward Looking Infra-Red) thermal imaging video camera, mounted under the nose of the helicopter, operated by an observer seated beside the pilot. A "Nightsun" searchlight was mounted under the rear fuselage section. A wide range of radio and microwave downlink equipment was installed in the Twin Ecureuil, which enabled both observers to communicate with Garda personnel and stations throughout the State.

One of the early problems encountered when operating the type was that there was only one machine available. The Twin Ecureuil had to be at constant readiness to fulfil Garda requirements, therefore limiting the amount of time available for Air Corps pilots deployed to the GASU for training on the helicopter.

In 2001 the annual report of the Comptroller and Auditor General considered the total operating costs of the GASU for 1997-2000 to be "far in advance of what was envisaged" in 1997. The split responsibility by the Air Corps and the Gardai for the operation of the GASU had an adverse effect on the financial management of the unit, according to the report. It was also revealed that the Twin Ecureuil, which comprised 7% of the helicopter fleet operated by the Air Corps, accounted for 19% of the total helicopter maintenance budget. After some negotiation, a service level agreement (SLA) was drawn up in 2004 between the Department of Justice, Equality and Law Reform and the Department of Defence covering all aspects of the Air Corps commitments to flying the Garda aircraft. Routine maintenance of the helicopters is now carried out by a private contractor with Air Corps personnel flying the machines.

During an overhaul in 2002 the door configuration on the right hand side was changed to match that on the left with a small forward door and large rear door. This was done as a result of a change in operational needs, and the necessity to carry specialist teams.

A small modification had been made previously to the entry steps, replacing a single step attached to the front of the skid with a longer rail step that ran almost the full width of the entry doors.

Over its ten years operational service with the GASU the AS.355N had flown a total of 7,321:24 flight hours and had responded to 10,905 incidents and contributed to the arrest of 1,612 suspects. The use of helicopters by the Gardai was deemed to be highly successful and a second machine in the form of an EC-135T1 was procured in 2002. This was later upgraded to T2 standard. See section 6.1 for details. After ten years in operation the AS.355N was withdrawn from use and replaced by another EC-135, this time a T2+ model in January 2008. In April 2009, the AS.355N was tendered for sale, complete with police role equipment, having accumulated 7,420 flying hours.

Colours & Markings

From 1999 to 2002 the Twin Ecureuil had an overall white paint scheme, with a horizontal yellow cheatline edged in blue running along the centre of the fuselage, from the nose along the boom to the stabilizer, The insignia of the Garda Siochana bisected the cheatline on the rear entrance door and the inscription "GARDA", in black, in two places on both sides of the fuselage and under the nose. A tricoloured fin flash was displayed on the fin and the Air Corps serial number, in black, was displayed on both sides of the gearbox housing. In 2002, during a major overhaul, the undersides of the Twin Ecureuil were painted dark blue up to the cheatline to match the high conspicuity livery of the newly purchased EC 135T1.

When it initially entered service the AS. 355N wore this attractive white colour scheme with a high visibility cheatline. The photo on right shows the original door configuration.
(T. Mansfield photo)

Left: Following a refit No. 255 is shown with it a new paint scheme similar to that of the EC-135 which ahd by this time entered service with the GASU. Note the new door configuration on the right hand side.
(T. Mansfield photo)

Left: No.255 again shortly before being retired from service in 2007. It could be used to carry small teams including dog handlers as well as its more usual surveillance role. (T. Mansfield photo)

5.6

Pilatus Britten-Norman BN-2T-4S Defender 4000 (1997 – date)

Anyone who has travelled by air to the Aran Islands off Ireland's west coast will almost certainly have flown in the well known Britten Norman Islander aircraft operated by Aer Arann. Less well known however is its larger derivative, the BN-2T-4S Defender 4000, the fixed wing equipment of the Garda Air Support Unit.

In April 1996, following the decision by the Irish Government to establish a dedicated Garda Air Support Unit the Inter-Departmental Technical Group was established to formulate specifications for a fixed-wing aircraft and a helicopter to equip this unit. On December 12, 1996 the Minister for Justice announced that a contract had been awarded to Pilatus Britten-Norman for a single BN-2T-4S Defender 4000, which was to be delivered in 1997, the Gardai becoming the launch customer for this type.

The Defender 4000 is a larger and more powerful derivative of the highly successful Britten Norman Islander range of small twin engine STOL airliners used throughout the world. Production of the BN-2A Islander, which had a number of aerodynamic refinements and other modifications over the original BN-2 commenced in 1969. Military variants of the BN-2A, named Defender, were also delivered to twenty air forces worldwide. Powered by two 320-shp Allison 250-B17C turboprop engines, a prototype (G-BPBN) flew for the first time on August 2, 1980, which was designated BN-2T Turbine Islander. Deliveries of the Turbine Islander to civil operators commenced in 1981 and a military variant, powered by the same turboprop engines, has also been delivered to coastguard and police forces worldwide.

In 1971, due to financial problems, Britten-Norman went into receivership and was acquired by the Belgian company, Fairey S.A. Production of the Islander was transferred from the Isle of Wight to Gosselies in Belgium, but Fairey S.A. went into receivership in 1977. Britten-Norman was acquired by the Swiss company, Pilatus Flugzeugwerke AG, in 1978 and the manufacture and assembly of the Islander and Defender on the Isle of Wight re-commenced in 1979.

The prototype BN-2T-4S Defender 4000 (c/n 4005) flew for the first time on August 17, 1994, powered by two 400-shp Allison B250-17F turboprop engines. By comparison with the Islander, the Defender 4000 has an increased all-up weight, an extended and strengthened fuselage and with a strengthened undercarriage. In addition it is fitted with a larger wing and a re-designed tailfin and tailplane. The aircraft is also equipped with advanced navigation and radio communications systems, with provision for a large radar antenna installed in the re-designed nose. The cabin can accommodate up to sixteen personnel in passenger configuration and the cockpit

Right: Defender No. 258 takes off from Waterford airport in 2008. Following a repaint it no longer carries the high visibility stripe. (P.J. Cummins photo)

No. 254 seen again at Waterford airport. (D. Leahy photo)

Below: No. 254 seen again just after take off. It is considerably larger than the Islander from which it is derived. (P. J. Cummins photo)

windscreen is deepened, to improve pilot visibility, with panoramic windows on both sides. It still maintains the short take off and landing capabilities for which the Islander is famous. It can loiter at around 80-100kts and has a stalling speed of 50kts.

As with the AS.355N helicopter operated by the same unit, the Gardai are responsible for operational control, while routine maintenance and provision of pilots to fly the aircraft is the responsibility of the Air Corps. Operating from Baldonnel throughout July and early August 1997, the prototype BN-2T-4S (G-SURV) was used by the Air Corps for pilot conversion courses and maintenance training for technicians. This aircraft, which was on loan from the company, did not have mission equipment installed.

On July 3, 1997 the first production BN-2T-4S Defender 4000 (c/n 4008) flew for the first time, and (as No. 255) was delivered to Casement Aerodrome on August 15, 1997. The Defender, which is available for 24 hour duties is normally used for covert surveillance at high altitudes during Garda support operations. An Air Corps pilot with two Garda observers are normally carried in the Defender during these operations but specialist operators can also be included, when required. The aircraft, which is equipped for IFR and has a maximum endurance of about six hours can fly to any region within the State without refuelling and using the aircraft's STOL capability can undertake Garda air support operations from all types of airstrips and airfields. The Defender is equipped to the same specification as the Eurocopter AS.355N Ecureuil 2, comprising forward Looking Infra-Red thermal imaging cameras in a retractable ventral pod, video recorders and advanced radio equipment.

Colours & Markings

The upper surfaces of the fuselage, wings, tailplane and tailfin of the Defender have an overall white finish, which had been initially bisected from the light grey undersides by a blue edged yellow cheatline running from the nose to the tailplane. The undersides of the engines, wings and tailplane are painted light grey. The Garda crest is displayed on the front doors while a tri-coloured fin flash is displayed on the tailfin. The nose radome and the serial numbers on both sides of the tailplane are painted black. Following a repaint in 2008, the Defender 4000 no longer carries the blue and yellow cheatline.

Irish Air Corps in the 21st Century

6.0

Irish Air Corps in the 21st Century

In 2000, the Irish government published the first-ever White Paper on Defence in Ireland. The White Paper set out the Government's medium term strategy for defence, covering the period up to 2010, based on the evolving national and international security environment. Bearing in mind that it was written prior to the September 11, 2001 attack on New York, and the subsequent wars in Afghanistan and Iraq, it nonetheless provided a useful framework for the development and restructuring of the Irish Defence Forces. Much of the groundwork for the White Paper had been carried out through the Price Waterhouse report on the Air Corps and Naval Service two years previously.

When it came to setting the international context for the country's defence policy, the White Paper stated that Ireland enjoyed a very benign external security environment, that Ireland faced virtually no risk of external military attack on its territory from another State, and that there was virtually no risk of externally instigated conflict in the country's immediate region. This remains true at the time of writing.

Nonetheless, the Irish Defence Forces bolstered their air defence capability with a purchase of twenty-four Bofors L70 anti-aircraft guns from the Royal Netherlands Air Force following the events of 11 September 2001. These weapons are controlled directly by eight 'Flycatcher' mobile air defence fire control radars, with a range of 20 km. The projected capability of these guns allows for the simultaneous protection of the country's four main airports, plus a reserve. The Defence Forces also have one 'Giraffe' mobile air defence radar, which has a range of up to 40 km, and six Bofors RBS missile launchers for use with this radar.

With regard to the Air Corps' role in air defence, the White Paper stated that Ireland has traditionally had a limited military air capability. Aspirations to broaden the range of available air-based capabilities had to be balanced against real world constraints. The generally favourable security climate resulted in the need for a very limited military air capability and to exceed this capability would require a level of investment in personnel, equipment and infrastructure which the Irish government believed could not be justified.

One of the Bofors 40mm AA guns purchased from the Dutch Armed Forces in 2002. (J. Maxwell photo)

The 'Good Friday Agreement' of 1998 was a major development in the Northern Ireland peace process, resulting in ceasefires and a general easing of tension between communities on both sides of the political divide. There nevertheless remains an on-going requirement for the Defence Forces to support the Garda Síochána, in particular providing support in response to potential actions of dissident groups. However, the White Paper recognised that at present there is no requirement to move large numbers of troops by air within the State, the need for such a capability being minimised by the small size of the country, the already geographically dispersed deployment of the Defence Forces, and the greatly improved roads infrastructure.

The Government also decided that the State would not seek to commit the Air Corps' limited equipment and resources to any overseas operation. This decision was to have unexpected consequences when the deployment of Irish troops to Chad in 2008 on EU (and subsequently UN) peacekeeping missions required the leasing of Mil Mi-8 helicopters from Moldova and Russia to support the Irish deployment.

The White Paper proposed that the then current broad profile of Air Corps roles should be maintained. The future development of the Air Corps was set out along the following lines, with clear recommendations as to how the policy should be implemented. The Air Corps was tasked with:

- Maintenance/generation of a 24 hour general helicopter capability for a variety of military and non-military tasks, including Garda support.
- The provision of SAR capabilities on the basis of agreed arrangements with the Department of Marine and Natural Resources.
- The provision of a Ministerial Air Transport service.
- The provision of fishery protection patrol services to standards agreed with the Department of the Marine and Natural Resources.
- The provision of an air ambulance service on the basis of agreed arrangements with the Department of Health and Children, and other transport services of a military or non-military kind.
- Provision of an appropriate capability to meet training requirements.

By late 2001, the Air Corps had undergone a major re-organisation, resulting in the appointment of more senior staff members, including an additional Colonel and an increase in senior NCO ranks; the revised establishment of 930 military personnel included, for the first time, an indigenous Military Police unit, while squadron numbering was introduced to replace the descriptive annotations previously used.

In the Defence Forces generally around this time, the financial reality meant that some installations were declared surplus to requirements and were simply withdrawn from use and sold to civilian developers. Air Station Gormanston in County Meath, where the Air Corps had been in residence for many years, ceased to function as an airbase by August 2001, although an Army infantry unit continues to occupy the facility at the time of writing. Adjacent to the Gormanston coast is Danger Area 1, still in use as an air firing range by the PC-9s and by army anti-aircraft artillery units, who practise firing at targets towed by the Cessnas which had been based there previously.

The retirement of the Fouga Magisters in 1999 brought the realisation that any new replacement type would have to encompass the roles of ab initio trainer, advanced flight trainer and light strike aircraft. It soon became obvious that a high-performance turboprop would be the most likely candidate and after exhaustive testing of available aircraft types, the Pilatus PC-9M was declared successful, with the first pair arriving at Baldonnel in April 2004. This brought to a close the career of the SIAI-Marchetti SF260s which had served since 1977; the last time that these aircraft had been were armed was in June 2004, when President George W. Bush visited the Shannon region. By the late 1990s, the primary SAR agency had become the Irish Coastguard, an element of the Department of the Marine, employing civilian-contracted Sikorsky S-61 helicopters. The Air Corps' own SAR asset, the Dauphin, was at that time based at Finner Camp in County Donegal, having been in a number of other locations over the preceding years. When a leased S-61 helicopter permitted the Air Corps to conduct medium-range SAR, Finner was considered lacking in hangar space and a move across the bay to Sligo Airport ensued.

Due to difficulties within the Air Corps vis-à-vis providing crews for the SAR mission, the Minister for Defence announced in December 2003 that the force would relinquish its SAR role, which it had pioneered for some four decades since the Alouette III's arrival. In that time, more than 1,400 people were assisted, of whom it is estimated that 861 represented actual lives saved. By way of recognition, a total of twenty-two Distinguished Service Medals had been awarded to helicopter crewmembers, four of them posthumously.

The 40th anniversary of the Alouette III's entry into service was noteworthy only in that it was largely ignored in Baldonnel, although the 30th anniversary had been well marked a decade earlier. However, the type's days were numbered, as the remaining airframes could not be maintained indefinitely, while the four remaining Dauphins were in need of expensive rebuilds were they to remain serviceable. In addition, the remaining Gazelle was almost twenty years old and no longer a state-of-the-art machine. A two-type helicopter fleet was envisaged and, after comprehensive selection processes, the successful contenders were the EC-135 and the AW-139, both being modern, advanced helicopters.

The helicopter fleet had already been increased by one airframe when the Gárda Air Support Unit

(GASU) received its second EC-135 in late 2002, a direct replacement for the Unit's 1997-vintage Squirrel, which had pioneered police air support in Ireland and which had logged a very high total of flying hours.

Maritime patrol remains an important role for the Air Corps, as it seeks to protect an important EU asset. In the period since the CASA CN-235's arrival, both aircraft have amassed a total flying time well in excess of 20,000 flying hours. As a result, both have undergone mid-life upgrades at the manufacturer's factory in Seville and are likely to remain in service for many years into the future.

Another addition to the fixed wing fleet was the second Ministerial Air Transport Service (MATS) jet, in the shape of a Learjet 45, delivered in late 2003 in order to augment the Gulfstream GIV and replace the Super King Air. Despite the Learjet's small size and relatively modest range, it has flown as far south as Liberia in West Africa where the Minister for Defence visited Irish troops on peacekeeping duties.

Service Level Agreements (SLAs) are in place between the Air Corps and the Departments of Justice, Equality and Law Reform (covering the provision of support to the GASU), Health and Children (covering Air Ambulance services), and Marine and Natural Resources (in relation to fisheries protection duties). The Air Corps has dedicated considerable resources to these roles in order to achieve the agreed targets. In particular, in meeting the GASU SLA requirements, Baldonnel now operates on a 24-hour basis, and 15 pilots are permanently deployed to the GASU operation.

It is worthy of mention that the airbase at Baldonnel has benefited greatly from significant recent funding, resulting in the installation of an instrument landing system (ILS), the complete resurfacing of the original runways, the erection of an entirely new hangar (Hangar 5), the re-cladding of the other four hangars and the opening of a PC-9 simulator building. A new twin-engined flight simulator should be operational by late 2009, thus easing the need to travel abroad for the advanced flying training phase of cadet pilot training. The Crash Rescue Service has been upgraded with a new fire fighting/rescue vehicle and crews trained to international standards. An on-site fire training/crash rescue training facility has also been installed and is now in service.

In passing, it should be remembered that as Ireland's sole military airbase, Baldonnel has seen a myriad military and civilian aircraft operate from its relatively confined runways over the years. In support of the Defence Forces' overseas commitments in more recent times, chartered civilian airliners have transported troops and materiel to many locations, including Africa, the Middle East and the Balkans. These airliners included various marks of Boeing 737, the Boeing 757 and even the odd DC-8, which gave the local spotters something a little different to see.

The Irish Air Corps, although small by international standards and lacking in firepower, is well equipped and well motivated to carry out its mission as outlined in Defence White Papers and elsewhere. It supports all elements of the Defence Forces both directly and indirectly, and is available for almost all airborne needs in support of the general population. What equipment purchases may be made in pursuit of future taskings remains a matter of speculation. At the time of writing, Ireland is facing into a major economic downturn and it is unlikely that there will be any new equipment purchased for the Air Corps in the foreseeable future.

Right: The Future is now! Although not an Air Corps operated craft, Orbiter UAV's operated by the Artillery Corps have been used operationally in Chad. With an effective range of about 18km they are a highly portable and inexpensive air surveillance system for use by ground troops. (K. Byrne photo)

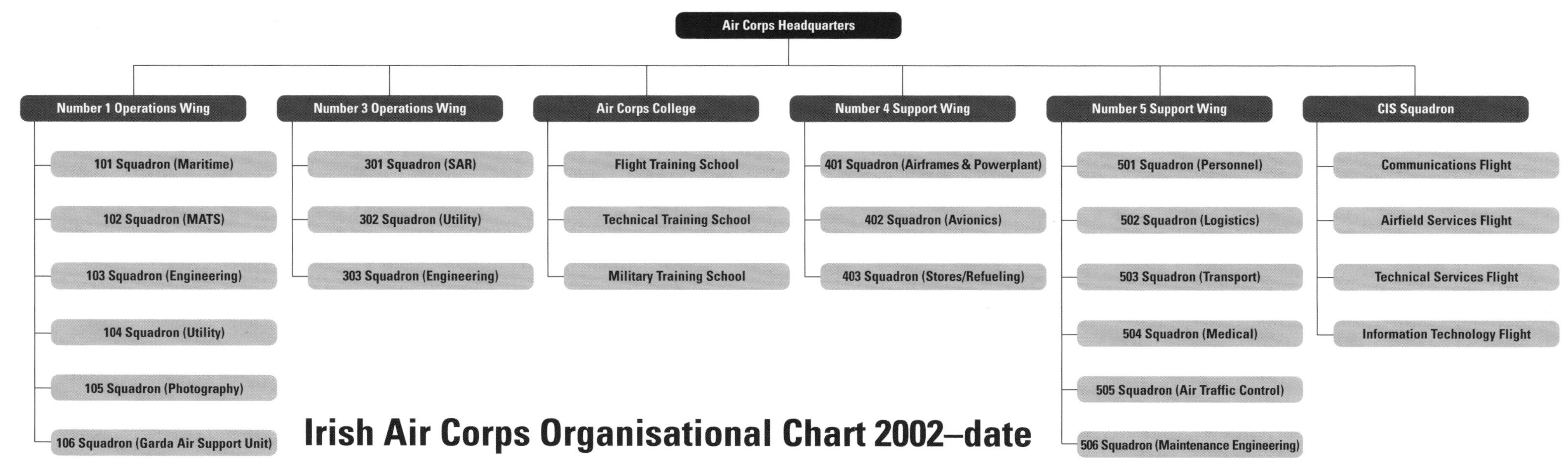

Air Corps Headquarters
Number 1 Operations Wing
101 Squadron (Maritime)
102 Squadron (MATS)
103 Squadron (Engineering)
104 Squadron (Utility)
105 Squadron (Photography)
106 Squadron (Garda Air Support Unit)
Number 3 Operations Wing
301 Squadron (SAR)
302 Squadron (Utility)
303 Squadron (Engineering)
Air Corps College
Flight Training School
Technical Training School
Military Training School
Number 4 Support Wing
401 Squadron (Airframes & Powerplant)
402 Squadron (Avionics)
403 Squadron (Stores/Refueling)
Number 5 Support Wing
501 Squadron (Personnel)
502 Squadron (Logistics)
503 Squadron (Transport)
504 Squadron (Medical)
505 Squadron (Air Traffic Control)
506 Squadron (Maintenance Engineering)
CIS Squadron
Communications Flight
Airfield Services Flight
Technical Services Flight
Information Technology Flight
Irish Air Corps Organisational Chart 2002–date

6.1

Eurocopter EC-135T and EC-135P (2002 – date)

Eurocopter was created in 1992 following the merger of MBB (Messerschmitt Bolkow Blohm), the helicopter division Deutsche Aerospace, of Germany and Aérospatiale of France. Each company had design strengths which were combined in the production of the EC-135 helicopter. This type started out as a technology demonstrator at MBB under the designation Bo-108 with a rigid main rotor and conventional tail rotor. A Fenestron tail was added where the tail rotor is built integrally with the tail fin resulting in improved safety for personnel on the ground as the blades are surrounded by a shroud. Considerable noise reduction is also possible by comparison with a conventional tail rotor and the support struts for the fan are spaced at unequal distances to prevent acoustic "beats". The fuselage has a large internal volume and the type has found favour with aeromedical helicopter operators and police forces. The helicopter weight has been kept to a minimum by extensive use of composite materials for the main fuselage and tail boom structure.

Eurocopter went on to produce two distinct models of this helicopter based around two different engines. The first was the EC135 T1 powered by two 435 kW (583 shp) Turbomeca Arrius 2B1A-1 engines. The second was designated the EC-135P1 powered by two 463 kW (621 shp) Pratt & Whitney Canada PW206B engines. Both sub types have been subject to continuous improvement resulting in higher take off weights and increased thermodynamic and mechanical one engine inoperative (OEI) ratings. EC135 P2+ and EC135T2+ are the designations for the latest production versions with 498 kW (667 shp) PW206B2 and 473 kW (634 shp) Arrius 2B2 engines respectively. The higher power ratings are as a result of a software upgrade to the Full Authority Digital Electronic Control (FADEC) system. These versions have higher maximum takeoff weights and extended component time between overhauls. A military version capable of carrying a wide range of armament is designated the EC635P2 or EC635T2 depending on the engine type selected by the customer.

McAlpine Helicopters Ltd, (now Eurocopter UK) the British agent for Eurocopter developed specialised underfuselage pods that can carry a wide range of surveillance and detection equipment to the specification of the police force acquiring the helicopter.

In November 1998 the Irish Government sought tenders to fulfil a requirement for a second helicopter to equip the GASU., which was to be delivered in 2001. The Eurocopter EC-135T1 was selected to fulfil this requirement at a cost of €5.5 million, according to contemporary news reports. The EC-135T1 (c/n 0149) for the GASU flew for the first time on

Right: EC-135 No. 256 takes off from Baldonnel on another Garda support mission. (G. Norman photo)

Left: the latest edition to the GASU is EC-135T2 No. 272. Detail differences from the first machine include heat shields fitted aft of the exhaust and a small window in the rear clamshell doors. The jeat shields were subsequently fitted to No. 256 also. (P.J.Cummins photo)

December 8, 2000, and was delivered (as D-HECK) on the following day to McAlpine Helicopters Ltd, Oxford, for the installation of specialised equipment for Garda operations. The EC-135T1 was expected to be delivered to the GASU in April 2001 and to be operational by June but remained instead at McAlpine Helicopters and registered to Eurocopter Deutschland GmbH (as G-BZRM). This was the first EC 135 to be fitted with a full autopilot instead of the common SAS (stability augmentation system as on previous EC 135s) and was the first to be certified up to 2,835kgs from the previous 2,720 Kgs.

In December 2001, following a study of GASU helicopter operations by an inter-departmental committee, the Department of Justice announced that the pilots for the EC-135T1 would be provided by the Air Corps but maintenance would be outsourced to a civilian agency. On February 8, 2002, the EC-135T1 was registered to An Garda Siochana, Phoenix Park, Dublin, but retained the British registration (G-BZRM).

Following conversion courses for Air Corps pilots on the helicopter, the EC-135T1 was delivered to Casement Aerodrome on December 5, 2002 and (as No. 256) entered service with 106 Squadron (GASU), No. 1 Operations Wing. A total of 46

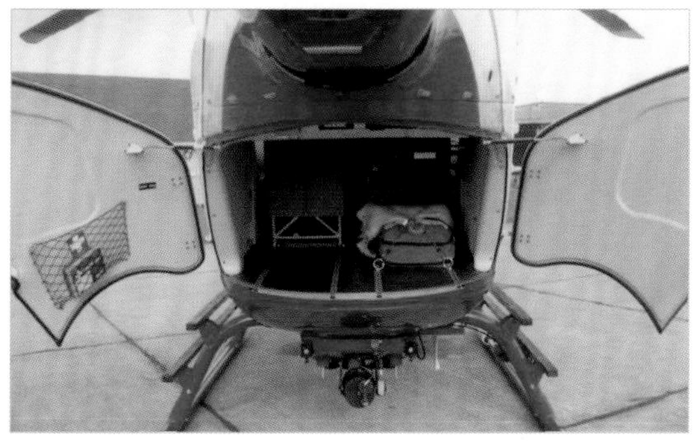

Left: Plenty of room for back packs and other equipment in the rear hold of the EC-135. (J. Maxwell photo)

flying hours was accumulated by the EC-135T1 in December 2002, providing 48 air support missions during Garda operations.

The EC-135T1 is operated by GASU by day and night, providing air support during Garda operations against criminal activities, crowd control and other surveillance duties. The type of equipment installed included a Leo 2 camera, SX5 Nightsun search light, Skyforce Moving Map, and Skyshout loudspearer / public address system. Commencing on January 1, 2004, a two year maintenance contract for the EC-135T was awarded to McAlpine Helicopters. By the end of 2008 No. 256 had flown over 5,270 hours in support of Garda operations responding 10,247 incidents and had contributed to the arrest of 1,588 suspects.

In April 2005 the Irish Government sought tenders for delivery of a second EC-135T for the GASU to replace the AS.355N. This was delivered on 14th November 2007 to Baldonnel and officially entered service 15th January 2008 with the serial number 272. This helicopter is the higher spec T2+ model and No. 256 was also modified previously, and brought up to the T2 standard. The most noticeable external difference between the two machines other than the serial number are the front camera pod and the different and distinctive night suns at the rear. There is also a small window in the rear clamshell doors on No. 272. A black heat shield has been placed directly behind the engine exhausts to prevent damage to the paintwork.

From 2000 onwards the maintenance of the three helicopter types (Alouette III, Gazelle and Dauphin) operated by the Irish Air Corps was becoming more difficult, due to intensive utilisation, lack of spare parts and obsolescence. In December 2003, following

Above right: Historic arrival of the first EC-135's for the Air Corps touching down at Waterford Airport for a refuelling stop prior to onward transit to Baldonnel on November 3, 2005. (P.J. Cummins photo)

a decision by the Irish Government to acquire new light utility and utility military helicopters to replace these helicopters, the evaluation of a number of modern helicopter types including the Agusta A109 and EC-135 was undertaken by an Air Corps procurement team to fulfil this requirement. The light utility helicopters were to be operated by the Air Corps for pilot, instructor and instrument training, air ambulance and army support duties.

On November 26, 2004 the Department of Defence announced that the EC-135P had been selected to fulfil the requirement for a light utility helicopter and two of these helicopters were ordered in January 2005, at a total cost of €12.5 million, for delivery by the end of the year.

The two EC-135P2s (c/n 0425 and 0431) were accepted by the Air Corps in September and October 2005 respectively and, following pre-delivery flight tests (as D-HECB and D-HECF), were then used for pilot conversion courses. The two EC-135P2s (as Nos. 270 and 271) were delivered to Baldonnel on November 3, 2005, after refuelling at Waterford Regional Airport, and entered service with 302 Squadron. The two EC-135P2s are equipped with a night vision goggle compatible glass cockpit, dual and single pilot IFR instrumentation, advanced navigation system, rescue hoist, cargo hook and fixed provisions for a forward looking infrared camera.

These aircraft have proven to have excellent reliability and achieved a total of 1,700 flying hours in the first year in service. They are ideal training helicopters for pilots starting out flying helicopters or transitioning onto the larger AW139 in that they have similar systems and have built in software for simulating a wide variety of emergencies. Compared to the Alouette that they replaced, the key difference is twin engine safety as the EC-135 is capable of safe flying on one engine in most flight regimes. It also requires less maintenance than the Alouette and is equipped with modern flat screen displays. The interior can be configured in a number of ways with five seats or a complete air ambulance suite of equipment. It also provides access to the rear of the cabin via two clamshell doors through which a stretcher or other items can be loaded.

The EC-135 is a very versatile machine and it has been used in a number of army support roles including fast-roping and support for the Army Ranger Wing. For carrying under slung loads a pylon is added to the underside of the fuselage. A winch can be fitted to either side of the cabin and it enables training for an overland SAR capability. For overwater deployments the EC-135 can be fitted with flotation gear on a special set of skids. The aircraft is

Left: Powered by two PW206 turboshaft engines, the EC-135 is capable of cruising at speeds up to 254 Km/h. The EC-135's are painted an overall matt green RAL 6031. (D. Leahy photo)

literally jacked up and the flotation equipped skids are bolted on in lieu of the standard skids. A first for an Irish operated helicopter was the provision of wire strike protection in the form of cable cutters mounted above and below the centreline and on the forward tips of the skids. The Air Corps is working on new roles in support of the Army using the EC-135 in the intelligence, surveillance, target acquisition and reconnaissance (ISTAR) role. It will be hard to beat the longevity of the Alouette III in Irish Air Corps service, some 43 years but it appears that the EC-135 is destined to have a successful future with the Air Corps.

Bottom Left: the cockpit in the EC-135 is fully digital with just a few back up analog instruments remaining. (A.C. Photographic Section)

Above: Crewman in the EC-135 steps out to get a better view! (A.C. Photographic Section)

Below: Demonstrating superb agility, this EC-135 is equipped with an under fuselage pylon used for carrying slung loads. (F. Grealish photo - Irishairpics.com)

Below: detail of the overhead instrument panel in the cockpit. (J. Maxwell photo)

Bottom right: For over water deployments, the EC-135 can be fitted with skids that have a built in emergency flotation system as seen here. This particular helicopter has been fitted with the modular Lifeport medical interior for air ambulance missions as evidenced by the panel blanking out the rear window. (P.J. Cummins photo)

6.2

Sikorsky S-61N (2003 – 2004)

The Sikorsky S-61N was developed from the company's military SH-3 Sea King design, to fulfil the conditions for certification by the US Federal Aviation Administration for overwater commercial operations. The Sea King's fuselage, with its amphibious sealed hull, was lengthened, and the flotation sponsons containing the retractable undercarriage were also enlarged. The tail rotor was mounted on a higher pylon, and a passenger door with folding steps was installed on the rear right-hand side of the fuselage, with a larger cargo door further forward. The S-61N, which flew for the first time on November 2, 1961, was delivered to commercial helicopter operators worldwide and was used for carrying passengers and freight, as well as for oil rig support and SAR operations. From 1971 onwards, the S-61N was being used by British commercial helicopter operators to provide coastal SAR services, under contract to Her Majesty's Coastguard. These helicopters were equipped with an auto hover system, variable speed rescue hoist and advanced radar systems. The S-61N was the first civil helicopter to receive Federal Aviation Administration certification for IFR operations. A total of 123 S-61Ns had been delivered when production ceased in 1979.

From 1975 onwards, the Air Corps had a requirement for a medium-lift helicopter capability for both military and SAR operations, which was briefly met with the curtailed lease of an Aérospatiale Puma in 1981-83; since then, the need for a medium-lift helicopter remained unfulfilled due to economic circumstances. However, in 1990, a 'Report and Review of Air/Sea Rescue Services' commissioned by the Irish government recommended the purchase of "two medium-range helicopters . . . for operation by the Air Corps". The report also recommended that "in the interim" a medium-range SAR service by a commercial helicopter operator under contract should be negotiated. Arising from these recommendations, an S-61N, operated by Irish Helicopters Ltd. from Shannon Airport, commenced a medium-range SAR service for the west coast in July 1991, under contract to the Department of the Marine, replacing the Aérospatiale SA.365F Dauphin which had been operated by the Irish Air Corps from the airport since September 1989.

Over the following decade a number of contracts were issued to private companies who had successfully tendered to operate maritime SAR services under contract to the Department of the Marine and Natural Resources. On July 1, 1998, another S-61N commenced medium-range SAR operations for the east coast of Ireland, operated by Bond Helicopters (Ireland) Ltd. from Dublin Airport, under contract to the Irish Marine Emergency Service, an agency of the Department of the Marine. (Bond helicopters

Right: The S-61N is a big helicopter, capable of lifting up to 20 survivors. (K. Byrne photo)

had previously taken over operations at Shannon from Irish Helicopters Ltd). It was originally intended that the Air Corps would provide the crews for the S-61N but due to a shortage of trained flight crews, the helicopter had to be operated by civilian personnel. A 24 hour, medium-range SAR service for the south-east by CHC (Ireland) Ltd., operating an S-61N from Waterford Regional Airport, commenced on July 1, 2002, under contract to the Irish Coastguard Service which had been formed out of the Irish Marine Emergency Service. Commencing in January 2002 and July 2003, respectively, this company was also awarded the contract to provide the medium-range SAR services from Shannon and Dublin airports, under contract to the Irish Coastguard Service.

Following a review of the Irish Naval Service and Air Corps in 1998 by the consultants Price Waterhouse, the Irish Government published a White Paper in 2000, which accepted that "the present broad profile of the Air Corps would be maintained". The review had also recommended a 24 hour general helicopter capability and SAR capabilities for the Air Corps, which could be fulfilled by the acquisition of four medium-lift helicopters. In July 2000, the Department of Defence requested tenders for a medium-lift helicopter to fulfil this requirement and, following a detailed evaluation of the helicopter types tendered, the Sikorsky S-92 was selected in January 2002. Three of these helicopters were to be acquired for SAR duties, at a cost of €100 million, with an option on two additional S-92s. Following a threat of litigation by Eurocopter, whose tender had not been successful, and financial restrictions caused by the economic downturn that followed the September 11, 2001 attack on New York, the order for the S-92s was cancelled in July 2002.

Despite the cancellation of the order for the S-92s, the Department of Defence remained favourably disposed towards a SAR role for the Air Corps and in this regard the Department of the Marine leased an S-61N for three years from CHC Helicopters (Ireland) Ltd. at a cost of €16 million, to be operated by the Air Corps in support of the Irish Coastguard to provide a medium-range SAR service for the north-west region. Maintenance and technical support for the helicopter would be provided by the company for the duration of the lease. Eight Air Corps pilots underwent conversion courses on the S-61N in Norway commencing in June 2002, According to newspaper reports at the time, the S-61N was to be delivered to the Air Corps in September 2002 and was expected to commence SAR operations two months later. An S-61N (c/n 61816), which had been constructed in 1978 and issued with an Irish civil registration (EI-CXS) in October 2002 was allocated to the Air Corps by the company for SAR operations. Throughout December 2002, a number of Air Corps aircrews underwent conversion courses on an S-61N (EI-CNL) of CHC Helicopters (Ireland) Ltd. at Baldonnel.

Above: The S-61N was a leased replacement of the Sikorsky S-92, two of which had been ordered but subsequently cancelled. A full scale mock up (top) and a company demonstrator were demonstrated to the Air Corps. (K. Byrne photos)

The delivery of the S-61N to the Air Corps was delayed until January 13, 2003, when the helicopter (as No. 257) entered service with 301 Squadron, 3 Operations Wing. Pilots and aircrews underwent an intensive training programme on the S-61N over the next four months at Casement Aerodrome, before the helicopter was deployed to Sligo Airport in May 2003. The facilities at Finner Military Camp were considered to be inadequate for the S-61N and the base for Air Corps SAR operations for the north-west region was relocated to Sligo Airport. In July 2003, the S-61N commenced daylight SAR operations from the airport while aircrew training continued throughout the summer to fulfil a declared objective of commencing a 24 hour service in November. From late September, due to crewing difficulties, only a limited service could be provided by the S-61N. These difficulties were not resolved, and in December 2003, following a direction by the Minister of Defence that the Air Corps was to cease off-shore SAR operations and that these services would in future be provided by civilian helicopter operators under contract to the Department of the Marine, the lease on the helicopter was terminated. The training of aircrews for the S-61N, and the setting up of the Air Corps base at Sligo Airport, had cost the Irish taxpayer approximately €11 million, according to newspaper reports at the time. The S-61N had carried out a total of 46 SAR missions, and accumulated a total of 76 flight hours, since its delivery to the Air Corps in July 2003.

Right: The complex strut arrangement that attaches the undercarriage sponsons to the airframe is shown in this view from the Observer's bubble window. (J. Maxwell photo)

Operating the Aérospatiale Dauphin from Sligo Airport, the Air Corps provided a limited SAR service for the region over the next nine months, terminating on October 11, 2004. During this period, the Department of the Marine was seeking tenders for a civilian helicopter operator to provide a medium-range SAR service for the region, which was eventually awarded to CHC Helicopters (Ireland) Ltd. Operating an S-61N from Sligo Airport, this company commenced SAR operations for the north-west region in November 2004.

While the Air Corps had a proud history in providing SAR services, it had come at a cost in terms of having to maintain a 24-hour service with a very small fleet of helicopters. The relinquishing of the overwater SAR role to a commercial operator allowed the Air Corps to redirect its limited resources in support of army operations.

Colours and markings

The Sikorsky S-61N was operated in a high visibility red and white colour scheme with two dayglo orange stripes on the underside of the fuselage. The St. Brendan badge was placed low down on the rear fuselage and a small tricolour was placed on the nose.

Right: Leased from a commercial operator, the S-61N received Air Corps markings as shown in the two photos. The black markings on the sponsons are a quick visual indicator in the event that ice forms on the air frame. (K. Byrne photos)

Right: Number 257 on a rare visit to Baldonnel following its deployment to Sligo. (K. Byrne photos)

The S-61N leads a Dauphin and an Alouette around the massive bulk of Ben Bulben in Co. Sligo.
(Air Corps Photo Section via B. Murran)

6.3

Bombardier Learjet 45 (2003 – date)

The name Learjet has been synonymous with executive aviation for more than 45 years. Originally designed in Switzerland using a wing planform similar to the Swiss P-16 fighter, the first of a long line of executive jets, the Learjet 23, first flew in 1963. This was a highly successful design, with a narrow, low-drag fuselage that reduced weight and permitted the aircraft to fly at altitudes of up to 45,000 ft. The aircraft was developed into a myriad of versions with extended fuselages, winglets replacing tip tanks, new engines and avionics. Learjet was bought by Bombardier of Canada in 1990, with a view to complementing its existing range of larger Challenger business jets. Bombardier also bought Shorts of Belfast in the same year. Development of the type has continued with Learjet 40, 45, 45XR and 60 models currently being marketed by the company.

With regard to the Learjet 45 model, design work on the development of a medium size variant of the Learjet was initiated in 1992; differences from earlier models included an increase in cabin height, accommodation for up to ten passengers and improved fuel efficiency. The prototype (carrying the US civil registration N45XL) flew for the first time on October 7, 1995, powered by two 3500 lb.s.t Allied Signal TFE731-20 turbofan engines. The prototype and four pre-production aircraft underwent an intensive test programme over the next two years, resulting in some alterations to the basic design, namely the fitting of a larger fin and rudder, smaller delta strakes and modified control surfaces on the wings. On September 22, 1997, after a number of delays, certification of the Learjet 45 was granted by the Federal Aviation Administration, with deliveries of the aircraft commencing in July 1998. One hundred Learjet 45s had been delivered by October 2000. Design, development and final assembly of the Learjet 45 was carried out at the Learjet facility in Wichita, Kansas, with the fuselage constructed by Short Brothers in Belfast, Northern Ireland, and the wings constructed by de Havilland Inc., Toronto, Canada.

In 2001, the Irish Government sought tenders from the aviation industry to fulfil a requirement for an aircraft to replace the Beechcraft Super King Air 200 in service with the Irish Air Corps. To fulfil this requirement, the aircraft would have to be capable of carrying seven passengers on a non-stop flight of not less than 1,500 nautical miles, after taking-off from a 4,800 foot runway. On July 23, 2003, following an intensive evaluation of various executive aircraft

Below: 102 Squadron provides the Ministerial Air transport Service using the Learjet 45 and the Gulfstream GIV. (A.C. Photographic Section)

Left: Up to date flight management systems are incorporated into the cockpit of the Learjet 45.
(K. Byrne photo)

types by the Air Corps from tenders submitted by six companies, the Irish Government announced that the Learjet 45 had been selected to fulfil this requirement. The Department of Defence ordered a Learjet 45 from Bombardier Aerospace on September 24, 2003, for delivery in December of that year, at a total cost of €8.4 million, to include spare parts and the training of Air Corps pilots and technicians. Another aircraft operator had agreed to a later delivery of the Learjet 45 to facilitate this rapid delivery to the Air Corps. The need for early delivery of the Learjet 45 arose from the necessity to carry out a significant number of ministerial flights throughout Europe from January to June 2004, when the Presidency of the EU was administered by the Irish government.

On December 15, 2003, a Learjet 45 (c/n 45-234) underwent a flight test (carrying the US civil registration N5009T) and a customer acceptance flight by the Air Corps. Four days later the Learjet 45 was delivered from the USA to Baldonnel and (as No. 258) entered service with 102 Squadron, No. 1 Operations Wing. Over the following four weeks, Air Corps personnel underwent an intensive training programme on the Learjet 45 and a series of test flights to destinations throughout Europe, before commencing operations with MATS. The first ministerial flight by the Learjet 45 occurred on January 21, 2004, transporting the Minister for Defence on a visit to the Irish Defence Forces detachment deployed on UN peacekeeping duties in Liberia. Operated on the Ministerial Air Transport Service (MATS) the Learjet 45 accumulated a total of 375 flying hours between January and June 2004, transporting ministers and officials who were engaged on business associated with the E.U. Presidency throughout Europe. Throughout 2004, there was criticism of the Learjet 45 by some of the national newspapers, claiming that the aircraft was too expensive, uneconomical and that passenger accommodation in the cabin was cramped. There was also media speculation that the Learjet 45 would be sold off after June 2004, when the EU Presidency was transferred to another state. A total of 600 flying hours was accumulated by the Learjet 45 throughout 2004, including 129 ministerial flights.

The Learjet 45 continued to be operated by MATS throughout 2005 and 2006 on short- and medium-range ministerial flights to destinations throughout Ireland and Europe, which enabled the Gulfstream IV to be used for long-range flights worldwide. The Beechcraft Super King Air 200, which had previously been used for ministerial flights throughout Ireland, could also be made available for use in twin-engined flight training and military support duties. The Learjet 45 is used on shorter routes around Europe, being more economical to operate than the Gulfstream IV also in service with the Air Corps. The Learjet complements the larger type, which has a much greater range and load carrying capacity. The Learjet 45 is fast; a typical run from Baldonnel to Shannon airport taking as little as 29 minutes.

Although the Learjet's role as ministerial transport tends to garner a lot of publicity in media circles, the aircraft is also used for air ambulance missions and a Lifeport Air Ambulance System is installed in the aircraft for these duties. This system, which was acquired with the Learjet 45, has all the necessary hospital equipment to keep a patient stable while in flight, and can be installed in the aircraft after the removal of three passenger seats. The aircraft's air ambulance role is less well known, but is very satisfying for those who fly it on these missions, while the increasing number of critical air ambulance flights undertaken by the type in recent years makes it a worthy addition to the Air Corps fleet.

Left: Flying low over the west coast of Ireland, the clean lines of the Learjet 45 are evident.
(A.C. Photographic Section)

6.4

Pilatus PC-9M (2004 – date)

Since its foundation in 1922, the Air Corps has always trained its own pilots. In the 1960s, three aircraft types were used for training, the Chipmunk for elementary training, the Provost for intermediate training and the Vampire for advanced training. In the mid-1970s, these aircraft types were phased out and replaced by the SIAI Marchetti SF260W for the elementary and basic stages of flight training, with advanced training being carried out on the twin-engined Fouga Magister. By 1999, the Fouga had been withdrawn and the training syllabus had been revised using the Marchetti, the twin engined Beech Super King Air and Gazelle helicopter.

This was not a wholly satisfactory arrangement and it quickly became clear that a new aircraft type was needed to replace the Marchetti and fulfil all of the training requirements of the Air Corps from elementary through to basic and on to advanced flying training. Initially the Air Corps had planned to replace the Fouga Magister with another jet, such as the Aero L.159, the Dassault-Dornier Alpha Jet or the British Aerospace Hawk. However, a number of turboprop trainers designed specifically to fulfil the training requirements of other air forces at the lowest possible cost were also on the market and were less expensive to both acquire and operate than their fast jet equivalents.

The Air Corps specification that eventually emerged called for a turboprop powered aircraft with a power output ranging from 750 shp to 1650 shp enabling, its use at altitudes of up to 30,000ft. The turbo-prop was also required by the specification to be very fuel efficient, an internal fuel endurance of 3.5 hours (which exceeds that of the Marchetti by one hour and that of the Fouga by two hours) being sought by the Air Corps. In addition, the aircraft would be required to have a high dive speed and limiting Mach number, as well as a high cruising speed, as close as possible to that of the Fouga Magister. The aircraftwas also required to be weapons-capable, with a variety of guns, rockets and fuel drop tanks capable of being mounted under the wings. Weapons sighting systems that included an air-to-air predicting facility were also specified, so as to restore the air Corps' ability to train in this role.

In June 2002, the Irish Government sought tenders to fulfil this requirement and a Fixed Wing Training Aircraft Project Group was established to evaluate the various aircraft types submitted, including the Embraer Super Tucano, Pilatus PC-9M and PC-9 Mk II. One of the prototype PC-9 Mk IIs (with the US civil registration N8284M) and a Pilatus PC-9 (bearing the Swiss civil registration HB-HPJ) had, even in advance of the tender, already been demonstrated to the Air Corps at Casement Aerodrome on October 29, 1996 and August 26, 2001, respectively.

Right: The large canopy of the PC-9 provides superb visibility for both crew members. (K. Byrne photo)

Left: The well laid out, front cockpit of the PC-9. Note the Head up Display (HUD) and the two rear view mirrors on each side of the instrument panel. (R. Brinzan photo)

Developed from the PC-7 tandem two seat trainer, of which more than 450 have been built, the PC-9 has a redesigned wing with six hardpoints and more advanced avionics. Powered by a 950-shp Pratt & Whitney of Canada PT6A-62 turboprop, the first pre-production PC-9 (c/n 001, with the Swiss civil registration HP-HBA) flew for the first time on May 7, 1984. The PC-9 was submitted to fulfil the requirements of specification AST-12 (Air Staff Target-412), issued by the RAF in 1984 for a training aircraft to replace the British Aerospace Jet Provost. The Shorts Tucano, itself a re-engined development of the Brazilian-built Embraer Tucano, was eventually selected to fulfil this requirement.

Production of the PC-9 commenced in 1985, with the first aircraft being deliveed to the Union of Burma Air Force in January 1986. Delivery of 30 PC-9s to the Royal Saudi Air Force commenced in December 1986, these aircraft having been ordered by the British Government as part of a wider agreement to supply aircraft to Royal Saudi Air Force. Cockpit instrumentation and other equipment compatible with the Panavia Tornado IDS and F.3 aircraft operated by the Saudis was installed by British Aerospace before delivery. Commencing in 1987, sixty seven PC-9s were delivered to the Royal Australian Air Force, while a further 10 aircraft equipped for target towing duties were acquired by a German civilian company. Designated PC-9B, these aircraft are operated under contract to the three German military services. The PC-9M is the latest version of the design to be offered by Pilatus, this variant being designed from the outset to have modular avionics so that each aircraft can be tailored to the needs of the customer.

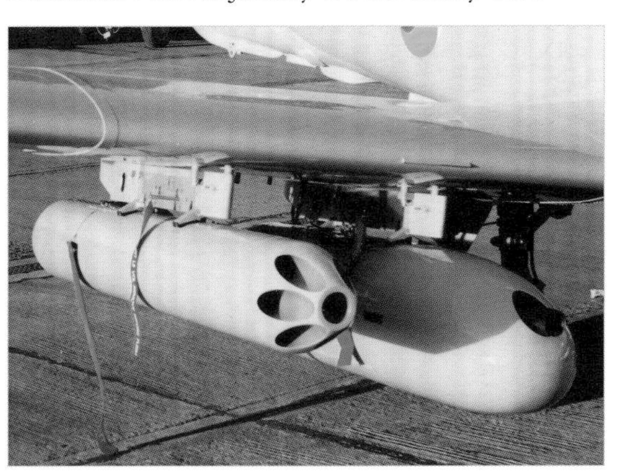

Left: The PC-9 can be armed with rocket pods and machine gun pods as shown here. (K. Byrne photo)

Following an agreement between Beechcraft Aircraft Corporation and Pilatus in 1990, the PC-9 Mk II was submitted to fulfil the requirements of JPATS (Joint Primary Aircraft Training System) to provide a basic training aircraft for the US Air Force and the US Navy. In 1994, Beechcraft became the Raytheon Aircraft Corporation and the JPATS contract was eventually awarded to the Raytheon/Pilatus proposal in June 1995, the type to be known as the Raytheon T-6 Texan II. Compared to the PC-9, these aircraft are almost completely redesigned to fulfil the requirements of JPATS; they are powered by a 1,700shp Pratt & Whitney PT6A-68 turboprop

Right: The PC-9 is only the second Air Corps type to be equipped with ejection seats, the other being the DH. Vampire T.55 of 1956. (S. Nolan photo)

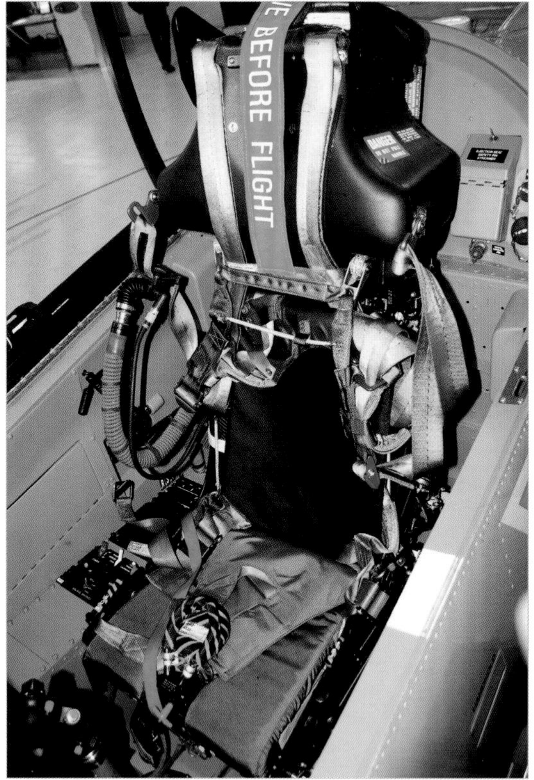

engine, have a pressurised cockpit with an enlarged, bird-resistant canopy, lightweight zero-zero ejection seats, single point refuelling, an enlarged ventral fin, and a strengthened rear fuselage, wings and tailplane. The first production aircraft flew for the first time on July 15, 1998 and deliveries to the U. S. Air Force commenced in 1999. A total of 700 T-6 Texan IIs is expected to be delivered to the US Air Force and the US Navy by 2017.

On completion of the tender process commence in June 2002, the Irish Air Corps selected the PC-9M to fulfil its requirement for a turboprop trainer, and a contract was signed on January 17, 2003 for the delivery of eight of these aircraft in 2004. This contract, which was worth approximately €60 million, also included ground based training systems and a complete integrated logistic support package.

Conversion courses on the PC-9M for pilots and technicians were conducted at the Pilatus factory in Switzerland before the aircraft were delivered to the Air Corps.

The first PC-9M (c/n 655) for the Air Corps made its first flight on February 6, 2004, having been allocated the Swiss civil registration HB-HQS, and was used by Pilatus for weapons trials in Austria before delivery (as No. 260) to the Air Corps on July 24, 2004. Accompanied by a Pilatus PC-12 carrying company support technical staff, the first PC-9Ms to actually arrive in Ireland were Nos. 261, 262 and 263, which were delivered to the Air Corps on April 21, 2004. Another PC-9M (c/n 660), was delivered to the Air Corps (as No. 265) on May 18, 2004, while the fifth and sixth examples of the type (c/ns 661 and 662) to be delivered to the Air Corps were Nos. 266 and 267, both of which arrived in Ireland on June 8, 2004. The seventh aircraft (c/n 659) was delivered on June 9, 2004, followed by the final machine No. 260) on July 24, 2004, as already mentioned in the preceding paragraph. The eight PC-9Ms entered service with Flight Training School, Air Corps College. The PC-9M is only the second aircraft type equipped with ejection seats (in this case, the Martin Baker CH-11A) to enter service with the Air Corps, the other being the De Havilland Vampire T.55 of 1956!

In 2004, the PC-9Ms participated in a number of air shows and rallies throughout the country, performing limited aerobatic displays and flypasts. The first weapons training exercises by the PC-9Ms over the Air Firing Range at Gormanston occurred in December 2004. Armed with 0.5-in. machine guns or 2.75-in. Folding Fin Aircraft Rockets (FFARs) contained in two underwing LAU-7 pods, the PC-9Ms carried out air–to ground attacks on targets during these exercises. In September 2005, the PC-9Ms participated in their first air show outside the State, with a display of close formation flying and aerobatics during an air display at Leuchars in Scotland.

Right: Seen here following a cross-country training flight to Waterford Airport, PC-9 No. 266 has been rigged for blind flying training with a cover inside the rear portion of the cockpit canopy. (P.J. Cummins photo)

Colours & Markings:

The PC-9Ms are painted in a highly effective two-tone grey camouflage, with RAL7040 on the upper surfaces and RAL 7035 underneath. Bright red paint is applied to the wingtips, tailfins and tailplanes of the PC-9Ms. From the wing leading edges received a coat of black erosion-resistant paint. This looks like a de-icer boot, and has the effect of increasing the visibility of the aircraft when viewed from head on.

Above: Banking away from the Learjet 45 from which this photo was taken, the underwing markings are clearly visible. (K. Byrne photo)

Left: The PC-9 has three hard-points under each wing but usually only two pylons are attached. (J. Maxwell photo)

Left: PC-9 No. 267 taxi's out for the return leg of a training flight to Dublin from Waterford. (D. Leahy photo)

6.5

AgustaWestland AW 139 (2006 – date)

Following the abortive attempt to procure medium-lift helicopters in the form of Sikorsky S-92s in 2002, the Air Corps' fleet of helicopters was nearing obsolescence and replacements were urgently required.

In December 2003, following recommendations by a procurement group that had been formed to investigate what helicopter type might be required, the Department of Defence sanctioned the necessary expenditure to replace all of the helicopters then in service with the Air Corps. A tender competition was initiated in May 2004 to fulfil one of the Air Corps requirements for utility helicopters, to be used for general military operational and training roles. Four helicopter types were evaluated to fulfil this requirement – the Agusta Bell AB139, the Eurocopter EC 145, and Sikorsky's S-76C and S-70A Blackhawk. The Agusta Bell AB139 (later re-designated AgustaWestland AW139) was declared the winner following this evaluation, and four were ordered in January 2005 at a total cost of €48.4 million, with an option to acquire two more later. Two of the four helicopters were to be delivered in 2006, followed by the remaining two in 2007.

The AW139 was designed by Agusta in 1997 as a replacement for the Bell family of light utility helicopters (205, 212 and 412) all of which were licensed built by Agusta in Italy. Bell joined the project in 1997 and the designation AB 139 was assigned to the new helicopter. It was anticipated that the helicopter would be suitable for a wide variety of civil and military roles including off-shore platform support, SAR, VIP transport, law enforcement and emergency medical services. After 54 airframes had been completed, Bell sold its 25% share in the programme to AgustaWestland and the helicopter was subsequently redesignated as the AW139.

On August 10, 2006 the first AW139 (c/n 31048) was formally handed over to Air Corps representatives at the company's factory in Italy, this representing the first delivery of the type to a military customer. Flying training for Air Corps AW 139 crews was carried out in Italy on this helicopter over the next three months, with the second AW 139 (c/n 31059) being handed over to the Air Corps in October 2006. Throughout this period, maintenance courses on the helicopter for Air Corps technicians were also being carried out at the Agusta Westland factory in Italy.

The AW 139 demonstrates suppressive fire at the Glen of Imaal range in Co. Wicklow. Note the muzzle flash.
(A.C. Photographic Section)

State of the art cockpit on the AW 139. (A.C. Photographic Section)

The two AW139s, flown by Air Corps crews, were finally delivered to Casement Aerodrome on November 23, 2006 and (as Nos. 274 and 275) entered service with 301 Squadron, No. 3 Operations Wing. Over the next six months, the Air Corps conducted an intensive training programme on the AW139, which included pilot training, army co-operation exercises and air gunnery trials over the Glen of Imaal, Co. Wicklow. The third AW139 (c/n 31076) was delivered to Casement Aerodrome on April 17, 2007, followed by the fourth AW139 (c/n 31078) on May 29, 2007, both helicopters also entering service with 301 Squadron (as Nos. 276 and 277 respectively).

Powered by two 1,679 hp Pratt & Whitney PT6C-67C turboshaft engines, with FADEC (Full Authority Digital Engine Control), the AW139 is equipped with advanced avionics and navigation systems. EFIS (Electronic Flight Instrumentation System), FMS (Flight Management System), autopilot, weather radar, TCAS (Traffic Alert and Collision Avoidance System) and GPWS (Ground Proximity Warning System) are all fitted, making the AW139 one of the most advanced helicopters in production.

The main roles of the AW139 are army support, air ambulance, military transport and general utility operations. Other duties include support for Garda operations, air ambulance, overland SAR, disaster relief and VIP transport tasks. The AW139 can be configured to provide seating for four, eight or twelve personnel; alternatively, nine military personnel with full equipment can be carried.

In addition, the aircraft can be used to transport government ministers and officials or other dignitaries in a six seat VIP configuration.

Dual 7.62mm general purpose machine guns can be installed in the AW 139, firing through the forward sliding windows, the first time that a helicopter operated by the Air Corps has been equipped with such weapons. The AW139 also has a fast roping capability from four special attachments on the side of the fuselage, allowing the deployment of eight soldiers at a time from the helicopter. Rapid deployment of an entire platoon can be accomplished by only three AW139s. In addition, a cargo sling can be attached to the underside of the aircraft to carry loads up to 2.5 tons – this limit would cover a single light 105mm artillery gun together with the gun team in the cabin.

For air ambulance missions a Lifeport air ambulance kit, which was delivered to the Air Corps in February 2008, can be installed in the AW139. The AW139s have been used on a number of occasions for air ambulance missions and for SAR operations in the Wicklow Mountains. One of these helicopters was also used to evacuate an injured person off Croagh Patrick in Co. Mayo, during the annual pilgrimage to the mountain's summit.

During 2007 the Department of Defence took up its option on two additional AW139s, for delivery in 2008. The first of these helicopters (c/n 31137) was delivered to Casement Aerodrome on July 26, 2008 and (as No. 278) entered service with 301 Squadron.

Right: Fitted with weight spreading skis on the wheels for landings on soft ground, this view of the AW-139 shows the wire strike protection afforded by the cable cutters mounted above and below the cockpit. (F. Goodman photo)

Right: Very much an Army support machine, the AW-139 can be equipped with a fast roping system to allow rapid deployment of troops. (J. Maxwell photo)

The second machine (c/n 31145) was delivered on November 15, 2008 to the Air Corps (as No. 279).

The AW 139 heralded a new era in Army support operations. It is the fastest helicopter to see service with the Air Corps, being capable of 167kts in level flight, whereas the Alouette III had a maximum speed of just 120kts. The biggest difference from previous helicopters operated by the Air Corps is the excess power available, which translates into a far superior load carrying capability and increased safety margins.

At time of writing in April 2009, one of the AW139 helicopters has been fitted with a FLIR system (though all of the fleet are wired to accept it) and training has commenced using night vision goggles. There are no current plans for overseas deployment of these helicopters, but the training they provide to regular army units going on UN or EU missions to areas where operating with large helicopters is the norm will prove extremely valuable.

Right: The first helicopter in Air Corps service designed from the outset to carry armament such as the 7.62mm machine gun shown here. (J. Maxwell photo)

Far right: A forward looking infra red turret has been fitted to this AW-139. (K. Byrne photo)

Above: The AW-139 is capable of carrying heavy loads including a 105mm artillery piece and it crew. (A.C. Photographic Section)

Below: The AW-139 fleet is painted in the same matt green RAL 6031 finish as the EC-135's. (A.C. Photographic Section)

Appendix 1 Irish Air Corps Individial Aircraft Histories

Air Corps Serial Number	Aircraft Type	Construction Number	Previous Identity	Service History
none	Martinsyde Type A Mk. II (1922-1927)	214	One of only four Martinsyde Type A Mk.IIs constructed by Martinsyde Ltd. in 1920. G-EAPN. First flight, 24.11.21. Stored at Croydon Aerodrome, 9.12.21.	Delivered in crates by sea to Dublin, 16.6.22. Named "Big Fella" (displayed on engine cowlings). Renamed "City of Dublin" (displayed on port side of engine cowling) and "Cathair Atha Cliath" (displayed on starboard side of engine cowling) in 1926. Withdrawn from use, 11.10.27. Broken up, January 1937.
I later B.I	Bristol (Type 14) F2B Fighter (1922-1935)	4014	E2411. From a batch of 500 (E2151-E2650; c/ns 3754-4253), constructed by the British and Colonial Aeroplane Co. Ltd. (later Bristol Aeroplane Co. Ltd) for the RAF in 1918. Arrived in Ireland on 25.3.19 and was in service with Nos. 2, 100 and 141 Squadrons and the Irish Flight, RAF, 1919-1921, operating from airfields at Baldonnel, Castlebar, Fermoy, Tallaght and Collinstown. Force-landed near Lucan, Co. Dublin, 5.6.19. Crash-landed at Castlebar, 6.8.20 and at Fermoy on 15.10.20. Repaired each time.	Delivered from the Irish Flight to Baldonnel Aerodrome, 5.7.22. To "B" Flight, No. 1 Squadron. Refuelled with "ordinary motor spirit" and force-landed near Limerick, August 1922. Repaired and returned to service. Crashed and "written-off", 14.2.24.
II later BF.II	Bristol (Type 14) F2B Fighter (1922-1935)	4968	H1251. From a batch of 150 (H1240-H1389; c/ns 4975-5106), constructed by the British and Colonial Aeroplane Co. Ltd., which were powered by a Sunbeam Arab engine and delivered to the RAF in 1918. RAF squadron service not known. A 300-hp Hispano engine was installed, 3.7.1922.	Purchased from the Aircraft Disposal Co. and delivered to Baldonnel Aerodrome, 4.7.22. To "B" Flight, No. 1 Squadron. Engine from BF.IV installed in this aircraft, 1.11.22. Crashed at Baldonnel Aerodrome, killing the pilot, 23.1.24. "Written-off".
III	Bristol (Type 14) F2B Fighter (1922-1935)	5202	H1485. From a batch of 282 (H1408-H1689; c/ns 5125-5406), constructed by the British and Colonial Aeroplane Co. Ltd. and delivered to the RAF in 1918. Powered by a Rolls-Royce Falcon engine. In service in Ireland with No. 2 Squadron and the Irish Flight, RAF, 1920-1921.	Delivered from the Irish Flight to Baldonnel Aerodrome, 10.7.22. To "B" Flight, No. 1 Squadron. Crashed at Naas, Co. Kildare, 17.7.22. "Written-off".
IV	Bristol (Type 14) F2B Fighter (1922-1935)	Not known, possibly none as the aircraft was not constructed by the parent company	E1958. From batch of 250 (E1901-E2150), constructed by Sir W. G. Armstrong Whitworth & Co. Ltd., which were powered by a Sunbeam Arab engine and delivered to the RAF in 1918. RAF squadron service not known.	Purchased from the Aircraft Disposal Co. but was damaged on landing after the delivery flight and had to be scrapped. Engine from this aircraft installed in BF.II, 1.11.22.
V later BF.V.	Bristol (Type 14) F2B Fighter (1922-1935)	3515	D7865. From batch of 300 (D7801-D8100; c/ns 3415-3750), constructed by the British and Colonial Aeroplane Co. Ltd. and delivered to the RAF in 1918. Powered by a Rolls-Royce Falcon engine. RAF squadron service not known.	Purchased from the Aircraft Disposal Co. and delivered to Baldonnel Aerodrome, 14.10.22. To "B" Flight, No. 1 Squadron. Crashed at Crumlin, Dublin, following engine failure over the city, 6.8.24. "Written-off".
VI later BF.VI	Bristol (Type 14) F2B Fighter (1922-1935)	3536	D7886. From batch of 300 (D7801-D8100; c/ns. 3451-3750), constructed by the British and Colonial Aeroplane Co. Ltd. and delivered to the RAF in 1918. Powered by a Rolls-Royce Falcon engine. RAF squadron service not known.	Purchased from the Aircraft Disposal Co. and delivered to Baldonnel Aerodrome, 13.10.22. To "B" Flight, No. 1 Squadron . Crashed, killing the pilot during military exercises at the Curragh, Co. Kildare, 22.9.25. "Written-off".
VII later BF.VII and 7	Bristol (Type 14) F2B Fighter (1922-1935)	3532	D7882. From batch of 300 (D7801-D8100; c/ns. 3451-3750), constructed by the British and Colonial Aeroplane Co. Ltd. and delivered to the RAF in 1918. Powered by a Rolls-Royce Falcon engine. RAF squadron service not known.	Purchased from the Aircraft Disposal Co. and delivered to Baldonnel Aerodrome, 22.11.22. To "B" Flight, No. 1 Squadron. Withdrawn from use, 27.4.32. Scrapped in June 1935 following an Air Corps survey of obsolete engines and aircraft held in storage.
VIII later BF.VIII	Bristol (Type 14) F2B Fighter (1922-1935)	3535	D7885. From batch of 300 (D7801-D8100; c/ns 3451-3750), constructed by the British and Colonial Aeroplane Co. Ltd. and delivered to the RAF in 1918. Powered by a Rolls-Royce Falcon engine. RAF squadron service not known.	Purchased from the Aircraft Disposal Co. and delivered to Baldonnel Aerodrome, 22.11.22. To "B" Flight, No. 1 Squadron. "Written-off" in a crash at Baldonnel, 3.8.28.
17	Bristol (Type 14) F2B Fighter Mk. II (1925-1935)	6858		First of a batch of six Bristol (Type 14) Fighter Mk.IIs, constructed by the Bristol Aeroplane Co. Ltd. in 1925, was ordered for the Irish Army Air Corps as replacements for the crashed F2B Fighters of the first batch. Delivered to Baldonnel Aerodrome, 24.10.25. To "B" Flight, No. 1 Squadron. Crashed at Hempstown, Co. Wicklow, during military exercises, killing the pilot and observer, 21.9.26. "Written-off".

18	Bristol (Type 14) F2B Fighter Mk. II (1925-1935)	6859		Delivered to Baldonnel Aerodrome, 24.10.25. To "B" Flight, No. 1 Squadron. Fitted with engine from Martinsyde A1 MkII in June 1928. Withdrawn from use, April 1935. Following an Air Corps survey of obsolete aircraft and engines held in storage, this aircraft was scrapped, June 1935.
19	Bristol (Type 14) F2B Fighter Mk. II (1925-1935)	6860		Delivered to Baldonnel Aerodrome, 10.11.25. To "B" Flight, No. 1 Squadron. Withdrawn from use, May 1935. Following an Air Corps survey of obsolete aircraft and engines held in storage, this aircraft was scrapped, June 1935.
20	Bristol (Type 14) F2B Fighter Mk. II (1925-1935)	6861		Delivered to Baldonnel Aerodrome, 4.11.25. To "B" Flight, No. 1 Squadron. Withdrawn from use, October 1931.
21	Bristol (Type 14) F2B Fighter Mk. II (1925-1935)	6862		Delivered to Baldonnel Aerodrome, 18.11.25. To "B" Flight, No. 1 Squadron. Withdrawn from use, July 1930.
22	Bristol (Type 14) F2B Fighter Mk. II (1925-1935)	6863		Delivered to Baldonnel Aerodrome, 9.11.25. To "B" Flight, No.1 Squadron. Withdrawn from use, May 1935. Scrapped, following an Air Corps survey of obsolete aircraft and engines held in storage.
I later MI	Martinsyde F.4 Buzzard (1922-1929)		D4285. From a batch off 150 (D4211-D4360), constructed by Martinsyde Ltd. for the RAF but did not enter service.	Purchased from the Aircraft Disposal Co. and delivered to Baldonnel Aerodrome, 15.8.22. To "B" Flight, No. 1 Squadron. Named "The Humming Bird". Force-landed near Killarney, Co. Kerry and later near Mallow, Co. Cork, due to engine failure, 14.10.22. Returned to service after repairs, 8.12.22. Crashed near Baldonnel and "written-off", 16.5.29.
II and later MII.	Martinsyde F.4 Buzzard (1922-1929)		D4281. From a batch of 150 (D4211-D4360), constructed by Martinsyde Ltd. for the RAF but did not enter service.	Purchased from the Aircraft Disposal Co. and delivered to Baldonnel Aerodrome, 14.10.22. To "B" Flight, No. 1 Squadron. Withdrawn from use, April 1929.
III later MIII	Martinsyde F.4 Buzzard (1922-1929)		D4298. From a batch of 150 (D4211-D4360) constructed by Martinsyde Ltd. for the RAF but did not enter service.	Purchased from the Aircraft Disposal Co. and delivered to Baldonnel Aerodrome, 14.10.22. To "B" Flight, No. 1 Squadron. Crashed and "written-off", 18.9.28.
IV later MIV	Martinsyde F.4 Buzzard (1922-1929)		D4274. From a batch of 150 (D4211-D4360), constructed by Martinsyde Ltd. for the RAF but did not enter service.	Purchased from the Aircraft Disposal Co. and delivered to Baldonnel Aerodrome, 14.10.22. To "B" Flight, No. 1 Squadron. Withdrawn from use, October 1925.
AI and I post 1924	Avro 504K (1922-1932)		H2500. From a batch of 500 (H2146-H2645), constructed by A.V.Roe & Co. Ltd. and delivered to the RAF in 1919.	Purchased from the Aircraft Disposal Co. and delivered to Baldonnel Aerodrome, 21.7.22. To "A" Flight, No. 1 Squadron. Crashed near Baldonnel Aerodrome, 18.3.27. "Written-off".
II and AII post 1924.	Avro 504K (1922-1932)		H2073. From a batch of 250 (H1896-H2145), ordered for the RAF from the Sunbeam Motor Car Co. Ltd., of which 70 were later cancelled and the majority were placed in storage to be withdrawn as complete airframes or for spares for the RAF	Purchased from the Aircraft Disposal Co. and delivered to Baldonnel Aerodrome, 11.10.22. To "A" Flight, No. 1 Squadron. Crashed and "written-off", 30.6.25.
III and AIII post 1924.	Avro 504K (1922-1932)		H2075. From a batch of 250 (H1896-H2145), ordered for the RAF from the Sunbeam Motor Car Co. Ltd., of which 70 were later cancelled and the majority were placed in storage to be withdrawn as complete airframes or for spares for the RAF	Purchased from the Aircraft Disposal Co. and delivered to Baldonnel Aerodrome, 14.10.22. To "A" Flight, No. 1 Squadron. Withdrawn from use, 2.6.31.
IV and AIV post 1924.	Avro 504K (1922-1932)		E359. From a batch of 205 (E301-E600), constructed by Harland and Wolff Ltd., Belfast and delivered to the RAF in 1918.	Purchased from the Aircraft Disposal Co. and delivered to Baldonnel Aerodrome, 14.10.22. To "A" Flight, No. 1 Squadron. This was the first and only aircraft manufactured in Ireland to enter service with the Irish Air Service or the Irish Air Corps. Withdrawn from use, 17.5.32.
V and AV post 1924.	Avro 504K (1922-1932)		H2505. From a batch of 500 (H2146-H2645), constructed by A.V.Roe & Co. Ltd. and delivered to the RAF in 1919.	Purchased from the Aircraft Disposal Co. and delivered to Baldonnel Aerodrome, 15.2.23. To "A" Flight, No.1 Squadron. Withdrawn from use, 3.7.28.
VI and AVI post 1924.	Avro 504K (1922-1932)		D7588. From a batch of 300 (D7501-D7800), constructed by A.V.Roe & Co. Ltd. and delivered to the RAF in 1918. Purchased by Central Aircraft Co. in 1919. Certificate of Airworthiness issued 6.6.19. G-EADQ. Expired June 1922.	Purchased from Central Aircraft Co. and delivered to Baldonnel Aerodrome, 11.6.23. To "A" Flight, No. 1 Squadron. Airdisco inline engine installed and possibly redesignated Avro 548. Crashed and "written-off", 3.9.26.

Air Corps Serial Number	Aircraft Type	Construction Number	Previous Identity	Service History
II. Some sources state no serial applied	Royal Aircraft Factory SE.5A (1922)		F5282. From a batch of 100 (F5249-F5348), constructed by Martinsyde Ltd. and delivered to the RAF in 1918. Did not enter service with RAF unit.	Purchased from the Aircraft Disposal Co. and delivered to Baldonnel Aerodrome, September 1922. Force-landed near Mallow, Co. Cork, due to engine failure and was destroyed by Anti-Treaty forces, October 1922.
I later DI.	Airco DH.9 (1923-1934)		H5797. From a batch of 345 (H5541-H5890), constructed by the Alliance Aeroplane Co. Ltd. (Waring and Gillow Ltd.) in 1918 for the RAF but apparently did not enter service with any squadron or other unit.	Purchased from the Aircraft Disposal Co. and delivered to Baldonnel Aerodrome, 1.1.23. To "B" Flight, No.1 Squadron. Crashed near Fermoy, Co. Cork, killing the observer, 25.6.23. "Written-off".
II later DII.	Airco DH.9 (1923-1934)		H5830. From a batch of 345 (H5541-H5890), constructed by the Alliance Aeroplane Co. Ltd. (Waring and Gillow Ltd) in 1918 for the RAF but apparently did not enter service with any squadron or other unit.	Purchased from the Aircraft Disposal Co. and delivered to Baldonnel Aerodrome, 1.1.23. To "B" Flight, No. 1 Squadron. Withdrawn from use, February 1930.
III later DIII.	Airco DH.9 (1923-1934)		H5774. From a batch of 345 (H5541-H5890), constructed by the Alliance Aeroplane Co. Ltd. (Waring and Gillow Ltd) in 1918 for the RAF but apparently did not enter service with any squadron or other unit.	Purchased from the Aircraft Disposal Co. and delivered to Baldonnel Aerodrome, 6.1.23. To "B" Flight, No. 1 Squadron. Withdrawn from use, September 1934. Scrapped, following an Air Corps survey of obsolete aircraft and engines held in storage, June 1935.
IV later DIV	Airco DH.9 (1923-1934)		H5869. From a batch of 345 (H5541-H5890), constructed by the Alliance Aeroplane Co. Ltd. (Waring and Gillow Ltd) in 1918 for the RAF but apparently did not enter service with any squadron or other unit.	Purchased from the Aircraft Disposal Co. and delivered to Baldonnel Aerodrome, 12.1.23. To "B" Flight, No. 1 Squadron. "Written-off"in crash , 18.1.23.
V later DV.	Airco DH.9 (1923-1934)		H5823. From a batch of 345 (H5541-H5890), constructed by the Alliance Aeroplane Co. Ltd (Waring and Gillow Ltd) in 1918 for the RAF but apparently did not enter service with any squadron or other unit.	Purchased from the Aircraft Disposal Co. and delivered to Baldonnel Aerodrome, 23.1.23. To "B" Flight, No. 1 Squadron. Crashed at Oughterard, Co. Galway, returning from an aerial search for a missing trawler off the west coast of Ireland, 26.6.26. "Written-off".
VI later DVI and 6	Airco DH.9 (1923-1934)		H9310. From a batch of 261 (H9113-H9412), constructed by the Aircraft Manufacturing Co. Ltd. (later de Havilland Aircraft Co. Ltd) in 1918 for the RAF but apparently did not enter service with any squadron or other unit.	Purchased from the Aircraft Disposal Co. and delivered to Baldonnel Aerodrome, 28.2.23. To "B" Flight, No. 1 Squadron. Converted to 2 seat trainer.Withdrawn from use, April 1931.
7	Airco DH.9 (1929-1935)		H9247. From a batch of 261 (H9113-H9412), constructed by the Aircraft Manufacturing Co. Ltd. (later de Havilland Aircraft Co. Ltd) in 1918 for the RAF but apparently did not enter service with any squadron or other unit.	Purchased from the Aircraft Disposal Co., apparently without an engine, as a replacement for the DH.9s that had crashed. Delivered to Baldonnel Aerodrome, 5.4.29. To "B" Flight, No. 1 Squadron. Withdrawn from use, September 1934. Following an Air Corps survey of obsolete aircraft and engines held in storage this aircraft was scrapped in June 1935.
8	Airco DH.9 (1929-1935)		H5862. From a batch of 345 (H5541-H5890), constructed by the Alliance Aeroplane Co. Ltd. (Waring and Gillow Ltd.) in 1918 for the RAF but apparently did not enter service with any squadron or other unit.	Purchased from the Aircraft Disposal Co., apparently without an engine, as a replacement for the DH.9s that had crashed. Delivered to Baldonnel Aerodrome, 5.4.29. To "B" Flight, No. 1 Squadron. Withdrawn from use, May 1932.
23	De Havilland DH 60 Cirrus Moth (1926-1935)	264		Delivered to Baldonnel Aerodrome, 12.7.26. To "A" Flight, No. 1 Squadron. Crashed and "written-off", 26.7.28.
24	De Havilland DH 60 Cirrus Moth (1926-1935)	265		Delivered to Baldonnel Aerodrome, 12.7.26. To "A" Flight, No. 1 Squadron. Crashed and "written-off", 4.6.28.
25	De Havilland DH 60 Cirrus Moth (1926-1935)	266		Delivered to Baldonnel Aerodrome, 12.7.26. To "A" Flight, No. 1 Squadron. This aircraft was scrapped in August 1935 following a review by the Air Corps of aircraft and engines held in storage that were obsolete or not required.
26	De Havilland DH 60 Cirrus Moth (1926-1935)	267		Delivered to Baldonnel Aerodrome, 12.7.26. To "A" Flight, No. 1 Squadron. Crashed and "written-off", 29.6.27.

None	Fairey IIIf Mk. Ii (1928-1934)	F968		One Fairey IIIF Mk. II was ordered for delivery to the Irish Army Air Corps, which was diverted from a batch of 13 (S1250-S1262; c/ns F956-F968), constructed for the Fleet Air Arm by the Fairey Aviation Co. Ltd. Delivered to Baldonnel Aerodrome, 20.3.28. Floats for this aircraft were also delivered, costing £1,450. To "B" Flight, No. 1 Squadron. Force-landed in Co. Cavan, but not damaged, 13.9.28. Returned to service after repairs. Crashed at Terenure, Dublin, 10.9.34. Two crew killed and one injured. "Written-off".
V1	Vickers Type 193 Vespa IV (1930-1934)			First flight, 25.3.30. Delivered to Baldonnel Aerodrome, 14.4.30. To "B" Flight, No. 1 Squadron. Crashed at Fermoy, Co. Cork, and "written-off", 6.7.34.
V2	Vickers Type 193 Vespa IV (1930-1934)			First flight, 27.3.30. Delivered to Baldonnel Aerodrome, 14.4.30. To "B" Flight, No. 1 Squadron. Crashed and "written-off", 31.8.32.
V3	Vickers Type 193 Vespa IV (1930-1934)			First flight, 7.4.30. Delivered to Baldonnel Aerodrome, 14.4.30. To "B" Flight, No. 1 Squadron. Crashed in the Foxford Mts., Co. Mayo, 18.5.31. "Written-off".
V4	Vickers Type 193 Vespa IV (1930-1934)			First flight, 2.4.30. Delivered to Baldonnel Aerodrome, 14.4.30. To "B" Flight, No. 1 Squadron. Crashed at the Curragh Military Camp, Co. Kildare, 9.4.31. "Written-off".
V5	Vickers Type 208 Vespa V (1931-1940)			First flight, 25.3.31. Delivered to Baldonnel Aerodrome, 5.4.31. To "B" Flight, No. 1 Squadron. To No. 1 Army Co-Operation Squadron, October 1934. Crashed and "written-off", 10.7.35.
V6	Vickers Type 208 Vespa V (1931-1940)			First flight, 26.3.31. Delivered to Baldonnel Aerodrome, 5.4.31. T "B" Flight, No. 1 Squadron. Crashed during an air show at the Phoenix Park, Dublin, killing the pilot and observer, 5.8.33. "Written-off".
V7	Vickers Type 208 Vespa V (1931-1940)			First flight, 30.3.31. Delivered to Baldonnel Aerodrome, 5.4.31. To "B" Flight, No. 1 Squadron. Damaged in a forced landing near Enniscorthy, Co. Wexford, 17.3.33. Repaired and returned to service, 1935. To No. 1 Army Co-Operation Squadron. Carried out a photographic survey over Rineanna, Co. Clare, for the Dept of Industry and Commerce, 15.7.35. Damaged in a landing accident, Baldonnel Aerodrome, 17.8.37. To Apprentice School as instructional airframe. Scrapped, 1942.
V8	Vickers Type 208 Vespa V (1931-1940)			First flight, 30.3.31. Delivered to Baldonnel Aerodrome, 5.4.31. To "B" Flight, No. 1 Squadron. Damaged in a forced landing at Baldonnel Aerodrome, September 1933. Repaired and returned to service, 1935. To No. 1 Army Co-Operation Squadron. Crashed and "written-off", 12.6.40.
A7	Avro 621 (1930-1937)	410		Delivered to Baldonnel Aerodrome, 23.3.30. To "A" Flight, No. 1 Squadron. Crashed at Bray Head, Co. Wicklow, 21.11.30. "Written-off".
A8	Avro 621 (1930-1937)	411		Delivered to Baldonnel Aerodrome, 5.4.30. To "A" Flight, No. 1 Squadron. To Air Corps Training Schools, October 1934. Withdrawn from use, August 1937.
A9	Avro 621 (1930-1937)	412		Delivered to Baldonnel Aerodrome, 17.4.30. To "A" Flight, No. 1 Squadron. Crashed at Maynooth, Co. Meath, 26.11.30. "Written-off".
C1 and No.1 post -1938.	Avro 631 Cadet (1932-1945)	581		Delivered to Baldonnel Aerodrome, 21.3.32. To "A" Flight, No. 1 Squadron. To Air Corps Training Schools, October 1934. Withdrawn from use, November 1941.
C2 and No.2 post -1938.	Avro 631 Cadet (1932-1945)	582		Delivered to Baldonnel Aerodrome, 21.3.32. To "A" Flight, No. 1 Squadron. To Air Corps Training Schools, October 1934. Crashed and "written-off", 26.7.42.
C3	Avro 631 Cadet (1932-1945)	583		Delivered to Baldonnel Aerodrome, 21.3.32. To "A" Flight, No. 1 Squadron. Crashed during formation flying practice for an air show, killing the pilot, at Belgard, Co. Dublin, 3.8.33.

Air Corps Serial Number	Aircraft Type	Construction Number	Previous Identity	Service History
C4	Avro 631 Cadet (1932-1945)	584		Delivered to Baldonnel Aerodrome, 2.4.32. To "A" Flight, No. 1 Squadron. To Air Corps Training Schools, October 1934. "Written-off" in a crash, 23.6.37.
C5 and No.5 post -1938.	Avro 631 Cadet (1932-1945)	585		Delivered to Baldonnel Aerodrome, 2.4.32. To "A" Flight, No. 1 Squadron. To Air Corps Training Schools, October 1934. Crashed and "written-off", 16.1.42.
C6 and No.6 post -1938	Avro 631 Cadet (1932-1945)	586		Delivered to Baldonnel Aerodrome, 2.4.32. To "A" Flight, No. 1 Squadron. To Air Corps Training Schools, October 1934. Crashed and "written-off", 23.2.42.
C7 and No.7 post-1938	Avro 631 Cadet (1934-1945)	730		Purchased as a replacement for the crashed Cadet (C3) and delivered to Baldonnel Aerodrome, 8.9.34. Fitted with an inverted fuel system. To Air Corps Training Schools. To No. 1 Coastal Patrol Squadron, 1940. Withdrawn from use, following accident on the ground, 1945. Purchased by civilian. EI-AFO, 10.11.50. No Certificate of Airworthiness issued. EI-AGO, 10.3.54. In storage to 1984. Sold in United Kingdom, 1984. G-ACFM. Sold in New Zealand, 1992. ZK-AVR. Flew again, 2000. Purchased by Dept of Defence and returned to Baldonnel 2007.
A10 and No.10 post-1938.	Avro 626 (1934-1941)	687		Delivered to Baldonnel Aerodrome, 20.4.34. To "A" Flight, No. 1 Squadron. To No. 1 Army Co-Operation Squadron, October 1934. Withdrawn from use, 14.4.39. To instructional airframe.
A11 and No.11 post-1938.	Avro 626 (1934-1941)	688		Delivered to Baldonnel Aerodrome, 19.4.34. To "A" Flight, No. 1 Squadron. To No. 1 Army Co-Operation Squadron, October 1934. Withdrawn from use, 20.5.41. To instructional airframe.
A12 and No.12 post-1938.	Avro 626 (1934-1941)	689		Delivered to Baldonnel Aerodrome, 21.4.34. To "A" Flight, No. 1 Squadron. To No. 1 Army Co-Operation Squadron, October 1934. Withdrawn from use, 26.7.40. To instructional airframe.
A13 and No.13 post-1938	Avro 626 (1934-1941)	690		Delivered to Baldonnel Aerodrome, 24.4.34. To "A" Flight, No. 1 Squadron. To No. 1 Army Co-Operation Squadron, October 1934. Crashed at Baldonnel Aerodrome, killing the pilot, 2.5.35. "Written-off".
A14 and No.14 post-1938.	Avro 636 (1935-1941)	863		Delivered to Baldonnel Aerodrome, 15.10.35. To Air Corps Training Schools. To No. 1 Fighter Squadron, 1940-1941. Withdrawn from use, 1941.
A15 and No.15 post-1938.	Avro 636 (1935-1941)	864		Delivered to Baldonnel Aerodrome, 16.10.35. To Air Corps Training Schools. Crashed due to engine failure at Baldonnel Aerodrome, 9.2.40. "Written-off".
A16 and No.16 post-1938.	Avro 636 (1935-1941)	865		Delivered to Baldonnel Aerodrome, 20.10.35. To Air Corps Training Schools. Crashed at Baldonnel Aerodrome, 14.3.38. "Written-off".
A17 and No.17 post-1938.	Avro 636 (1935-1941)	866		Delivered to Baldonnel Aerodrome, 20.10.35. To Air Corps Training Schools. To No. 1 Fighter Squadron, 1940-1941. Withdrawn from use, October 1941.
DH18 and No.18 post-1938	De Havilland DH.84 Dragon 2 (1937-1941)	6071	G-ACNI. Certificate of Airworthiness issued, 23.3.34. Delivered to Jersey Airways, March 1934. Named "Bonne Nuit Bay". To United Airways Ltd., April 1935. To British Airways Ltd., October 1935. Sold to Airwork Ltd., August 1936 and converted to target tug for the Irish Army Air Corps.	Delivered to Baldonnel Aerodrome, 17.3.37. To No. 1 Reconnaissance and Medium Bombing Squadron. The Dragon 2 was the first twin-engined aircraft to enter service with the Air Corps and was the first aircraft delivered to this squadron, which was formed in the same year. Crashed at Baldonnel Aerodrome, 16.12.41. "Written-off".
19	Avro 652A Anson I (1937-1948)	980		Delivered to Baldonnel Aerodrome, 20.3.37. To No. 1 Reconnaissance and Medium Bombing Squadron. To General Purpose Flight, 1944. Withdrawn from use, June 1946.
20	Avro 652A Anson I (1937-1948)	981		Delivered to Baldonnel Aerodrome, 20.3.37. To No. 1 Reconnaissance and Medium Bombing Squadron. Withdrawn from use, November 1943.

21	Avro 652A Anson I (1937-1948)	1033	K8846. Second last Anson I from a batch of 106 ordered for the RAF	Delivered to Baldonnel Aerodrome, 19.1.38. To No. 1 Reconnaissance and Medium Bombing Squadron. To General Purpose Flight, 1944. Crashed at Rineanna, 1.6.45. "Written-off".
22	Avro 652A Anson I (1937-1948)	1034	K8847. Last Anson I from a batch of 106 for the RAF	Delivered to Baldonnel Aerodrome, 19.1.38. To No. 1 Reconnaissance and Medium Bombing Squadron. Crashed at Boher, Co. Limerick, 29.9.41. "Written-off".
23	Gloster Gladiator I (1938-1944)			Delivered to Baldonnel Aerodrome, 9.3.38. To No. 1 Army Co-Operation Squadron. Crashed near Baldonnel Aerodrome and "written-off", 20.10.38.
24	Gloster Gladiator I (1938-1944)			Delivered to Baldonnel Aerodrome, 9.3.38. To No. 1 Army Co-Operation Squadron. To No. 1 Fighter Squadron, January 1939. Crashed at Celbridge, Co. Kildare, 21.1.44. "Written-off"
25	Gloster Gladiator I (1938-1944)			Delivered to Baldonnel Aerodrome, 9.3.38. To No. 1 Army Co-Operation Squadron. To No. 1 Fighter Squadron, January 1939. Withdrawn from use, August 1943.
26	Gloster Gladiator I (1938-1944)			Delivered to Baldonnel Aerodrome, 9.3.38. To No. 1 Army Co-Operation Squadron. Crash-landed at Baldonnel Aerodrome, 2.6.38. Repaired and returned to service, July 1940. To No. 1 Fighter Squadron. Withdrawn from use, November 1943.
27-30	Gloster Gladiator I (1938-1944)		A further twelve Gladiator Is (allotted serial nos. 27-30 and 53-60) were ordered for the Air Corps but were not delivered due to a wartime embargo imposed by the British Government.	
31	Miles M.14A Magister I (1939-1952)	1025	N5389. Did not enter service with the RAF	Delivered to Baldonnel Aerodrome, 22.2.39. To Air Corps Training Schools. Crashed and damaged beyond repair, January 1946. "Written-off".
32	Miles M.14A Magister I (1939-1952)	1026	N5390. Did not enter service with the RAF	Delivered to Baldonnel Aerodrome, 22.3.39. To Air Corps Training Schools. Withdrawn from use, January 1946.
33	Miles M.14A Magister I (1939-1952)	1027	N5391. Did not enter service with the RAF	Delivered to Baldonnel Aerodrome, 22.3.39. To Air Corps Training Schools. Crashed and "written-off", 1.7.42.
34	Miles M.14A Magister I (1939-1952)	1028	N5392. Did not enter service with the RAF	Delivered to Baldonnel Aerodrome, 22.3.39. To Air Corps Training Schools. Withdrawn from use, 11.3.52. To instructional airframe until 1968. Refurbished and delivered to Irish Aviation Museum, 1981. To Irish Air Corps Museum, 1996. Currently on display at the national Museum, Collins Barracks, Dublin.
35	Miles M.14A Magister I (1939-1952)	1029	N5393. Did not enter service with the RAF	Delivered to Baldonnel Aerodrome, 22.3.39. To Air Corps Training Schools. Crashed and "written-off", 6.9.42.
36	Miles M.14A Magister I (1939-1952)	1036	N5400. Did not enter service with the RAF	Delivered to Baldonnel Aerodrome, 8.3.39. To Air Corps Training Schools. Withdrawn from use, September 1946.
37	Miles M.14A Magister I (1939-1952)	1037	N5401. Did not enter service with the RAF	Delivered to Baldonnel Aerodrome, 8.3.39. To Air Corps Training Schools. Crashed and "written-off", 15.5.44.
38	Miles M.14A Magister I (1939-1952)	1038	N5402. Did not enter service with the RAF	Delivered to Baldonnel Aerodrome, 8.3.39. To Air Corps Training Schools. Crashed and "written-off", 28.2.44.
39	Miles M.14A Magister I (1939-1952)	1039	N5403. Did not enter service with the RAF	Delivered to Baldonnel Aerodrome, 8.3.39. To Air Corps Training Schools. Withdrawn from use, August 1946.
40	Miles M.14A Magister I (1939-1952)	1040	N5404. Did not enter service with the RAF	Delivered to Baldonnel Aerodrome, 8.3.39. To Air Corps Training Schools. Withdrawn from use, February 1946.
41	Avro Anson I (1939-1948)		N4863. Did not enter service with the RAF	Delivered to Baldonnel Aerodrome, 2.2.39. To No. 1 Reconnaissance and Medium Bombing Squadron. This was the second aircraft to land at the new airfield at Rineanna, Co. Clare, Withdrawn from use, January 1944.

Air Corps Serial Number	Aircraft Type	Construction Number	Previous Identity	Service History
42	Avro Anson I (1939-1948)		N4864. Did not enter service with the RAF	Delivered to Baldonnel Aerodrome, 2.2.39. To No. 1 Reconnaissance and Medium Bombing Squadron. Force-landed at Buttevant, Co. Cork, 31.8.42. Repaired and returned to service, August 1943. To General Purpose Flight, 1944. Withdrawn from use, March 1948.
43	Avro Anson I (1939-1948)		N4865. Did not enter service with the RAF	Delivered to Baldonnel Aerodrome, 2.2.39. To No. 1 Reconnaissance and Medium Bombing Squadron. This was the first aircraft to land at the new airfield at Rineanna, Co. Clare, 18.5.39. Crashed in Galway Bay and damaged beyond repair, 19.12.39. "Written-off".
44	Avro Anson I (1939-1948)		N4866. Did not enter service with the RAF	Delivered to Baldonnel Aerodrome, 2.2.39.To No. 1 Reconnaissance and Medium Bombing Squadron. Force-landed near Nenagh, Co. Tipperary, 10.10.39. Repaired and returned to service., June 1945. Withdrawn from use, July 1946.
45	Avro Anson I (1939-1948)		N4867. Did not enter service with the RAF	Delivered to Baldonnel Aerodrome, 2.2 39. To No. 1 Reconnaissance and Medium Bombing Squadron. Crashed and damaged beyond repair near Dingle, Co. Kerry, 8.9.39. "Written-off".
46-52	Avro Anson I (1939-1948)		The remaining seven Anson Is (N5290, N5300, N5320, N5340, N5365, N5380 and N9540) were being delivered to Baldonnel Aerodrome in September 1939 when the wartime embargo was imposed. These aircraft had been allotted Air Corps serial numbers (Nos. 46–52) before delivery. These serial numbers were not allotted to any other aircraft in service with the Air Corps.	
53-60	Gloster Gladiator I (1938-1944)		A further twelve Gladiator Is (allotted serial nos. 27-30 and 53-60) were ordered for the Air Corps but were not delivered due to a wartime embargo imposed by the British Government.	
N18 later 18	Supermarine Type 236 Walrus I (1939-1945)	6S/21840.	L2301. First flight, 24.2.39. Did not enter service with the Fleet Air Arm.	Force-landed during delivery flight, due to engine failure, near Ballytrent, Co. Wexford, 3.3.39. Upper wing structure damaged and transported by road to Baldonnel Aerodrome for repairs. Did not enter service until 1941 when wings from another Walrus I (N19) were fitted. To No. 1 Coastal Patrol Squadron. To General Purpose Flight, 1944. Withdrawn from use, 8.8.45. To Aer Lingus as EI-ACC. Purchased for No. 615 Squadron, R.Auxiliary A.F., March 1947. G-AIZG. Sold for scrap, 1949. Restored for static display at Fleet Air Arm Museum, Yeovilton, 1963-1966.
N19	Supermarine Type 236 Walrus I (1939-1945)	No Known	L2302. First flight, 10.1.39. Did not enter service with the Fleet Air Arm.	Delivered to Baldonnel Aerodrome, 4.3.39. To No. 1 Coastal Patrol Squadron. Crash-landed at Baldonnel Aerodrome, 18.9.40. Hull damaged and wings fitted to Walrus I (N18).
N20, later 20	Supermarine Type 236 Walrus I (1939-1945)		L2303	Delivered to Baldonnel Aerodrome, 4.3.39. To No. 1 Coastal Patrol Squadron. Crashed and "written-off", 3.9.42.
61	Westland Lysander II (1939-1947)			First flight, 8.6.39. Delivered to Baldonnel Aerodrome, 15.7.39. To Air Corps Training Schools. To No. 1 Fighter Squadron, August 1939. Converted to target-tug , September 1944. Re-designated Lysander TT.II. To General Purpose Flight. Withdrawn from use, December 1946.
62	Westland Lysander II (1939-1947)			Delivered to Baldonnel Aerodrome, 15.7.39. To Air Corps Training Schools. To No. 1 Fighter Squadron, August 1939. Crashed and "written-off", 8.7.41.
63	Westland Lysander II (1939-1947)			Delivered to Baldonnel Aerodrome, 15.7.39. To Air Corps Training Schools. To No. 1 Fighter Squadron, August 1939. Crashed and "written-off", 15.4.47.
64	Westland Lysander II (1939-1947)			Delivered to Baldonnel Aerodrome, 15.7.39. To Air Corps Training Schools. To No. 1 Fighter Squadron, August 1939. Crashed and "written-off", 2.1.42.

65	Westland Lysander II (1939-1947)			Delivered to Baldonnel Aerodrome, 15.7.39. To Air Corps Training Schools. To No. 1 Fighter Squadron, August 1939. Crashed and "written-off",13.7.41.
66	Westland Lysander II (1939-1947)			Delivered to Baldonnel Aerodrome, 15.7.39. To Air Corps Training Schools. To No. 1 Fighter Squadron, August 1939. Converted to target-tug , September 1944. Re-designated Lysander TT.II. To General Purpose Flight. Withdrawn from use October 1946.
67	Hawker Hind I (1940-1944)		K5446. From a batch of 193 (K5368-K5560), constructed by Hawker Aircraft Ltd., and delivered to the RAF between January and August 1936. To No. 21 Squadron. Converted to dual control training aircraft by General Aircraft Ltd, October 1938. To No. 43 Elementary and Reserve Flying Training School, June 1939. To No. 5 Service Flying Training School, November 1939. To 12 and 47 Maintenance Units, March and May, 1940.	Delivered to Baldonnel Aerodrome, 1.6.40. To Air Corps Training Schools. To No. 1 Fighter Squadron, 1942/1943. Withdrawn from use, October 1944.
68	Hawker Hind I (1940-1944)		K5559. From a batch of 193 (K5368-K5560), constructed by Hawker Aircraft Ltd., and delivered to the RAF between January and August 1936. To No. 15 Squadron, August 1936 and No. 106 Squadron, June 1938. Converted to dual control training aircraft by General Aircraft Ltd., July 1938. To No. 32 Elementary and Reserve Flying Training School, April 1939. To No. 5 Service Flying Training School, September 1939. To 12 and 47 Maintenance Units, March and May 1940.	SERVICE HISTORY: Delivered to Baldonnel Aerodrome, 1.6.40. To Air Corps Training Schools. To No. 1 Fighter Squadron, 1942/1943. Withdrawn from use, November 1943.
69	Hawker Hind I (1940-1944)		K6712. From a batch of 244 (K6613-K6856), constructed by Hawker Aircraft Ltd., and delivered to the RAF between October 1936 and June 1937. To No. 139 Squadron, February 1937 and No. 104 Squadron, August 1937. Converted to dual control training aircraft by General Aircraft Ltd., October 1938. To No.35 Elementary and Reserve Flying Training School, May 1939. To No. 5 Service Flying Training School, November 1939. To 12 and 47 Maintenance Units, March and May 1940.	Delivered to Baldonnel Aerodrome, 1.6.40. Withdrawn from use, June 1940.
70	Hawker Hind I (1940-1944)		K5415. From a batch of 193 (K5368-K5560), constructed by Hawker Aircraft Ltd., and delivered to the RAF between January and August 1936. To No. 44 Squadron, March 1937 and No. 62 Squadron, January 1938. To 24 and 47 Maintenance Units, March and May, 1940.	Delivered to Baldonnel Aerodrome, 1.6.40. To Air Corps Training Schools. Crashed at Laytown, Co. Meath, killing both crew, 27.7.40. "Written-off".
71	Hawker Hind I (1940-1944)		K6755. From a batch of 244 (K6613-K6856), constructed by Hawker Aircraft Ltd., and delivered to the RAF between October 1936 and June 1937. To No. 218 Squadron, April 1937 and No. 603 Squadron, February 1938. To 24 and 47 Maintenance Units, March 1938 and May 1940.	Delivered to Baldonnel Aerodrome, 1.6.40. To Air Corps Training Schools. Crashed and "written-off", 27.9.40.
72	Hawker Hind I (1940-1944)		K6781. From a batch of 244 (K6613-K6856), constructed by Hawker Aircraft Ltd., and delivered to the RAF between October 1936 and June 1937. To No. 62 Squadron, April 1937. To 24 and 47 Maintenance Units, March 1938 and May 1940.	Delivered to Baldonnel Aerodrome, 1.6.40. To Air Corps Training Schools. To No. 1 Fighter Squadron, 1942/1943. Withdrawn from use, August 1944.
73	Miles M.14A Magister I (1940-1946)	524	L6903. From a batch of 24 (L6894-L6919, c/ns 331-559), constructed by Phillips and Powis Aircraft Ltd., for the RAF in 1938. To Nos. 9 and 3 Elementary and Reserve Training Schools. To 47 Maintenance Unit.	Delivered to Baldonnel Aerodrome, 7.6.40. To Air Corps Training Schools. Withdrawn from use, March 1946.
74	Miles M.14A Magister I (1940-1946)	1784	P6440. From a batch of 100 (P6343-P6382, c/ns 1711-1810), constructed by Phillips and Powis Aircraft Ltd., for the RAF in 1939. To 47 Maintenance Unit but did not enter service with the RAF	Delivered to Baldonnel Aerodrome, 7.6.40. To Air Corps Training Schools. Withdrawn from use, September 1945.
75	Miles M.14A Magister I (1940-1946)	942	N3901. From a batch of 204 (N3773-N3991, c/ns 821-1024), constructed by Phillips and Powis Aircraft Ltd., for the RAF in 1938. To 47 Maintenance Unit but did not enter service with the RAF	Delivered to Baldonnel Aerodrome, 7.6.40. To Air Corps Training Schools. Withdrawn from use, August 1946.
76	Miles M.14A Magister I (1940-1946)	1769	P6414. From a batch of 100 (P6346-P6466, c/ns 1711-1810), constructed by Phillips and Powis Aircraft Ltd., for the RAF in 1939. To 47 Maintenance Unit but did not enter service with the RAF	Delivered to Baldonnel Aerodrome, 7.6.40. To Air Corps Training Schools. Crashed and "written-off", 7.10.41.

Air Corps Serial Number	Aircraft Type	Construction Number	Previous Identity	Service History
77	Miles M.14A Magister I (1940-1946)	1777	P6422. From a batch of 100 (P6346-P6466, c/ns 1711-1810), constructed by Phillips and Powis Aircraft Ltd., for the RAF in 1938. To 47 Maintenance Unit but did not enter service with the RAF	Delivered to Baldonnel Aerodrome, 7.6.40. To Air Corps Training Schools. Withdrawn from use, August 1946.
78	Hawker Hector I (1941-1943)		K8098. From a batch of 78 (K8090-K8167), constructed by Westland Aircraft Ltd., and delivered to the RAF between February and June 1937. To No. 4 Squadron, March 1937 and No. 13 squadron, April 1937. To 10 and 46 Maintenance Units, February 1939 and June 1940.	Delivered to Baldonnel Aerodrome, 16.5.41. To Air Corps Training Schools. Withdrawn from use, October 1943.
79	Hawker Hector I (1941-1943)		K8102. From a batch of 78 (K8090-K8167), constructed by Westland Aircraft Ltd., and delivered to the RAF between February and June 1937. To 615 Squadron, February 1938 and No. 613 Squadron, November 1939. To 45 Maintenance Unit, June 1940.	Delivered to Baldonnel Aerodrome, 16.5.41. To Air Corps Training Schools. Withdrawn from use, July 1943.
80	Hawker Hector I (1941-1943)		K8105. From a batch of 78 (K8090-K8167), constructed by Westland Aircraft Ltd., and delivered to the RAF between February and June 1937. To No. 615 Squadron, April 1937. To 5 Maintenance Unit, February and September 1939. To Practice Flying Unit, March 1940.	Reported to have been converted to dual-control training aircraft. Delivered to Baldonnel Aerodrome, 16.5.41. To Air Corps Training Schools. Withdrawn from use, August 1943.
81	Hawker Hector I (1941-1943)		K8114. From a batch of 78 (K8090-K8167), constructed by Westland Aircraft Ltd., and delivered to the RAF between February and June 1937. To No. 4 Squadron, April 1937 and No. 13 Squadron, May 1939. To 10 and 46 Maintenance Units, February 1939 and June 1940.	Delivered to Baldonnel Aerodrome, 16.5.41. To Air Corps Training Schools. "Written-off" in a collision with another Hector (No. 83) at Gormanston Military Camp, Co. Meath, 4.9.41.
82	Hawker Hector I (1941-1943)		K8115. From a batch of 78 (K8090-K8167), constructed by Westland Aircraft Ltd., and delivered to the RAF between February and June 1937. To RAF College, May 1938 and No. 615 Squadron, August 1938. To 9, 5 and 45 Maintenance Units, December 1938, February 1939 and May 1941.	Reported to have been converted to dual-control training aircraft. Delivered to Baldonnel Aerodrome, 16.5.41. To Air Corps Training Schools. Withdrawn from use, October 1943.
83	Hawker Hector I (1941-1943)		K8117. From a batch of 78 (K8090-K8167), constructed by Westland Aircraft Ltd., and delivered to the RAF between February and June 1937. To RAF College, May 1938 and No. 615 Squadron, August 1938. To 9 Maintenance Unit, December 1938. To Practice Flying Unit, April 1940.	Delivered to Baldonnel Aerodrome, 16.5.41. To Air Corps Training Schools. "Written-off" in a collision with another Hector (No. 81) at Gormanston Military Camp, Co. Meath, 4.9.41.
84	Hawker Hector I (1941-1943)		K8148. From a batch of 78 (K8090-K8167), constructed by Westland Aircraft Ltd., and delivered to the RAF between February and June 1937. To 5 Maintenance Unit, March and September 1939. To Practice Flying Unit, March 1940.	Reported to have been converted to dual-control training aircraft. Delivered to Baldonnel Aerodrome, 16.5.41. To Air Corps Training Schools. Withdrawn from use, September 1943.
85	Hawker Hector I (1941-1943)		K9697. From a batch of 100 (K9687-K9786), constructed by Westland Aircraft Ltd., and delivered to the RAF between July and December 1937. To No. 53 Squadron, July 1937. To 5 Maintenance Unit, May and September 1937. To Practice Flying Unit, May 1940. To 46 Maintenance Unit, July 1940.	Delivered to Baldonnel Aerodrome, 16.5.41. To Air Corps Training Schools. Crashed and "written-off", Rathduff, Co. Tipperary, 28.8.42.
86	Hawker Hector I (1941-1943)		K9725. From a batch of 100 (K9687-K9786), constructed by Westland Aircraft Ltd., and delivered to the RAF between July and December 1937. To No. 26 Squadron, August 1937. To 19, 8 and 45 Maintenance Units, January to December 1940. To 45 Maintenance Unit, May 1941.	Reported to have been converted to dual-control training aircraft. Delivered to Baldonnel Aerodrome, 16.5.41. To Air Corps Training Schools. Withdrawn from use, November 1943 and later scrapped.
87	Hawker Hector I (1941-1943)		K9715. From a batch of 100 (K9687-K9786), constructed by Westland Aircraft Ltd., and delivered to the RAF Between July and December 1937. To No. 26 Squadron, August 1937. To 9 and 45 Maintenance Units, February and March 1940.	Delivered to Baldonnel Aerodrome, 28.5.41. To Air Corps Training Schools. Crashed and "written-off", 21.7.41.
88	Hawker Hector I (1941-1943)		K8130. From a batch of 78 (K8090-K8167), constructed by Westland Aircraft Ltd., and delivered to the RAF between February and June 1937. To RAF College, May 1938. To 27 Maintenance Unit, August 1938.	Delivered to Baldonnel Aerodrome, 13.1.42. To Air Corps Training Schools. Withdrawn from use, September 1942 and later scrapped.
89	Hawker Hector I (1941-1943)		K8159. From a batch of 78 (K8090-K81670, constructed by Westland Aircraft Ltd., and delivered to the RAF between February and June 1937.To 6 and 12 Maintenance Units, January and December 1939. To 18 Maintenance Unit, August 1940.	Delivered to Baldonnel Aerodrome, 13.1.42. To Air Corps Training Schools. Withdrawn from use, October 1943 and later scrapped.

90	Hawker Hector I (1941-1943)		K9761. From a batch of 100 (K9687-K9786), constructed by Westland Aircraft Ltd., and delivered to the RAF Between July and December 1937. To No. 602 Squadron, December 1938. To 6 Maintenance Unit, January 1939. To Newtownards airfield, December 1941.	Delivered to Baldonnel Aerodrome, 13.1.42. To Air Corps Training Schools. Withdrawn from use, October 1943 and later scrapped.
91	Lockheed L.214 Hudson I. (1941-1945)	1812	P5123. From a batch of fifty (P5116-P5165), constructed by the Lockheed Aircraft Corporation, and delivered to the RAF in 1939. To No. 233 Squadron. ZS-W. Crash-landed at Skreen, Co. Sligo, due to fuel shortage, during a convoy patrol mission, 24.1.41.	To No. 1 Reconnaissance and Medium Bombing Squadron after being overhauled and repaired by the Air Corps. The Hudson I was the first American aircraft to enter service with the Air Corps. To General Purpose Flight, 1944. Withdrawn from use, August 1945.Purchased by Aer Lingus as EI-ACB. Certificate of Airworthiness not issued and remained in storage until 1947. Purchase by John Mathieu Aviation. OO-API. Scrapped 1954.
92	Fairy Battle T.T.I (1941-1946)		V1222. From a batch of fifty (V1201-V1250), constructed by the Austin Motor Co., and delivered to the RAF in 1940. To No. 4 Bombing and Gunnery Flight, No. 8. Crash-landed at Tramore, Co. Waterford, on April 24, 1941, during a training flight.	To Air Corps Training Schools as a target tug, after being overhauled by the Air Corps. Withdrawn from use, May 1946 and later scrapped.
93	Hawker Hurricane I (1940-1945)		P5178. From a batch of forty (P5170-P5209), constructed by the Canadian Car and Foundry Corporation, and delivered to the RAF in 1940. To No. 79 Squadron, 1.9.40. Following the interception of Heinkel He 111Ps of Kampfgeschwader 55 over the Irish Sea, and after shooting down one of the German bombers, this fighter had to crash-land in Co. Wexford due to fuel shortage, 29.9.40.	To Advanced Training Section, Air Corps Training Schools after being repaired by the Air Corps, 9.5.42. To No. 1 Fighter Squadron, 1943. Withdrawn from use, August 1945 and later scrapped.
94	Hawker Hurricane IIa (1941-1943)		Z2832. From a batch of 50 (Z2791-Z840), constructed by Hawker Aircraft Ltd., and delivered to the RAF between January and July 1941. To No. 32 Squadron. GZ-M. Displayed inscription "McConnell's Squadron 17"under cockpit. Force-landed at Whitestown, Co. Waterford due to a fuel shortage after shooting down a Heinkel He 111H-3 of Wekusta 51, 10.6.41	Repaired and made airworthy again by the Air Corps. To Advanced Training Section, Air Corps Training Schools, March 1943. Returned to the RAF, 7.7.43. Restored to Z2832. To No. 55 Operational Training Unit, 16.7.43. To No. 196 Squadron, 9.8.44. To Wethersfield Station Flight. Withdrawn from use, 31.3.45 and later scrapped.
95	Hawker Hurricane IIb (1941-1943)		Z5070. From a batch of 417 (Z4990-Z5693), constructed by the Gloster Aircraft Co. Ltd., and delivered to the RAF between March and September 1941. Crash-landed at Athboy, Co. Meath during a delivery flight to Scotland, 21.8.41. Did not enter service with the RAF	Repaired and made airworthy again by the Air Corps. To Advanced Training Section, Air Corps Training Schools late 1942. Returned to the RAF, 7.7.43. Restored to Z5070. To No. 55 Operational Training Unit, July 1943. To No. 527 Squadron, July 1944. Withdrawn from use, 9.8.46 and later scrapped.
96	Miles M.9a Master I (1940)		N8009. From batch of 500 (N7408-N9017), constructed by Phillips and Powis Aircraft Ltd., and delivered to the RAF in 1939. To No. 307 Squadron. Force-landed at Dungooley, Co. Louth, due to navigational error, 21.12.40.	Unable to be made airworthy again by the Air Corps due to large crack discovered in a wing spar. To instructional airframe. No. A5.
97	Miles M.19 Master II (1943-1949)		DM260. From a batch of 38 (DM258-DM295), constructed by Phillips and Powis Aircraft Ltd. in 1942. Did not enter service with the RAF	Delivered to Baldonnel Aerodrome, 10.2.43. To No. 1 Fighter Squadron. To Air Corps Training Schools, 1944. Withdrawn from use, October 1949.
98	Miles M.19 Master II (1943-1949)		W9028. From a batch of 36 (W9004-W9039), constructed by Phillips and Powis Aircraft Ltd., in 1942. Did not enter service with the RAF	Delivered to Baldonnel Aerodrome, 10.2.43. To No. 1 Fighter Squadron. To Air Corps Training Schools, 1944. Withdrawn from use, July 1946 and later scrapped.
99	Miles M.19 Master II (1943-1949)		DM258. From a batch of 38 (DM258-DM295), constructed by Phillips and Powis Aircraft Ltd., in 1942. Did not enter service with the RAF	Delivered to Baldonnel Aerodrome, 10.2.43. To No. 1 Fighter Squadron. To Air Corps Training Schools, 1944. Withdrawn from use, August 1945 and later scrapped.
100	Miles M.19 Master II (1943-1949)		DL352. From a batch of 48 (DL326-DL373), constructed by Phillips and Powis Aircraft Ltd., in 1942. Did not enter service with the RAF	Delivered to Baldonnel Aerodrome, 10.2.43. To Air Corps Training Schools. Crashed near Naas, Co. Kildare, killing the pilot, 23.3.49.
101	Miles M.19 Master II (1943-1949)		AZ741. From a batch of 525 (AZ104-AZ856), constructed by Phillips and Powis Aircraft Ltd., in 1942. Did not enter service with the RAF	Delivered to Baldonnel Aerodrome, 12.2.43. To Air Corps Training Schools. Crashed at Baldonnel Aerodrome, killing the pilot, 19.8.46.
102	Miles M.19 Master II (1943-1949)		DM261. From a batch of 38 (DM258-DM295), constructed by Phillips and Powis Aircraft Ltd., in 1942. Did not enter RAF service.	Delivered to Baldonnel Aerodrome, 10.2.43. To Air Corps Training Schools. Withdrawn from use, August 1946 and later scrapped.
103	Hawker Hurricane I (1943-1946)		V6613. From a batch of 50 (V6600-V6649), constructed by the Gloster Aircraft Co. Ltd., between July and November 1940. To No. 111 Squadron, September 1940. To 59 Operational Training Unit.	Delivered to Baldonnel Aerodrome, 7.7.43. To No. 1 Fighter Squadron. Withdrawn from use, December 1945.

Air Corps Serial Number	Aircraft Type	Construction Number	Previous Identity	Service History
104	Hawker Hurricane I (1943-1946)		V7411. From a batch of 47 (V4700-V7446), constructed by Hawker Aircraft Ltd. and delivered to the RAF in 1940. To Nos. 151 and 229 Squadrons. Damaged in combat, 30.9.40. Repaired and to 52, 56, 55 Operational training Units. To No. 182 Squadron.	Delivered to Baldonnel Aerodrome, 7.7.43. To No. 1 Fighter Squadron. Withdrawn from use, September 1946.
105	Hawker Hurricane I (1943-1946)		V7540. From a batch of 40 (V7533-V7572), constructed by Hawker Aircraft Ltd. and delivered to the RAF in 1940. To Nos. 605, 501, 286, 182 Squadrons, 10 Group, Army Air Corps, 55 Operational Training Unit.	Delivered to Baldonnel Aerodrome, 7.7.43. To No. 1 Fighter Squadron. Withdrawn from use, September 1946.
106	Hawker Hurricane I (1943-1946)		Z4037. From a batch of 40 (Z4022-Z4071), constructed by the Gloster Aircraft Co. Ltd., between February and June 1941. To 1423 Flight and No. 87 Squadron.	Delivered to Baldonnel Aerodrome, 7.7.43. To No. 1 Fighter Squadron. Withdrawn from use, March 1946.
107	Hawker Hurricane I (1943-1946)		P2968. From a batch of 50 (P2946-P2995), constructed by the Gloster Aircraft Co. Ltd., between December 1939 and April 1940. To Nos. 32, 151 and 46 Squadrons. To No. 9 Flying Training School, August 1941. To No. 9 (Pilots) Advanced Flying Unit. To instructional airframe, November 1943.	Delivered to Baldonnel Aerodrome, 29.11.43. To No. 1 Fighter Squadron. Withdrawn from use, July 1946.
108	Hawker Hurricane I (1943-1946)		P3416. From a batch of 50 (P3380-P3429), constructed by Hawker Aircraft Ltd., between February and July 1940. To Nos. 3 Squadron, 5 and 55 Operational Training Units. To 9 Flying Training Unit. To 9 (Pilots) Advanced Flying Unit.	Delivered to Baldonnel Aerodrome, 29.11.43. To No. 1 Fighter Squadron. Withdrawn from use, July 1946.
109	Hawker Hurricane I (1943-1946)		V7173. From a batch of 40 (V7156-V7195), constructed by the Gloster Aircraft Co. Ltd., between July and November 1940. To No. 85 Squadron, 52, 59 Operational Training Unit. MF-X34.	Delivered to Baldonnel Aerodrome, 29.11.43. To No. 1 Fighter Squadron. Withdrawn from use, September 1946.
110	Hawker Hurricane I (1943-1946)		Z7158. From a batch of 20 (Z7143-Z7162), constructed by the Canadian Car and Foundry Corporation, between November 1940 and April 1941. To 56 Operational Training Unit and Station Flight, Newtownards, Co. Down.	Delivered to Baldonnel Aerodrome, 21.2.44. To No. 1 Fighter Squadron. Crash-landed in Co. Wexford, November 1945 and Withdrawn from use.
111	Hawker Hurricane I (1943-1946)		V6576. From a batch of 50 (V6533-V6582), constructed by the Gloster Aircraft Co. Ltd., between July and November 1940. To Nos. 242, 504, 133, 257, 59 Squadrons and 59 O.T.U.	Delivered to Baldonnel Aerodrome, 30.3.44. To No. 1 Fighter Squadron. Withdrawn from use, August 1946.
112	Hawker Hurricane I (1943-1946)		V7435. From a batch of 47 (V7400-V7446), constructed by Hawker Aircraft Ltd. and delivered to the RAF in 1940. To Nos. 56, 71 Squadrons, 56 Operational Training Unit.	Delivered to Baldonnel Aerodrome, 30.3.44. To No. 1 Fighter Squadron. Withdrawn from use, August 1946.
113	Not Allocated			
114	Hawker Hurricane I (1943-1946)		V7463. From a batch of 50 (V7461-V7510), constructed by Hawker Aircraft Ltd. and delivered to the RAF in 1940. To Nos. 73, 85, 32, 247 Squadrons, 55 and 41 Operational Training Units.	Delivered to Baldonnel Aerodrome, 30.3.44. To No. 1 Fighter Squadron. Withdrawn from use, August 1946.
115	Hawker Hurricane IIc (1945-1947)		LF536. From a batch of 14 (LF529-LF542), constructed by Hawker Aircraft Ltd., for the RAF in 1944. To 1689 Flight.	Delivered to Baldonnel Aerodrome, 28.3.45. To No. 1 Fighter Squadron. Withdrawn from use, June 1946 and later scrapped.
116	Hawker Hurricane IIc (1945-1947)		LF541. From a batch of 14 (LF529-LF542), constructed by Hawker Aircraft Ltd., for the RAF in 1944. To 1689 Flight.	Delivered to Baldonnel Aerodrome, 7.3.45. To No. 1 Fighter Squadron. Withdrawn from use, July 1947 and later scrapped.
117	Hawker Hurricane IIc (1945-1947)		LF566. From a batch of 43 (LF559-LF601), constructed by Hawker Aircraft Ltd., for the RAF in 1944. To 1690 Flight.	Delivered to Baldonnel Aerodrome, 7.3.45. To No. 1 Fighter Squadron. "Written-off" in a crash, June 1947.
118	Hawker Hurricane IIc (1945-1947)		LF624. From a batch of 41 (LF620-LF660), constructed by Hawker Aircraft Ltd., for the RAF in 1944. To No. 679 and 691 Squadrons.	Delivered to Baldonnel Aerodrome, 7.3.45. To No. 1 Fighter Squadron. Withdrawn from use, March 1947 and later scrapped.
119	Hawker Hurricane IIc (1945-1947)		LF770. From a batch of 38 (LF737-LF774), constructed by Hawker Aircraft Ltd., for the RAF in 1944. To No. 1697 Air Despatch Letter Service Flight. DR-G. May 1944.	Delivered to Baldonnel Aerodrome, 7.3.45. To No. 1 Fighter Squadron. Withdrawn from use, January 1947 and later scrapped.

120	Hawker Hurricane IIc (1945-1947)		PZ796. From a batch of 45 (PZ791-PZ835), constructed by Hawker Aircraft Ltd., for the RAF in 1944.	Delivered to Baldonnel Aerodrome, 28.3.45. To No. 1 Fighter Squadron. Withdrawn from use, November 1947 and later scrapped.
121	Miles M.19 Master II (1945-1949)		DL194. From a batch of 36 (DL169-DL204), constructed by Phillips and Powis Aircraft Ltd. in 1941. To RAF College. To Nos. 5 and 7 (Pilots) Advanced Flying Units. To No. 4 Armament Practice Camp.	Delivered to Baldonnel Aerodrome, 31.5.45. To Air Corps Training Schools. "Written-off" in a mid-air collision with another Master II (No. 124), killing the pilot, 3.2.49.
122	Miles M.19 Master II (1945-1949)		DK835. From a batch of 44 (DK800-DK843), constructed by Phillips and Powis Aircraft Ltd. in 1941. To RAF College. To No. 5 (Pilots) Advanced Flying Unit. To No. 4 Armament Practice Camp.	Delivered to Baldonnel Aerodrome, 31.5.45. To Air Corps Training Schools. Withdrawn from use, 1.9.49 and later scrapped.
123	Miles M.19 Master II (1945-1949)		DK934. From a batch of 49 (DK909-DK957), constructed by Phillips and Powis Aircraft Ltd. in 1941. To Nos 5 and 17 (Pilots) Advanced Flying Units.	Delivered to Baldonnel Aerodrome, 31.5.45. To Air Corps Training Schools. Withdrawn from use, 21.7.47 and later scrapped.
124	Miles M.19 Master II (1945-1949)		DM220. From a batch of 46 (DM200-DM245), constructed by Phillips and Powis Aircraft Ltd. in 1942. To RAF College. To No. 2 Flying Instructors School. To No. 5 (Pilots) Advanced Flying Unit.	Delivered to Baldonnel Aerodrome, 15.6.45. To Air Corps Training Schools. "Written-off" in a mid-air collision with another Master II (No. 121), killing the pilot, 3.2.49.
125	Miles M.19 Master II (1945-1949)		DL405. From a batch of 41 (DL395-DL435), constructed by Phillips and Powis Aircraft Ltd. in 1941. To No. 2 Flying Instructors School. To No. 5 (Pilots) Advanced Flying Unit. To No. 4 Armament Practice Camp.	Delivered to Baldonnel Aerodrome, 15.6.45. To Air Corps Flying Schools. Withdrawn from use, 13.9.49 and later scrapped.
126	Miles M.19 Master II (1945-1949)		AZ250. From a batch of 45 (AZ245-AZ289), constructed by Phillips and Powis Aircraft Ltd. in 1940. To No. 8 Flying Training School. To No. 2 Flying Instructors School. To No. 5 (Pilots) Advanced Flying Unit.	Delivered to Baldonnel Aerodrome, 15.6.45. To Air Corps Training Schools. Withdrawn from use, 16.9.49 and later scrapped.
127	Miles M.14 Magister I (1946-1953)		P6424. From a batch of 29 (P6396-P6424), constructed by Phillips and Powis Aircraft Ltd. in 1939. To Nos. 15 and 7 Elementary Flying Training Schools. To Nos. 7 and 2 Flying Instructors Schools. To No. 604 Squadron. Refurbished by Miles Aircraft Ltd., 1945. Certificate of Airworthiness No. 8260 issued, 14.2.46.	Delivered to Baldonnel Aerodrome, 17.2.46. To Air Corps Training Schools. Withdrawn from use, May 1952 and later scrapped.
128	Miles M.14 Magister I (1946-1953)	1827	R1826. From a batch of 60 (R1810-R1859), constructed by Phillips and Powis Aircraft Ltd. in 1939. To Nos. 5 and 16 Elementary Flying Training Schools. To Empire Central Flying School. Purchased by Miles Aircraft Ltd., 1944 and refurbished, 1945. Certificate of Airworthiness No. 8261 issued, 14.2.46.	Delivered to Baldonnel Aerodrome, 17.2.46. To Air Corps Training Schools. Withdrawn from use, November 1951 and later scrapped.
129	Miles M.14 Magister I (1946-1953)	2000	T9733. From a batch of 40 (T9729-T9768), constructed by Phillips and Powis Aircraft Ltd. in 1940. To Empire Central Flying School. Purchased by Miles Aircraft Ltd., 1944 and refurbished, 1945. Certificate of Airworthiness No. 8262 issued, 14.2.46.	Delivered to Baldonnel Aerodrome, 17.2.46. To Air Corps Training Schools. Withdrawn from use, December 1952 and later scrapped.
130	Miles M.14 Magister I (1946-1953)	915	N3869. From a batch of 50 (N3820-N3869), constructed by Phillips and Powis Aircraft Ltd. in 1939. To Conversion Flight (Woodley). Refurbished by Miles Aircraft Ltd., 1945. Certificate of Airworthiness No. 8263 issued, 14.2.46.	Delivered to Baldonnel Aerodrome, 17.2.46. To Air Corps Training Schools. Withdrawn from use, January 1953 and later scrapped.
131	Miles M.14 Magister I (1946-1953)	768	L3842. From a batch of 34 (L8326-L8359), constructed by Phillips and Powis Aircraft Ltd. in 1938. To Air Transport Auxiliary. Refurbished by Miles Aircraft Ltd., 1945. Certificate of Airworthiness No. 8264 issued, 14.2.46.	Delivered to Baldonnel Aerodrome, 9.3.46. To Air Corps Training Schools. Withdrawn from use, June 1952 and later scrapped.
132	Miles M.14 Magister I (1946-1953)	2044	T9807.From a batch of 50 (T9799-T9848), constructed by Phillips and Powis Aircraft Ltd. in 1940. To Empire Central Flying School. Purchased by Miles Aircraft Ltd., 1944 and refurbished, 1945. Certificate of Airworthiness No. 8265 issued, 14.2.46.	Delivered to Baldonnel Aerodrome, 20.2.46. to Air Corps Training Schools. Withdrawn from use, September 1953 and later scrapped.
133	Miles M.14 Magister I (1946-1953)	2242	V1089. From a batch of 40 (V1063-V1102), constructed by Phillips and Powis Aircraft Ltd. in 1941. Refurbished by Miles Aircraft Ltd., 1945. Certificate of Airworthiness No. 8266 issued, 14.2.46.	Delivered to Baldonnel Aerodrome, 20.2.46. To Air Corps Training Schools. "Written-off" in a crash at Gormanston Military Camp, 7.2.47.
134	Miles M.14 Magister I (1946-1953)	2189	V1016. From a batch of 40 (V1003-V1042), constructed by Phillips and Powis Aircraft Ltd. in 1941. To Air Transport Auxiliary. Refurbished by Miles Aircraft Ltd., 1945. Certificate of Airworthiness No. 8267 issued, 14.2.46.	Delivered to Baldonnel Aerodrome, 20.2.46. To Air Corps Training Schools. Withdrawn from use, January 1953 and later scrapped.

Air Corps Serial Number	Aircraft Type	Construction Number	Previous Identity	Service History
135	Miles M.14 Magister I (1946-1953)	2040	T9803. From a batch of 50 (T9799-T9848), constructed by Phillips and Powis Aircraft Ltd. in 1940. To Air Transport Auxiliary. Refurbished by Miles Aircraft Ltd., 1945. Certificate of Airworthiness No. 8268 issued 14.2.46.	Delivered to Baldonnel Aerodrome, 9.3.46. To Air Corps Training Schools. Withdrawn from use, August 1951 and later scrapped.
136	Miles M.14 Magister I (1946-1953)	2247	V1094. From a batch of 40 (V1063-V1102), constructed by Phillips and Powis Aircraft Ltd. in 1941. Refurbished by Miles Aircraft Ltd., 1945. Certificate of Airworthiness No. 8269 issued, 14.2.46.	Delivered to Baldonnel Aerodrome, 9.3.46. To Air Corps Training Schools. Withdrawn from use, November 1952 and later scrapped.
137	Miles M.14 Magister I (1946-1953)	778	L8352. From a batch of 34 (L8326-L8359), constructed by Phillips and Powis Aircraft ltd. in 1938. Refurbished by Miles Aircraft Ltd., 1945. Certificate of Airworthiness No. 8270 issued, 14.2.46.	Delivered to Baldonnel Aerodrome, 9.3.46. To Air Corps Training Schools. Withdrawn from use, November 1952 and later scrapped.
138	Miles M.14 Magister I (1946-1953)	1835	R1834. From a batch of 60 (R1810-R1859), constructed by Phillips and Powis Aircraft Ltd. in 1939. To Nos. 253 and 614 Squadrons. To Nos. 15 and 21 Elementary Flying Training Schools. To Flying Training Command. Refurbished by Miles Aircraft Ltd., 1945. Certificate of Airworthiness No. 8271 issued, 14.2.46.	Delivered to Baldonnel Aerodrome, 9.3.46. To Air Corps Training Schools. Withdrawn from use, June 1952 and later scrapped.
139	Not Allocated		Some sources have suggested that these numbers were originally allocated to the two Miles M.25 Martinet T.T.Is.	
140	Not Allocated			
141	Avro XIX Series I (1946-1962)	1313		Delivered to Baldonnel Aerodrome, 10.4.46. To Advanced Training Flight. To General Purpose Flight. Withdrawn from use, to Technical Training Squadron as instructional airframe, 20.1.62. In storage at Baldonnel Aerodrome from 1974. To Irish Aviation Museum, 1981. To Air Corps Museum, 1995.
142	Avro XIX Series I (1946-1962)	1314		Delivered to Baldonnel Aerodrome, 10.4.46. To Advanced Training Flight. To General Purpose Flight. Damaged when undercarriage collapsed at Baldonnel Aerodrome, 31.1.58. Withdrawn from use. To Technical Training Squadron as instructional airframe. Withdrawn from use and scrapped, 1962.
143	Avro XIX Series I (1946-1962)	1315		Delivered to Baldonnel Aerodrome, 10.4.46. To Advanced Training Flight. To General Purpose Flight. "Written-off" in a crash at Shannon Airport, Co. Clare, 8.5.53.
144	Miles M.25 Martinet T.T.I (1946-1958)		not Known	Delivered to Baldonnel Aerodrome, 5.7.46. To General Purpose Flight. "Written-off" in a crash, 25.5.52.
145	Miles M.25 Martinet T.T.I (1946-1958)		not Known	Delivered to Baldonnel Aerodrome, 5.7.46. To General Purpose Flight. Withdrawn from use. To Technical Training Squadron as instructional airframe, December 1958. Withdrawn from use and scrapped, 1964.
146	Vickers Supermarine Seafire LF.III (1947-1955)		PR302. From a batch of 50 (PR285-PR334), constructed by Westland Aircraft Ltd. To British Pacific Fleet, March 1945. Acquired by Vickers Supermarine, 1946.	First flight as Seafire LF.III, 4.12.46. Accepted by Air Corps, 24.1.47. Delivered to Baldonnel Aerodrome, 17.2.47. To No. 1 Fighter Squadron. Withdrawn from use, 16.6.54. To Technical Training Squadron as instructional airframe. Scrapped, 1962.
147	Vickers Supermarine Seafire LF.III (1947-1955)		PR315. From a batch of 50 (PR285-PR334), constructed by Westland Aircraft Ltd. To British Pacific Fleet, March 1945. To No. 879 Squadron, June 1945. Acquired by Vickers Supermarine, 1946.	First flight as Seafire LF.III, 2.9.46. Accepted by Air Corps, 24.1.47. Delivered to Baldonnel Aerodrome, 17.2.47. To No. 1 Fighter Squadron. "Written-off" in a crash at Gormanston Military Camp, Co. Meath, 5.9.47.
148	Vickers Supermarine Seafire LF.III (1947-1955)		PX950. From a batch of 50 (PX913-PX962), constructed by Cunliffe Owen Ltd. and delivered to the Fleet Air Arm, 26.3.45.. To No. 761 Squadron, April 1945. To No. 2 School of Naval Air Fighting.	First flight as Seafire LF.III, 30.12.46. Accepted by Air Corps, 24.1.47. Delivered to Baldonnel Aerodrome, 17.2.47. "Written-off" in a crash into the sea off Gormanston, Co. Meath, killing the pilot, 22.5.53.
149	Vickers Supermarine Seafire LF.III (1947-1955)		PX948. From a batch of 50 (PX913-PX962), constructed by Cunliffe Owen Ltd. To British Pacific Fleet, 1945. Acquired by Vickers Supermarine, 1946..	First flight as Seafire LF.III, 3.12.46. Accepted by Air Corps, 24.1.47. Delivered to Baldonnel Aerodrome, 17.2.47. To No. 1 Fighter Squadron. Withdrawn from use, 15.5.54. To Technical Training Squadron as instructional airframe. Scrapped, 1960.

150	Vickers Supermarine Seafire LF.III (1947-1955)		RX210. From a batch of 47 (RX210-RX256), constructed by Westland Aircraft Ltd. To British Pacific Fleet, April 1945. Acquired by Vickers Supermarine, 1946.	First flight as Seafire LF.III, 15.4.47. Delivered to Baldonnel Aerodrome, 11.7.47. To No. 1 Fighter Squadron. Withdrawn from use, 11.3.55. To Technical Training Squadron as instructional airframe. Scrapped, 1960.
151	Vickers Supermarine Seafire LF.III (1947-1955)		PX941. From a batch of 50 (PX913-PX962), constructed by Cunliffe Owen Ltd. To British Pacific Fleet, 1945. Acquired by Vickers Supermarine, 1946.	First flight as Seafire LF.III, 15.5.47. Delivered to Baldonnel Aerodrome, 11.7.47. To No. 1 Fighter Squadron. "Written-off" in a crash in Co. Meath, 29.6.51.
152	Vickers Supermarine Seafire LF.III (1947-1955)		PX929. From a batch of 50 (PX913-PX962), constructed by Cunliffe Owen Ltd. and delivered to the Fleet Air Arm, 3.3.45. To 39 Maintenance Unit. Acquired by Vickers Supermarine, 1946.	First flight as Seafire LF.III, June 1947. Delivered to Baldonnel Aerodrome, 11.7.47. To No. 1 Fighter Squadron. "Written-off" in a forced-landing at Gormanston Military Camp, Co. Meath, 1.9.49. Airframe used for fire practice at Dublin Airport. Scrapped, 1962.
153	Vickers Supermarine Seafire LF.III (1947-1955)		PX924. From a batch of 50 (PX913-PX962), constructed by Cunliffe Owen Ltd. To British Pacific Fleet, 1.3.45. Acquired by Vickers Supermarine, 1946.	Delivered to Baldonnel Aerodrome, 11.7.47. To No. 1 Fighter Squadron. Withdrawn from use, June 1954. To Technical Training Squadron as instructional airframe. Scrapped, 1962.
154	Vickers Supermarine Seafire LF.III (1947-1955)		PX915. From a batch of 50 (PX913-PX962), constructed by Cunliffe Owen Ltd. and delivered to the Fleet Air Arm, 22.2.45. Acquired by Vickers Supermarine, 1946.	First flight as Seafire LF.III, 8.8.47. Delivered to Baldonnel Aerodrome, 27.9.47. To No. 1 Fighter Squadron. "Written-off" in a crash at Kilbride, Co. Wicklow, killing the pilot, 28.5.51.
155	Vickers Supermarine Seafire LF.III (1947-1955)		PR236. From a batch of 44 (PR228-PR271), constructed by Westland Aircraft Ltd. and delivered to the Fleet Air Arm, 30.11.44. To No. 880 Squadron, April 1945. Acquired by Vickers Supermarine, 1946.	This aircraft was fitted with the wings from another Seafire III (NF566) before delivery to the Air Corps as a Seafire LF.III. Delivered to Baldonnel Aerodrome, 27.9.47. To No. 1 Fighter Squadron. Withdrawn from use, August 1954. To Technical Training Squadron as instructional airframe. Scrapped, 1962.
156	Vickers Supermarine Seafire LF.III (1947-1955)		PX936. From a batch of 50 (PX913-PX962), constructed by Cunliffe Owen Ltd. and delivered to the Fleet Air Arm, 5.3.45. This aircraft was a replacement for another Seafire III (PX 959) which had been selected for delivery to the Air Corps but was "written-off" in a crash during the delivery flight to the company factory.	First flight as Seafire LF.III, 28.4.47. Delivered to Baldonnel Aerodrome, 27.9.47. To No. 1 Fighter Squadron. Withdrawn from use, 12.6.54. To Technical Training Squadron as instructional airframe. Scrapped 1962.
157	Vickers Supermarine Seafire LF.III (1947-1955)		RX168. From a batch of 39 (RX156-RX194), constructed by Westland Aircraft Ltd. To British Pacific Fleet, 1945. Acquired by Vickers Supermarine, 1946.	First flight as Seafire LF.III, 12.9.47. Delivered to Baldonnel Aerodrome, 27.949. To No. 1 Fighter Squadron. Withdrawn from use, October 1953. To Technical Training Squadron as instructional airframe.Purchased by College of Technology, Dublin, 11.3.61. Used as an instructional airframe. Apparently scrapped circa 1963. Parts sold in United Kingdom for restoration of Seafire III. G-BWEM, June 1995.
158	Vickers Supermarine Spitfire Tr.9 (1951-1961)	CBAF 7122	MJ627. From a batch of 45 (MJ602-MJ646), constructed by Vickers Armstrong (Supermarine) Ltd. and delivered as Spitfire LF.IX to the RAF, December 1943. To 9 Maintenance Unit. To No. 83 Ground Support Unit. March 1944. No. 441 Squadron, September 1944. Damaged in accident, March 1945. To Air Service Training for repairs. To 29 Maintenance Unit. Purchased by the company, July 19.2.50. Converted to Spitfire Tr.9. G-15-171.	Delivered to Baldonnel Aerodrome, 5.6.51. To 'B' Flight, Air Corps Training Schools. To No. 1 Fighter Squadron, 1955. Withdrawn from use, 20.4.60. To Technical Training Squadron as instructional airframe. Sold in United Kingdom, 1963. G-ASOZ, later cancelled. Wings fitted to another Spitfire T.9 (ex No.159) Fuselage stored until 1977. Long-term restoration commenced, which was completed 1995.
159	Vickers Supermarine Spitfire Tr.9 (1951-1961)	CBAF7269	MJ772. From a batch of 33 (MJ769-MJ801), constructed by Vickers Armstrong (Supermarine) Ltd. and delivered as Spitfire LF.IX to the RAF, December 1943. To 33 Maintenance Unit. To No. 341 Squadron, January 1944. Damaged in combat, June 1944. Repaired. To No. 340 Squadron, June 1944. To No. 84 Ground Support Unit, August 1944. Damaged in flying accident, January 1945. To No. 83 Ground Support Unit. To 29 Maintenance Unit, September 1945. Purchased by the company, 19.2.50. Converted to Spitfire Tr.9. G-15-172.	Delivered to Baldonnel Aerodrome, 5.6.51. To 'B' Flight, Air Corps Training Schools. To No. 1 Fighter Squadron, 1955. Withdrawn from use, 27.1.60. To Technical Training Squadron as instructional airframe. Sold in United Kingdom, 1963. In storage until 1969. G-AVAV. Restored with wings from another Spitfire T.9 (ex No. 158) Sold in U.S.A., December 1974. N8R.
160	Vickers Supermarine Spitfire Tr.9 (1951-1961)	not known	MK721. From a batch of 44 (MK713-MK756), constructed by Vickers Armstrong (Supermarine) Ltd. and delivered as Spitfire LF.IX to the RAF, April 1944. To 4 Maintenance Unit. No. 401 Squadron, June 1944. Damaged in combat, July 1944. Repaired. To No. 411 Squadron, 14.7.44. To No. 401 Squadron, October 1944. Damaged, 24.10.44. To Miles Aircraft Ltd. for repairs. To No. 3 Armament Practice Camp, April 1945. To 33, 16 and 29 Maintenance Units. Purchased by the company, 19.2.50. Converted to Spitfire Tr.9. G-15-173.	Delivered to Baldonnel Aerodrome, 29.6.51. To 'B' Flight, Air Corps Training Schools. To No. 1 Fighter Squadron, 1955. "Written-off" in an accident at Baldonnel Aerodrome, 15.2.57.

Air Corps Serial Number	Aircraft Type	Construction Number	Previous Identity	Service History
161	Vickers Supermarine Spitfire Tr.9 (1951-1961)	CBAF 9590	PV202. From a batch of 42 (PV174-PV215), constructed by Vickers Armstrong (Supermarine) Ltd. and delivered as Spitfire LF.IX to the RAF, September 1944.To 33 Maintenance Unit. To No. 84 Ground Support Unit, October and December 1944. To No. 412 Squadron, March 1945. No. 83 Ground Support Unit, May 1945. To 29 Maintenance Unit, March 1946. Purchased by the company, 19.2. 50. Converted to Spitfire Tr.9. G-15-174.	Delivered to Baldonnel Aerodrome, 29.6.51. To 'B' Flight, Air Corps Training Schools. To No. 1 Fighter Squadron, 1955. Withdrawn from use, December 1960. To Technical Training Squadron as instructional airframe. Sold in United Kingdom, 1968. In storage until 1979. Sold again, 1980. G-BHGH, later cancelled. Restoration commenced, 1980. G-TRIX. Airworthy again, 1990. Written-off in crash, 8.4.2000. returned to airwothy status and flew in 2005 marked as 161. Currently marked as Royal Netherlands Air Force H-98
162	Vickers Supermarine Spitfire Tr.9 (1951-1961)	CBAF 8463.	ML407. From a batch of 33 (ML396-ML428), constructed by Vickers Armstrong (Supermarine) Ltd. and delivered as Spitfire LF.IX to the RAF, April 1944. To 33 Maintenance Unit. No. 485 Squadron, April 1944. Damaged, 12. 10 44. Repaired. To Nos. 485, 341, 131, 349, 485, 345, and 332 Squadrons, April 1944 – April 1945. Purchased by the company, 19.2.50. Converted to Spitfire Tr.9. G-15-175.	Delivered to Baldonnel Aerodrome, 30.7.51. To 'B' Flight, Air Corps Training Schools. To No. 1 Fighter Squadron, 1955. Withdrawn from use, 28.6.60. To Technical Training Squadron as instructional airframe. Sold in United Kingdom, 1968. Sold to Strathallen Museum, 1979. Restoration commenced and airworthy again, 1985. G-LFIX.
163	Vickers Supermarine Spitfire Tr.9 (1951-1961)	CBAF11432	TE308. From a batch of 7 (TE303-TE309), constructed by Vickers Armstrong (Supermarine) Ltd. and delivered as Spitfire HF.IX to the RAF in 1945. Purchased by the company, 19.2.50. Converted to Spitfire Tr.9. G-15-176.	Delivered to Baldonnel Aerodrome, 30.7.51. To 'B' Flight, Air Corps Training Schools. To No. 1 Fighter Squadron, 1955. Withdrawn from use, 12.9.61, after the last operational flight by a Spitfire T.9 in service with the Air Corps. To Technical Training Squadron as instructional airframe. Sold in the United Kingdom, 1968. G-AWGB, later cancelled. In storage until April 1970. Sold in Canada. CF-RAF. Sold in U.S.A., 1975. N92477.
164	De Havilland DHC-1 Chipmunk T.20 (1952-1980)	C1-0450.		Delivered to Baldonnel Aerodrome, 16.1.52. To Air Corps Training Schools. To No. 1 Fighter Squadron, March 1955. To Basic Flying Training School, 1956. To Advanced Flying Training School, 1974. To Basic Flying Training School, 1980. Withdrawn from use, 1981. To Technical Training Squadron as instructional airframe. To Air Corps Museum, 1995.
165	De Havilland DHC-1 Chipmunk T.20 (1952-1980)	C1-0452		Delivered to Baldonnel Aerodrome, 16.1.52. To Air Corps Training Schools. To No. 1 Fighter Squadron, March 1955. To Basic Flying Training School, 1956. Crashed at Laytown, Co. Dublin, 14.6.56. To Technical Training Squadron as instructional airframe. Scrapped 1961.
166	De Havilland DHC-1 Chipmunk T.20 (1952-1980)	C1-0453		Delivered to Baldonnel Aerodrome, 16.1.52. To Air Corps Training Schools. To No. 1 Fighter Squadron, March 1955. To Basic Flying Training School, 1980. To Advanced Flying Training School, 1974. To Basic Flying Training School, 1980.Withdrawn from use, August 1980 and later scrapped.
167	De Havilland DHC-1 Chipmunk T.20 (1952-1980)	C1-0463		Delivered to Baldonnel Aerodrome, 31.1.52. To Air Corps Training Schools. To No.1 Fighter Squadron, March 1955. To Basic Flying Training School, 1956. Force-landed at Clondalkin, Co. Dublin, 8.9.59. To Technical Training Squadron as instructional airframe until 1968. Scrapped, 1979.
168	De Havilland DHC-1 Chipmunk T.20 (1952-1980)	C1-0464		Delivered to Baldonnel Aerodrome, 31.1.52. To Air Corps Training Schools. To No. 1 Fighter Squadron, March 1955. To Basic Flying Training School, 1956. To Advanced Flying Training School, 1974. Withdrawn from use, 1980. In storage at Air Corps Station, Gormanston until 1989. Following refurbishment it flew again, November 1989. Remained airworthy, 1998.
169	De Havilland DHC-1 Chipmunk T.20 (1952-1980)	C1-0552		Delivered to Baldonnel Aerodrome, 31.1 52. To Air Corps Training Schools. To No. 1 Fighter Squadron, March 1955. To Basic Flying Training School, 1956. To Advanced Flying Training School, 1974. Withdrawn from use, 1980 and later scrapped.
170	De Havilland DHC-1 Chipmunk T.20 (1952-1980)	C1-0724.		Delivered to Baldonnel Aerodrome, 26.9.52. To Air Corps Training Schools. To No. 1 Fighter Squadron, March 1955. To Basic Flying Training School, 1956. Withdrawn from use, 1975 and later scrapped.
171	De Havilland DHC-1 Chipmunk T.20 (1952-1980)	C1-0732.		Delivered to Baldonnel Aerodrome, 26.9.52. To Air Corps Training Schools. To No. 1 Fighter Squadron March 1955. To Basic Flying Training School, 1956. To Advanced Flying Training School, 1974. Withdrawn from use, 1980. Scrapped, 1985.

172	De Havilland DHC-1 Chipmunk T.20 (1952-1980)	C1-0745.		Delivered to Baldonnel Aerodrome, 26.9.52. To Air Corps Training Schools. To No. 1 Fighter Squadron, March 1955. To Basic Flying Training School, 1956. To Advanced Flying Training School, 1974. Withdrawn from use, August 1979. To Technical Training Squadron as instructional airframe. Scrapped mid-1984.
173	De Havilland DHC-1 Chipmunk T.20 (1952-1980)	C1-0746.		Delivered to Baldonnel Aerodrome, 26.9.52. To Air Corps Training Schools. To No. 1 Fighter Squadron, March 1955. To Basic Flying Training School, 1956. To Advanced Flying Training School, 1974. Withdrawn from use, 19.12.78. In storage at Air Corps Station, Gormanston until 1985. To South-East Aviation Museum, Waterford, 17.7.85. later to moved to Cavan & Leitrim Railway Museum, Dromod, Co. Leitrim
174	De Havilland DHC-1 Chipmunk T.20 (1952-1980)	C1-0753.		Delivered to Baldonnel Aerodrome, 26.9.52. To Air Corps Training Schools. To No. 1 Fighter Squadron, March 1955. To Basic Flying Training School, 1956. "Written-off" in a crash at Air Corps Station, Gormanston, 5.5.63.
175	De Havilland DHC-1 Chipmunk T.20 (1952-1980)	C1-0754.		Delivered to Baldonnel Aerodrome, 26.9.52. To Air Corps Training Schools. To No. 1 Fighter Squadron, March 1955. To Basic Flying Training School, 1956. "Written-off" in a crash at Air Corps Station, Gormanston, 29.3.63.
176	De Havilland DH.104 Dove Srs 4 (1953-1970)	04368		Delivered to Baldonnel Aerodrome, 22.2.53. To General Purpose Flight. Withdrawn from use, following a heavy landing at Baldonnel Aerodrome, August 1970. In storage at Baldonnel Aerodrome and used as a spares source for the other Doves in service with the Air Corps until 1980. To Civil Defence School, Phoenix Park, Dublin, 1980. Used for aircraft rescue training.
177	Hunting Percival P.56 Provost T.51 (1954-1976)			Delivered to Baldonnel Aerodrome, 26.3.54. To Air Corps Training Schools. To Advanced Flying Training School, 1956. Withdrawn from use, 1976. In storage at Baldonnel Aerodrome until 1981. Sold in the United Kingdom, 1981. G-BLIW, 12.6.85.
178	Hunting Percival P.56 Provost T.51 (1954-1976)	157		Delivered to Baldonnel Aerodrome, 27.7.54. To Air Corps Training Schools. To Advanced Flying Training School, 1956. Withdrawn from use, 1976. In storage at Baldonnel Aerodrome until 1981. Sold in the United Kingdom, December 1981. G-EIRE, later cancelled. Restoration commenced, 1984. Flew again, August 1989. G-BKOS. Destroyed in a crash, 19.5.91.
179	Hunting Percival P.56 Provost T.51 (1954-1976)	160		Delivered to Baldonnel Aerodrome, 27.7.54. To Air Corps Training Schools. To Advanced Flying Training School, 1956. "Written-off" in a crash at Glenmalure, Co. Wicklow, killing the pilot, 7.3.57.
180	Hunting Percival P.56 Provost T.51 (1954-1976)	179		Delivered to Baldonnel Aerodrome, 6.7.54. To Air Corps Training Schools. To Advanced Flying Training School, 1956. "Written-off" in a crash at Baldonnel Aerodrome, June 1968.
181	Hunting Percival P.56 Provost T.53 (1955-1976)	400		Delivered to Baldonnel Aerodrome, 21.7.55. To Air Corps Training Schools. To Advanced Flying Training School, 1956. Withdrawn from use, 1976. Used for fire practice by Crash Rescue Service at Baldonnel Aerodrome until 1981.
182	Hunting Percival P.56 Provost T.53 (1955-1976)	403		Delivered to Baldonnel Aerodrome, 20.9.55. To Air Corps Training Schools. To Advanced Flying Training School, 1956. "Written-off" in a crash at Fermoy, Co. Cork, 3.1.57.
183	Hunting Percival P.56 Provost T.53 (1955-1976)	406		Delivered to Baldonnel Aerodrome, 21.10.55. To Air Corps Training Schools. To Advanced Flying Training School, 1956. Withdrawn from use after carrying out the last flight by a Provost, in service with the Air Corps, June 1976. In storage at Baldonnel Aerodrome until 1985. To Irish Aviation Museum after restoration by the Air Corps, with wings from another Provost, 22.2.85. To Air Corps Museum, 1996.

Air Corps Serial Number	Aircraft Type	Construction Number	Previous Identity	Service History
184	Hunting Percival P.56 Provost T.53 (1955-1976)	408		Delivered to Baldonnel Aerodrome, 21.10.55. To Air Corps Training Schools. To Advanced Flying Training School, 1956. Withdrawn from use, 1976. In storage, mainly external, at Baldonnel Aerodrome to 1987. To South-East Aviation Museum, with wings from another Provost T.53 (No. 183), 1987. later moved to Cavan & Leitrim Railway Museum, Dromod, Co. Leitrim
185	De Havilland DH.115 Vampire T.55 (1956-1976)	15775		Delivered to Baldonnel Aerodrome, 21.7.56. To No. 1 Fighter Squadron. Withdrawn from use, 1975. In storage at Baldonnel Aerodrome until 1978. Delivered to the French aviation museum, Le Musee de l'Air, aboard a Transall C.160, February and March, 1978
186	De Havilland DH.115 Vampire T.55 (1956-1976)	15765		Delivered to Baldonnel Aerodrome, 21.7.56. To No. 1 Fighter Squadron. Withdrawn from use, 1974. In storage at Baldonnel Aerodrome until 1979. (An ejection seat was used for the first time from an aircraft in service with the Air Corps when a student pilot ejected from this Vampire, 5.5.61. The Vampire returned safely to Baldonnel Aerodrome after the ejection) Sold in the U.S.A., December 1979. To U.S. Department of Defence. N4861K. Various owners up to 1985.
187	De Havilland DH.115 Vampire T.55. (1956-1976)	15766		Delivered to Baldonnel Aerodrome, 21.7.56. To No. 1 Fighter Squadron. Withdrawn from use, 1974. Internal and external storage at Baldonnel Aerodrome, until 1987. Scrapped.
188	De Havilland DH.104 Dove Srs 5 (1959-1961)	04503		Delivered to Baldonnel Aerodrome, 24.3.59. To General Purpose Flight. "Written-off" in a crash near Shannon Airport, killing three on board, 27.1.61.
189	Hunting Percival P.56 Provost T.53 (1960-1972)	460		Delivered to Baldonnel Aerodrome, 23.3.60. To Advanced Flying Training School. "Written-off" after the fuselage was damaged in a forced-landing at Maynooth, Co. Meath, 14.4.62. Fuselage to Technical Training Squadron as instructional airframe. Scrapped, 1977. In 1966 the wings from this Provost were used with the fuselage of a Provost T.1 (XF846) to construct a Provost T.53 (No. 189A).
189A	Hunting Percival P.56 Provost T.53 (1960-1972)	352	XF846. From a batch of 19 Provost T.1s (XF836-XF854), constructed by Hunting Percival Aircraft Ltd. in 1955. Did not enter service with any RAF unit.	Fuselage delivered to Baldonnel Aerodrome, July 1964. Wings from a Provost T.53 (No. 189) attached to fuselage. To Advanced Flying Training School as Provost T.53, 21.2.66. "Written-off" after collision on the ground with a Provost T.51 at Baldonnel Aerodrome, 15.5.69. Scrapped by 1977.
190	Hunting Percival P.56 Provost T.53 (1960-1972)	461		Delivered to Baldonnel Aerodrome, 13.4.60. To Advanced Flying Training School. Withdrawn from use, 1976. Scrapped, 1979.
191	De Havilland DH.115 Vampire T.55 (1961-1976)	15815		Delivered to Baldonnel Aerodrome, 18.1.61. Fitted with underwing drop-tanks. To No. 1 Fighter Squadron. Withdrawn from use, after the last operational flight by a Vampire T.55 in service with the Air Corps, 2.3.76.
192	De Havilland DH.115 Vampire T.55 (1961-1976)	15816		Delivered to Baldonnel Aerodrome, 16.3.61. To No. 1 Fighter Squadron. Withdrawn from use, 1976. In open storage at Baldonnel Aerodrome until 1987.
193	De Havilland DH.115 Vampire T.55 (1961-1976)	15817		Delivered to Baldonnel Aerodrome, 16.3.61. To No. 1 Fighter Squadron. Withdrawn from use, 1976. In open storage at Baldonnel Aerodrome until 1987. Fuselage to South-East Aviation Museum, Waterford, 1987.
194	De Havilland DH.104 Dove Srs 7 (1962-1978)	04530		Delivered to Baldonnel Aerodrome, 11.7.62. To General Purpose Flight. Withdrawn from use, March 1978. In storage at Baldonnel Aerodrome until 1980. Sold in the United Kingdom, September 1980. G-ARVE. Sold in Germany, October 1983. D-IKER. Certificate of Airworthiness not issued and registration cancelled, April 1984. To museum in Germany, 1993.

195	Aérospatiale (Sud Aviation) SE.3160/ SA.316B Alouette III (1963-2007)	1151	F-WJDH. During flight-testing and training programme for Air Corps personnel in France.	Delivered to Baldonnel Aerodrome, 25.11.63. To Helicopter Flight. To Helicopter Squadron, November 1974. Damaged in crash-landing at Baldonnel Aerodrome, 26.5.76. Repaired and returned to service, August 1978. To Helicopter Squadron, No. 1 Support Wing, 1980. To Army Support Squadron, No. 3 Support Wing, 1986. To SAR Squadron, No. 3 Support Wing, 1989. To 302 Squadron, No. 3 Operations Wing, 2001. Withdrawn from use 21.9.07
196	Aérospatiale (Sud Aviation) SE.3160/ SA.316B Alouette III (1963-2007)	1153	F-WKQB. During flight-testing and training programme for Air Corps personnel in France.	Delivered to Baldonnel Aerodrome, 25.11.63. To Helicopter Flight. To Helicopter Squadron, November 1974. To Helicopter Squadron, No. 1 Support Wing, 1980. To Army Support Squadron, No. 3 Support Wing, 1986. To SAR Squadron , No. 3 Support Wing, 1989. To 302 Squadron, No. 3 Operations Wing, 2001. Withdrawn from use 21.9.07
197	Aérospatiale (Sud Aviation) SE.3160/ SA.316B Alouette III (1963-2007)	1194		Delivered to Baldonnel Aerodrome, 13.5.64. To Helicopter Flight. To Helicopter Squadron, November 1974. To Helicopter Squadron, No. 1 Support Wing, 1980. To Army Support Squadron, No. 3 Support Wing, 1986. To SAR Squadron, No. 3 Support Wing, 1989. To 302 Squadron, No. 3 Operations Wing, 2001. Withdrawn from use 21.9.07
198	De Havilland DH.115 Vampire T.11 (1963-1978)	15563	XE977. From a batch of 24, constructed by de Havilland Aircraft Co. Ltd., delivered to the RAF in 1955. To No. 8 Flying Training School (No. 60). Withdrawn from service, 1963.	Delivered to Baldonnel Aerodrome, 30.8.63. To Technical Training Squadron. Remained in RAF markings and the allotted Air Corps serial number was not applied to this aircraft. As "gate guardian" outside Officer's Mess, Baldonnel Aerodrome from 1978. To Air Corps Museum, 1995. currently on display at National Museum, Collins Barracks, Dublin
199	De Havilland DHC-1 Chipmunk T.22 (1965-1980)	C1-0013/C1-0392.	WB561/WG320. Constructed from these two Chipmunk T.10s by Derby Aviation Ltd., 1964. Certificate of Airworthiness issued, February 1965. WB561. From a batch of 40 (WB549-WB88), constructed by de Havilland Aircraft Co. Ltd., delivered to the RAF in February 1950. To Oxford University Air Squadron, 1950. "Written-off" in a crash, August 1955. Fuselage used in construction of the Chipmunk T.22. WG320. From a batch of 68 (WG299-WG366), constructed by de Havilland Aircraft Co. Ltd., delivered to the RAF in July 1951. To No. 18 Reserve Flying School, 1951. Purchased by Derby Aviation Ltd., 1959. G-APTF. Wings and other parts used in the construction of the Chipmunk T.22.	Delivered to Baldonnel Aerodrome, 26.2.65. To Basic Flying Training School. To Advanced Flying Training School, 1974. Withdrawn from use, 1979.
200	De Havilland DHC-1 Chipmunk T.22 (1965-1980)	C1/0061	WB620. From a batch of 36 (WB600-WB635), constructed by de Havilland Aircraft Co. Ltd., delivered to the RAF in April 1950. Withdrawn from service, 1954. Purchased by Iona Engineering Works, Dublin, 1956. Certificate of Airworthiness issued, 1956. EI-AJC. To United Kingdom, 1958. G-APMW. Returned to Ireland, April 1962. EI-AMH. Purchased by Derby Aviation Ltd., November 1964. G-APMW.	Delivered to Baldonnel Aerodrome, 26.2.65. To Basic Flying Training School. To Advanced Flying Training School, 1974. "Written-off" in a crash at Air Corps Station, Gormanston, killing both crew, 25.4.80.
201	De Havilland DH.104 Dove Srs. 8a (1970-1978)	04525	Constructed by de Havilland Aircraft Co. Ltd. in 1961. G-ARSN. Sold to the Department of Transport and Power, August 1967. EI-ARV.	Delivered to Baldonnel Aerodrome, 10.12.70. To General Purpose Flight. Withdrawn from use, December 1977. Sold in United Kingdom, September 1980. G-ARSN. Sold again, March 1983. G-LIDD. Sold in Australia, 1987. VH-OBI.
202	Aérospatiale SA.316B Alouette III (1972-1995)	1973		Delivered to Baldonnel Aerodrome, 24.3.72. To Helicopter Flight. To Helicopter Squadron, November 1974. To Helicopter Squadron, No. 3 Support Wing, 1986. To SAR Squadron, No. 3 Support Wing, 1989. Crashed into Lough Eske, Co. Donegal, 20.10.95. In storage at Baldonnel Aerodrome, 1999. Restored to static display condition and donated to the Ulster Aviation Museum.
203	Reims-Cessna FR.172H Rocket (1972-)	0343		Delivered to Baldonnel Aerodrome, 4.10.72. To Advanced Flying Training School. To Basic Flying Training School, 1973. To Army Co-Operation Squadron, No. 2 Support Wing, 1980. To Army Co-Operation Squadron, 1986. To 104 Squadron, No. 1 Operations Wing, 2001.

Air Corps Serial Number	Aircraft Type	Construction Number	Previous Identity	Service History
204	Reims-Cessna FR.172H Rocket (1972-)	0344		Delivered to Baldonnel Aerodrome, 4.10.72. To Advanced Flying Training School. To Basic Flying Training School, 1973. "Written-off" in a crash in the Shannon Estuary, 20.9.78.
205	Reims-Cessna FR.172H Rocket (1972-)	0345		Delivered to Baldonnel Aerodrome, 4.10.72. To Advanced Flying Training School. To Basic Flying Training School, 1973. To Army Co-Operation Squadron, No. 2 Support Wing, 1980. To Army Co-Operation Squadron, 1986. To 104 Squadron, No. 1 Operations Wing, 2001.
206	Reims-Cessna FR.172H Rocket (1972-)	0346		Delivered to Baldonnel Aerodrome, 4.10.72. To Advanced Flying Training School. To Basic Flying Training School, 1973. Modified for parachute training, 1979. To Army Co-Operation Squadron, No. 2 Support Wing, 1980. To Army Co-Operation Squadron, 1986. To 104 Squadron, No. 1 Operations Wing, 2001.
207	Reims-Cessna FR.172H Rocket (1972-)	0347		Delivered to Baldonnel Aerodrome, 13.10.72. To Advanced Flying Training School. To Basic Flying Training School, 1973. To Army Co-Operation Squadron, No. 2 Support Wing, 1980. To Army Co-Operation Squadron, 1986. Force-landed in the sea off Gormanston due to engine failure, 2.3.90. Withdrawn from use. To Apprentice School as instructional airframe.
208	Reims-Cessna FR.172H Rocket (1972-)	0348		Delivered to Baldonnel Aerodrome, 13.10.72. To Advanced Flying Training School. To Basic Flying Training School, 1973. To Army Co-Operation Squadron, No. 2 Support Wing, 1980. To Army Co-Operation Squadron, 1986. To 104 Squadron, No. 1 Operations Wing, 2001.
209	Reims-Cessna FR.172H Rocket (1972-)	0349		Delivered to Baldonnel Aerodrome, 13.10.72. To Advanced Flying Training School. To Basic Flying Training School, 1973. Modified for parachute jumps, 1979. To Army Co-Operation Squadron, No. 2 Support Wing, 1980. To Army Co-Operation Squadron, 1986. Force-landed near Gormanston, 10.11.89. Repaired and returned to service. "Written-off" after being damaged in a landing at Air Corps Station, Finner, Co. Donegal, 10.11.93.
210	Reims-Cessna FR.172H Rocket (1972-)	0350		Delivered to Baldonnel Aerodrome, 13.10.72. To Advanced Flying Training School. To Basic Flying Training School, 1973. To Army Co-Operation Squadron, No. 2 Support Wing, 1980. To Army Co-Operation Squadron, 1986. Force-landed near Bandon, Co. Cork, 31.1.91. Repaired and returned to service. To 104 Squadron, No. 1 Operations Wing, 2001.
211	Aérospatiale SA.316B Alouette III (1973-2007)	1983		Delivered to Baldonnel Aerodrome, 4.2.73. To Helicopter Flight. To Helicopter Squadron, November 1974. To Helicopter Squadron, No. 3 Support Wing, 1986. To SAR Squadron, No. 3 Support Wing, 1989. To 302 Squadron, No. 3 Operations Wing, 2001. Withdrawn from use 21.9.07
212	Aérospatiale SA.316B Alouette III (1973-2007)	1984		Delivered to Baldonnel Aerodrome, 29.3.73. To Helicopter Flight. To Helicopter Squadron, November 1974. To Helicopter Squadron, No. 3 Support Wing, 1986. To SAR Squadron, No. 3 Support Wing, 1989. To 302 Squadron, No. 3 Operations Wing, 2001. Withdrawn from use 21.9.07
213	Aérospatiale SA.316B Alouette III (1973-2007)	2116		Delivered to Baldonnel Aerodrome, 6.12.73. To Helicopter Flight. To Helicopter Squadron, November 1974. To Helicopter Squadron, No. 3 Support Wing, 1986. To SAR Squadron, No. 3 Support Wing, 1989. To 302 Squadron, No. 3 Operations Wing, 2001. Withdrawn from use 21.9.07
214	Aérospatiale SA.316B Alouette III (1973-2007)	2122		Delivered to Baldonnel Aerodrome, 25.3.74. To Helicopter Flight. To Helicopter Squadron, November 1974. To Helicopter Squadron, No. 3 Support Wing, 1986. To SAR Squadron, No. 3 Support Wing, 1989. To 302 Squadron, No. 3 Operations Wing, 2001. Withdrawn from use 21.9.07

215	Aérospatiale (Fouga) CM.170-2 Super Magister (1975-1999)	357	Delivered as CM.170-1 Magister to the Osterreichische Luftstreitkrafte (Austrian Air Force), 15.10.62. 4D-YJ. To Fliegerschulkompanie 1 (Flying School Company 1). To Jaboschulstaffel (Fighter Bomber Training Squadron), 1963. To 1 Staffel/Schulgeschwader 2/Fliegerregiment 2 (1st Squadron/Training Wing/Air Regiment 2), 1966. To Dusenschulstaffel (Jet Training Squadron), 1968. Withdrawn from use, 1972. Purchased by Aérospatiale and placed in storage in France, 1972.	Delivered to Baldonnel Aerodrome, 11.9.75. To No. 1 Fighter Squadron. To Light Strike Squadron, No. 1 Support Wing, 1980. Withdrawn from use, 19.12.97. Used by Dublin Institute of Technology as an instructional airframe.
216	Aérospatiale (Fouga) CM.170-2 Super Magister (1975-1999)	358	Delivered as CM.170-1 Magister to the Osterreichische Luftstreitkrafte (Austrian Air Force), 12.10.62. 4D-YK. To Fliegerschulkompanie 1 (Flying School Company 1). To Jaboschulstaffel (Fighter Bomber Training Squadron), 1963. To 1 Staffel/Schulgeschwader 2/Fliegerregiment 2 (1st Squadron/Training Wing/Air Regiment 2), 1966. To Dusenschulstaffel (Jet Training Squadron), 1968. Withdrawn from use, 1972. Purchased by Aérospatiale and placed in storage in France, 1972.	Delivered to Baldonnel Aerodrome, 11.9.75. To No. 1 Fighter Squadron. To Light Strike Squadron, No. 1 Support Wing, 1980. Withdrawn from use, 19.12.97. Currently located at the Air Corps Museum, Baldonnel.
217	Aérospatiale (Fouga) CM.170-2 Super Magister (1975-1999)	359	Delivered as CM.170-1 Magister to the Osterreichische Luftstreitkrafte (Austrian Air Force), 15.10.62. 4D-YL. To Fliegerschulkompanie 1 (Flying School Company 1). To Jaboschulstaffel (Fighter Bomber Training Squadron), 1963. To 1 Staffel/Schulgeschwader 2/Fliegerregiment 2 (1st Squadron/Training Wing/Air Regiment 2), 1966. To Dusenschulstaffel (Jet Training Squadron), 1968. Withdrawn from use, 25.10.71. Purchased by Aérospatiale and placed in storage in France, 1972.	Delivered to Baldonnel Aerodrome, 16.2.76. To No. 1 Fighter Squadron. To Light Strike Squadron, No. 1 Support Wing, 1980. Withdrawn from use, 24.4.98. To mark the occasion of their 50th Anniversary o, this aircraft was presented to the Austrian Air Force and placed on display in the Austrian Air Force Museum at Linz on 30th March 2005. It is repainted in its original Austrian markings.
218	Aérospatiale (Fouga) CM.170-2 Super Magister (1975-1999)	390	Delivered as CM.170-1 Magister to the Osterreichische Luftstreitkrafte (Austrian Air Force), 11.4.63. 4D-YU. To Fliegerschulkompanie 1 (Flying School Company 1). To Jaboschulstaffel (Fighter Bomber Training Squadron), 1963. To 1 Staffel/Schulgeschwader 2/Fliegerregiment 2 (1st Squadron/Training Wing/Air Regiment 2), 1966. To Dusenschulstaffel (Jet Training Squadron), 1968. Withdrawn from use, 1972. Purchased by Aérospatiale and placed in storage in France, 1972.	Delivered to Baldonnel Aerodrome, 16.2.76. To No. 1 Fighter Squadron. To Light Strike Squadron, No. 1 Support Wing, 1980. Withdrawn from use, 23.5.98. Currently located at FÁS in Shannon, Co. Clare.
219	Aérospatiale (Fouga) CM.170-2 Super Magister (1975-1999)	298	One of nine CM.170-1 Magisters (c/ns 294-302) secretly diverted from a batch of forty five, constructed by Potez Air Fouga between January 1960 and January 1962, for the Force Aerienne Belge (Belgian Air Force). The nine CM.170-1 Magisters were to be delivered to the Force Aerienne Katanga but only three of these aircraft entered service with that air force. The remaining six CM.170-1 Magisters were placed in storage in France until 1973 and were then overhauled and refurbished by Aérospatiale.	Delivered to Baldonnel Aerodrome, 13.11.76. To No. 1 Fighter Squadron. To Light Strike Squadron, No. 1 Support Wing, 1980. Withdrawn from use, 1998. Currently located at the Air Corps Museum, Baldonnel.
220	Aérospatiale (Fouga) CM.170-2 Super Magister (1975-1999)	299	One of nine CM.170-1 Magisters (c/ns 294-302) secretly diverted from a batch of forty five, constructed by Potez Air Fouga between January 1960 and January 1962, for the Force Aerienne Belge (Belgian Air Force). The nine CM.170-1 Magisters were to be delivered to the Force Aerienne Katanga but only three of these aircraft entered service with that air force. The remaining six CM.170-1 Magisters were placed in storage in France until 1973 and were then overhauled and refurbished by Aérospatiale.	Delivered to Baldonnel Aerodrome, 13.11.76. To No. 1 Fighter Squadron. To Light Strike Squadron, No. 1 Support Wing, 1980. Withdrawn from use, June 1999. Currently located at the Institute of Technology, Carlow.
221	Aérospatiale (Fouga) CM.170-2 Super Magister (1975-1999)	79	Delivered to Armee de l'Air, 1957. To Escadron de Convoyage (Ferry Squadron). Air Attache, Stockholm, Sweden. TY/Groupement Instruction. 2-HJ. 3-KE. Damaged in force-landing, 13.11.74.	Delivered to Dublin Airport in Nord Noratlas, 8.9.75. To Technical Training Squadron as instructional airframe. Remained in Armee de l'Air markings and the allotted Air Corps serial number was not applied to this aircraft. To Apprentice School, Training Wing, 1980. Dismantled in hangar, Baldonnel Aerodrome, 1994.
222	Siai-Marchetti SF.260WE Warrior (1977-2006)	24-01/289		Delivered to Baldonnel Aerodrome, 4.3.77. To Basic and Advanced Flying Training Schools. To Basic Flying Training School, Training Wing, 1980. To Basic Flying Training School, Air Corps College, 2001. Sold to Airpower Aviation Resources in 2006
223	Siai-Marchetti SF.260WE Warrior (1977-2006)	24-02/290		Delivered to Baldonnel Aerodrome, 4.3.77. To Basic and Advanced Flying Training Schools. To Basic Flying Training School, Training Wing, 1980. "Written-off" in a crash at Virginia, Co. Cavan, killing the pilot, 13.12.90.

Air Corps Serial Number	Aircraft Type	Construction Number	Previous Identity	Service History
224	Siai-Marchetti SF.260WE Warrior (1977-2006)	24-03/291		Delivered to Baldonnel Aerodrome, 4.3.77. To Basic and Advanced Flying Training Schools. To Basic Flying Training School, Training Wing, 1980. "Written-off" in a crash at Baldonnel Aerodrome, 24.1.78.
225	Siai-Marchetti SF.260WE Warrior (1977-2006)	24-04/292		Delivered to Baldonnel Aerodrome, 4.3.77. To Basic and Advanced Flying Training Schools. To Basic Flying Training School, Training Wing, 1980. To Basic Flying Training School, Air Corps College, 2001. Sold to Airpower Aviation Resources in 2006
226	Siai-Marchetti SF.260WE Warrior (1977-2006)	24-05/293		Delivered to Baldonnel Aerodrome, 16.4.77. To Basic and Advanced Flying Training Schools. To Basic Flying Training School, Training Wing, 1980. To Basic Flying Training School, Air Corps College, 2001. Sold to Airpower Aviation Resources in 2006
227	Siai-Marchetti SF.260WE Warrior (1977-2006)	24-06/294		Delivered to Baldonnel Aerodrome, 16.4.77. To Basic and Advanced Flying Training Schools. To Basic Flying Training School, Training Wing, 1980. Damaged in a force-landing at Clane, Co. Kildare, 21.2.91. Returned to manufacturers in Italy, 17.10.91. Repaired and returned to service. To Basic Flying Training School, Air Corps College, 2001. Sold to Airpower Aviation Resources in 2006
228	Siai-Marchetti SF.260WE Warrior (1977-2006)	24-07/295		Delivered to Baldonnel Aerodrome, 16.4.77. To Basic and Advanced Flying Training Schools. To Basic Flying Training School, Training Wing, 1980. "Written-off" in a crash at Clondalkin, Co. Dublin, 23.8.93.
229	Siai-Marchetti SF.260WE Warrior (1977-2006)	24-08/296		Delivered to Baldonnel Aerodrome, 16.4.77. To Basic and Advanced Flying Training Schools. To Basic Flying Training School, Training Wing, 1980. To Basic Flying Training School, Air Corps College, 2001. Sold to Airpower Aviation Resources in 2006
230	Siai-Marchetti SF.260WE Warrior (1977-2006)	24-09/297		Delivered to Baldonnel Aerodrome, 16.4.77. To Basic and Advanced Flying Training Schools. To Basic Flying Training School, Training Wing, 1980. Damaged in an accident at Baldonnel Aerodrome, 20.7.89. Repaired and returned to service. To Basic Flying Training School, Air Corps College, 2001. Sold to Airpower Aviation Resources in 2006
231	Siai-Marchetti SF.260WE Warrior (1977-2006)	24-10/298		Delivered to Baldonnel Aerodrome, 16.4.77. To Basic and Advanced Flying Training Schools. To Basic Flying Training School, Training Wing, 1980. To Basic Flying Training School, Air Corps College, 2001. Currently on display at Air Corps Museum, Baldonnel.
232	Beechcraft Super King Air 200 (1977-1990)	BB-208	First flight, December 1976. To United Beechcraft Sweden. SE-GRR. Leased to Irish Government, April 1977 registered as EI-BCY. Purchased for Air Corps, December 1979.	After purchase by the Irish Government it was allocated the serial 232. Originally allocated to the General Purpose Flight, it was subsequently allocated to the Maritime Squadron, No. 1 Support Wing, in 1980. The aircraft was withdrawn from use in May 1990, and sold to American Sales Aircraft International, U.S.A., in January 1992, and registered as N60MK.
233	Siai-Marchetti SF.260MC (1977-)	11-09	I-SJAS. To Force Aerienne Zairoise (Zaire Air Force). AT-109.	Delivered to Baldonnel Aerodrome, 3.3.77. To Technical Training Squadron. To Apprentice School, Training Wing, 1980, as instructional airframe.
234	Beechcraft Super King Air 200 (1978-1991)	BB-376	N4914M. To United Beechcraft Sweden. Leased to Irish Government, August 1978. EI-BFJ. Purchased for Air Corps, December 1979.	Delivered to Baldonnel Aerodrome, 17.8.78. To General Purpose Flight. To Maritime Squadron, No. 1 Support Wing, 1980. Withdrawn from use, 1991. To Gannt Aviation, U.S.A., November 1991. N409GA. It was reregistered N376RC and operated by BAM Aircraft Leasing LLC.
235	Siai-Marchetti SF.260WE Warrior (1979-1982)	24-11/373		Delivered to Baldonnel Aerodrome, 2.4.79. To Basic and Advanced Flying Training Schools. To Basic Flying Training School, 1980. "Written-off" in a crash at Dunboyne, Co. Meath, killing the pilot, 10.2.82.
236	Hawker Siddeley Hs.125-600b (1979)	25256	Prototype HS.125-600B. First flight, 21.171. G-AYBH. To Civil Aviation Authority. 1974. G-5-13. To Philippines Airways, November 1974. RP-C111. Returned to British Aerospace, 1978. G-AYBH.	Delivered to Baldonnel Aerodrome, 1.6.79. To Ministerial Transport Service. Damaged in aborted take-off at Baldonnel Aerodrome, 27.1.79. Withdrawn from use and returned to British Aerospace, 17.1.80.

237	Aérospatiale SA.342L Gazelle (1979-2002)	1772		Delivered to Baldonnel Aerodrome, 30.12.79. To Helicopter Squadron, No. 1 Support Wing, 1980. To Helicopter School, No. 3 Support Wing, 1987. "Written-off" in a crash-landing at Baldonnel Aerodrome, August 16, 2002.
238	British Aerospace BAe 125-700B (1980-1992)			Delivered to Baldonnel Aerodrome, 2.2.80. To Ministerial Air Transport Service, Transport and Training Squadron, No. 1 Support Wing. Withdrawn from use, October 1992. Sold in Mexico and delivered, 2.12.92. XA-TCB.
239	Hawker Siddeley HS.125-600B (1979-1980)	256015	First flight, 1973. G-BBCL, G-BJCB and 9K-ACZ. Returned to British Aerospace, 1979. G-BBCL.	Delivered to Baldonnel Aerodrome, 6.12.79 as a replacement for the HS.125-600B that had been damaged in the aborted take-off in the same year.. To Ministerial Air Transport Service. Training and Transport Squadron, No. 1 Support Wing. Returned to British Aerospace, 28.2.80.
240	Beechcraft Super King Air 200 (1980-)	BB-672		Delivered to Baldonnel Aerodrome, 7.5.80. To Transport and Training Squadron, No. 1 Support Wing. To 102 Squadron, No. 1 Operations Wing, 2001.
241	Aérospatiale SA.342L Gazelle (1979-2005)	1854		Delivered to Baldonnel Aerodrome, 14.1.81. To Helicopter Squadron, No. 1 Support Wing. To Helicopter School, No. 3 Support Wing, 1987. To Flight Training School, Air Corps College, 2001. Withdrawn from use 31.12.2005. It was subsequently sold to a private owner and is now based in the UK with the Hungarian registration HA-LFQ.
242	Aérospatiale SA.330L Puma (1981-1983)	1240	First flight, 1973. To Ethiopian Air Force, 18.12.73. No. 850. Returned to Aérospatiale, 1976. Converted to SA.330L Puma. F-BRQK.	Delivered to Baldonnel Aerodrome, 22.7.81. To Helicopter Squadron, No. 1 Support Wing. Withdrawn from use and returned to Aérospatiale, 26.2.83. This particular Puma remains in use today for experimental test programmes with the Centre d'Essais en Vol (CEV) in France carrying the civil registration F-ZLAT.
243	Reims-Cessna FR.172K Rocket (1981-2004)	671		Delivered to Baldonnel Aerodrome, 7.4.81. To Army Co-Operation Squadron, No. 2 Support Wing. To Army Co-Operation Squadron, 1986. To 104 Squadron, No. 1 Operations Wing, 2001. "Written-off" in crash at Clonbullogue, Co. Offaly, May 6, 2004.
244	Aérospatiale Sa.365f Dauphin 2 (1986-2005)	6124	First flight, 19.9.84. F-ZKBZ. Equipped for naval operations. Used by Aérospatiale for flight certification and testing the advanced navigation and guidance systems installed to fulfil Air Corps specifications. Also used for deck landing trials on the L.E.Eithne.	Delivered to Baldonnel Aerodrome, 25.6.86. To Naval Squadron, No. 3 Support Wing. To 301 Squadron, No. 3. Operations Wing, 2001. Withdrawn from use 31.12.05
245	Aérospatiale SA.365Fi Dauphin 2 (1986-2005)	6168	First flight, 1985. F-ZKBJ. Equipped for naval operations. Used for flight certification and testing of equipment installed. On static display at the 1985 Paris Air Salon.	Delivered to Baldonnel Aerodrome, 18.7.86. To Naval Squadron, No. 3 Support Wing. To 301 Squadron, No. 3. Operations Wing, 2001. Withdrawn from use 31.12.05
246	Aérospatiale SA.365Fi Dauphin 2 (1986-2005)	6181		Delivered to Baldonnel Aerodrome, 25.6.86. To Search and Rescue Squadron, No. 3 Support Wing. To 301 Squadron, No. 3. Operations Wing, 2001. Withdrawn from use 31.12.05
247	Aérospatiale SA.365Fi Dauphin 2 (1986-2005)	6202	F-ZKBW	Delivered to Baldonnel Aerodrome, 21.8.86. To Search and Rescue Squadron, No. 3 Support Wing. To 301 Squadron, No. 3. Operations Wing, 2001. Withdrawn from use 31.12.05
248	Aérospatiale SA.365Fi Dauphin 2 (1986-1999)	6203		Delivered to Baldonnel Aerodrome, 19.12.86. To Search and Rescue Squadron, No. 3 Support Wing. Destroyed in a crash at Tramore, Co. Waterford, 1.7.1999.
249	Grumman Aerospace G.1159a Gulfstream III (1990-1992)	413	First flight, 1983. N357GA. To J.E.Seagram, January 1984. N77SW. To Federal Aviation Administration, August 1988 to May 1989. N1. To September 1989. N8266M. Returned to company.	Delivered to Baldonnel Aerodrome, 4.1.90 To Ministerial Air Transport Service, Transport and Training Squadron, No. 1 Support Wing. Withdrawn from use and returned to company, 6.3.92.
250	CASA CN.235M-100 (1991-1995)	C019	EC330. Used as a demonstration aircraft by the company.	Delivered to Baldonnel Aerodrome, 6.6.91. To Maritime Squadron, No. 1 Support Wing. Withdrawn from use and returned to company, 16.1.95.
251	Gulfstream Aerospace G.1159c Gulfstream IV-SP (1991-)	1160	First flight, 26.2.91. N17584.	Delivered to Baldonnel Aerodrome, 20.12.91. To Ministerial Air Transport Service, Transport and Training Squadron, No. 1 Support Wing. To 102 Squadron, No. 1 Operations Wing, 2001.

Air Corps Serial Number	Aircraft Type	Construction Number	Previous Identity	Service History
252	Airtech (CASA) CN.235-100M (1991-)	085		Delivered to Baldonnel Aerodrome, 8.12.94. To Maritime Squadron, No. 1 Support Wing. To 101 Squadron, No. 1 Operations Wing, 2001.
253	Airtech (CASA) CN.235-100M (1991-)	094		Delivered to Baldonnel Aerodrome, 8.12.94. Returned to the manufacturers, 10.12.94. Entered service, 28.1.95. To Maritime Squadron, No. 1 Support Wing. To 101 Squadron, No. 1 Operations Wing, 2001.
254	Pilatus Britten-Norman BN-2T-4S Defender 4000 (1997-)	4008	First flight, 3.7.97. G-BWPN	Delivered to Baldonnel Aerodrome, 15.8.97. To Garda Air Support Unit. To 106 Squadron, No. 1 Operations Wing, 2001.
255	Eurocopter AA.335N Twin Ecureuil (1997-2007)	5633	G-BXEV. Delivered to McAlpine Helicopters Ltd. for installation of equipment and training of Air Corps personnel, 24.4.97.	Delivered to Baldonnel Aerodrome, 22.8.97. To Garda Air Support Unit. To 106 Squadron, No. 1 Operations Wing, 2001. Withdrawn from use in December 2007.
256	Eurocopter EC-135T1	0149	First flight as F-HECK 08.12.00, Delivered to McAlpine Helicopters Ltd. for installation of equipment. Re-registered G-BZRM.	Delivered to Baldonnel 05.12.02 operated by GASU (No. 106 Squadron)
257	Sikorsky S-61N	61816	Constucted in 1978. To Helikopter Service AS, Norway. LN-OQU. G-CBKZ, April 2002. To CHC Helicopters. EI-CKS, October 2002.	Leased to Air Corps, 13.1.2003. To 301 Sqdn, 3 Ops Wing. Lease terminated Dec. 2003.
258	Bombardier Learjet 45 (2003 -)	45-234	N5009T.	Delivered to Baldonnel Aerodrome, 19.12.2003. To 102 Squadron, (Air Transport), No. 1 Operations Wing.
259	Not Allocated			
260	Pilatus PC-9M (2004-)	655	First flight, February 6, 2004. HB-HQS. Used for weapons trials in Austria.	Delivered to Baldonnel Aerodrome, 24.7.2004. To Flight Training School, Air Corps College.
261	Pilatus PC-9M (2004-)	656	HB-HQT	Delivered to Baldonnel Aerodrome, 21.4.2004. To Flight Training School, Air Corps College.
262	Pilatus PC-9M (2004-)	657	HB-HQU	Delivered to Baldonnel Aerodrome, 21.4.2004. To Flight Training School, Air Corps College.
263	Pilatus PC-9M (2004-)	658	HB-HQV	Delivered to Baldonnel Aerodrome, 21.4.2004. To Flight Training School, Air Corps College.
264	Pilatus PC-9M (2004-)	659	HB-HQW	Delivered to Baldonnel Aerodrome, 9.6.2004. To Flight Training School, Air Corps College.
265	Pilatus PC-9M (2004-)	660	HB-HQX	Delivered to Baldonnel Aerodrome, 18.5.2004. To Flight Training School, Air Corps College.
266	Pilatus PC-9M (2004-)	661	HB-HQY	Delivered to Baldonnel Aerodrome, 8.6.2004. To Flight Training School, Air Corps College.
267	Pilatus PC-9M (2004-)	662	HB-HQZ	Delivered to Baldonnel Aerodrome, 8.6.2004. To Flight Training School, Air Corps College.
268	Not Allocated			
269	Not Allocated			
270	Eurocopter EC-135P2	0425	D-HECB	Delivered to Baldonnel Aerodrome, 03.11.05. In service with 302 Squadron
271	Eurocopter EC-135P2	0431	D-HECF	Delivered to Baldonnel Aerodrome, 03.11.05. In service with 302 Squadron
272	Eurocopter EC-135T2	0478		Delivered to Baldonnel Aerodrome, 05.12.07 Officially entered service 15.01.08 operated by GASU (No. 106 Squadron)

273	Not Allocated			
274	AgustaWestland AW139	31048		Delivered Baldonnel Aerodrome, 23.11.06. To 301 Sqdn., No. 3. Ops Wing
275	AgustaWestland AW139	31059		Delivered Baldonnel Aerodrome, 23.11.06. To 301 Sqdn., No. 3. Ops Wing
276	AgustaWestland AW139	31076		Delivered Baldonnel Aerodrome, 17.04.07. To 301 Sqdn., No. 3. Ops Wing
277	AgustaWestland AW139	31078		Delivered Baldonnel Aerodrome, 29.05.07. To 301 Sqdn., No. 3. Ops Wing
278	AgustaWestland AW139	31137		Delivered Baldonnel Aerodrome, 26.07.08. To 301 Sqdn., No. 3. Ops Wing
279	AgustaWestland AW139	31145		Delivered Baldonnel Aerodrome, 15.11.08. To 301 Sqdn., No. 3. Ops Wing
Other aircraft operated by the Air Corps but not registered as such.				
none	Siai-Marchetti SF.260D (1991-1992)	707	N402FD. Evaluated for Enhanced Flight Screener contract by U.S. Air Force.	Delivered to Baldonnel Aerodrome, 3.6.91. To Training Wing. Leased for a further six month period, May 1992. To Training Wing. Withdrawn from use, November 1992.
none	Siai-Marchetti SF.260D (1991-1992)	770	N405FD. Evaluated for Enhanced Flight Screener contract by U.S. Air Force.	Delivered to Baldonnel Aerodrome, 3.6.91. To Training Wing. Leased for a further six month period, May 1992. To Training Wing. Withdrawn from use, November 1992.
none	Siai-Marchetti SF.260D (1991-1992)	772	N407FD. Evaluated for Enhanced Flight Screener contract by U.S. Air Force.	Delivered to Baldonnel Aerodrome, 3.6.91. To Training Wing. Leased for a further six month period, May 1992. To Training Wing. Withdrawn from use, November 1992.

Appendix 2

Irish Air Corps Fatalities 1922-2004 – Ar dheis Dé go raibh a n-anamacha

Date	Name	Aircraft Type	Location
25.6.1923.	Lieut. K.M. Mcdonagh (Observer)	Airco DH.9 (DH.1)	Fermoy, Co. Cork.
23.1.1924.	Lieut. R.T. Nevin (Pilot)	Bristol F2B Fighter (BF.II).	Baldonnel Aerodrome, Co. Dublin
22.9.1925.	Comdt. Thos. Moloney (Pilot)	Bristol F2B Fighter (BF.VI)	Curragh, Co. Kildare.
21.9.1926.	Second Lieut. Timothy J. Prenderville (Pilot)	Bristol F2B Fighter (No. 17)	Hempstown, Co. Wicklow.
	Lieut. Edward O'Reilly (Observer)		
3.8.1933.	Lieut. J.P. Twohig (Pilot)	Avro 631 Cadet (C.3)	Belgard, Co. Dublin
5.8.1933.	Capt. Oscar Heron (Pilot)	Vickers Vespa V (V.6)	Phoenix Park, Dublin.
	Pvt. Tobin (Observer)		
19.9.1934	Lieut. Arthur Russell (Pilot)	Fairey IIIF Mk.II (F968)	Terenure Rd. East, Dublin.
	Pvt. Daniel Toomey (Observer)		
2.5.1935.	Lieut. Michael Kennedy (Pilot)	Avro 626 (A13)	Baldonnel Aerodrome, Co. Dublin.
27.7.1940	Lieut. Michael J. Ryan (Pilot)	Hawker Hind I (No.70)	Laytown, Co. Meath.
	Pvt. Patrick Power (Observer)		
15.5.1944.	Pvt. Arthur Casserly (Pilot)	Miles Magister I (No. 37)	
19.8.1946.	Capt. Maurice Quinlan (Pilot)	Miles Master II (No. 101)	Castlebaggot, Co. Dublin.
3.2.1949.	Lieut. P.G. McCabe (Pilot)	Miles Master II (No. 121)	Brownstown, Saggart, Co. Dublin.
3.2.1949.	Capt. H.T. Houston (Pilot)	Miles Master II (No. 124)	Brownstown, Saggart, Co. Dublin.
23.3.1949.	Sgt. Plt. Michael McLaughlin (Pilot)	Miles Master II (No. 100)	Sillagh, Ballymore Eustace, Co. Kildare.

28.5.1951	Capt. William Ryan (Pilot)	Vickers Supermarine Seafire L.F.III. (No. 154)	Kilbride, Co. Wicklow.
22.5.1953.	Lieut. F.J. Coghlan (Pilot)	Vickers Supermarine Seafire L.F.III. (No. 148)	Gormanston, Co. Meath.
3.1.1957.	Lieut. Michael Flynn (Pilot)	Hunting Percival Provost T.53. (No. 182)	Fermoy, Co. Cork.
	Airman Thomas Breslin		
7.3.1957.	Lieut. Patrick O'Connor (Pilot)	Hunting Percival Provost T.53. (No. 179)	Glenmalure, Co. Wicklow.
27.1.1961.	Capt. James Liddy (Pilot)	De Havilland Dove Srs. 5 (No. 189)	Shannon Airport, Co. Clare.
	Lieut. Brian Corr		
	Lieut. Donal Brady		
	Two Civilian A.T.C. Assistants		
25.4.1980.	Lieut. Alan Hickey (Pilot)	De Havilland Chipmunk T.22 (No. 200)	Gormanston, Co. Meath.
	Cpl. Johan Monaghan		
10.2.1982.	Lieut. Edward Barry (Pilot)	Siai Marchetti SF.260WE Warrior (No. 235)	Dunboyne, Co. Meath.
13.12.1990.	Second Lieut. Gavin Foyne (Pilot)	Siai Marchetti SF.260WE Warrior (No. 223)	Virginia, Co. Cavan.
1.7.1999.	Capt. David O'Flaherty (Pilot)	Aérospatiale SA.365F Dauphin 2 (No. 248)	Tramore Strand, Co. Waterford.
	Capt. Michael Baker (Co-Pilot)		
	Sgt. Patrick Mooney (Winchman)		
	Cpl. Niall Byrne (Winchman)		
6.5.2004.	Second Lieut. Raymond Heery (Pilot)	Reims (Cessna) FR.172K Rocket (No. 243)	Clonbullogue, Co. Offaly.

Appendix 3

Flying Units of The Irish Air Service And Irish Air Corps, 1922-2002

No. 1 Squadron (1922-1934).
A Flight.
B Flight.

No. 1 Army Co-Operation Squadron (1934-1939).
A Flight.
B Flight.
C Flight.

Air Corps Schools, No. 2 Section: Flying Training (1934-1956).
Elementary Training Flight.
Intermediate Training Flight.
Advanced Training Flight.

No. 1 Reconnaissance And Medium Bombing Squadron (1937-1944).
A Flight.
B Flight.

No. 1 Coastal Patrol Squadron (1939-1944).

General Purpose Flight (1944-1980).

Basic and Advanced Flying Schools (1956-1980).

Helicopter Flight (1963-1974).

Helicopter Squadron (1974-1980).

Training Wing (1980-2002).

Basic Flying Training School.

No. 1 Support Wing (1980-2002).
Light Strike Squadron.
Transport And Training Squadron
(Ministerial Air Transport Service).
Maritime Squadron.
Helicopter Squadron.

No. 2 Support Wing (1980-1986).
Army Co-Operation Squadron.

No. 3 Support Wing (1986-2002).
Search And Rescue Squadron
Naval Support Squadron.
Army Support Squadron.
Helicopter School.

Army Co-Operation Squadron (1986-2002).

Garda Air Support Unit (1997-2002).

No. 1 Operations Wing (2002-).

101 Squadron (Maritime).
102 Squadron (Air Transport).
104 Squadron (Army Co-Operation).
106 Squadron (Garda Air Support).

No. 3 Operations Wing (2002-).
301 Squadron (Search And Rescue).
302 Squadron (Army Support).
A And B Flights.

Air Corps College (2002-).
Flight Training School.

Bibliography

Files consulted at Irish Military Archives

AC/1/3/4 Four co-operation aircraft
AC/1/3/5 Cirrus moths
AC/1/3/6 Avro 626
AC/1/3/7 Rebuild of Vickers Vespa
AC/1/3/8 File concerning two gliders for the Air Corps
AC/1/3/9 Purchase of Avro's
AC/1/4/3 File concerning the request for Air Corps aircraft for use on Everest expedition
AC/1/6/2 File on a Potez aircraft
AC/1/6/4 File on Seversky aircraft
AC/1/6/5 File on Bristol Bulldog aircraft
AC/1/10/3 Repairs to Vespa
AC/2/1/23 Servicing aircraft at Shannon 1939-43
AC/2/2/1 Purchase of aircraft by McSweeney
AC/2/2/10 Purchase of 2 Ansons £17,000
AC/2/2/13 Purchase of training aircraft 1938 £2250
AC/2/2/27 Purchase of Merryweather Fire Tender 1939
AC/2/2/28 Purchase of 7 Ansons
AC/2/2/30 Lysander Purchase
AC/2/2/35 Gladiator purchase
AC/2/2/37 Purchase of launches 1940-44
AC/2/2/39 Lysander Spares 10/4/1940- 20/5/1950
AC/2/2/41 Hawker Hind aircraft
AC/2/2/51 Hawker Hector purchase
AC/2/2/53 Purchase of bombs in 1941-42
AC/2/2/71 Master II aircraft
AC/2/2/76 Purchase of Hurricanes
AC/2/2/97 Purchase of Seafires
AC/2/2/98 Fokker S.11
AC/2/2/101 Spitfire Tr.9 purchase 1949-50
AC/2/2/102 Balliol
AC/2/2/105 Martinet engine 1951
AC/2/2/107 Seafire Spares
AC/2/2/108 Seafire Spares
AC/2/2/112 Chipmunk purchase
AC/2/2/113 Possible purchase of Fokker S.14 Jet trainer
AC/2/4/12 Launch at Gormanston 1935-41
AC/2/4/33 Modifications to Martinet and Master
AC/2/4/36 Modifications to Martinet and Master
AC/2/4/47 Maintenance of Miles Magister
AC2/4/51 Spitfire Trainer
AC2/4/62 HP JPR2
AC2/6/38 Sergeant Pilots course
AC2/6/56 Fighter leader Course Comdt P. Swan
AC2/6/67 Radar course
AC2/6/83 1952 report on special air defence course at Old Sarum
AC2/6/114 50 year account of Air Corps
AC2/8/9 GCI duties 1949-50
AC/2/8/32 Proposal for civilian SAR auxiliary
AC/2/9/18 Statistics for 1943
AC/2/10/2 Low flying complaints 1938-50

Books:

The Irish Air Corps Celebrates 100 years of Flight, 2003, ISBN 0-9546669-0-9
Spying on Ireland, British Intelligence and Irish Neutrality During the Second world War, Eunan O'Halpin, Oxford University Press. ISBN 978-0-19-925329-6
Guarding Neutral Ireland, The Coast watching Service and Military Intelligence, 1939-1045, Michael Kennedy, Four Courts Press, ISBN 978-1-84682-097-7
Defending Ireland, The Irish state and its Enemies since 1922, Eunan O'Halpin, Oxford University Press, ISBN 0-19-820426-4
The Emergency, Neutral Ireland 1939-45, Bernard Share, Gill & Macmillan, 1978 ISBN 7171 1516 X
A History of the Irish Army. John P. Duggan, Gill & Macmillan 1991, ISBN 978 071711 9578
The Irish Sword – The Emergency 1939-45. The Journal of the Military History Society of Ireland in association with the Military Archives. Vol. XIX Nos. 75 & 76. 1993-94.
Gormanston Camp 1917- 86 by Lt. Col. M. O'Malley
In Time of War: Ireland, Ulster and the Price of Neutrality, 1939-45. Robert Fisk ISBN: 9780717124114
Irish Air Corps- A view from the Tower, Comdt. Peter Tormey & Capt. Kevin Byrne, Defence Forces Printing Press, 1991.
Wings Over Ireland, The story of the Irish Air Corps, Donal MacCarron, Midland Publishing, 1996, ISBN 1-85780-057-5
A View from Above- 200 years of Aviation in Ireland. Donal MacCarron, O'Brien Press, 2000, ISBN 0-86278-662-2
A History of the Royal Air Force and United States Naval Air Service in Ireland 1913-1923, Karl E. Hayes in association with Irish Air letter, 1988.
Defending the Future, Defence White paper Submission from the Representative Association of Commissioned Officers.
History of Aviation in Ireland, Liam Byrne, Blackwater, Dublin , 1980, ISBN 0-905471 10 5
Air Spectaculars, Air displays in Ireland, Madeleine O'Rourke, Glendale, 1989, ISBN 0 907606 57 1
Mayday! Mayday! Heroic Air-Sea rescues in Irish Waters, Lorna Siggins, Gill & MacMillan, 2004, ISBN 0-7171-3529-2
Nine Lives, David Courtney, Mercier press 2008, ISBN 978 1 85635 602 2
The Filght of the Iolar- the Aer lingus Experience 1936-1986, Bernard Share, Gill and MacMillan, 1986, ISBN 7171 1457 0.
IPMS Color Cross-Reference Guide, David H. Klaus, 1988 ISBN 0-9629146-0-6
The Encyclopaedia of World Air Power, Bill Gunston, 1981 Temple Press Aerospace, ISBN 0-600-34989 6
The Encyclopaedia of the Worlds Combat aircraft, Bill Gunston, Salamander Books 1976 ISBN 0-600-33144 X
Camouflage & markings No.1, RAF fighters 1945-50 UK based. Guideline Publications Ltd.
Camouflage & markings No. 2 – The Battle for Britain-RAF May-December 1940, Paul Lucas, Guideline Publications Ltd. ISBN 0-9539040-0-8
Fleet Air Arm Camouflage and Markings – Atlantic & Mediterranean Theatres 1937-41, Stuart Lloyd, Dalrymple & Verdun Publishing, ISBN 978-1-905414-08-6
Heroes of Jadotville, The Soldiers' Story, Rose Doyle with Leo Quinlan, New Island Publishing 2006, ISBN 1-905494-31-9
Dublin Airport - The History, 50th anniversary 1940-1990, Hugh Oram, Aer Rianta ISBN 0-9516193-0-6

Fermoy 1891 to 1940. A local History by Niall Brunciardi, 1979.
The Irish Air Corps Today, Capt. Kevin Byrne,
Irish Aviator 1987, ISBN 1 871573 01 7
Avro Aircraft since 1908, A.J.Jackson ISBN: 0851778348,
ISBN 13: 9780851777979
British military aircraft serials, 1878-1987 by Robertson, Bruce Published in 1987, Midland Counties Publications (Leicester) ISBN 10: 090459761X
The SE5A File Ray Sturtivant, Air-Britain (Historians) Ltd, 1996,
ISBN 0-85130-246-7
De Havilland Aircraft Of World War I: Vol I D.H.1-D.H.4 by Colin Owers,
Flying Machines press, ISBN 978-1-89126-817-5
Vickers Aircraft Since 1908, Author: A. F. Andrews, January 1969,
ISBN-10: 0370000056, ISBN-13: 9780370000053
The Anson File, Ray Sturtivant, Air-Britain (Historians) Ltd,
ISBN 0-85130-156-8
Royal Air Force aircraft P1000 - R9999 by James J Halley; Air-Britain (Historians) Ltd, 1996, ISBN: 0851302351 9780851302355
Supermarine Aircraft since 1914,Brassey's: Putnam Aeronautical;
2nd Revised edition edition (May 2003) ISBN-10: 0851778003,
ISBN-13: 978-0851778006
Hawker Aircraft Since 1920 (Putnam Aeronautical Books) by Francis K. Mason ISBN13 / EAN: 9780851778396 ,ISBN10: 0851778399
4+ publications, Westland Lysander, ISBN 80-902559-1-4
4+ publications, Miles Magister, ISBN 80-902559-4-9
An Irishman's Aviation Sketchbook by R.W. O'Sullivan published by Irish Aviator, Dublin 2, 1988.
Spitfire International, Helmut Terbeck, Harry van der Meer & Ray Sturtivant, Air-Britain Publications,2002, ISBN 0-85130-250-5.
T-41 Mescalero – The Military Cessna 172, Walt Shiel, Jan Forsgren, Mike Little, Slip down Mountain Publications 2006, ISBN 0-9746533-3-3
Bristol Fighter in Action, Squadron Signal Publications No. 137,
ISBN 0-89747-301-9

Magazines and Other Publications

Irish Air Letter - various issues
Flying in Ireland - various issues
Irish Aviator - various issues
Irish Air Corps Celebrating 30 years of Helicopter Operations 1963-1993, published by Helicopter Wing, Casement Aerodrome, Baldonnel, 1993. Editor Capt. David Swan.
The Irish Air Corps 1922-1997 75th Anniversary Official Souvenir Publication
Scale Aircraft Modelling, July 1981, The Irish Air Corps, its history and markings by A.P.Kearns
Scale Aircraft Modelling , August 2003, Irish Air Corps SA365F Dauphin in Close Up by P.J. Cummins, Guideline Publications Ltd.
Scale Aircraft Modelling, December 1996, Camouflage & Markings Irish Air Corps Update by Comdt. Kevin Byrne. Guideline Publications Ltd.
Scale Aircraft Modelling, April 2005. Irish Air Corps in the 21st Century, Lt. Col. Kevin Byrne.
The Irish Defence Forces handbook 1988, An Cosantoir.
An Cosantoir, March 1985, Air Corps Edition celebrating 21 years of Helicopter service
Airfan Magazine, September 1993.
An Cosantoir, January 1990. Light Strike Squadron
Air Pictorial, March 1997, Irish Air Corps Today
Flight International, 30 July 1988, The Irish Indentity
Air International, October 1977, Ireland's Air Force
Air International, March 1982, Eire's Expanding Air Force
Air International, October 1998, Vigilant and Loyal, The Irish Air Corps
Air Forces Monthly, August 1998, Irish Air Corps Silver Swallows.
Air Enthusiast, March 1973, Epitome of an Era... the RAF's last fighting biplane (Gloster Gladiator)
Warpaint Series No. 37 Gloster Gladiator by Tom Spencer
Air International, January 1984, Westland Lysander
Air International, February 1984, Westland Lysander
Combat Colours No. 2 the Hawker Hurricane 1939-45 in RAF, Commonwealth and FAA service, Guideline Publications Ltd.
Scale Aircraft Modelling, October 1997, Miles Military Trainers.
Warpaint Series No. 53 Avro Anson Mks 1-22, Alan W. Hall
An Cosantoir, July-August 1995, The hawker Hurricane.
Aviation Guide No. 1, Fairey Battle by Ian D. Huntley, Sam Publications.
Scale Aircraft Modelling, April 1986, Supermarine Walrus.
Scale Aircraft Modelling, March 2002, Merlin Engined Seafires.
Scale Aircraft Modelling, October 1998, De Havilland DH.104. Dove & Devon.
Scale Aircraft Modelling, February 1988, Hunting Percival Provost
Air International, May 1996, Timeless Trainer from Toronto (DHC-1 Chipmunk)
Warpaint series No. 27, de Havilland Vampire by W.A. Harrison
Aeroplane monthly, November 2007, Vampire in detail
Air International ,October 1978, Spitfires with Sea legs, (Seafire III)
Aeroplane Monthly, January 2009, The Grace Spifire.
Flying in Ireland, October 2005, IAC 161 Sptifire T.9 returns to Ireland.
Air International, April 1999, SIAI Marchetti SF260.
Air International, September 1977, Fans for the Hs. 125
Air International, December 1977, Franco-British Antelope, first ten years of the Aérospatiale/Westland Gazelle
Irish independent August 7, 1933 report on funeral of Lt. Twohig.
Air Enthusiast, March 1972 Armstrong Whitworth Scimitar (forerunner of the Avro 636)
The Illustrated Encyclopaedia of Aircraft, Vol. 13; Air Britain, M.P.Filmore.
Pamphlet, Air Corps Museum Baldonnel, commemorating the 50th Anniversary of the Ending of the Emergency, 1996.

Newspapers

Irish times – various issues
Irish Independent – various issues
Irish Press – various issues

Websites:

http://historical-debates.oireachtas.ie/en.toc.dail.html
Historical Dáil Debates transcripts
www.irishairpics.com – Irish Aircraft Photographs
www.flightglobal.com – Flight International on-line archive going back to 1908

About the Authors

Joe Maxwell is an aviation enthusiast and scale modeller. Joe produced the Max decals range of model aircraft decal sheets and contributed drawings to The Irish Air Corps Celebrates 100 years of Flight book that was published in 2003. He was an active member of the Dublin Wicklow Mountain Rescue Team in the 1990s where he witnessed firsthand the extraordinary work of the Air Corps helicopter crews. Joe is married with two daughters and lives in Dublin.

Patrick. J. Cummins is an aviation historian who has published many articles on aviation subjects. A member of Air Britain, his first book, "Emergency" Air incidents South East Ireland 1940-1945 was very well received. Patrick is married with three children and lives in Waterford.

WATERFORD CITY AND COUNTY LIBRARIES
WITHDRAWN